Restructuring the Soviet Economy

Restructuring the Soviet Economy

In Search of the Market

Nicolas Spulber

Ann Arbor

THE UNIVERSITY OF MICHIGAN PRESS

Library of Congress Cataloguing-in-Publication Data

Spulber, Nicolas.
    Restructuring the Soviet economy : in search of the market /
Nicolas Spulber.
      p. cm.
    Includes bibliographical references and index.
    ISBN 0-472-10229-X (cloth : alk.)
    1. Soviet Union—Economic policy—1986–   2. Soviet Union—Economic
conditions—1985–   I. Title.
HC336.26.S737   1991
338.947—dc20   90-27429
                                                              CIP

To Pauline, with love

Acknowledgments

The study for this book was carried out with the help of two grants-in-aid from the Office of Research and Graduate Development of Indiana University. I am deeply grateful to Professor Kenneth R. R. Gros Louis, the vice president of the university, who responded rapidly and generously to my research requests.

I am greatly indebted to a number of my colleagues, in particular professors Robert A. Becker, Roy J. Gardner, H. Scott Gordon, Elmus R. Wicker, and Willard E. Witte, who have carefully read either parts of or the entire manuscript in its various versions, and who have made invaluable suggestions for its improvement. I have also benefited enormously from access to the personal collection of Soviet economic books and periodicals of my colleague, Professor Robert Campbell. These resources have completed, whenever needed, the great collections of Soviet materials at the Indiana University Main Library.

My thanks go finally to Susan Hall of the Graphics Department, Audio Visual Center of Indiana University, who drew with great ability and understanding the charts included in the text, to Ruth Fishel who typed with patience and admirable diligence the several versions of the manuscript, and to Stephen Cole for his competent and precious editorial help on the final version.

Any remaining errors are mine alone.

Contents

Introduction

For decades the centralized, Stalinist, administrative planning system drove the USSR and its East European satellites along the path of intensive autarkic industrialization. Immense efforts were made there in order to industrialize each country on parallel lines, on the centralist "Soviet model," aloof from the trends in the world market and in defiance of the international division of labor. By the middle of the 1980s, however, the Soviet leadership's perception of the economic results of the centralist system started to change radically. It became increasingly clear that the gap between the USSR and market-directed economies was growing incessantly with respect to modernization, technological progress, social productivities, and standards of living. It became clear, and the leaders began to say so publicly, that the USSR had developed a vast but obsolete and inefficient industrial machine, that it was commanding a devastated agriculture, an alienated labor force, and a disgruntled, ill-fed, ill-clothed, and poorly housed population.

Since then, new economic directions have been mapped out in the USSR as well as in the East European countries. The new economic paths are set to lead from a centrally directed economy either to a *mixed* economy, combining a central planning core with a broadly decentralized state administration and regulated markets, or to a fully *market-directed* economy. To understand the basic issues involved in these processes, it is useful to recall briefly the ways in which the flows of production and income relate to the state administration in the old centralist model.

In the old system the state intervened directly on the two fundamental sides of yearly national economic activity: the production of goods and services and the distribution of the incomes generated by that production. In regard to the volume and mix of consumer and producer goods, the national economic plan set obligatory targets, in both physical and value terms, for each type of output and for each firm and organization in manufacturing and agriculture, as well as various other targets for the supporting sectors and branches: construction, transport and communication, trade, and financial services. On the side of incomes, the state dictated the level of wages and determined the volume of the so-called social surplus it assigned to itself. It then attempted roughly to match the low level of wages with the low level (and poor assortment) of consumer goods at centrally established prices and also the large volume of the social surplus with a continuously expanding volume of investment goods. In order to insure that its commands would be followed by firms and organizations, the state nationalized—that is, socialized—industry, transport, trade, and the banks, and it collectivized the peasants. Put differently, it expropriated the private owners, large and small, and became the universal owner of the means of production and of financial institutions.

In a market-directed economy the state administration does not command what, how, and by whom goods should be produced. Instead, producer and other firms attempt to respond to the preferences of the buyers of goods and services. On the side of incomes, the state administration intervenes only indirectly via the utilization of public finance instruments (for example, taxes and transfers to household) and of money and credit instruments (volume of currency issue, interest rates, and lending and borrowing).

The transmutation of a centrally administered economy into either a mixed plan and market economy or into a fully market-directed one posits vast changes in the relations of the state administration to both production and income distribution and in its use of instruments of management. On the side of production, the transition requires the deliverance of producer firms and organizations from the strictures of state ownership, of centralized tutelage, and of administrative injunctions concerning inputs, outputs, and the distribution of goods. On the side of finance and income distribution, it posits a shift away from the attempts to match physical production and income flows at manipulated state prices. It also involves the cessation of the use of instruments of direct control in favor of indirect instruments of public finance and of money and credit.

Such changes are complex and difficult to carry out without bringing about enormous dislocations, maladjustments, and instabilities—whether the goal is the step-by-step creation of a mixed system of central planning and of controlled markets, as the president of the USSR, Mikhail Gorbachev, is trying to achieve, or a radical transition to a full market-determined economy, as the president of the Russian republic, Boris Yeltsin, is insistently propounding. Indeed, replacement of managers and of administrators trained either to issue centralized commands or to submit to them and true emancipation of producers from state ownership and tutelage require time, involve many difficulties, and can take a variety of forms. Outright denationalization, dismantling of industrial ministries and monopolistic conglomerates, and widespread privatization raise complex issues, to start with, the question of how could the state sell its assets when there are no market prices to guide choices. Extensive privatization has as yet not been envisaged by the country's central leaders, even in the case of agriculture—the first sector in which privatization is usually attempted in the process of a disengagement from centralized administration. What is incessantly emphasized in the USSR under the name of *radical reform* is a vast expansion of leasing in all forms, both in manufacturing and in agriculture, and a systematic devolution of various economic powers from the center to the republics, regions, and local authorities. Only a part of the Soviet leadership seems willing to cross over the divide between a centrally directed economy and a market-dominated one in order to break the system's inertia and to allow the resurgence of markets within and at the borders of the state's "commanding heights."

On the side of income distribution, the shift to indirect methods is also slow and hesitant. Even in some of the former Soviet-type socialist countries undergoing a transition, the state administrations seem reluctant to abandon a whole set of controls, including the control over wages and the power to arbitrarily manipulate the division between private and public income shares. The fiscal systems still rely on haphazard mixes of subsidies and sales taxes and on tight control of financial operations, many of which remain geared toward the fulfillment of still ill-defined national economic goals. What results from this mix are various hybrid and unstable arrangements between central plans and centrally guided sectors and branches, neither fully controlled nor really responsive to market supply and demand signals.

During Stalin's administrative planning and management system (1928–53) it was possible to impose on the Soviet economy and society the tasks of fulfilling a few top-priority targets, of controlling, in a more or less meaningful fashion, the input-output connections within its enterprises, of compelling the labor force to work by means of terror, of regimenting the countryside, and of reducing the demands of the population to bare essentials. As the economy grew and diversified, possibilities for the enterprises to thwart central decisions increased, and terror was progressively lifted and the infamous labor camps (*gulags*) were disbanded, the population's expectations for a higher standard of living and for more and better goods and services rose incessantly. Faced with this situation, the Soviet policymakers and planners felt compelled at various points in time to engage in a number of reforms of the old administrative planning system. One of the most important of the reforms was carried out in the mid-1960s, exactly twenty years before the policy of broad restructuring was started by Gorbachev. It attempted to orient the producing enterprises toward achieving results more congruent with central objectives by enlarging their options, changing the ways of measuring (and of rewarding) their performances, modifying the system of incentives, and revising the methods of central price formation. However, the basic changes introduced in the mid-1960s—at times revised, retracted, then again advanced and reshaped in different ways—did not yield the hoped-for results. Indeed, slippages between goals set at the center and the actual movement of goods grew. Gaps expanded between the central objectives and the performance of manufacturing enterprises, productivity of the work force, outputs of agriculture, patterns of saving and spending, and the integration and cooperation of ethnic components in the Soviet mosaic. These ever-increasing slippages made, from 1985 on, Mikhail Gorbachev's moves toward restructuring (*perestroika*) a necessity and forced the continual enlargement of both its scope and intensity in relation to the more limited and less decisive reforms of the mid-1960s.

What exactly are the long-range objectives of the Soviet leader's policy of restructuring? Does it eventually open the way toward a truly market-directed economy? How does the unfolding of this policy affect the role of Communist managers and administrators, the forms of ownership on which their leading role has been predicated, the relations between the center of decision making and the enterprises, and the traditional priorities of production over consumption? In what ways do the instruments used and the measures envisaged differ from those already tried in the past in the USSR and other socialist countries? Can the projected changes with regard to the retooling and modernization of the economy be carried out? Can these measures arrest the fall in its growth rates, eliminate the widening slippages, surmount the imbalances in production, supply, and distribution? Can these changes prevent the further progress of black markets, restore confidence in the currency, overcome the deep-seated alienation of the work force, and open new and broad ways toward the restoration of markets, albeit regulated ones, or will additional measures be necessary? What additional measures must actually be implemented in order to create an efficient system?

The divided Soviet leadership agonizes about what features of the centralized system to conserve or discard, while at the same time it grapples with the question of what economic powers it should devolve to the lower administrative levels of the state and what paths it should open toward the utilization of market mechanisms. The processes of dismantling and restructuring the system in the USSR as well as in its former satellites are neither smooth nor simple, neither quick nor devoid of risks. Their implementation as well as their analysis raise problems as difficult and challenging as those that were raised when this kind of system was first created and put into place.

In the course of the discussion I refer to Mikhail Gorbachev's perestroika. Historically, he is the initiator of the process of broad restructuring that started in the USSR in 1985 and eventually helped to bring about accelerated structural changes in its former East European satellites. Eventually, under an enormous conjunction of domestic and international pressures, the entire Soviet leadership has been drawn, willy-nilly, in the process of change. Whatever Gorbachev's personal ups and downs, the problems of the complete restructuring of the Soviet system has already become part and parcel not only of the history of the USSR and communism, but also of the study of the complex issues involved in all processes of modernization and economic growth and change.

This book focuses only on the economic changes in the USSR. It is divided into four main parts: (1) the modifications of underlying principles in the centralized economic system of planning and management envisaged by the Soviet architects of economic restructuring; (2) the overhauling of the economy's directive center and the limits established by the administration's policy with respect to the traditional functions of this center; (3) the scope of structural shifts in the economy's component units and of the changes in the method of their guidance; and (4) socialist searches as well as Western proposals for shaping a "workable" socialist system.

Part 1 contains two chapters. The first chapter focuses on measures taken from the mid-1980s on to reshape the conceptual foundations of the Soviet economic mechanism and to modify the administrative model devised under Stalin. Chapter 2 examines the commodity space and the ways in which firms and households interact given a set of constraints that are unlikely to be removed fully, under the basic directions imparted from the center to the restructuring policy.

Part 2 consists of six chapters. The first two chapters assess the scope and the impact of restructuring on the ways in which the directive center of the economy formulates and implements its policies. Since the end of the 1980s this directive center is comprised, on the one hand, of a newly established president of the USSR, his advisory Presidential Council, and his executive arm, the Council of Ministers of the USSR; and, on the other hand, by a legislative body, the bicameral Supreme Soviet crowning the administrative state apparatus, which consists of elected Soviets. In addition, the component republics of the USSR try to assert their own autonomy in various directions, but the scope of their authority is still limited in regard to many economic issues. Chapter 3 shows how the center tries to determine the economy's "basic directions of development" with the support of a politically diminished Communist party. Chapters 4, 5, 6, and 7 indicate how the central core program of capital construction, manpower planning, and financial operations (budget and banks) still determine the basic developmental options. The concluding chapter of part 2, chapter 8, presents Soviet and Western methods of evaluating the economy's performance.

Part 3's four chapters examine the modifications introduced in sectoral arrangements, the scope and the instruments of management at the levels of manufacturing enterprises and associations (chap. 9), state and collective farms (chap. 10), supply and distribution networks (chap. 11), and foreign trade organs (chap. 12). The focus is both on the interrelations between the decisions and the activities of the center and the developing activities of the state, private, and semi-private firms—namely industrial cooperatives, individual small-scale enterprises, personal auxiliary farms, legal and illegal trade networks, and joint companies with foreign capital. Special attention is paid to the ways in which the center's policies attempt to preserve the planning framework while opening ways to the resurgence of markets. In many cases, the result is the creation of unstable, hybrid arrangements, which will have to be modified subsequently, particularly in regard to the rights, forms, and scope of private ownership.

Part 4, the concluding section of the book, focuses on the interrelations between the crucial Marxian concept of the centralized, conscious organization of "socialized production" on the basis of the suppression of the market, and the variations in the Soviet implementations of that schemata. Since the revolution the Soviet Union has constructed a vastly centralized administrative economy during War Communism (1918–20) and under Stalin's reign (1928–53). It has made a variety of departures from the original Marxian tenets, including various forms of reliance on market mechanisms during the New Economic Policy (NEP) (1921–28) and, even more so, since the launching of the policy of restructuring from the middle of 1985 on. Chapter 13, the first chapter of part 4, presents the Marxian schemata, the main characteristics of its implementation during War Communism and under Stalin, various methods attempted for its improvement, and the subsequent Soviet assessments and critique of this model. Chapter 14, the concluding chapter of part 4 and of the entire book, presents the steps that must be taken in the process of dismantling this model, and it examines the actual steps taken both during the NEP and since the start of the policy of restructuring, the impact of these and related measures on the West, and the redefinition of *socialism* in the conditions of perestroika and the collapse of the socialist system in Eastern Europe.

Many readers will perhaps be familiar with my previous text on the *Soviet Economy: Structure Principles and Problems* (published in the 1960s). Since then momentous changes have taken place in the USSR. To start with, since the Soviet turn toward openness (*glasnost*) and economic restructuring have taken place, a vast amount of data, analyses, comments, proposals, and counterproposals of reform have come out of the USSR on all of the topics discussed in this book. At no time before the mid-1980s would it have been possible to have access to such a wealth of information and such candid evaluations from Soviet sources as we now have available. The present book is altogether new—with a new structure, new information, and a new focus: the scope, development, and difficulties of restructuring the Soviet economy. (Only about 5 percent of the previous work has been used in this one.) To facilitate reading, I have chosen to dispense with footnotes. Instead, whenever necessary or expedient, I give the reference directly in the text and, in addition, provide an extensive References and Bibliography keyed to each subsection of each chapter.

While Soviet restructuring policies begun in the mid-1980s are evolving in various directions, and while the processes they began will be influenced by the deep changes unfolding in all present or former centrally administered states, it is already possible to grasp their inner logic, to map their basic directions, and to evaluate their prospects. But these as well as the broader, complex issues of the failure of the traditional Soviet economic mechanism, of the disconcerting inefficiency of its planners and managers, of the USSR's deep and widening internal dislocations, of the abject collapse of the socialist economic satellites of Eastern Europe, cannot be fully understood without a patient, methodic, and detailed inventory and analysis of the specific courses of action and of the instruments devised and used by the Communist rulers in the pursuit of the elusive goal of directing and controlling all the aspects of economic activity. The analysis of these procedures and instruments presented herein should prove interesting to students of Soviet economics, comparative economics, and economics in general, political science, and contemporary history and international relations. The momentous Soviet transformations are also of great interest to a larger public, indeed, to any informed person concerned with the vital modification of a major part of the world in which we live.

Part 1
Adjusting the "Economic Mechanism"

Four key characteristics defined the Soviet economic system emerging after the Russian revolution of 1917. The first of these was the integration, under the direction of the Communist party, of the summits of the party itself, the state administration (in the Soviet Union as a whole and in each of its republics and regions), and the economy. The party officials controlled and supervised all levels of administration and management. The second basic feature of the system was the socialization (nationalization) of the economy's commanding heights (in industry, banking, transport, and wholesale trade). The third key feature was the organization of a centralized bureaucratic system of economic coordination, using mandatory planning of inputs, outputs, costs, profits, technologies, involving the state enterprises, and reducing market mechanisms to subsidiary roles. The fourth and final basic trait was the assertion of the primacy of society over the individual and of production over consumption.

Under Josef Stalin's leadership (1928–53) the party's command functions were expanded to control all the activities of society; socialization was extended to all economic sectors, including agriculture (in combination with peasants' collectivization) and retail trade; administrative coordination, relying on central mandatory plans, superseded the use of most market mechanisms; and the primacy of production over consumption was inflexibly imposed. Over time, a variety of reforms were carried out with respect to prices, incentives, and the linkages between the center and the production entities, but the basic concepts underlying the administrative economic system put in place by Stalin continued under his successors until March 1985.

Then, the new general-secretary of the party, Mikhail Gorbachev, launched a broad program of political and economic restructuring (perestroika) aimed at modifying some of the principles and instruments of Stalin's economic system in a series of successive stages to continue over the balance of the century and possibly beyond. The original objective of this restructuring has been to bring about new economic conditions in which the central will of the policymakers and planners will express itself primarily through decisions on the basic directions of development, the allocation of the bulk of investments, and the use of economic levers (rather than commands) to force the economy's sectors to conform to directions mapped out for them. These efforts should create new conditions allowing the economy's component units to discharge their activities more efficiently than in the past.

To start with, Gorbachev demarcated the functions of the party and of the state administration. From the late 1980s the party's apparatus started to be purged and reorganized, while its direct controls over the state bureaucracy and the economy's managers were progressively eliminated. The party's top leadership—which coincides with the state's top administration—kept in its hands the authority to determine the broad directions of development of the country, while first reducing and then eliminating the power of the party as such, to supervise and control the economic organs and to form local and regional coalitions counteracting the center's decisions. Accordingly, from 1989 on, first the administrative powers were shifted from the party to the hierarchy of elected Soviets (councils), crowned by a bicameral Supreme Soviet and endowed with real legislative authority. Then, the executive powers were shifted to a newly established president, to his personal advisory council, and to his Council of Ministers. Eventually, the scope of socialization was redefined to allow a broad field of operation for mixed ownerships, communal ownerships, cooperative and private ownerships, and various long-term leasing arrangements of state properties around the core formed by state ownership. Administrative commands were reduced, various economic functions were devolved to the republic, regional, and local authorities, and a number of new economic instruments were called into play. Central planning decisions—the objectives of the center's industrial policy—and the expanding enterprises' autonomy were scheduled to be brought into harmony primarily via economic and financial levers, namely, centrally planned prices, centrally established norms for the use of enterprises' funds, and credit policies. Markets for some materials and for consumer goods and services were to remain subsidiary transacting mechanisms for the implementation of the basic objectives of the central policy and not alternatives to the central plan. Finally, more attention was to be paid to consumer preferences at the levels of the republics, regions, and localities, while the center focuses on the retooling of the country's basic industries so as to bring the entire economy onto a higher technological plateau. Actually, the attempts to coordinate central decisions with the enterprises' activities break down often while the central commands appear to be increasingly ineffective.

Chapter 1 presents the historic characteristics of the system and indicates how each of these features has been modified and how they might change in the future. Chapter 2 examines the prevailing constraints on producers and households and points to limits of the proposed transmutations. Part 1 concludes by drawing attention to the critical role of centrally determined prices in both traditional and projected frameworks.

CHAPTER 1

Basic Principles

Party, State, and the Economy

The Communist Party of the Soviet Union (CPSU) was referred to by the Soviet Union's constitution of 1977 as "the guiding and directing force of the Soviet society and the nucleus of its political system and of all state and public organizations." In the system that evolved under Stalin, the party's general-secretary became indeed the country's real prime minister; the party's top political decision-making institution, the Politburo, became his cabinet; and the party's congresses (and, between congresses, the party's Central Committee) became a kind of parliament, usually with secret debating procedures. Historically, the state's administration, officially constituted by a hierarchy of Soviets, became a mere appendix of the party, subservient to its direction, controls, and staffing. While the slogan of the Bolshevik revolution in 1917 had been "All Power to the Soviets" and, eventually, Russia changed its name to *Soviet* Union, from the beginning of Bolshevik rule the party became the locus of real power.

As it evolved historically, the administration of the Soviet state has consisted of a hierarchical pyramid whose base has been comprised of so-called local Soviets, namely the Soviets of villages, settlements, cities, regional units (*oblasts*), autonomous republics, and other administrative-territorial subdivisions (*krai, okrug,* and *raion*). As of 1987 there were some 52,000 such local Soviets. The middle part of the pyramid has consisted of fifteen Supreme Soviets of the fifteen Union Republics comprising the USSR. The top of the pyramid has been embodied in the Supreme Soviet of the USSR, comprised of two chambers: the Soviet of the Union (whose members have been elected by an equal number of inhabitants) and the Soviet of Nationalities (comprised of a given number of representatives from each Union Republic, autonomous regions, and autonomous areas). Between the Supreme Soviet's sessions its functions have been discharged by its presidium. The chairman of the presidium has played the role of head of state. The Supreme Soviet has held the power of appointing the Council of Ministers of the USSR.

Traditionally, the Council of Ministers of the USSR has been comprised of All-Union ministries and Union-Republic ministries, the chairmen of various ministerial agencies, bureaus, and committees, and the fifteen chairmen of the Councils of Ministers of the fifteen republics. The council has also always chosen its own presidium authorized to speak in its name and to handle executive and administrative issues of the highest significance. In Stalin's institutional arrangement, the Council of Ministers of the USSR was entrusted with both the short-term supervision and the long-term management of the economy as a whole. It discharged these functions through a complexly structured hierarchy involving the indicated ministries as well as functional agencies among which the crucial ones became the USSR planning agency, *Gosplan*, and the USSR agency in charge of "material technical supply," *Gossnab*, both of which evolved into large, complex, and very powerful organizations. Traditionally, the Union ministries were in charge of the heavy industrial branches', while the Union-Republic ministries directed the light industries and trade, as well as the republic and territorial authorities and, through them, the industries of regional and local significance.

As indicated above, the Soviet hierarchy has been under the party's all-encompassing control. The party not only directed and provided its key personnel but also supervised it with both a regional administrative structure of committees (for localities-districts-territories-provinces-republics) and with primary party organizations at each level of the administrative apparatus. The basic sources of legitimacy of the party's powers have been its accession to power through the 1917 revolution, its self-proclaimed role of "vanguard of the proletariat," and its purported mandate from the proletariat to install in its name a "class dictatorship." This dictatorship, established by the 1917 revolution in lieu of what Lenin called "the dictatorship of the bourgeoisie," was said, from the 1960s on, to have evolved first into a "state of all the people" and later into "mature and advanced socialism." The party's Marxist-Leninist ideology—its assumptions, contentions, constructs, and language—became the framework of communication in the society between the rulers and the ruled from the beginning of the Soviet system. While a large part of the officialdom's (and, of course, the population's) system of beliefs came to be at increasing variance with Marxism-Leninism in all the latter's evolving interpretations, it is this ideology, with its shibboleth and its myths about "socialist values," that still holds together the core of the ruling elite, and it is its conceptualizations—concerning the forms of ownership, planning, and the market—that remain embedded in the key institutions of the Soviet system. Without a good understanding of Marxian ideological roots, of its language and symbols, many of the Soviet Union's decisions and tendencies might easily be misinterpreted.

In Stalin's system, the Central Committee's Secretariat became the key instrument for controlling and staffing both the party's and the state's hierarchies. As Stalin indicated at the 12th Congress of the Soviet Communist Party in 1923, he appointed and removed the party's officials following the principle that "officials must be selected in such a way that positions should be held by people who will know how to apply directives, will understand the directives, and will transform these directives into realities." Thereafter, the party established secret lists of the most important positions at each echelon (called *nomenklatura*) and corresponding selected party members assigned to fill the positions.

The entire system, and the bureaucracy it spawned, became known as the *nomenklatura* system. In 1988 the uppermost layer of the *nomenklatura* comprised some 1.8 million positions. Moreover, there were at the time an additional 13.1 million people in the managerial-technical staffs of enterprises and associations, thus reaching a total of close to 15 million supervisors of the economy, or, as Gorbachev put it derisively a year earlier (in a speech in Murmansk), "a manager for every six or seven people . . . an inordinately bloated apparatus" (see table 1-1).

After the death of Stalin in 1953 the state bureaucracy—the Soviet administrative hierarchs, the judiciary, the militia and the secret police, and the military officers—acquired increasing stability and with it increasing con-

TABLE 1-1. Structure of the Soviet Union's Executive-Managerial Administration, 1988

Executive-Managerial Administration	Number (in thousands)	Percentages
Total administration[a]	14,962	100.0
Managerial personnel of enterprises and organizations	13,131	87.8
Apparatus of ministries and of administrative-management agencies	1,831	12.2
Supreme Soviet Presidium and executive committees	311	2.0
Public and cooperative organizations	341	2.3
Various agencies	99	0.7
Apparatus of ministries, committees, and administrations	1,080	7.2
Union	85	0.6
Republic	108	0.7
Autonomous-republic, territory, and province	265	1.8
Regional-district-city	477	3.2
Trusts, offices (economic apparatus)	145	0.9

Source: Based on *Izvestia*, March 7, 1989.
[a]Excluding security and lower office personnel.

fidence in its own ability to run the country's administration. Eventually, the deterioration of the economy's performance, particularly from the 1970s on, provided the leadership of the party and of the state with the occasion to implement a proposal already made in the late 1950s under Nikita Khrushchev, namely, that of curtailing the party's control over the state's administration. This time Gorbachev pushed for the elimination of this particular role for the party's machine. With the necessary endorsement of the Politburo and of a broader ad hoc party conference assembled in June 1988, the shift of emphasis from the operational-controlling role of the party apparatus to the Soviets as full-fledged bodies of people's power took place under the appearance of a return to the "Leninist" system. Actually, the crux of the matter was both to disentangle the party from universal responsibility for everything that went wrong in the economy and society and to shift power (along with more responsibilities) to a refurbished state administration, with the Soviets as its core. As Gorbachev indicated at that conference, "henceforth not a single question concerning the state, the economy, or the social fabric can be decided if the Soviets are bypassed." The disengagement from the party's tutelage and the increased erosion of the privileges and status of its medium and lower party ranks were sanctioned by the oft-repeated assertion of the full and independent authority of the Soviets in managing the development of the areas run by them.

From 1989, at the apex of the new state structure was placed in the Congress of the USSR People's Deputies. The June 1988 conference accepted that from 1989 on, and each five years thereafter, such a popularly elected congress, convening annually, would elect a bicameral Supreme Soviet and would debate and decide on all legislative, administrative, and other important issues. The first congress, consisting of 2,250 members, met in May 1989. Fifteen hundred of its deputies were elected from territorial and national districts from multicandidates though not from multiparty lists. The choices of the electorate were confirmed or rejected by the district party hierarchs. These fifteen hundred were joined by half as many deputies selected by the CPSU from the governing bodies of the state, unions, and youth and other organizations. The congress elected Mikhail Gorbachev as its first chairman and empowered him to submit for nomination the chairman of the USSR Council of Ministers. In October 1989, only a few months after its establishment, the Soviet legislature voted to eliminate special seats for the Communist party and other official organizations in national and local elections. The legislators also passed measures that would allow direct elections for president in each of the fifteen constituent republics.

The final measures in the process of dislodging the party from the position of supreme controller of the state apparatus and ending the duplication of party and state bureaucracies were taken in February 1990. A plenum of the

Central Committee of the Communist party preparing the platform for the Party's 28th Congress (summer 1990) decided to redefine the party as "a democratically reorganized force" whose status could not be "imposed through constitutional endorsement." In order to "get rid of everything that tied the party to the authoritarian-bureaucratic system"—as Gorbachev put it in his speech at the plenum—the platform specified that the party "does not claim a monopoly of power" and that it did not "preclude the possibility of the formation of parties" according to legal procedures to be established (*Izvestia*, February 13, 1990). The plenum also recommended the institution of the post of head of state—president—endowed with extensive powers and responsible to the Congress of USSR People's Deputies. The latter then decided to institute a popularly elected president for a five-year term—but only after a transition of four years during which Mikhail Gorbachev assumed the post after election by the People's Congress.

The official renunciation of the party's power monopoly (article 6 of the 1977 constitution) and the creation of the powerful executive position of USSR president and of a personal advisory Presidential Council (of some sixteen members) brings to an end the organizational system created by Lenin and Stalin and shifts the locus of power to the indicated Congress and to the head of the state's administration. While these changes give certain rights to the Soviet electorate and allow it to observe the inner workings of the Congress of the USSR People's Deputies and of the Supreme Soviet, they *do not* imply that the Soviet people or its vastly diverse ethnic groups actually have been granted the rights of changing the structure and content of the state and the government. Still, a new situation has been created in regard to the structure of power at the center of the Soviet system. The elected Congress of the People's Deputies, the elected president of the country, and his personally appointed Presidential Council displace and replace, respectively, the party's Congress, its general-secretary, and its Politburo. The parallel is not entirely fortuitous: within the new framework the system keeps its familiar hierarchical structures.

Most executive powers and the main economic management tasks continue to be discharged by the USSR Council of Ministers, while the legislative power is in the hands of the Supreme Soviet, and certain administrative and economic powers are entrusted to the hierarchy of elected Soviets. The party as such retains only a diminished advisory role. But the newly elected administrative apparatus must still function according to the old and tried principle of democratic centralism. The "democratic" component of this traditional Bolshevik principle refers to the electability of all representative organs from the bottom to the top of the pyramid. The second component of the principle refers to the obligation of the lower organs to conform to the basic decisions of their higher authorities—above all, of the center. It is still uncertain to what extent the centralized Soviet administration of an ethnic conglomerate that is increasingly torn by centrifugal forces will acquire real republic, regional, and local autonomy; flexibility; adaptability to new conditions; and the thrust for initiative sought by the reform. One may wonder whether professionalism, merit rules, and acceptance of responsibility at all the levels of the revamped state apparatus will actually take hold and supersede old ties nurtured by the party's interests, goals, and criteria. One might question finally whether the party's cadres, who always knew so well how to control elections, select even multicandidates called to occupy positions in the Soviets, and impose their will in their bailiwicks, will now hold back, adjust to, or circumvent the rising powers of Soviet hierarchy in the republics, districts, and local levels.

It is interesting to recall that sixty-five years before this, Leon Trotsky, then still a key leader of the party in power, proposed in a famous political tract entitled *New Course* that the party disengage itself from the state administration in order to save itself from "bureaucratic degeneration" and "concentration solely upon questions of administration." Now Gorbachev aims to save the state administration from the overbearing day-to-day controls of the party's cadres and to create new ways of interacting between the so-called vanguard party and the Soviets. But he also aims by this move to whitewash the thoroughly corrupt and discredited party and endow it with some kind of new life while simultaneously shifting both the responsibility and the blame for the country's plight onto the revamped state apparatus alone. One may doubt, however, whether the population at large will readily reconcile itself with the idea of "humane, democratic socialism," exempt the party qua party from its historic responsibilities for the country's disastrous state, and shift the blame onto only the ministries, departments, republics, regions, districts, and local authorities.

Extent and Consequences of "Socialization"

In the Marxian frame of reference the Soviet Union is a socialist state, a historically new political and socioeconomic institution based on new relations among the people engaged in production. The act that engendered this new entity in Russia and its empire was the socialization of the means of production—that is, the expropriation of the private owners of the economy's "commanding heights." A century and a half ago Marx and Engels asserted in the *Communist Manifesto* that "modern bourgeois private property" was "the final and most complete expression of the system of production and appropriation based on class antagonisms" and that the communist theory could be summed up in a single sentence: "Abolition of private property." This abolition was never viewed as a legal measure only; in the Marxian conception it was the instrument of a crucial social and economic change of great historical import and of vast consequences. The "abolition of capital as a social power" and the resulting creation of common property were stated to engender new harmonious social and production relationships, create the conditions for a rational, conscious organization of the economy and society, and firmly establish the priority of social needs and wants over the preferences of the individual.

From the very beginning the Communist party grounded the system it created on the socialization of nonlabor production factors. Since then, state ownership—in Soviet parlance, "the property of the whole people"—has been defined as having either an exclusive or a nonexclusive character. The land and its mineral wealth, waters, and forests are the exclusive property of the state. The basic means of production in industry, construction, agriculture, transportation and communication, banks, property of commercial and communal enterprises, housing, and other types of property are of the nonexclusive kind, since collective farms and cooperatives and even private persons have the right to acquire certain means of production necessary to their activity. Until perestroika, collective ownership had been confined primarily to agriculture—collective farms (*kolkhozy*)—and to the sectors in which small-scale ownership had been widespread before the Soviet regime. As a rule, personal income has been limited to income from work, ownership of a dwelling house and/or an apartment and a summer home, as well as to household articles and goods for personal use. The sphere of personal ownership has also included the right to inherit personal property.

The scope of personal activity and rewards has been larger in agriculture and in some cooperative fields. Given the inability of the state and collective farms to produce sufficient food supplies, the collective farmers have been allowed to tend the small plots of land granted to their households by the collective farms. Eventually, they have been permitted to raise various kinds of livestock for their own needs, as well as for supplemental income, and also to own agricultural implements and some equipment. The state farm workers and non–farm workers and employees located in small towns and cities have also been granted the right to tend state-owned small plots of land and have been given permission to raise livestock in order to alleviate the shortage of meat, milk, and eggs. Since Gorbachev's accession to power the entire system of so-called personal subsidiary farms has been scheduled for development in a number of ways—namely, large utilization of leases of state-owned land and increased access to larger and better machinery, seeds, and pasture land. It should be noted here that, already by the late 1980s, the subsidiary farms system involved forty-five million families (collective farm families, workers and employees of state farms, and other workers and retirees). Moreover, the regime also has encouraged the development of family owned and operated small-scale artisanal workshops and industrial or trade cooperatives for the production of consumer goods and services (restaurants, homemade arts and crafts, household repairs, photographic labs, and taxi driving).

Stalin's expansion of socialization and restriction of private property has not engendered a harmonious, "nonantagonistic" society in which individual and collective interests would coincide. Indeed, it became increasingly evident, particularly from the 1960s on, that the socialist society was deeply fragmented, just as its predecessors had been, by divisions of social labor. Diverse strata of society, such as government bureaucrats of all shades and occupations, managers, scientists, engineers, technicians, factory workers, and laborers on state and collective farms, could not be held together by an overriding, abstract preoccupation with the common good. In fact, Soviet society is rigidly structured and hierarchy conscious. There are no less than thirty categories of technical, professional, and executive personnel above the mass of the workers. There are ten echelons of technicians, accountants, and dispatchers; above them, ten echelons of specialists with higher education and engineering-technical personnel; and, higher up, ten echelons of managers of enterprises and sections of enterprises—with different interests and a different scale of rewards. Old Soviet textbooks asserted dogmatically that the abolition of private property relegated the interests it engendered to the past and that under socialism the interests of those who own the means of production and those who work are no longer opposed since they are one and the same. Such claims might still be made, ritualistically, from time to time, but nobody seems to believe them anymore.

The first open challenge to this fundamental Marxian tenet was raised in Czechoslovakia by the economist Ota Šik and his followers who brought about that unique phenomenon, the Prague Spring of 1968. Šik stressed that the main driving forces of socialist, like capitalist, society are personal and group interests rather than abstract social needs. The very structuring of the Soviet order involves a fractionizing of interest groups. It is not the alleged identity but the divergence of interests that must be seized upon if the economy is to progress. From this crucial shift in emphasis cogently pointed out by Šik and then many others, a number of decisive changes must be carried out with respect to the goals and structure of production, the material incentives, the workers' rights in the enterprise and the society at large, and the general policies of the state toward individual interests. The same challenge—but without reference to the Prague Spring—was also raised in the USSR by Gorbachev when launching perestroika in 1985. Indeed, he was keen to point out repeatedly that socialization had not generated real concern for social property—quite the contrary. As he put it, for instance, in a report to the CPSU Central Committee on January 27, 1987: "Departmental and parochial attitudes eroded socialist property, it became 'no one's' free, belonging to no real owner, and in many cases was used to derive unearned income." In the same report, he added that various "elements of social corrosion" had eroded moral values, while corruption, bribe taking, arbitrariness in establishing wage scales, and ineffective incentive schemes have helped the spread of "amorality and skepticism." Simultaneously, a powerful, complex, and thriving "shadow economy," nourished to no mean extent by widespread pilfering of the legal economy, grew up alongside the latter and has sapped its strength and vitality. In *The Economic Challenge of Perestroika* (1988), Abel Agenbegyan remarks that, without "all-embracing measures" including "the whole of society and all sectors of the economy"—that is, both "base and superstructure" (in Marxian parlance)—the future cannot be but bleak. Yet the central Soviet leadership is reluctant to seriously dismantle the core of the system—state ownership of the means of production. What it tries to do instead is to allow limited "privatization" of state property, small-scale individual and cooperative production and trade in capital goods, along with widespread leasing of state property in all sectors of the economy as a means of increasing output and productivity and overcoming alienation and indifference toward work. As we shall see in chapters 9 and 10, however, the attempt to use leasing as a substitute for outright denationalizations is not achieving the hoped-for results.

Organization and Steering Methods

In Marxian theory, socialization was supposedly the unavoidable outcome of a historical process leading to a centralized, consciously directed system along "rational" lines, an extraordinarily productive and growing economy able to pursue the full utilization of all of its human and material resources at all times. The Soviet reorganization of the economy as a single, centrally run, multibranch, multiplant corporation was, allegedly, the necessary result of a process that had begun with the appearance of the modern factory and machine manufacture. Indeed, Marx, and then Engels, asserted that with the modern factory's replacement of individual by social production, social rather than private coordination will eventually become imperative. The private owners of factories were supposedly coalescing into trusts and holding companies in order to replace "obsolete" market competition. According to the founders of Marxism, however, capitalism could not carry out the process to its logical end; it could not overcome crises and waste of resources. It could not reconcile socialized production and organization with individual appropriation. Only the Communists could open the appropriate way by expropriating the private owners of the means of production. Then, during a transitional stage leading from the discarded capitalism to the Communist future, the Communists would create a harmonious, rationally directed, fully employed, planned socialist economy.

The leaders of the Soviet party-state debated extensively in the 1920s about just how such an economy could be organized and operated. To what extent should each state-owned enterprise orient itself independently? Should these enterprises compete with one another? What role should be left to the market? Eventually, by the end of the 1920s, the idea of rigorous centralization and full dependence on a single center of command prevailed. Through the following decades, although the Soviet leaders felt compelled to restructure the institutional arrangements in various ways and to modify certain rules for formulating and implementing the center's decisions, they remained convinced until the mid-1980s that the Soviet economy could be managed like a unified railroad network, that is, like a self-sufficient technical entity. They viewed the economy as an integrated, mechanically controllable system with predictable, disciplined responses at all levels. Stalin treated the Soviet economy as a kind of servo-mechanism (see fig. 1-1). In this system his commands (x) to the "computer," C_1—say, the Council of Ministers and its Gosplan— would produce, in accordance with a mandatory program, signals to be transmitted to the "actuator," A_1—the plant managers—whose own signals would drive the processing plant, P (the economy as a whole), exactly as desired. The resulting performance (y), measured and identified by various party and administration committees, I_1, would be fed back to C_1 whose signals would be adjusted to avoid any deviation from the originally set targets. Since a central plan contains not only an overall primary objective but also a set of objectives—namely, secondary, tertiary, and n objectives—the centralized planning and control system was eventually conceptualized as being a mechanical system provided with parallel loops (for example, C_2, A_2, I_2, . . . , C_n, A_n, I_n) each for one objective, adjusting the values of free parameters in C so that any and all of the additional objectives assumed to be mutually compatible would be met. Stalin's Council of Ministers, comprised of numerous industrial ministries and of functional bodies (for example, Gosplan and Gossnab) became the locus of centralized day-to-day management of the economy as a whole and each branch, region, and organizational level of the enterprises (see fig. 1-2).

After Stalin's death, the chain of control over the economy was reorganized in various ways (with changing emphases on the branch or region principle), but the core concept that the economy as a whole must be run as an integrated, single complex on the basis of a system of commands was not officially questioned. The idea was kept alive even when, in the mid-1960s, various changes were undertaken in regard to the utilization of monetary and financial instruments and mathematical techniques in planning, as we shall see later on. Throughout these attempts, the idea of the economy as a single, centrally commanded complex continued to be emphasized and even to be enshrined in the 1977 constitution (article 16), notwithstanding the obvious

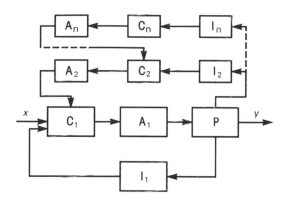

Fig. 1-1. The "single national economic complex"

discrepancies between the ponderously elaborated plans and the results achieved in their implementation. Numerous official books of the mid-1980s—for instance, a massive collective work of leading Soviet economists entitled *The Socialist Economic System*—continued to assert that the Soviet economy had become an integrated "single national economic complex" (*edinyi narodnokhoziaistvennyi kompleks [ENKhK]*), thanks to the construction of an appropriate technological basis created in the conditions of "adequately developed socialism." Allegedly, the ENKhK, a "new manifestation of the law of planned development of the national economy," had surmounted all the so-called particularisms of the industrial branches and regions. This unitary, command-guided economy was supposedly in the process of integration at all levels thanks to the formation of an all-encompassing statewide system of information processing supported by a system of interconnected computing centers.

By the mid-1980s, however, the idea of a fully integrated economy guided step by step by instructions from the center lost the official stamp of approval. The deteriorating economic performance—in terms of growth rates, productivity, availability of goods, and work-force morale— prompted the new Soviet leadership to put the emphasis on decentralizing economic responsibilities, expanding the options left to enterprises and farms, changing some of the central instruments used for guiding them, and increasing the responsibility of their employees (so-called work collective). For the purpose, in a report to the Central Committee (published in *Pravda* on June 26, 1987) Gorbachev unearthed a study written more than twenty years before by the

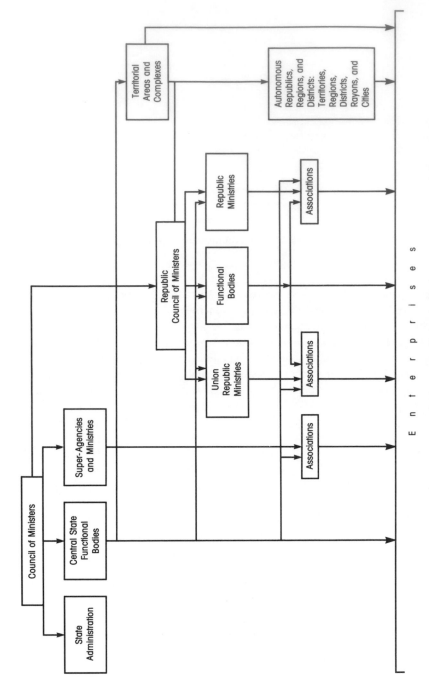

Fig. 1-2. The executive-administrative chain of control over the functioning of the economy

late academician Vasilii S. Nemchinov and published in the party's theoretical journal, *Kommunist,* in 1964. In the study the Soviet academician asserted that it was *not* necessary to make all the economy's systems "mechanically and arithmetically identical." Rather, it was more appropriate to create a new, more flexible mechanism and to discard the old "ossified mechanistic system relying on quotas from top to bottom." In the Nemchinov system, the centrally established mandatory plan-target assignments would be replaced by state orders backed by freely negotiated contracts for which the state enterprises would compete among themselves. Gorbachev affirmed his full agreement with Nemchinov's vision of the economy and his advocacy of expanded contractual relations among enterprises. He embodied some of these ideas in his perestroika, along with various other concepts of reform suggested or put into practice in certain socialist countries (for example, Hungary in the late 1960s). In this new economic mechanism the Council of Ministers retains its role of supreme economic manager, but the scope of its activities and the instruments to carry them out are modified. We should not forget that the Soviet government, like any other government, has at its disposal a vast array of instruments—both direct and indirect, of public finance, money and credit, and institutional change—with which it can affect the operation of the economy's components in a variety of ways. Many possibilities are open to it for transiting from the administrative, mandatory system of directives to other methods for carrying out the center's will, as, for instance, the methods proposed by Nemchinov and those implemented by other socialist states. The Hungarian New Economic Mechanism (NEM), evolved in the late 1960s, indeed foreshadowed key elements of the perestroika involving various shifts toward more indirect methods for guiding enterprises in ways that will be examined in detail in chapters 3 and 9.

"Laws," Policies, and Priorities

The Bolshevik economic theoretician Nikolay Bukharin—killed by Stalin in 1938 and "rehabilitated" postmortem fifty years later by Gorbachev—affirmed at the dawn of the Soviet system (in *The ABC of Communism* [1919]) that the Marxian economic methodology had three components: an objective social point of view; a material-production approach; and a dialectical-historical conception of major socioeconomic changes. The first, he noted, posited the primacy of society over the individual; the second, the primacy of material production (that is, of material supply as the determinant of the scope and pattern of demand); and the third, the existence of different economic laws (that is, of different regularities) in differing socioeconomic systems. The Communists asserted the primacy of society over the individual first of all by expropriating the private owners of capital. With respect to the tenet of the primacy of material production, they formulated and applied industrial policies aiming at the rapid growth of certain producer goods (intermediate products and industrial equipment) to the neglect of consumer goods and services—policies supported by the massive channeling of the country's investable resources toward the selected priority branches. They upheld their beliefs in the existence of new economic laws under socialism by disregarding cost-price calculations and trying to impose on the economy the policy-makers' arbitrary choices concerning the rates and scope of economic growth and change. Stalin erected into permanent socialist commandments the three presumptions of the Marxian methodology: he nationalized virtually the entire production and distribution sectors; he inflexibly pursued the expansion of producer goods and disregarded the needs of consumption and services; he sanctified the "voluntaristic" approach to planning as the expression of a so-called new economic law, the "law of planned proportional development of the economy." His doctrinal interpretations reigned supreme until the 1980s. While, up to then, the emphasis was placed on the progress achieved thanks to Stalin's vision and thrust toward forced industrialization, since it has been increasingly noted, as Fiodor Burlatski put it in the *Literaturnaia gazeta* in February, 1988, that all these policies had in fact left "an increasingly impoverished and essentially half-destroyed countryside, technically backward industry, grave shortage of housing, the population's low standard of living, millions of prisoners in jails and camps, the country's isolation from the outside world."

The rehabilitation of Bukharin by the Gorbachev leadership expressed the latter's identification not with the Bukharin of the earliest years of the revolution, but with the Bukharin of the mid-1920s. At that time Bukharin and his followers opposed the push of the so-called left superindustrializers, and argued instead in favor of the encouragement of small-scale private property in agriculture and trade, expansion of consumer goods outputs, recognition of the importance of cost-price considerations and economic accounting. Gorbachev's chief economic adviser, Abel Aganbegyan, asserted in the late 1980s that only a true reversal of priorities leading to "the subordination of production to consumer demand" could put a halt to the perennial production of shoddy and unwanted goods and the wastage of resources and bring about a rapid increase in the quality and quantity of the goods produced. But such a reversal is slow in coming. Gorbachev has focused first of all on priorities of the centrally determined industrial policy. Stalin had emphasized the coal-iron-steel orientation. In the late 1950s and early 1960s Nikita Khrushchev emphasized fuel oil and chemicals (polymer materials). Gorbachev shifted the emphasis from raw and intermediate products to machine building, in particular, viewed by him as the key lever for transforming the economy, accelerating its pace of growth, and bringing it onto a higher development plateau. Again, this emphasis is claimed to be indispensable for raising the economy's productivity before the policymakers could envisage a decisive shift in favor of the consumer.

The Marxists have dismissed the attempts to analyze economic phenomena from the side of demand as subjectivist and ahistorical. As we shall see in detail later on, in Soviet planning, statistics, and accounting procedures, manufacturing production (based on planners' goals) has always held the pride of place. This production has traditionally been divided into groups A and B, which roughly correspond to the Marxian division of production into Department I (producer goods) and Department II (consumer goods)—of Marx's celebrated schema of reproduction (growth) published in *Capital*. Emphasis has been placed on the rate of growth of group A vs. B, even though the scope of what should be included in A or B has never been free of definitional contradictions. While since the mid-1980s the growth rate of B has been officially stated to increase significantly, and while Aganbegyan has warned that socialism must by all means turn its face toward the consumer's needs for goods *and* services, priority continues to remain with material production and, within it, with machine tools. The emphasis might reflect Marx's view of capitalism (in the *Communist Manifesto*) as having been extraordinarily successful in creating "constant capital"—and his neglect of such things as human capital and the division of labor as factors generating economic growth.

Concluding Comments

The four constitutive principles of what Soviet economists call the Soviet economic mechanism and what Western Sovietologists have tended to designate as the Soviet economic model have been finally drawn into what appears to be a long process of reevaluation and modification: (1) Below the top levels, the state administration is disengaging itself from the party's dominance; (2) The socialization of the means of production is shrinking, while at its borders and in its interstices various forms of ownership (municipal-communal and private) and various commercial-market relations for goods and services (but not for capital) are in the process of development; (3) The relationships between the center and the enterprises continue to be restructured, changing from a system of commands to a system of centrally established norms (concerning prices, wages, and the distribution of profits); (4) The primacy of production and capital goods is not abandoned, but its premises are challenged while its consequences are reappraised and reevaluated more realistically.

The progressive injection of transitional elements and correctives between the functions of the center, the responsibilities of the republics, regions, and local authorities, and the market's impulses does not mean that the central controls have been entirely abandoned. The controls continue in the allocation of the bulk of investable resources, the movement of labor, the scope and structure of the producing units, and the connections of the latter with suppliers and buyers. The system, authoritarian in its foundations and its approaches to change, is hesitant and uncertain in many respects, but it is departing from Stalin's centralized administrative methods.

The shortcomings of the latter system were exposed and modified in various ways in Eastern Europe *before* the advent of Gorbachev—notably in Yugoslavia in the 1950s and in Hungary during the second half of the 1960s— and many of the debates on these issues help to clarify them and foreshadow some Soviet changes. The outright discarding of the basic tenets of Soviet-type economies in Eastern Europe in the latter half of the 1980s also influences Soviet policymakers and planners. But, unlike the East European countries, the vast Soviet Union also must cope with the exacerbated problems of an ethnically explosive empire, a complex, well-entrenched, and obdurate bureaucracy, a class of managers raised for decades in the spirit of submission to plan instructions, a disgruntled and alienated work force, and a still-large and distrustful rural population.

The candid recognition by the leadership of the Soviet Union of the increasingly deteriorating performance of its economy is of great importance not only for partisans of socialism but also for the world at large. Certainly, the greatest interest lies in examining how and why this continuous decline has taken place, how the top leaders of the party-state of this pivot of socialism attempt to modify it in various stages, how they try to displace the locus of power (below the top echelons) from the party to the refurbished state administration, how they try to handle the traditional limits set on private ownership, how they search to modify the planning mechanisms and to awaken each enterprise to an environment responsive to the other firms' demands, how they strive to connect the national and the world markets, and how, in general, they hope to improve the overall functioning of the failing Soviet economy. It is certainly a vast process with portentous consequences for the very existence of socialism as a distinct economic system.

CHAPTER 2

Commodities and Prices

Commodity Space

Traditionally, Soviet economic textbooks, rooted in Marxian theory, have contended that no capitalist-like "buying and selling" operations existed under socialism, that capitalist "extraction of surplus value" (real profits) had long since vanished in the USSR, and that economic categories, such as commodities, money, price, profit, and interest, have all acquired entirely new meanings and new functions. On closer observation, however, one can note that, Soviet definitions often vary, some of the categories in question have changed their content over time, and various other changes are likely to occur there in the future.

At the beginning of the centralized planning system in the late 1920s, Soviet policymakers and Soviet economists asserted that the existence of buying and selling and commodity-monetary relations was thenceforth to be confined only to the sale and purchase of goods destined for consumption by the population. No such relations could exist in the transactions taking place among state-owned (socialized) firms, since these transactions did not involve a change of ownership. In the latter cases, the exchange concerned *simple products* whose transfer from one state firm to another reflected itself only in bookkeeping and banking changes. Indeed, in Marxian theory, as socialism advanced to its highest stage, all the goods produced would eventually turn into simple products involving state production and distribution without the use of money. Toward the mid-1960s, however, the basic segregation of total output into products and commodities (produced, respectively, by Department I—producer goods—and by Department II—consumer goods) was discarded. From then on commodities were said to be produced and sold by both departments whether such transactions involved bank transfers, credits, or cash.

Significant differences continue to exist, however, between the quantity, quality, and assortment of commodities produced and sold in a Soviet-type economy and those produced and sold in a market-directed economy. To start with, in such an economy the production and sale of commodities are subject to many important policy-making decisions. The priorities of policymakers

29

and *not* commodity-market relations determine the allocation of the bulk of investable resources among sectors, branches, and enterprises. What the Marxians call the law of value—namely, the "spontaneous," "elemental" determination of the exchangeable value of commodities, that is, their *prices*—is still kept under an array of controls. Planned prices, along with various controls on inputs and outputs, still determine the basic flows of goods and their composition. As recently as 1984, an official Soviet guide, *Teaching of Political Economy* edited by A. D. Smirnov, V. V. Golosov, and V. F. Maximova, asserted that, in fact, the plan and the market could not coexist as opposing "principles of regulation." The Gorbachev policy, as we shall see in more detail later on, has taken as its goal the idea of blending these two principles. As in Stalin's time, the center will continue to determine the allocation of most investable resources and the pace and direction of development of the economy, while contractual relations among the producing-distributing enterprises increasingly will shape the structure of a large part of interfirm transactions and the final bill of goods. Put differently, while the policymakers will decide how to allocate the bulk of investments and how and in which directions to map the expansion of the economy, the producing enterprises will determine to an appreciable degree their own inputs and outputs in conformity with both the plan and the consumers' demand (the consumers being represented first of all by priority demands of the main state organs followed by those of other state enterprises responding to consumers' preferences). The leaders of the USSR seem still inclined to believe that such a combination of central decisions with contractual impulses under price controls will eliminate in time most of the shortcomings of the highly centralized Stalinist system—namely, excess demand for capital goods and raw materials from the producing enterprises, chronic shortages and poor quality of all products (and, in particular, consumer goods), and ineffective and wasteful distribution systems. These changes, however, might not necessarily be quite the final result, as we might surmise when taking a closer look at the specific constraints under which producers and households must continue to operate, even as Gorbachev's perestroika started to unfold in various directions.

Constraints on Producers

The leading Soviet business institute, the Academy of National Economy in Moscow, trains the Soviet Union's most senior bureaucrats and executives of state-owned enterprises and coordinates the instruction of some sixty other business institutes. In the spring of 1988 a Soviet delegation led by the director of the academy, Eugeni K. Smirnitsky, visited some American business schools. According to the *New York Times* (May 2, 1988), the visitors showed great interest in the American business schools' management programs, the marketing expertise the business schools could offer, and the use of incentives to improve worker productivity. Thomas H. Naylor of the Fuqua School of Business at Duke University felt the visit showed that the Soviet leaders "realized that the foremost obstacle to Gorbachev's reforms are Soviet managers' lack of knowledge of Western-style management practices." And Naylor added that, "within two years at least one hundred senior Soviet managers will be in American business schools' executive management programs." The Russians seem to confirm Naylor's belief. The number of Soviet management training programs has increased since then, not only abroad but in the Soviet Union itself, with on-the-spot training by Western managers.

These developments might convey the false impression that Western-style management practices, to be dispensed and absorbed in ad hoc seminars, could be easily grafted onto Soviet practices. Actually, vast differences exist in the position and functions of managers in the two economies. And, as long as the Soviet enterprises are compelled to work under the tutelage of higher administrative organs, Western managerial practices could be transferred from our framework to the Soviet one only in a very limited way. Certainly, in both systems the firms (or enterprises) are *cooperative* forms of organization that take advantage of specialization and the division of labor within prevailing technologies. As Oliver E. Williamson has noted, all firms can be broadly classified into three basic structures: unitary firms (*U* form) created around classic business functions such as manufacturing, finance, and marketing; holding firms (*H* form) grouping a large number of unrelated firms, each treated as a profit or investment center; and multidivisional firms (*M* form), which are, in essence, partially diversified business divisions. Until the 1960s, the typical Soviet firms were of the *U* and *M* forms. Since the 1970s impetus has been given to the development of the *H* type, called in the USSR "enterprises' associations" and often organized around a *head* enterprise. Whatever the type and whatever the changes introduced there since the second half of the 1980s, at the beginning of the 1990s the Soviet firms were still operating under the supervision of a ministry, a central agency, or a ministerial department. To grasp the meaning of such constraints and to understand what problems their removal would elicit, let us consider the differences that exist in managerial tasks, initiatives, allocative powers, and obligations, as well as the contrast that prevails in the kinds of information on which the managers operating in one or the other economy must base their decisions.

Let us recall briefly that the modern capitalist corporation produces for and distributes its products in a variety of markets. The latter involve complex interactions among (mostly) privately owned firms, all responding primarily to households' demand. The firms sell their products in order to recover outlays and realize a profit. Whatever the type of firm, its executives must create and maintain a demand for its products; in order to do this, they must try to assess not only the immediate prospects in the firm's surroundings and its potential markets but also the dominant conditions in the economy as a whole and the specific conditions prevalent in the given industry (or industries) and in its markets. Concerning the general outlook, executives will have to take into consideration the possible impacts of prospective changes in such indicators as growth and employment rates, government budget and trade deficits, interest rates, stock and bond yields, and government regulations and rules. The decision makers of the firm further will have to forecast carefully the possible quantity-price relationships for each of its scheduled products and the impacts of the price of similar and related competitive products, advertising expenditures, and the prospective consumer income. They will also have to acquire information about the prices and availability of factor inputs, assuming that they are familiar with the production technologies available to the firm. They will have to determine how to allocate the company's resources across its set of divisions or businesses, whether the internal financing resources are sufficient for the purpose or they will have to resort to the capital markets via the issue of stocks and bonds, and whether it is necessary to acquire new businesses or, instead, it is imperative to divest some of the businesses that do not offer growth potential and the prospect of substantial amounts of revenue. On the basis of goals, evaluations of the general outlook, forecasts of demand and supply, analyses of competitors' prices and strategies, and choices involved in portfolio management, a host of *operative* decisions will finally be taken. Aside from the firm's organizational structure design, they will concern which factors of production should be bought and of what type and in what quantities, which products should be produced and in what quantities and assortments, which technological combinations should be resorted to, what kind of incentives should be called into play, how production should be scheduled, and toward which particular markets the firms' principal effort should be directed.

In a market-directed economy managerial decision making thus involves undivided attention to the interrelated problems of what, how, and for whom to produce, combining long-range and day-to-day choices that require many types of information, along with the freedom to exercise initiative and ingenuity in their interpretation and utilization. Diversification and development of multiproduct, multifunction industrial enterprises have brought about a distinction between top management—which formulates policy (or strategy), appraises performance, and coordinates the activity of the enterprise as a whole—and the operations managers, whose tasks are determined by the daily conduct of operations and functions for which they are responsible. As pointed out by Alfred Chandler in his *Essays toward a Historical Theory of Big Business* (1988), the problems facing top management are the formulation of the prime objectives of the business as to products and markets, the determination of the desirability and type of expansion, the provision of the capital for operations, and the distribution of its profits between profits retained and the amount paid out as dividends. The division heads, which now discharge functions quite similar to those of the senior executive of a single-product, multifunction enterprise are appraised by the success on the return on investment and the market share they conquer. The need for large, interdepartmental communication has brought pressures on the large-scale enterprise to predict the future in addition to gauging past performance. Ultimately, the total product flow through all departments is determined by demand. Hence, the more accurately demand is forecasted, the more evenly the product flow can be assured and coordinated, and the more the overall organization can operate closer to maximum capacity.

In contrast to the privately owned capitalist firms, which must operate under risk and uncertainty, the managers of the majority of state-owned Soviet enterprises, even after the unfolding of perestroika, have to work in the seemingly "safe" and "settled" framework of a state plan that determines to a large extent each one's inputs, outputs, and distribution. We will examine later on the case of the private partnerships functioning on the territory of the USSR since 1987. What is at issue here is how perestroika might change the parameters within which the managers of state firms have been accustomed to function. Under perestroika, all state enterprises and associations of enterprises—that is the overwhelming number of enterprises now in operation in the USSR—are supposed to achieve complete financial autonomy and depend on self-financing. But their expansion or contraction is still at the discretion of their supervisory agency, ministry, or department—a function of policy decisions taken at a higher level. Whether a state enterprise or group of enterprises carry on their activity in manufacturing, agriculture, construction, transport, commerce, scientific work, or services of any kind (excluding, of course, cooperatives, which are not state owned), the scope of self-financing activity is determined by a supervisory agency—ministry or ministerial department. The internal structure of an association—for instance, the organization of its components—is determined by the associations' officers, while a plant's internal structuring is decided by its executive officers. But the size and number of firms engaged in the economy are still the result of decisions of policymakers and planners concerning the creation, grouping, or amalgamation of firms according to centrally perceived needs and objectives involving organizational convenience and control only, not demand.

One should note, however, that functional patterns of enterprise creation, along with centralized decisions on exit, entry, amalgamations, and the "streamlining" of this or that structural design of an industry and of the methods of its control do not necessarily yield an efficient industrial structure.

To minimize production costs might require either fewer firms of large scale or more firms of a smaller scale with different specialization. The state firms cannot decide by themselves to merge with other firms to save on and/or better use their inputs and respond more efficiently to demand, nor can they appeal for private capital via the issue of stocks and bonds. People working in state enterprises cannot engage in self-employed work (an exception is made for artisans). Pensioners, students, and a few other people can do so. The self-employed cannot hire others for a wage, which is considered to be exploitation. Following the adoption on June 4, 1990, of a "Law on Enterprises in the USSR," the Supreme Soviet of the USSR has opened the door, as of January 1, 1990, to the formation of all kind of private enterprises—individual, family, cooperative enterprises, partnerships, joint-stock companies and association. But their sphere of activity is constrained by the centralized control of *inputs* that remains in the hands of the so-called material technical supply system.

On the threshold of the 1990s, decisions on scheduled outputs are still predicated on past performance rather than eventual shifts in demand. The state enterprises' mergers and amalgamation are not resorted to in order to protect or expand markets, to out-compete other firms, to reduce the cost of financing and/or of inputs. Evaluation of consumer demand and acceptance of consumer preferences are still in the future, while assessments of suppliers' pricing strategies and risk analysis are irrelevant in the existing conditions. The key economic choices are still administrative decisions motivated by a preoccupation with better planning, controlling, and coordinating production via the organization of state production into complexes or associations on a national or regional basis and via the establishment of one, two, or more levels of coordination. However, changes are bound to take place in the future, as more and more private owned enterprises take advantage of the rights spelled out in the June 4, 1990, "Law on Enterprises in the USSR," and as they expand both their domestic and import-export operations.

Before the second half of the 1980s enterprises were commanded to obey very detailed directives concerning their inputs and assignments concerning their outputs, both of which had been worked out within the rigid framework of centrally managed, yearly state plans. From July 1987 on, following the adoption of the Law of the State Enterprise, a more flexible framework was put into place, allowing, in principle, more freedom to the input and output choices of the state enterprises. Functioning on the basis of economic accountability and financial autonomy, they were set henceforth to work out their own five-year and yearly plans on the basis of plan guidelines for five years. The strategy of the state enterprises' managers concerning expansion and the allocation of their finances continues, however, to be constrained, on the one hand, by policy decisions that determine state ceilings concerning capital construction in the economy as a whole and, on the other hand, by norms concerning the allocations of their own resources to the wage fund, incentives, taxation, depreciation, and construction of new facilities, as we will see later on. Even in their operational activities, the Soviet state enterprises' executives have to face serious handicaps. In an attempt at democratization, the executives are scheduled to be elected by the enterprises' labor collectives and, therefore, depend largely on their wishes. Even a schematic representation of the ways in which the firm is managed in a market environment and is to be managed in the restructured Soviet environment shows the enormous differences between the *qualitative* conditions in which the state firms have to function. One wonders what the students of Eugeni K. Smirnitsky would learn in the American management seminars that they could actually apply in the USSR before a real shift—from emphasis on production to emphasis on demand, domestic and foreign—occurs there. (See fig. 2-1.)

In contrast to the state nonagricultural firms, farm managers are supposed to have more autonomy concerning production varieties, area, and timing, and are to be subjected only to the plan of deliveries to the state (procurement plan). In practice, however, tight and detailed sales plans put the agricultural enterprise also in a bind. The state has certainly no reasonable interest in ascertaining which particular farm produce and which particular outputs will be produced as long as it can be certain that it will obtain the total and the overall assortment of farm produce that it deems necessary. But, for a number of years to come, neither planners nor the farm authorities at all levels seem to be ready to give up the control of marketing quotas, output, and procurement prices, and to rely instead on freely negotiated contracts and prices and quantities determined by supply and demand. A proposal for free sales of agricultural outputs was put forward in the 1960s, but few prices have been rendered flexible since then. As we will see in detail further on, as long as the centrally manipulated prices continue to distort the farms' decision making, inputs are centrally allocated, and the system of detailed procurement targets remain in place, one cannot expect that the agricultural sector as a whole will effectively respond to opportunities to improve its input and output mixes.

Constraints on Households

In one of his *Essays on Consumption and Econometrics* (1987), James Tobin pointed out that a household, like a business firm, can be thought to have two related accounts: one for income and one for capital. The income account is composed of flows over a period of time; the capital account consists of stocks at a moment in time. The shape of the first account is determined by the household's decisions concerning work and leisure, present consumption

Private Firms, Market-Directed Environment	State Firms, Plan-Directed Environment

Prospects Evaluation
    Consideration of:
—General prospects (growth, employment, and budget and trade deficits)
—Financial prospects (interest rates, stock and bond yields, returns on investments)
—Legal framework (regulations, other laws)
	Prospects Evaluation
	    Consideration of:
	—Five-Year State Economic Plan (with branch and sector assignments broken down by year)

Demand and Supply Evaluation
    Consideration of:
—Product-demand forecasting models
—Evaluation of competitors and designing promotion programs
—Supply forecasting (prices and availability of factor inputs)
—Risk analysis
	Demand and Supply Evaluation
	    Consideration of:
	—Control figures (general output indices); scope of state orders (for top priority requirements); other state assignments; contracted commercial orders
	—Scope of centralized supply pricing and of supervised contract pricing
	—Scope of centralized supply procedures plus independent contracting for other input and output deliveries

Strategy Formulation
    Consideration of:
—Allocation of available resources
—Evaluation of capacities and of cost of capital
—Financing (internal and/or external)
—Acquisitions and/or divestitures
	Strategy Formulation
	    Consideration of:
	—Centralized financing for reconstruction and expansion
	—Marginal internal financing powers for various facilities
	—Any reorganization (merger and annexation, for example) envisaged in function of central policy decisions

Operational Measures
    Decisions by the firm's divisions executives:
—Organizational structures design
—Choice of production techniques
—Cost analyses and choices
—Supply analyses and choices
—Personnel choice (efficiency and incentives)
—Production scheduling
—Research and development (R & D)
—Marketing
	Operational Measures
	    Decision divided between the center and the "firm":
	—Uniform technical policies determined centrally for the entire branch
	—Centralized controls on "scarce" supplies
	—Organizational structures designed within the enterprise for the enterprise only
	—Savings on materials and wage fund allocation decided within the firm
	—Personnel selection and placement decided jointly by the firm's management and the party organization
	—Production scheduling set by the firm's executives within the plan targets
	—R & D technological improvement and modernization decided within the firm

Control —Accounting systems for control —Budgeting control —Profit and loss accounts	*Control* —Accounting autonomy within fixed rules and obligations —Management–party–trade union—regional and local authorities' controls

Fig. 2-1. Nature and scope of management decision making in the firm in two environments

needs and future needs (namely, savings for housing, appliances, auto, recreation, and retirement). The shape of the second account is determined by decisions concerning the structure of assets (namely, residence, appliances, auto, cash and savings, debts, and professional assets of the self-employed).

The Soviet household is constrained in a wide variety of ways as far as its income and capital accounts are concerned. As we saw in chapter 1, the limits placed on private ownership are severe. The Soviet citizen who does not belong to a licensed individual or cooperative enterprise cannot own more than an apartment, a summer home, household appliances, and a car. The scope of ownership is somewhat larger in agriculture, but it, too, is clearly limited. In the case of cooperatives (as we will see in chap. 9), access to credit is restricted, hiring of help is prohibited, and income generated is highly taxed. Artisanal work is hampered by various restrictions on the supply of materials and equipment, and a number of incongruous regulations push many activities onto the black market. The low level of wages stimulates pilfering of state property, clandestine production, and extensive trafficking in all kinds of goods and services. Consider further the question of wages versus leisure. A Soviet citizen cannot freely or easily decide how much to work, in what kind of job, and where. Since 1950 he or she is free to change jobs in response to higher wages: but a citizen cannot move freely within the country or go abroad. Internal passports are mandatory, residence permits in certain cities are very hard to get, housing is very scarce, and traveling abroad is a privilege reserved to the higher layers of the nomenklatura. Domestic travel is facilitated when the worker agrees to move to high-priority developing areas and industries. A citizen is still not free to decide to work or not to work if he or she is in a working-age bracket; leisure is "parasitism." These constraints will eventually be changed since the Soviet leadership has given up its commitment to full employment and since it faces the need to lay off a large number of workers in various industries.

The basic division of the national income between *consumption* and *savings* is decided centrally and implemented through an array of direct and indirect measures, which determine the broad structure of both of them and places numerous constraints on consumer's freedom of choice and utility maximization. The reduced availability of scarce inputs needed for the production of consumer goods, the obsolete and deteriorating character of the equipment of many light industries, the ups and downs of agricultural outputs, the priority claims of exports, and, last but not least, the incapacity of distributors to choose among producers and to select among their products— except in the case of the shops reserved for the nomenklatura—severely limit the access to goods and the range of choice among them left to ordinary households. The system thus imposes multiple constraints instead of a single budget constraint on the maximization of the utility of the consumer (see fig.

In the Market-Directed Environment

max $U(C_1,C_2,C_3)$
Subject to
$p_1C_1 + p_2C_2 + p_3C_3 = M$
$C_1,C_2,C_3 \geqslant 0.$

In the Plan-Directed Environment

max $U(C_1,C_2,C_3)$
Subject to
$p_1C_1 + p_2C_2 + p_3C_3 = M$
$a > a' \geqslant C_1 \geqslant 0,$
$b > b' \geqslant C_2 \geqslant 0,$
$c > c' \geqslant C_3 \geqslant 0.$

Example of a Reduction in the Opportunity Set

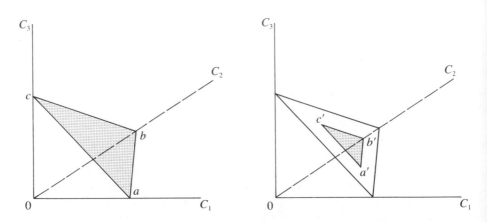

**Fig. 2-2. The utility maximization of the consumer in two environments.
The figure illustrates utility maximization with three commodities. Let
C_1, C_2, and C, denote these commodities and p_1, p_2, and p, their prices.
The market income of the consumer is given by M and $U(C_1,C_2,C_3)$ is
the agent's utility function. The left-hand diagram represents the case in
a market-directed environment. The point a represents the amount of
good one available if the entire budget is spent on the first good. Points
b and c have a similar interpretation. The right-hand diagram represents
the case of a plan-directed environment. The constraints of the market
model are now expanded to include quota constraints. The maximum
amount of good one allowed for purchase is $a' < a$; points b' and c' have
similar interpretations.**

2-2). Foreign as well as Soviet analyses of the supply of consumer goods
stress the narrowness of choice with respect to style, design, assortment,
quality, durability, convenience, reliability, and attractiveness of the goods
offered to the consumer. Pervasive disequilibria between supply and demand
lead to shortages of certain basic products and to random surpluses of others.

The imbalance forces the consumer to spend inordinate amounts of time searching for products, trudging from store to store, and standing in line— and, eventually, it pushes him or her to resort to black markets. As Basile Kerblay and Marie Lavigne aptly summed this up (in their book on Soviet Citizens of the 1980s [*Les sovietiques des annees 1980,* 1985]), "the life of the Soviet consumer is first of all a struggle of every instant against 'short-age.'" As in all systems with open or hidden rationed goods, the black market establishes the effective price of the goods under ration or in scarce supply for whatever reason.

Goods available only to privileged bureaucrats, either in their special stores or from trips abroad, are resold at black market prices involving, in certain cases, significant income changes in favor of the seller (for instance, in the resale of a recently purchased car or scarce foreign goods). Not only the supply of goods but also everyday services fall short of demand, and their quality is poor. This is true for such things as tailoring and repair of clothing, shoes, repair and maintenance of appliances and furniture, and help for diverse household needs. Also in short supply are services such as laundries, cleaners, barber services, recreational and cultural services, and many other facilities, including hotels, motels, and rooming houses.

For most Soviet citizens, however, the worst problem is housing. Most urban families live in crowded, state-owned, subsidized apartments; a full quarter of the population lives in communal housing with communal facilities. The typical rural family lives in small two or three-room farmhouses devoid of modern facilities. The "housing norm" is five square meters of habitable surface per family member, and it takes years of waiting to obtain an apartment. It is estimated that it would take no less than a doubling of the existing housing stock over the balance of the century, along with an "equitable distribution system," to provide every family with a separate apartment. As of the 1980s, all new construction was of poor quality and in need of *immediate* repair. New housing lacked retail facilities, and convenient public transport was often absent. The provision of retail facilities continues to differ widely between large and small cities, regions and areas; moreover, most of the retail network employs cumbersome methods and lacks modern equipment. Health care, except for the nomenklatura, leaves much to be desired in terms of quality and ready access; clinics and hospitals are crowded, often dirty, and poorly equipped. The "Basic Provisions and Tasks of the Comprehensive Program for the Development of Consumer Goods Production and Service Sphere in 1986–2000" (worked out after the 27th CPSU Congress as a component part of the *Basic Guidelines* concerning economic development up to the year 2000) spelled out in great detail many old promises to households concerning "an all-out increase in the production of consumer goods, and in the expansion of their assortment and improvements in their quality," as well as in the availability and range of services and the organization of wholesale and retail trade. Similar promises were included again in the 13th Five-Year Plan (1990–95), proceeding from the alleged aim of "saturating the consumer market." Actually, as indicated in the report on the plan of the then-premier N. I. Ryzkov at the Congress of People's Deputies (*Pravda,* December 14, 1989) the scheduled rate of growth of consumer goods is quite modest.

The economic levers used for "guiding private consumption" include not only the determination of proportions between the overall size and structure of consumption and savings and the projection of growth rates of the industrial groups A (producer goods) and B (consumer goods, including a great part of agricultural output) but also controls over the wage fund and the volume of money and credit available to households. Planning of prospective consumption involves a vast array of normative models concerning "rational" levels of consumption for different commodities, investigation of consumption typologies involving characteristic consumption types created under certain postulated conditions of the consumer's life and explored with the help of various statistical techniques, and, finally, multiple calculations concerning the balances between incomes and outlays of the population by social categories. Yet plans and results fail to mesh even more in regard to consumer goods than with respect to priority producer goods where the fit between the pace of plant construction and that of the delivery of machinery and equipment has traditionally been out of phase. With regard to consumer goods, the leadership has traditionally emphasized the importance of matching the pace of consumer goods output (at established retail prices) with the growth of the income of the population in order to stifle inflationary pressures and avoid the dampening effect of unfulfilled consumer demand on incentives and productivity. Yet wide discrepancies have always developed between the supply and demand of consumer goods, as reflected in sharp increases at certain moments in the volume of the population's saving deposits (equal to unsatisfied demand plus savings for unexpected opportunities or for major cash purchases). Thus, for instance, between 1965 and 1978—a time of sharply reduced growth rates in the food-processing industries—the savings of the population grew no less than sevenfold, reaching a worrisome sum equal to 55 percent of the value of the retail sales in that year. In short, households face a vast array of constraints on their incomes, capital accounts, and choices of goods. Their opportunity sets are vastly reduced (see fig. 2-2).

In the perestroika scheme, the centralized prospective planning of consumption and its interrelations with the distribution of income, on the one hand, and the market impulses registered in interfirm commercial relations, on the other, are to be brought into agreement via centralized price formation and price controls. Let us see how and whether or not centralized prices can discharge this role assigned to them.

The Role of Prices

In Vasilii Nemchinov's planning schema, published in *Kommunist* in 1964 and endorsed by Gorbachev in 1987, planned prices play a crucial role. According to Nemchinov, bourgeois economists are convinced that the regulating power of prices is so great that they counterpose price to plan and proclaim the slogan "Price in place of Plan." Soviet economists, continued Nemchinov, often veer in the opposite direction and proclaim "Plan in place of Price." The correct solution, affirmed Nemchinov, is instead a "purposeful combination of plan and price," since "prices can be subject to planning." The search for this purposeful combination is also viewed as necessary by Gorbachev, who stated a number of times that the planning of prices was indeed a crucial component of socialist management. In his report to the Central Committee of the party in June 1987, he specified that "prices for the most important types of output must, of course, be determined in a centralized way, as part of the process of drawing up the state plan. But, at the same time, under the new mechanism it is expedient to broaden the use of contract prices in order to facilitate an expansion of the rights and economic independence of the enterprises."

Since the beginning of the centralized planning system, the setting of prices has been influenced by two sets of factors: the complex and contradictory objectives assigned to prices by the planners and a host of theoretical considerations, or, more accurately, ideological ways of thought rooted in the Marxian concepts concerning value and price. The Soviet economists have never been unanimous about either the objectives that planned prices were supposed to fulfill or the appropriate theoretical frameworks that were to be used for the formation of these prices. A general consensus exists, however, that planned prices provide basic connecting links among the state plan, the enterprises' economic accounting, the budget and financial balances, and, finally, consumers. Most Soviet economic studies on money and prices assert that prices serve to measure the expenditures on the output of production—as stimuli for lowering costs, tools for dividing and distributing income, and instruments for balancing supply and demand. Prices and wages must "reflect and monitor the effectiveness of planning decisions." In order to do this, prices must remain *unchanged* for the length of the planning period—say, five years and even more. Price stability must be tempered when needed, however, with price flexibility. Thus, wholesale prices can be lowered at appropriate moments in order to spur the producing enterprises to use their reserves of raw materials and unused capacities; on the other hand, prices can be increased in order to raise the income and profits of the enterprises so as to provide them with the funds they need to meet their financial obligations toward the budget and the banks.

Consider now questions of the calculation of the rates of return on the socialist property used by enterprises and the formation of prices of production. In Marx's analysis of the capitalist system, the price of production is said to be derived from labor value. But, on the other hand, Marx asserts that the distribution of capital determines the distribution of social labor. This production price is not to be confused with the market price. The latter is said to fluctuate above or below the production price, which is theoretically defined as the center of equilibrium, the "regulator" of the market price. How is this production price arrived at under capitalism? According to Marx, the components of price (or of gross output) are constant capital (cost of raw materials and depreciation—c), wages (v), and surplus (m) (in Western accounting terms, interest, rent, and profits). Following Marx, the new value created in production $v + m$ is entirely due to labor but is split between the worker and the capitalist (the owner of the means of production). Changes in c/v reflect changes in "capital intensity"; changes in m/v reflect changes in the exploitation of labor as well as in the value of commodities consumed by labor. The capitalist is primarily interested in the ratio $m/(c + v)$, that is, on the return on his total outlays.

These ideas, amended by experimentation, have served as the theoretical matrix for the determination of Soviet centrally planned prices. Up to the 1960s, the planned markup for the social surplus m needed for investment was assumed to be equal to the amount of the payroll in any given material production (excluding services). The ratio was apparently based on Marx's arbitrary assumption that $m/v = 1$ under capitalism. Eventually, the shortcomings of this approach became obvious. (Indeed, they had been evident after 1867 in the critiques of vol. 1 of *Capital*.) As should have been expected, capital-intensive industries, such as electric energy, yielded a low surplus, while labor-intensive industries, such as the light industries, yielded a high surplus "over and above their (planned) need for further growth." The markup $m/v = 1$ was finally changed after a large number of Soviet economists recommended that m be related to total outlays ($c + v$) and not labor's wage (v). In any case, up to that moment the total surplus of the economy was collected in the consumer goods industries since the producers' goods industries were allegedly producing only simple products rather than commodities. So, in 1967 it was decided as a general rule that m will be computed in *all* industries in relation to their $c + v$. The markup was so computed as to reduce also the large percentage (about 25 percent) of all industries operating until then at a planned loss.

In the course of the thorough revision of prices that took place at the

TABLE 2-1. Structure of Costs in the Soviet Industry in 1987, in Percentage

	$c + v$	c						v
	Total Cost	Raw Materials	Other Materials	Fuel	Electricity	Depreciation	Other Expenditures	Wages and Social Insurance
Total industry	100.0	63.1	4.3	4.0	2.7	9.0	3.0	13.9
Heavy industry	100.0	54.4	4.7	5.2	3.6	11.5	3.9	16.7
Machine tools complex	100.0	59.6	3.4	1.2	2.0	8.3	4.5	21.0
Light industry	100.0	84.7	2.8	0.5	0.7	2.2	0.6	8.5

Sources: Promyshlenost' SSSR. Statisticheskii sbornik (The Industry of the USSR. A Statistical Manual), (Moscow: Finansy i statistika, 1988), 43. For the preceding year, see Nerodnoe khoziaistvo SSSR za 70 let. (The National Economy during Seventy Years) (Moscow: Finansy i statistika, 1987), 159.

TABLE 2-2. The Production Price

Items		Coefficients Related to the Item
c_i	cost of production of good i	α_i
v_i	wages for good i	β_i
$(C + V)$	total outlays in the economy as a whole	γ_i
C'	cost of fixed funds in the economy	δ_i
C''	cost of circulating funds in the economy	ϵ_i
I	investments	ζ_i
A	cost of government apparatus, etc.	η_i
R_i	rent for good i	θ_i

Models

Model 1. $p_i = c_i + \beta_i v_i$ $\qquad\qquad$ $m_i = \beta_i - 1$
(*m* proportional to living labor)

Model 2. $p_i = \alpha_i(c_i + v_i)$ $\qquad\qquad$ $m_i = \alpha_i - 1$
(*m* proportional to outlays for given good in given branch)

Model 3. $p_i = c_i + v_i + \gamma_i(C + V)$ $\qquad\qquad$ $m_i = \gamma_i(C + V)$
(*m* proportional to outlays for good i in the economy as a whole)

Model 4. $p_i = c_i + v_i + \delta_i C' + \epsilon_i C''$ $\qquad\qquad$ $m_i = \delta_i C' + \epsilon_i C''$
(*m* proportional to the capital outlays for good i in the economy as a whole)

Model 5. $p_i = c_i + v_i + \gamma_i(C + V) + \zeta_i I + \eta_i A + \theta_i R_i$ $\quad$ $m_i = \gamma_i(C + V) + \zeta_i I + \eta_i A + \theta_i R_i$
(*m* proportional to an increasing variety of outlays)

time, it was perceived that the new general rule was also deficient given the differences among branches between fixed assets and the sizes of their outlays on raw materials—a distinction not worked out in Marx's model. The structure of costs in industry in 1987, for instance, can be seen in table 2-1. These differences led to the allowance of a flexible utilization of the rule. Permission was granted to each production branch to adjust the surplus entering in its planned price so as to cover the funds needed for its payments to the budget for the use of fixed assets, for the advances needed for purchasing the material inputs, and for its own incentive funds. Other proposals were also made then to include in *m* various other charges for meeting such expenditures as the upkeep of the state apparatus, the army, and social insurance. Essentially, then, the planned production prices have acquired in time the following structures. Let the components of the production price p_i of good i consist of the *items* and the *coefficients* related to them entering in the calculation of *m* as given, for instance, in table 2-2: then, evidently, a vast number of price models are possible, each one with its own legitimate defenders and detractors, leaving the planner and the policymaker in a quandary. Cutting through these differences, the official 1989 textbook, *Political Economy,* which was used in the Soviet schools, defines price as consisting of cost of production plus the net income (*m*) computed on the basis of *norms* related to labor, assets, and resource utilization (somewhat as in models 4, 5).

Now, the production price is the cornerstone of planned prices. The average production price is the price of production of a given branch: the *producer's price*. On its basis are constructed two other sets of prices: the *wholesale price of an industry* and the *retail prices* of the goods entering into the state retail network. The wholesale price of an industry is the price charged by the distribution system. This is the *purchaser's price*. This price includes three additional charges over and above the producer's price: the turnover tax—a sales tax depending on the type of commodity involved—and the markup by the wholesale organization, consisting of handling charges and its planned profit. Finally, the retail price contains, on top of the wholesale price, the markup of the trade network for handling the goods plus a planned profit. Since the components of the wholesale prices of industry as well as those of the retail prices can be manipulated to discourage or encourage the use of certain resources or products or to bring supply and demand into line, certain wholesale or retail prices will sharply deviate from costs, a deviation that in certain cases can be very large. Thus, in the 1980s, 75 percent of the turnover tax was yielded by four groups of commodities, namely, alcoholic beverages, sugar, tobacco, and textile products. On the other hand, the retail prices of certain agricultural goods, such as meat, butter, vegetables, and potatoes, were kept stable in the face of rising costs and, therefore, required large subsidies; indeed, in certain years, these subsidies were three to four times larger than total investment in agriculture. With respect to various commodities, wide discrepancies developed between innumerable price zones; by the beginning of the 1980s, there were forty-eight price zones for grain, ninety-two price zones for milk, and additional differentials were in place between groups of farms in each zone. According to stated policy, in time, all the centrally determined prices will be devoid of subsidies.

Given constraints on most producers and households, various "correcting" items have supplemented the planned prices. Gifts for producers or distributors of severely needed inputs (allocated on the basis of authorizations of delivery by the material-technical supply system) acted as payments for the *reduction of delays* of deliveries—delays that are essentially rationing devices. On the other hand, planned *discounts* for mass-produced unsalable goods acted as inducements for the purchase of unwanted, defective goods. The real price of consumers goods is *not* the official price but that price supplemented by the value of the time and income lost in waiting in line or hunting for scarce goods, bribes for storekeepers to obtain the goods under the counter, and payments for "fixing" new but defectively produced goods.

A properly functioning price mechanism is, inter alia, supposed to signal comparative scarcities, represent a reliable means of accounting, and eliminate the need of the "double coincidence of wants." Prices distorted in a variety of ways do not signal relative scarcities and are not the same unit of account in all circumstances; they induce error in the planning of production systems and harm the consumer. Given the various schemes of rationing of producers and consumers (for instance, in favor of the state administrators) both barter and black markets develop among state enterprises as well as among households. In a barter economy there is the need of a double coincidence of wants, which a proper price system eliminates; thus, when bartering, if someone has a small apartment and wishes to acquire a larger one, he or she must find someone else who has a large apartment and who prefers a smaller one, plus some other good that the holder of the smaller apartment is able to furnish. Thus, the roles of price and the monetary system are reduced to subsidiary ones. A highly placed state administrator who purchases a good in short supply and in high demand below cost (at a subsidized price) fetches an appreciable additional gain when he or she resells the good on the black market (this is often the case with new or slightly used automobiles, available mostly to the nomenklatura). Finally, the planners want the physical flows of goods at planned prices ($P \, Q$) to match the stock of money and its velocity ($M \, V$) released to producers and consumers—as if money could stay attached to the goods produced without making rounds of its own and as if there were no rising state prices for "new" goods introduced in the planning periods for new equipment and materials, no massive output of unwanted and unsold goods, no creeping prices in the collective farm market, no prolonged dearth of goods of mass consumption, no black markets, and no inflation. In the market-directed economies no one pretends, as the central planners do, that there is actually a price system that would *guarantee* that aggregate demand (what the consumers want to purchase and the firms want to invest) would equal aggregate supply.

A vast effort was supposed to be deployed in order to restructure prices in the framework of the general reconstruction program started at the beginning of 1985. Production prices were to be reconstructed to ensure both better use of resources and adequate self-financing of the enterprises, while other prices—namely, retail prices of goods of mass consumption—were to lose their subsidies, which have long weighed heavily on the budget. Gorbachev asserted in a variety of speeches that what the perestroika of prices was to accomplish was an increase in the incentive role of planned prices so as to improve the use of resources, reduce outlays, increase quality, and accelerate scientific-technical progress. To guarantee the solvency of the fuel and power complex and eliminate the illusion of cheapness and inexhaustibility of resources, the prices of oil, gas, and electric power were set to increase. On the other hand, in order to reduce "unjustifiably high levels of profitability" in various other branches, their planned prices were set to decrease. What was supposed to be innovative in all this was the eventual decrease in the amount of centrally determined prices and the corresponding increase in the importance of contractual prices among enterprises. The latter, incidentally, would be either directly or indirectly controlled prices—for example, prices set by the state enterprises themselves under conditions of strict adherence to an approved method of calculating such prices. All this did not depart from Nemchinov's schema, which was noted earlier. Fixed planned prices would be established for a limited number of goods, namely, those that determine "the population's material and cultural standard of living and the level of production outlays." The majority of remaining goods would be sold and bought under price controls, while the rest would be priced by the enterprises following centrally approved methods.

The 1980s came and went without much price restructuring. To make the point in this respect it is interesting to recall here the proposals of the Organizational Committee of the All-Union Scientific-Practical Conference on Problems of Radical Economic Reform (published in *Ekonomicheskaia gazeta*, no. 43, October 1989). According to these "radical" proposals, price reform should be undertaken step by step as follows. Three types of prices should be introduced: *fixed* prices, determined by the USSR Council of Ministers, chiefly for primary resources; *controlled* (ceiling) prices, determined by state authorities placing state orders; and *free* contractual prices as agreed to by the parties. The fixed wholesale prices in the raw material sectors should be raised "in a coordinated manner" over four to five years as of 1990, in a direction consistent with world prices for raw materials and energy. Controlled prices should change, "proceeding from the requirements of a consistent transition to wholesale trade." In regard to agriculture, the reform of prices should take into account the local authorities' determinations of rental payments, given the abandonment of direct state intervention in the determination of price levels for specific products. Retail prices should be left to react to supply and demand, but in the following order: first, in regard to luxury items and imported, high-quality foods; then, in regard to basic foodstuffs, depending on their quality and maintaining the present prices of lower grades; finally, until market balance is achieved, "the authorities should be free to resort to rationing."

Clearly, as of the beginning of the 1990s, Soviet policymakers were still incapable of breaking loose from Nemchinov's schema. Certainly, economists such as Nikolai Shmelev and Abel Aganbegyan consistently pointed out that the only solution in regard to all prices—including those of producer goods—was to rely on market forces, but their advice remained unheeded.

Concluding Comments

In a thoughtful article published in the *Columbia Law Review* in October, 1985, Richard Posner formulates a brilliant "Economic Theory of the Criminal Law" in a market-directed framework. "The major function of criminal law in a capitalist society," wrote Posner, "is to prevent people from bypassing the system of voluntary, compensated exchange"—the market, explicitly or implicitly—in situations where, because transaction costs are low, "the market is a more efficient method of allocating resources than forced exchange." In the Soviet economy, before as well as after the unfolding of perestroika, the function of criminal law is to prevent people from bypassing forced (planned) exchange at planned or controlled prices by fully engaging in voluntary, compensated exchange (that is, in "nonauthorized" markets) that would, by definition, jeopardize the centrally determined directions of economic development. The question of efficiency is weighed and interpreted in entirely different ways in the two frameworks. If and only if Soviet central planning assumes an *indicative* character in respect to the directions of development—that is, if and only if the center ceases to mortgage the bulk of the country's investable resources and lifts its controls over physical outputs and construction programs—will the prevailing rules of Soviet criminal law become outdated and forgotten.

Part 2
Reshaping the Directive Center

Part 2 deals with changes in the ways in which the economy's directive center and executive arm, the Council of Ministers of the USSR (its ministries, departments, and agencies), attempts to set the country's direction of development and implement the central priorities via investments and capital construction programs, while using economic levers (instead of commands) to guide the economy.

In Stalin's economic system the center spelled out the priority tasks of the economy in physical terms. The instrument of implementation was a detailed yearly operational plan (and quarterly subdivisions) approximating current operations and constructed on the basis of an array of product balances (input-output balances of sources and uses). Ministries, departments, and agencies specified physical input-output interrelations for each level and apportioned supplies. As noted, since the mid-1980s central planning has been involved in a complex process of reevaluating and transforming the system. Emphasis has shifted from a yearly operational plan to a central five-year "perspective" plan, as well as toward fifteen-to-twenty-year expansion plans. The center's Control Figures, calculated for the perspective period of five years on the basis of selected interrelations (proportions) among sectors and branches, set the limits within which enterprises and associations must form yearly input-output-sales plans. Concurrently, the center orients enterprises via central limits and norms concerning new construction, ceilings on resources, payments to the budget, and size of the wage fund and incentive funds.

As in the past, the newly restructured center tries to decide the direction of the country's development — that is, it attempts to define an industrial policy and to specify the patterns of technological change. It hopes to map out the scheduled changes with the help of loosely interconnected physical and monetary balances. The product balances are supposed to play a subordinate role. Emphasis is placed on a central core of capital constructions—much smaller than in the traditional planning system—and on the centrally needed resources. A gamut of financial levers supporting the selected package are to be used in regard to the "basic" manufacturing establishments and other economic sectors, the management of money and credit, government receipts and outlays, and the creation, distribution, and redistribution of the national income and product.

Part 2 opens with an analysis of the industrial policies—that is, of the strategy for selecting the direction of change, priorities, and the determination of intersector, interbranch economic proportions. From the 1920s on, Soviet strategy for economic growth has been predicated on the allocation of a large part of resources to incessant increases of means of production (in the Marxian concept, industrial inputs and machinery). The strategy has been based on the Marxian model of steady state and growth included in the second volume of *Capital*. This strategy has come under criticism from a variety of quarters, but its assumption and logic, as yet, have not been questioned. Under Gorbachev, emphasis has continued to be placed on heavy industry, but on the machine-building branches rather than on raw materials and intermediate products, while responsibility for the bulk of consumer goods and light-industry products has been transferred to the republics, regions, and local authorities.

Part 2 moves from a discussion of strategy and options to an examination of economic balances, and proposals by mathematical economists for an "optimally functioning socialist economy" are considered. Changes in devices for carrying out intersector and interbranch relations are noted, and an evaluation of both traditional and Gorbachev's "national economic proportions" and priorities are discussed.

Chapters 4 and 5 focus on fulcrums of the Soviet efforts to determine economic and technological development, namely, planning the program of core capital constructions and the use of manpower. The central capital investment package is shaped by planned volume of national income in its material production phase and by policy decisions concerning division into accumulation and consumption. The monetary forms of distribution and redistribution of national income are treated as separate from investment decisions; in the Soviet conception, the central investment package is only loosely connected to volume and intensiveness of the use of production assets, charges for capital use, and norms governing depreciation. This virtual divorce justifies the attention given in chapter 4 to the management of the core of capital constructions and in chapters 6 and 7 to financial management in general. Chapter 4 explores the controlling role of the capital investments package, capital budgeting, discrepancies between plan norms and achievements, and, finally, the current status of Stalin's industrial showpieces as well as the effects of this legacy. Chapter 5 presents mechanisms of manpower planning, schemas of manpower balances, and approaches to the wage fund. It examines characteristics of the Soviet labor market, structure of wages, salaries, and privileges of party-selected "movers and shakers," the nomenklatura. It evaluates the possible effects of abandoning the traditional Soviet tenet of full employment under socialism.

Chapters 6 and 7 focus on financial management. Specifically, chapter 6 analyzes characteristics of the state budget. After examining Soviet concepts with regard to the budget, direct and indirect taxes, budgetary controls over the economy, and the question of budget deficit, the chapter examines historical trends of government receipts and outlays. Chapter 7 presents Soviet conceptions of money and credit, measures for restructuring the banking system, and the consequences of efforts (made or planned) for intensifying, as adjuncts to central planning choices, commodity-monetary relations, and overcoming financial disequilibria and inflationary pressures plaguing the economy.

Chapter 8 concludes part 2 with a discussion of the performance of the Soviet economy. Gorbachev's policies were supposed to accelerate growth while achieving a new quality of development via retooling the economy's branches and components and intensifying production. Why has acceleration become such an issue, and what are the rates of growth? To answer these questions, chapter 8 looks at methodological and statistical characteristics of national income accounting and stresses reasons why its results are not acceptable. It is important to consider also the methodologies proposed in the West concerning the conversion of the Soviet system of balances to the United Nations system of national accounts and recomputations undertaken in the West on the basis of the so-called adjusted factor cost standard. The issues of growth rates and changes and the relations of growth to standard of living are also relevant to the discussion. All this comes down to the failed Soviet objective of "reaching and surpassing" the U.S. economy.

Part 2 is thus focused on Soviet conceptions concerning the functions and activities of the directive center; shifts in central policies, new principles of centralized management, and the center's investments and construction programs. Part 3 will focus on ways of guiding and of restructuring the components of each economic sector (industrial, agricultural, and domestic and foreign trade) so that these activities would not conflict with changes decided centrally and would allow the utilization, whenever expedient, of market mechanisms.

CHAPTER 3

Setting the Economic Proportions

Planning Strategy

The Soviet drive for economic growth was launched in 1929 by Soviet policy-makers and planners with the objectives of equipping the USSR with a vast and powerful heavy industry, enabling it to catch up with and surpass, in the shortest possible time, "the highest indices of capitalism" (that is, those of the United States) and endowing it with a defense establishment second to none. Which specific industry choices—that is, which specific industrial priorities—and which investment patterns could secure these ambitious results? Upon close examination, the industrial policies and views of the Bolshevik leadership on these issues in the 1930s appear to have been based on their readings of the evolution of capitalism in the nineteenth century and on a rather simplistic perception of developed capitalism in the twentieth century. Their views and perceptions were buttressed, as one might expect, with ample quotations from Marx's writings. But general quotations do not shape a definite policy, and, probably more than anything else in his writings, Marx's equations, embodied in his model of steady state and growth in volume 2 of *Capital,* served to shape and define Soviet thinking and choices in these matters.

Soviet strategy for growth and development, planning techniques, accounting methods, and pricing theories, which were debated in the 1920s and formulated in their essentials in the 1930s, and which still play a decisive role in the management concepts of the Soviet economy, can be understood more easily if one refers to Marx's celebrated two-sector economic model. On the basis of its destination, Marx divided the *physical output* of the economy into two categories: producers' goods (i_g) and consumers' goods (c_g), produced, respectively, by producers' goods industries—or industries of sector I—and consumers' goods industries—or industries of sector II. Producers' goods embrace both raw materials and capital goods. Each output is in turn equated to depreciation plus raw materials used (c), wage bill (v), and surplus value (m) (that is, property income, although Marx does not define it in this way). The two-sector model seeks to portray the mutual relations between the components of each output and the demand and supply of producers' and consumers' goods in either "simple reproduction" (in conditions of zero net investment) or "enlarged reproduction" (in conditions of positive net investment). Total output under the schema is equal to

$$c_1 + v_1 + m_1 = i_g$$
$$c_2 + v_2 + m_2 = c_g$$
$$\overline{c \ + v \ + m \ = i_g + c_g}$$

Under repetitive stationary conditions, the output of sector I must match the capital consumption and raw materials used up in both sectors, that is, $i_g = c_1 + c_2$, whereas consumers' goods output must equal the grand total of wages and the entire surplus. From this, it follows that the condition for the steady state is that the investment demand in the second sector should equal the net income in the first sector ($c_2 = v_1 + m_1$). Simple and enlarged reproduction can be effected smoothly if certain mutual relationships between the components of the national (physical) product and the outputs of the two sectors are realized. Thus, to achieve growth, the output of sector I must be larger than replacements—that is, larger than $c_1 + c_2$—by, say, Δc. In the second (expanded) cycle of production, the total demand for producers' goods, say, c' (that is, $c_1 + c_2 + \Delta c_1 + \Delta c_2$) must equal the output produced by sector I during the first cycle (that is, $c'_1 + c'_2 = c_1 + v_1 + m_1 = i_g$). Further, the demand for consumers' goods in the second cycle—represented by the wage bill v' (that is, $v_1 + v_2 + \Delta v_1 + \Delta v_2$) and the consumption outlays of the nonproductive sphere, m_r—must equal the output of consumers' goods produced during the first cycle (that is, $v'_1 + v'_2 + m_{r1} + m_{r2} = c_2 + v_2 + m_2 = c_g$).

The model is based on constant returns to scale. In Marx's numerical examples of the model, the organic composition of capital (the ratio of c to v) remains unchanged, and the output of the two sectors develops at an unchanged rate. The proportions in which new investment is distributed between the two sectors can, however, be varied, and the growth rate of total output can be increased, kept constant, or decreased. Lenin grasped this idea in his work, *The Development of Capitalism in Russia* [1899]. He stressed there that the development of consumers' goods industries might even be completely arrested while heavy industry forged continuously ahead. Using the Marxian model, he stated that: (1) the growth limits of the economy are set by the excess of the output of producers' goods over replacement needs—under capitalism, the larger share of demand is made up of demand for producers' goods—and, consequently, expansion of sector I is always larger than that of sector II; and (2) the organic composition of capital necessarily grows, and, as a result, the increment of expenditures on capital goods necessarily exceeds the increment of expenditures on labor. Lenin concluded that the basic contradiction of capitalism lies precisely in the urge to "limitless expansion of production and limited consumption." Even though Marx is supposed to have examined the processes of steady state and growth in a specific historical setting, namely capitalism, Marx's model and Lenin's propositions derived from that schema were subsequently declared to have disclosed the universal mechanism of the growth process and, therefore, to be appropriate for the conscious guidance of a program of industrialization within a centrally directed socialist economy.

Concentrations of the investable resources in heavy industry—to start with, in the production of electricity, iron and steel, and machinery—became the hallmark of the Soviet system of industrialization. The Soviet party congresses and economic textbooks denounced incessantly any questioning of the "determining role of production in relation to consumption and of the necessity for the priority growth under socialism of the production of means of production" as a "vulgarized, narrow consumers' approach." A collective of Soviet economists led by A. I. Zalkind, for instance, pointed out as late as 1984 in a study on national economic proportions that the party congresses had continually stressed the need to step up "the tempos of heavy industry—the basis of expanded reproduction" while placing the investment emphases on the "progressive structural links of the economy," namely, on "electroenergy, metallurgy, machine building, chemicals, as well as on transportation and construction." The Zalkind collective, too, dismissed as utterly false the idea of those who considered the priority development of means of production as only a transitory orientation and not as an *objective law* also in force under developed socialism.

Numerous Western economists have questioned the general validity of Marx's schema because of its confusion of stocks (c) and flows ($v + m$), its abstraction with respect to internal interchanges in the two sectors, and the vagueness of the dividing line between investment and consumers' goods industries according to the destination of their products. Furthermore, the theoretical foundation of the schema has been shown to have technical flaws when one moves from values (in the Marxian sense of materialized labor) to prices, which diverge from values, and when one drops the unrealistic assumption concerning the identity of the organic composition of capital in all branches of industry. It has also been pointed out that Lenin's assumption that technological progress necessarily means an increase in the organic composition of capital is questionable. Technological progress may be achieved through replacement of worn-out equipment—that is, at a zero (or even negative) rate of growth of sector I, and hence, a fortiori, at any rate of growth of sector I. On the other hand, the unlimited pursuit of a pattern that posits a growing investment rate would obviously make investment in the end absorb the whole of national income. (In Lenin's study, investment expanded at an increasing rate, but Lenin did not carry out his demonstration beyond a few numerical examples.)

It is not, however, the theoretical neatness of the schema but its broad implications that have attracted Soviet policymakers and planners. The late Joan Robinson—who, incidentally, formulated some of the very criticisms just cited—also noted that the schema provided after all "a simple and indispensable approach to the problem of saving and investment and the balances between production of capital goods and demand for consumer goods."

The allocation of Soviet investable resources during successive five-year plans indeed displayed a broad consistency as far as "basic" choices are concerned (see table 3-1). From 72 to 80 percent of the total investable resources have been allocated to material production, while, correspondingly, a decreasing share of 28 to 20 percent has been left for the nonproductive sphere (that is, for services excluding trade and transport, which, in Soviet statistics, are included in material production). Systematically, more than a third of the country's total investments have gone to manufacturing, and, within manufacturing, as much as 90 percent of them have been provided for Group A, the producer of intermediate products and equipment. However, these basic choices at times have been accompanied by significant shifts in emphases concerning the *composition* of investments within and between sectors, branches, and groups of industries.

As can be expected, the country's capital stock has acquired a skewed structure. According to official data (compare the quote, cited earlier, from the *National Economy of the USSR During 70 Years*, 154), between 1970 and 1986 heavy industry's share of the country's industrial capital stock rose from 87.4 percent of the total to 89.1 percent while, correspondingly, that of light and food industries dropped from 12.6 percent to less than 11 percent. Within the heavy industry group various shifts took place among shares of the "complexes" of fuel and power, metallurgy, chemicals and petrochemicals, and machine building. Thus, for instance, between 1970 and 1986 the relative share of metallurgy decreased and that of machine building increased, while the share of the other complexes remained relatively unchanged.

Consider now the changing emphases in the composition of investments between sectors and branches. Agriculture, for instance, has received an increasing relative share of investments from the Seventh Five-Year Plan on, and particularly so in the Ninth and Tenth Five-Year Plans, but the increases ceased with the Eleventh Five-Year Plan. On the other hand, the relative share of housing has shrunk continuously from the Seventh Five-Year Plan on. Gorbachev hoped to be able to shift the allocation within Group A away from fuel and power, metallurgy, chemicals, and building materials toward the ensemble of engineering branches. Typically, and in accordance with Marx's

TABLE 3-1. Soviet Investments Allocation over the Five-Year Plans (FYP) 1956–85, Percentage Distribution

	Sixth FYP	Seventh FYP	Eighth FYP	Ninth FYP	Tenth FYP	Eleventh FYP
Material Production	71.5	74.9	76.3	79.0	80.7	80.2
Manufacturing	36.0	36.5	35.1	34.8	35.0	35.7
Group A	32.7	31.7	29.9	30.1	30.7	31.4
Group B	3.3	4.8	5.2	4.7	4.3	4.3
Other Material Production	35.5	38.4	41.2	44.2	45.7	44.5
Agriculture	13.9	15.2	16.7	19.8	20.0	18.5
Construction	3.0	2.6	3.3	3.7	3.9	3.6
Transport and Communications	9.0	10.0	9.5	10.7	11.8	12.4
Trade and Other	9.6	10.6	11.7	10.0	10.0	10.0
Nonproductive Sphere	28.5	25.1	23.7	21.0	19.3	19.8
Housing	23.5	18.9	17.7	15.8	14.2	15.1
Science and Education	5.0	6.2	6.0	5.2	5.1	4.7

Source: Narodnoe khoziaisvo SSSR za 70 let., 328–29.
Note: Underlying data are at constant prices.

conception, the output structure of Group A had consistently kept a rather stable composition (in percentages):

	1975	1980	1985	1987
Raw materials and intermediate products ("objects of work")	80.6	79.7	80.6	79.5
Machinery and equipment ("means of work")	19.4	20.3	19.4	20.5

From 1985 on, Gorbachev denounced the policy of incessantly commissioning the building of new productive assets, emphasized the need to renovate the existing ones, recommended reductions in the fuel and raw materials bases, and pointed to the need for conservation and better use of the outputs available. Asserting that growth depended to a crucial degree on machine building, which embodies fundamental scientific and technological ideas, he pushed for a vaster concentration of investable resources in the engineering branches than ever before. As already noted, Stalin made the coal-iron-steel complex the pivot of his industrialization drive. Khrushchev asserted instead that fundamental scientific and technological results were to be reaped from the development of oil and chemicals. Gorbachev, and along with him the 27th Party Congress (1986), asserted that engineering was the priority sector to which large investments must be allocated. Yet, obviously peremptory, one-sided, top-priority industrial choices imposed on an entire economy can lead to vast dislocations, wastage of resources, and other irreversible and deleterious side effects.

Proportions and Balances

From its inception, centralized Soviet management and planning has relied on a series of economic balances conceived and developed, on the one hand, under pressure to balance the supply and allocation of certain scarce products and, on the other hand, under the impetus of developing some kind of consolidated frame of *national* accounts consistent with the Marxian concepts of production and distribution of the national product. The first balances of supply and distribution of various products were indeed formulated in the early 1920s. If X_i is the total, scarce (physical) supply of a given good, x_{ij} the parts of this output used either in the same productive sector or in another sector (j), and x_i, the surplus available for households, exports, and reserves, the central managers must adjust the items of the two sides of the balance to produce equality between total supplied (X_i) and total allocated ($x_{ij} + x_i$) (see table 3-2). A number of outstanding Soviet economists of the time—P. I. Popov, L. N. Litoshenko, M. Barengol'ts, to mention a few—pioneered in social accounting and input-output analysis, and, under their direction or with their cooperation, the Central Statistical Administration produced in 1926 a

TABLE 3-2. A Soviet Balance of Resources and Allocation

Resources (X_1)	Allocation	
	x_{ij}	x_i
Production	Used by the producing firm	Marketed
Imports	and other firms	Exports
Reserves and		Reserves and Inventories
inventories		

$$X_i = \sum_{j=1}^{n} x_{ij} + x_i \qquad (i = 1, \ldots , n)$$

highly original work, *The Balance of the National Economy of the USSR for 1923–24.* However, this pioneering effort, the first and still unique complete balance of the national economy published by the Soviets for any year, was dismissed by Stalin as "a game with figures." Input–output analysis was subsequently expanded and perfected—but in the West, by Wassily Leontief. Soviet planning developed in the meantime into a vast system of loosely interconnected balances focused on specific products, branches, and sectors only tenuously consistent with one another. The goal of creating a single complex of truly integrated balances and models encompassing *both* ongoing activities of the economy, financial flows, and planned developments has eluded the Soviet economists.

Traditionally, the physical plans have been predicated on estimated achievements in some key, or leading level, industries and on "guesstimates" as to what would be achievable given an appropriate allocation of investable resources—resources determined on the basis of the scheduled growth of the *gross value of output*, detailed in an all-encompassing Financial Plan, and distributed through the state budget and credit system. The physical balances have been the principal levers of plan formulation and implementation. Constructed with the help of various technical coefficients (norms) and integrated by the help of assumptions concerning projected growth rates, they have aimed first of all at balancing available and scheduled supplies of scarce products with their mandated utilization by designated users (ministries, branches, and enterprises). These balances have been neither consistent nor amenable to coordination in the process of implementation. In fact, they have not been able to ensure the realization of even the broadest interbranch and intersector operational connections. This failure has led in practice to situations in which various branches or enterprises could operate with significant overt or covert reserves, while other enterprises would run headlong into insuperable bottlenecks.

Sources of Products

Production by individual enterprises and branches of material production

Uses of Products by Industries and Sectors

Producer goods
—Objects of labor (raw materials; fuels; electricity; other)
—Implements of labor (machinery; equipment; instruments)
Consumer goods
—Foodstuffs; clothing; durables; nondurables

Sources of Net Income in Material Production

Primary incomes of the gainfully employed and the enterprises ("social surplus")

Uses: Distribution and Redistribution

Distribution
—Final consumption
—Net capital formation ("accumulation")
Redistribution
—through the financial and credit system and the budget
—outside the above redistribution, between economic units and households

Additional Tabulations

Itemized lists of capital construction projects
Sources of manpower

Consolidated Tabulations

Balance of incomes and outlays of the population
Balance of incomes and credit of the banks
Balance of receipts and expenditures of the government
Balance of foreign trade
Consolidated input-output table of gross product and income

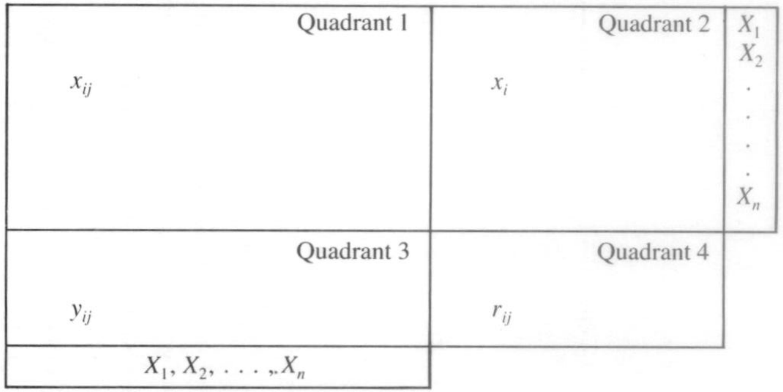

		X_1 X_2 $\cdot$ $\cdot$ $\cdot$ X_n
Quadrant I	Quadrant 2	
x_{ij}	x_i	
Quadrant 3	Quadrant 4	
y_{ij}	r_{ij}	
$X_1, X_2, \ldots, X_n$		

$X_1, X_2, \ldots, X_n =$ gross outputs $(x_{ij} + x_i)$
$x_{ij} =$ interindustry flows
$x_i =$ final demand
$y_{ij} =$ primary incomes $(y_{ij} = x_i)$
$r_{ij} =$ redistribution of incomes in the "nonmaterial sphere"

Fig. 3-1. Schematic representation of the system of balances of the national economy

The Gorbachev administration has decided to shift the focus of central planning away from direct assignments of inputs and injunctions on output mixes, away from the imperative of the physical balances, and toward the use of economic levers—that is, toward a broader and more flexible use of the balances in *value* terms dealing with income flows (see fig. 3-1). But, alas, the latter balances are predicated on the former. Gosplan and Gossnab still have to construct (though not publicize) the physical balances henceforth officially reduced to a secondary role. Gaps and inconsistencies continue within and between these balances, just as before. Moreover, the shift in emphasis from the operational day-to-day aspects to a longer "perspective" horizon does not imply a real change in the basic *concepts* of plan construction. The perspective plans are still constructed as a function of some so-called leading links, be they specific industries and/or some critical development projects selected by policymakers toward which most of the investable resources must be allocated. The top of the hierarchy of plan equations must still be taken by certain leading product balances loosely linked to the other supporting physical balances. The Soviet planning process remains in many respects as dubious a process as the one described by the Hungarian economist Janos Kornai, who remarked (in a 1967 study, *Mathematical Planning of Structural Decisions*) that the Soviet-type plan "actually tries to solve the immense equation system with a kind of guesswork, with repeated trials although we are all aware of the fact that equation systems with considerably fewer variables and equations cannot be solved by mere guessing."

As we have pointed out, Soviet plans traditionally have been differentiated and then loosely coordinated according to objective, time span, and the organizational strictures of the economy—a procedure akin in a number of respects to planning procedures in the West, for example, in France. The outstanding apparent difference has been the *directive* role of each of the Soviet plan choices concerning input and output mixes. Yet the discarding of the emphasis on commands and the shift away from yearly operational plans should not be construed as implying a shift toward a Western-type *indicative* planning. The perspective five-year plans and the expansion plans of fifteen years or more will not form an indicative framework embodying the *expectations* of the country's producing units. They must still embody the prospective changes mandated by the decision center. It is the latter who, as in the past, backs up its selected choices by determining the allocation of the bulk of investments. Thus, while Gorbachev has reduced the scope of the center's interferences in the day-to-day operation of the economy's component units, he has tried to keep the privilege of mapping the economy's evolving goals, priorities, structural proportions, and technological choices. Moreover, while the underlying economic balances are not to be used for setting detailed targets or imposing solutions to a multiplicity of partial questions, they are still supposed to serve as the frame of reference for working out the economic norms and the parameters that constrain the scope of the activities of the main producing units.

Controls and Optimization

Ever since the death of Stalin in 1953, and more so since the end of Khrushchev's reign in 1964, the Soviet leadership has engaged in a series of intensive efforts aimed at improving the directive center's choice decisions and the economy's performance. Some of these efforts can best be understood with the help of concepts used in engineering and the theory of systems regulation and adoptive control (cybernetics); others can be better gauged within the framework of the theory of rational policy choice associated with the work of Jan Tinbergen. The two approaches, which apply to the same means-ends analysis, have played a prominent role in Soviet economic thinking, particularly from the late 1960s to the early 1980s. The crucial difference between the two approaches is that they yield different insights into the problems of economic planning and management.

Associated with and influenced by the cybernetic approach have been a series of models and proposals concerning the achievement of an *optimally functioning economic system*. Optimality conditions have been explored in two basic directions: in respect to the planning and determination of the path of development of the economy as a whole, and in regard to the redesigning of the static and dynamic linkages of the system's basic components. A number of economists associated with the country's leading research institutes— notably the Central Economic Mathematical Institute (TsEMI)—have deployed a vast modeling effort of the processes of planning, the regulation of the activities of various economic subsystems, and the organization and transmission of information concerning planning, statistics, material-technical supply, prices, and scientific and technological data. Concerning planning, the efforts have centered on the specification of optimal paths under different assumptions concerning sectoral or overall growth rates, coordination of the indicators of national development with the indicators of the enterprises association, branches and regions, determination of interbranch, intersectoral, and interregional proportions. Comprehensive organizational-economic models involving optimization calculations within each component unit of the economy were to lead eventually to the creation of a single complex of interconnected models for the economy as a whole. In the words of the great Soviet mathematician Leonid V. Kantorovich, the management of the Soviet economy required not only the planned articulation of the basic directions of its development but also the reciprocally coordinated management of the activity of individual links, branch and territorial agencies, and associations and enterprises.

Yet much of these intensive modeling efforts yielded only limited results. Some of the mathematical models—for example, variants of interbranch input-output models—were used by Gosplan, particularly for the calculation of long-range national plans, while other models found some application in optimization calculations in a number of branches and in the monitoring of certain project constructions (such as the Baikal-Amur Mainline). Research concerning the use of mathematical economics remained, however, confined by and large to a narrow circle of scholars and institutes only marginally influencing the main project design organizations of ministries and departments. The crowning concept of mathematical economics—the forging of a unified economic mechanism integrating all forms, methods, and means of management with centralized planning playing the leading role—finally lost much of its appeal by the mid-1980s. The fetishization of computer technology, underestimation of the complexity of an efficient centralized-decentralized management and control system, disregard of conflicting interests, overemphasis on techniques and the concurrent neglect of the human factor started to be viewed as manifestations of past errors and misconceptions. As previously noted, the goal of creating a single complex of interconnected optimization models encompassing *all* current and planned activities of "the single national economic complex" (*edinyi narodnokhoziaistvennyi komplex*), so highly emphasized until the mid-1980s, has been slowly but surely dissipating.

When the Soviet Union entered the "all-around planning era" in 1929, its First Five-Year Plan was viewed even in the West as a bold experiment in the management of an entire economy. On January 1, 1933, Stalin proclaimed the plan "completed" in four years. Actually, as it is now pointed out, the rate of growth of total output during the years of the plan fell far short of the targets set; moreover, the annual rate of increase of industrial production—the crux of the plan—declined in relation to the rate achieved during the preceding period, that of the New Economic Policy. At the end of the Second Five-Year Plan, Stalin proclaimed the achievement of socialism in the USSR was complete. This date is still looked upon by Soviet officialdom as a benchmark. Certain Soviet writers such as Vasilii Seliunin now point out, however, that the entire economic development preceding World War II (1929–41) "saw the beginning of the disproportions that continue to torment our economy," disproportions between sectors, branches, incomes, and goods available ("Sources," *Novyi Mir*, May, 1988). The other Five-Year Plans completed were the fourth, fifth, and then seventh through twelfth (1961–90). Two plans have been discontinued; the third was interrupted by World War II, and the sixth, abandoned in 1958, was followed by the Seven-Year Plan modified after the fall of Khrushchev.

Associated with and influenced by the concepts and analyses of rational policy choices have been various efforts to modify the interrelations of policy

Fig. 3-2. Interrelation of Soviet objectives and instruments

OBJECTIVES / INSTRUMENTS

INSTRUMENTS	Implementing the "Economic Proportions"	Expanding Production (faster growth)	Increasing Productivity	Improving Output Quality	Controlling Input Demand	Improving the Balance of Payments	Overhauling Production Techniques	Changing Income Distribution	Other Objectives
Instruments of Direct Control									
A. Enterprises									
Control of type, size, association, location	+	+							
"Control Figures" (plans)	+	+							
Control of investment	+	+	+						
Control of production techniques	+	+					+		
System of norms and central allocation of resources	+	+	+		+		+		
State orders for "top priorities"	+	+					+		
Price fixing; cost and profitability controls	+	+	+		+				
Wages and incentives controls	+	+	+		+		+		
Quality and standard controls				+			+		
B. Branches and Sectors									
Control of investment	+	+	+		+				
Inputs allocation	+	+			+				
Prices and wage controls	+		+						
Output and distribution controls							+		
C. Foreign Trade									
Imp. and exp. trading (prices, volume, and mixes)						+			
Exchange control						+			
Immigration and foreign travel control									+
Instruments of Public Finance									
A. Related to Direct Controls									
Direct and indirect taxes on, and subsidies of, enterprise	+		+						
Public consumption								+	
Financing central investments	+	+							
Payments to banks for loan financing	+	+							
Budget surplus or deficit	+	+							+

INSTRUMENTS	Implementing the "Economic Proportions"	Expanding Production (faster growth)	Increasing Productivity	Improving Output Quality	Controlling Input Demand	Improving the Balance of Payments	Overhauling Production Techniques	Changing Income Distribution	Other Objectives
Instruments of Public Finance (continued)									
B. Other									
Taxes on households	+								
Taxes on collective farms, cooperatives, and organizations	+	+							
Transfers to households								+	+
Foreign aid									+
Custom duties						+			+
Legal imposition of interest rates	+								
Instruments of Money and Credit									
A. Related to Direct Controls									
Govt. guarantees of loans	+								
Control of state enterprises borrowing	+	+							
Control of collective farm and cooperative borrowing		+							
Other directives	+								+
B. Other									
Lending abroad	+								
Borrowing from abroad	+								
Devaluation	+								
Revaluation	+								
Changes in Institutional Framework									
A. Affecting Other Instruments									
Changes in the system of direct controls	+	+							
Changes in the system of subsidies to enterprises	+				+				
Changes in the tax system	+	+	+	+					
Changes in the court system				+					
B. Affecting the Production Framework									
Changes in extent of public ownership	+	+	+	+				+	+
Changes in labor's role in management	+		+						
Creation of new institutions	+	+	+						+

goals and instruments (economic levers). As is the case for any government, the Soviet government has at its disposal actions that can affect the institutional framework, as well as an array of public finance and money and credit instruments, besides instruments of direct control. Direct controls affect the size and location of enterprises, their inputs, investment, prices and wages, as well as the quality of classification of their outputs. Taxes, subsidies, credits, and budget surpluses or deficits can play their familiar roles in that economy (see fig. 3-2). Since the mid-1960s a series of reforms have been carried out aimed at bringing the use of instruments more in tune with planners' goals—notably, rendering the price system more responsive to the needs of efficient use of resources and the incentive system more capable of eliciting from the workers more intensive efforts to fulfill plans. The price reforms have consisted in administrative manipulation and rules involving the inclusion in prices of various markups for the use of fixed and working capital (either in the enterprise or in the economy at large), rent, and profit—all computed within the more or less orthodox Marxian frame of reference of the labor theory of value (see table 2-2). The modifications of the incentive system have involved changes aiming to affect the size, structure, and scope of enterprises' incentive funds from retained profits, transfers to and from the wage fund, and bonuses related to changing plan indicators such as amount of sales (instead of total output), profitability, reduction of cost per unit of output, productivity, and proportions of quality goods in total output. The limited results achieved are illustrated by the continuous shaping and reshaping of such reforms along the same conceptual lines. As an American analyst of these reforms, Gertrude E. Schroeder, aptly put it (in *Soviet Economy in a Time of Change* [1979]), since the mid-1960s the Soviet economy has been on a "treadmill of 'reforms,'" a treadmill whose endless belt is trodden also by the leaders of the perestroika, who, in respect to prices or incentives, do not seem to muster more imagination than their predecessors. We will return to these issues in more detail in chapter 9.

Overhauling the Directive Center

Though the central policy-making and planning bodies still control the allocation of the bulk of investable resources, determine the scale and scope of the main capital constructions, and dispose of a vast variety of instruments of guidance or for enforcing their goals, great deviations occur with respect to selected proportions, following discrepancies among the pace—*timing* and *volume*—in which enterprises, branches, and sectors underfulfill, fulfill, or overfulfill their plans. Could such failures be avoided?

To carry out the basic tasks set, avoid the dangers of interbranch lack of coordination, and cope with the fact that at least certain "crucial" plan goals would not mesh, Stalin relied on the so-called *vertical principle* of management and planning, namely, on the centralized organization of the economy by industrial branches. All-Union ministries forwarded mandatory plan assignments within the branch; materials involved in the production of key types of goods were centrally distributed; and ceilings were fixed on the use of other resources (such as electric power, construction materials, transport facilities, and working capital). This rigorously centralized system along vertical lines was replaced by Khrushchev in 1957 with a *horizontal principle* of managerial organization, a system for organizing production and distribution by regional (territorial) councils of the national economy (*Sovnarkhozy*). Stalin's branch system was discarded in part for political and also economic reasons— namely, for having led to the growth of "deleterious tendencies" toward branch self-sufficiency, duplication of facilities between branches, preoccupation with branch technology and not with interbranch technological change, neglect of local-territorial problems and consumer needs, and, finally, dominance of the military-industrial complex's priorities.

The Sovnarkhozy system was in its turn disbanded in 1965 for both political and economic reasons. Management and planning were reorganized again along the vertical principle, but this time in combination with devolution to republic and local levels of some controls over the regional and local industries. Symmetrically, Sovnarkhozy were condemned for having encouraged tendencies toward regional self-sufficiency, duplication of facilities between regions, preoccupation with regional technological development and not with interregional technological change, neglect of national interests, and excessive concern with consumer goods and service to the detriment of the production of producer goods. In the process of returning to the vertical principle, numerous industrial enterprises were merged into large associations meant to achieve economies of scale and to save on administrative costs.

Given the increasingly poor performance of the economy from the middle of the 1960s on, however, the Gorbachev administration proceeded to overhaul the system of centralized management via the establishment of a small number of super high-level ministerial organizations. It consolidated some branch ministries into "complexes" supervised by interministerial bureaus (for example, the Bureau for the Fuel-Energy Complex) and topped the reorganized agro-industrial complex with a new and powerful State Commission for Agricultural Purchases and Food. These kinds of reorganization at the levels of the USSR Council of Ministers and newly constituted large-scale cost accounting production structures have allowed the elimination of a number of ministries and departments. But this did not reduce appreciably the total number of the managerial bureaucracy, since many former top managers were simply shifted to lower positions. Be that as it may, Gorbachev has continuously stressed since his accession to power that the top managerial apparatus had grown enormously, encompassing almost one hundred union and eight hundred republic ministries and departments (by the end of the 1960s there were only fifty Sovnarkhozy in operation). Further, the central ministerial agencies had grown to vast proportions, and their tasks had enormously expanded. In the mid-1980s Gosplan and its multiple departments planned the coordination of the country's flow of goods through the compilation of some eighteen hundred yearly product balances and four hundred five-year balances. In turn, Gossnab detailed the items to be distributed through thirteen thousand balances transmitted to the industrial ministries. The latter disaggregated these balances into forty thousand balances covering the scheduled allocations to enterprises and associations. Finally, when assigning the actual supplies to customers, Gossnab enlarged the total of balances ten to fifteen times. In the perestroika scheme, these processes were simplified. In 1988 Gosplan reduced the scope of its balanced estimates to 950 products, and in the 1990s its calculations were to encompass only four hundred key items, while Gossnab was to develop better forms of supply and marketing.

Fyodor I. Kushnirsky, who had firsthand experience with Soviet planning, rightly noted (in *Soviet Economic Planning* [1982]) that "the real power of [the Soviet] planning authorities lies in their ability to distribute resources," and it is this distribution that inevitably led to intricate processes of bargaining, swapping, bribing, padding, and reports of falsification within ministries and between ministries and the central agencies. The practical results have been innumerable compromises, while the official illusion that the solutions adopted were not subjective but objective outcomes of plan calculations was dutifully cultivated. Gorbachev hoped that the bickering would subside as contractual relations among the center and the state enterprises, and among the enterprises themselves, expanded. In the meantime, however, as was noted, the center has continued to rely, as far as its military needs and the basic producers' goods are concerned, on state orders addressed to the appropriate large state enterprises, orders accompanied with guaranteed supplies for specified outputs. Even in a longer perspective, the center still nourishes the hope of exercising effective controls over certain key branches, while using less direct forms of centralized controls—via interbranch and territorial-branch associations—that would hopefully take over "the entire research-investment-production-marketing-servicing." Finally, tens of thousands of medium-sized and small enterprises, including cooperatives, will develop under republic and local jurisdictions for republic and local needs.

The idea that industrial production units must strive for income and profit has not been fully extended to agriculture. The emphasis in that sector remains on how to guarantee state acquisition of the lion's share of the final produce rather than how to develop output. The crucial underlying assumption is still that the state knows best how and for whom this produce is to be produced and distributed. (These issues will be examined in chapter 10.) At certain times (in the mid-1950s and mid-1960s) there were some efforts to raise the state purchase prices of agricultural produce, cancel farms' debts, decrease the tax burden on agriculture, and cut back on the administrative tutelage of this sector. The fact that farms did not respond with increased deliveries was blamed on many factors, except on the most obvious one, namely, that not much could be purchased with the money received. Subsequently, capital investments were sharply increased in this sector, but the results remained disappointing. Central policymakers are still not receptive to the idea that "commodity-market relations" need to be applied widely to this sector.

Much hinges on the centrally determined proportions, which are supposed to express the necessary conditions for the desired "expanded reproduction." It is important to note, however, as the central planner O. Iun' has pointed out, that the planned prices do not stem from the centrally established proportions and therefore cannot stimulate their implementation (*Kommunist*, 1985). The last industrial wholesale prices established before the advent of the Gorbachev administration were introduced on January 1, 1982. They were formulated at the level of 1980 costs and had nothing to do with the proportions established in the Eleventh Five-Year Plan (1981–85). The targets of that plan were approved in old prices, and the conversion to new prices necessarily changed *all* the value proportions. The Thirteenth Five-Year Plan (1991–95) has also been drafted independently of the thorough price reform scheduled first for the early and then the middle 1990s. Again, there are no valid correspondences between the planned physical proportions and the actual value proportions.

Concluding Comments

A number of Soviet economists have expressed doubts about the leadership's capacity to select the national economic proportions that could lessen rather than further aggravate the glaring imbalances already existing between heavy and light industries, manufacturing and agriculture, material production and services, and incomes received and goods available, along with the obvious technological disproportions predicated on the protracted maintenance of a vast sphere of technically obsolete and inefficient economic entities. The very idea that policymakers and planners could prescribe from above the country's most appropriate priorities and specific industry choices on the basis of some peculiar wisdom or of some special techniques has been challenged, for instance, by Vasilii Seliunin. He pointed out that Soviet planners themselves "belie this idea when they carefully study world trends, which are determined by market forces, in order to plan what we should produce. Thus they tacitly admit that there is a better means than ours for regulation, or self-regulation of the economy" (*Novyi mir,* May, 1988). As another Soviet economist, Gavriil Popov, remarked earlier, "the decision makers, possessing no objective criteria, inevitably become hostages to foreign countries: what is already being used there is always correct" (*Management of Socialist Production,* 1986).

On the other hand, one must not forget that the reluctance to accept fully the play of market forces within the Soviet economy still shapes the thinking of a considerable number of officials and of high-ranking scholars. Years after the launching of perestroika, while some popular politicians such as Boris Yeltsin and prestigious publications stress incessantly the need of moving resolutely toward the expansion of markets, other no less prestigious journals continue to print nostalgic proposals about the possibility of "sterilizing" the commodity turnover, "washing it clean" of money, and setting accounts in, say, "units of energy." The paradox of perestroika is that it must be carried out by the very members of the apparatus who have been formed and educated by the administrative system that they are supposed to overcome. As the Soviet poet Andrei Voznesensky put it, referring to the uncouth, nouveau riche Ermolai Alexeevich Lopakhin, who becomes the master and then destroyer of a beautiful orchard in Anton Chekhov's play, *The Cherry Orchard:* "We are now reaping the fruits of what was done in the Soviet Union by people who were versions of Lopakhin in *The Cherry Orchard.* But the paradox is that only new Lopakhins can now pull us out of the swamp" (*New York Times Book Review,* November 27, 1987).

CHAPTER 4

Capital Management

Planning Capital Formation

The centrally determined program of capital construction still constitutes the core of Soviet planning. Though the size of the central package has been sharply reduced, still on its basis are mapped the growth and development of material production, and, secondarily, housing and public utilities, education and culture, and health services and social welfare. In turn, the implementation of the central package of capital construction depends on the performance of all branches of material production, the adequacy and timing of all types of supplies (including, first of all, machinery and equipment), and building materials. While any projection of the Soviet national income and product is clouded more than ever by uncertainty, the planners must still make tentative calculations about the rates of growth of output of all branches and sectors of the economy and about the stipulated distribution of supplies among them and among the economy's nonproductive sphere (see table 4-1). As long as market relations do not play the determined role, the planners must make provisions for the renewal or expansion of production capacities so as to insure that the posited growth rates and mandated proportions will be implemented. The plans must further embody thrusts toward a higher technology, as well as "rational" and "judicious" choices with respect to the distribution of productive capacities among cities, regions, and republics. Given its role of chief nexus among all the plans, the plan of capital construction should, in principle, be the best considered plan, the best formulated, and the most tightly balanced as far as scheduled resources and uses are concerned. This status, however, is far from the actual case. As we will see, vast differences exist between the directions *chosen* by the central policymakers and the actual directions taken in project making and construction, between the planners' choices and norms and the actual completion of the projects and of their course, and, last but not least, between ambitious targets and the quite inadequate means available to carry them out.

The capital investment plans are drawn up separately by branches, ministries, agencies, complexes, and republics for *centralized* as well as *decentralized* investments (enterprise funds, bank credits, deductions from local

71

TABLE 4-1. Net Fixed Capital Formation by Economic and Social Sectors

Row Number	Economic Sectors	Total (2 + 8)	Socialist Sector	Social Sectors					Private Sector
				Including					
				State Sector	Cooperative Sector and Collective Farms	Social Organizations	Personal Plots of Employees	Personal Plots of Members of Collective Farms	
		1	2	3	4	5	6	7	8
01	Total net fixed capital formation (02 + 11 + 15 + 16)								
02	Material Production Sphere								
03	Industry								
04	Construction								
05	Agriculture								
06	Forestry								
07	Transport								
08	Communications								
09	Trade								
10	Other material production								

11	Nonproductive sphere
12	Housing and public utilities
13	Education, culture, and art
14	Health services, social welfare, and sports
15	Collective needs of the communities (including science, finance, credit and insurance, general government, and other needs of nonproductive sphere)
16	Population

Source: U.N. Statistical Office, *Basic Principles of the System of Balances of the National Economy*, Studies in Methods, Ser. F, no. 17 (New York: United Nations, 1971), 77; and *Narodnce khoziaistvo za 70 let.*, 100.

revenues, and other sources). Consideration is also given to capital investments from collective farm funds, cooperatives, and social organizations, as well as for investments in residential buildings financed by individuals. Roughly 85 to 90 percent of all investments are still made by the state and state enterprises, and the remaining 10 to 15 percent by the collective farms and individuals. Consolidated calculations for overall investments and for successive periods of implementation during the course of a plan are made with the help of a variety of norms and indices concerning the allocation of funds to structures and/or equipment, to maintaining the capacities of existing enterprises or for new construction, and to the material sphere and/or to the nonproductive sphere. As we will see, the implementation of this huge, extremely complex, and detailed plan is often beset by innumerable discrepancies between set planning standards and actual results, between the projected outputs and distributions and their de facto interlocking, and between the sluggish pace of construction of structures and that of the production and delivery of equipment. Before focusing (in the next section) on the Soviet meaning of a "construction project" and on Soviet methods of capital budgeting, it is useful to note that, from the beginning of the so-called all-around planning era in 1929, the Soviet leadership has striven to create a veritable mystique of central planning in general and of the five-year plan (*piatiletka*) in particular, a legend of the latter's coherence and rationality and a shrill saga of each of its alleged accomplishments.

While every Five-Year Plan launched thousands of construction projects, each plan was identified for propaganda purposes with some gigantic, pharaonic-type pyramid building—the "greatest project of the century"—to which everything else had to be subordinated. The First Five-Year Plan (1929–32), which was proclaimed to be completed in four years, had as its centerpiece the establishment of Stalin's gigantic iron city, Magnitogorsk, the Soviet Pittsburgh behind the Urals, on the divide between Europe and Asia. The Second Five-Year Plan (1933–37) centered its claim to fame on the building of the Ural-Kuznetsk metallurgical combine as well as on the opening of the Moscow-Volga and the White Sea–Baltic Sea canals and the creation of new industrial centers in Siberia. At the time a new "industrial fictional literature" came into being, and a new set of Soviet literary heroes made their appearance: the enthusiastic "shock-worker," the daring engineer, and the energetic director of giant industrial projects, always "en garde" against foreign sabotage. Soviet writers such as Marietta Shaginian celebrated *Hydrocentral;* Valentin Kataev, in *Time Forward,* hallowed Magnitogorsk; Fiodor Gladkov glorified *Energy;* Nikolai Ostrovski waxed lyrical on *How Steel Was Tempered,* while, in *Scutarevsky,* Leonid Leonov denounced the evils of foreign industrial sabotage. Finally, Alexei Tolstoi praised Stalin, under the guise of glorifying Peter the Great, for dragging a reluctant, backward Russia into modernity. The last pre–World War II plan, the Third Five-Year Plan (1938–42), had as its showpieces the constructions of the Petrovsk-Zabaikalski metallurgical factory, the Balkash and Sredneuralsk smelting works, and the huge Uralchimmash combine. After destruction caused by the war, the first postwar Five-Year Plan, the fourth in number (1946–50), returned to the kind of shrill advertisement of Soviet projects witnessed in the mid-1930s. Besides reconstruction, it exalted the building of the Trans-Caucasus metallurgical factory, the Ust-Kamenogorsk combine, and the Kolomna heavy machine tools works. The Fifth Five-Year Plan (1951–55) was marked by new ambitious emphases on hydropower and water conservation projects. The sixth (1956–60) announced the completion of the Volga Lenin Hydroplant and the Irkutsk and Novosibirsk power stations, and the Seventh Five-Year Plan celebrated the opening of the "world's largest electric power station," the mammoth Bratsk hydroelectric plant, and the first major northward penetration of the Siberian forest, whose inauguration was saluted by the well-known poet Eugenii Yevtushenko in a long lyrical poem.

After the fall of Nikita Khrushchev in 1964—because of his irrepressible drive for change, his alleged mistakes concerning the reorganization of the party-state machine, the poor results of his policies involving the reorganization of the economy on territorial lines, the push for the reequipment of industry and the priority of chemicals, and, last but not least, his pet scheme concerning the "virgin lands"—policymakers turned their attention to the pressing need to improve pricing and cost accounting and to end wasteful capital allocations for huge hydropower stations. Yet, with the Eighth Five-Year Plan (1966–70), the traditional campaigns of exalting great projects were back on track; the eighth plan emphasized not only a vast expansion of the network of Siberian gas and oil pipelines but also the commissioning of such showpieces as the Krasnoiarsk hydropower station. The Ninth Five-Year Plan (1971–75) and the tenth (1975–80) were supposed to assign large resources to improve living standards. But very soon their emphases shifted to other kinds of objectives. The ninth plan turned much of the country's efforts toward changing the USSR into "the world's largest producer of building materials," while the tenth celebrated as "a great feat of the party and the people" the commissioning of yet another project of the century, the two-thousand-mile rail line along the Trans-Siberian route, the Baikal-Amur Mainline (BAM)—a giant project of stations, tunnels, towns, and other large facilities (some of which had to be postponed subsequently to the year 2000 and beyond). The tenth plan was also exalted for having earmarked vast sums of money for the development of a territorial production complex based on the mineral resources of the Kursk Magnetic Anomaly, which, as Lenin himself had predicted, was capable "of revolutionizing the whole of metallurgy." The last plan before Gorbachev's accession to power, the Eleventh Five-Year Plan

(1981–85), also stressed various ambitious developments, notably of nuclear power and oil and gas outputs meant to turn the USSR into the "world's largest producer of fuels."

As soon as he came to power, Gorbachev announced his decision to break with the old patterns and shift the emphasis to new directions. Taking account of the increasing "difficulties that have been felt in the country's overall economic development since the beginning of the seventies" (that is, the steady decline in the country's economic growth rates), Gorbachev declared in his inaugural speech of July 24, 1985, that he wanted to put an end to the preceding "policy of inertia" based on "extensive methods of growth" and absorbing an ever-increasing amount of resources, that he intended to terminate the commissioning of "ever newer and newer large enterprises," that he wished to end the dispersal of forces and, accordingly, would extract guarantees from planners and managers that "the large outlays by the state yield a rapid return and are not frozen in the Siberian soil," and that his goal was to *reshape, retool, and advance* the economy onto a higher technological plane. His wholesale indictment of the wasteful "gigantomania" of the preceding five-year plans and their ever vaster drives for the expansion and consumption of resources displaced from the center of the Gorbachev plans the building of new pyramid-like showcase projects. The Twelfth Five-Year Plan (1986–90) stressed the need of "laying the foundation for the rise in the growth rate of the country's development" and, for this purpose, increasing "considerably" investments in the engineering complex "in which scientific and technological progress is embodied." The Thirteenth Five-Year Plan (1991–95), while again emphasizing the need of requirement—particularly, in order to strengthen "the nucleus of the national economy, which is made up of such science-intensive branches as electronics, the production of computer systems, information systems, and communications systems, and the aerospace industry"—also affirmed the necessity to saturate the consumer market, perhaps in the period 1993–95. As we will see below, it would be erroneous to assume that these tasks are in any way less ambitious than the preceding economic plans or that they are likely to be carried out even to the extent that it was customary to do it in the past.

Capital Budgeting

Aggregative decisions about allocation of resources have to be implemented in detail. Numerous alternatives, however, confront planners and policymakers, who must formalize decisions for action. Choices must be made among competing branches even within the same industry (for example, types of machine tools), alternative processes (capital- or labor-intensive), and present and postponable outlays. In turn, choices among these alternatives, as suggested by the project-making offices of the ministries and administrations, will influence the final choices of capital expenditures, though the projects will not set the ceiling for total investment, since that depends on what is considered politically feasible.

Although the theoretical solution to the "efficiency"—or productivity—of investments is complicated by the prevailing distortions in pricing and costing, top management, like the project makers, engineers, and operative managers who have the task of preparing the projects, needs some objective standards for measuring the economic effectiveness of each investment proposal in comparative terms. The crux of the matter is the choice of an adequate yardstick, which is by no means simple. Soviet managers, like capitalist entrepreneurs, are plagued by the economics of capital budgeting; failure to measure the worth of each proposal, lack of adequate standards, and reliance on intuition, which often turns out to be a disregard for alternatives, are shortcomings that collectivist managers share with their counterparts in other systems.

After many years of soul searching, the Soviets have placed the stamp of official approval on two well-known types of indicators: the *incremental output to capital ratio* and the *payoff period*. The first concerns the relation between changes in output (Y) and changes in capital investment (K). Indicators of this type are rough guides for calculating the effectiveness of investments for the national economy, republics, branches, or complexes as a whole. The second indicator, the payoff period, is the number of years needed to recoup an original investment outlay. The form of the payoff depends on how both the initial investment and the revenues that "pay it back" are defined; its application consists then in making choices among production alternatives. Numerous official Soviet "Guidelines on Methods" (*Metodicheskie ukazaniia*) for the compilation of plans provide a variety of formulas for the purpose. Thus, pairs of processes can be evaluated by contrasting their respective operating expenses and capital outlays and comparing the results with some given norm.

Let K_1 and K_2 be capital outlays, C_1 and C_2 the operating expenses, T the payoff period needed by the more expensive alternative to pay out the additional investment outlays it requires through savings in yearly operating expenses, and T_s the norm or standard payoff period. With $(K_1 - K_2)/(C_2 - C_1) = T$, preference will be given to the expensive alternative; if $T > T_s$, to the cheaper one. In practice, the reciprocal of the payoff period ($1/T$) is the estimate of the proposal's rate of return. The Soviets call it the coefficient of effectiveness (E). If capital expenditures for the mutually exclusive alternatives are to be made at different periods, it has been suggested that the normative coefficient of effectiveness might be used as a discounting factor; that is, investment outlays at future dates can be discounted to the present by multiplying them by $1/(1 + E)$. Other suggested payback formulas contrast the profit P_f achieved in the final year of a project due to the capital outlay K, with the profit P_b realized in the preplan year—that is, $T = K/P_f - P_b$, and $E = P_f - P_b/K$. The preference will be given to the fastest payback ($T < T_s$). For *construction* projects, official recommendations suggest the formula $T = K/P_r - C$, where P_r is the yearly revenue (that is, the annual *planned* output of the constructed enterprise at its wholesale price [excluding the turnover tax]), and C is the yearly production costs. For the selection of *locational* alternatives, the calculations are to be based on the formulas $C_o + E_s K_o + T_r = \min.$; and $K_o + T_s C_o + T_r = \min.$, where C_o is the cost per unit of output, E_s is the standard coefficient of effectiveness, K_o is the investment per unit of output, and T_r stands for the transport outlays incurred for delivering a unit of output to the plan addressees. In drawing up the plans, calculations of effectiveness are required also with respect to the basic directions of capital investments, namely: (a) new construction (*novoe stroitel'stvo*); (b) expansion (*rashirenie*) of existing production faculties; (c) reconstruction (*rekonstruktsiia*) of the production facilities; and (d) technical retooling (*technicheskoe perevooruzhenie*). These directions are considered decisive for planning.

In market-directed economies the payback method is used only as a secondary tool of analysis. Projects are usually ranked on the basis of their present values (PV) or their internal rates of return (IRR). PV is equal to revenue less disbursed costs over the life of the asset, discounted to the present at the prevailing rate of interest. The firm will undertake projects with a positive PV. The IRR is the discount rate at which the present value of the cash flow generated by a project just equals the cost of that project. The IRR method converts the cash flow information to a rate of return directly comparable to the cost of capital; investments will be made in all projects in which IRR $> r$, where r is the cost of acquiring the funds. The PV, IRR, or payback methods used in market-directed economies are only superficially comparable to the methods used in the Soviet economy. In the latter, the problem with the official yardsticks is that the underlying costs, prices, profits, and standard recoupment periods are manipulated by policymakers and planners. Soviet planning gives preference not only to certain branches in terms of investment but also within these branches to capital-intensive processes. Hence, for planning capital investments the permissible coefficients of efficiency are quite low for priority branches and high for others. Yet, the indicated coefficients play one of the key roles of interest rates in the West, namely, that of a screening device or a means of rationing investment funds. The official recognition of the need for such a device implies that the planners do in fact take into account both the services of nonlabor factors and, within each branch at least, the opportunity costs of investment outlays.

Each and every project of construction, expansion, reconstruction, and technical retooling is supposed to be carefully prepared with respect to the planned volume of operations by the appropriate planners of investment, designing and surveying design organizations, and construction and assembly organizations. Their calculations involve the use of physical and value indicators based on officially established norms (or standards) for every aspect of construction work and assembly operation, putting the facilities into operation, producing the major inputs required, and even settling accounts between client and contracting firms. The capital construction projects drafted and approved in conformity with established procedures are then integrated into Title Lists (*titul' nye spiski*), "the fundamental initial document of the plan of capital construction." The Title Lists include the complete characterization of each project—its name, location, period of completion, estimated costs, and date at which it begins operation.

"Acceleration" vs. Bottlenecks

Like the early five-year plans of the Stalin era, the planning guidelines for 1986 90 and the period ending in 2000 projected a radical transformation of the structure of the economy as well as a rapid acceleration of the growth of its output and to intensify its efficiency. The core of this policy, the crucial "starting point for shaping the pace and proportions of enlarged reproduction" (that is, of growth), was the restructuring of the machine-building complex (MBC), supposed to provide both the machines necessary to rebuild itself on a higher technological level and the advanced equipment needed to enable all the sectors of the economy to be rebuilt so as to achieve a massive step forward. According to the guidelines and subsequent planning documents, as much as 60 percent of the basic assets of the engineering industry were to be replaced by 1990; the use of available capacity was to be doubled; the metal content, the use of specialized steel products, and the power consumption per unit was to be sharply curtailed; and output of the machine-building and metalworking industries was to increase by 40–45 percent, while labor productivity would increase by the same amount and costs would fall by some 10 percent. Concomitantly, the quality of engineering production was supposed to sharply increase so that 80–95 percent of its product would meet "world standards" (as against some 20–25 percent in 1985).

Were these extraordinary goals realistic? Consider first the structure of the machine-building complex and the bottlenecks it faced during the last half of the 1980s in terms of quantity and quality of machines and other inputs and, next, the discrepancies between the norms set by planners and the project's actual achievements with respect to design, construction, the putting into operation of facilities, and the replacement of equipment.

TABLE 4-2. Structure of the Soviet Inventory of Machinery and Equipment in 1986, by Technical Parameters in Percentage of Total

Total Machinery and Equipment	Highest World Standard	At Prevailing Standard	Below Contemporary Standards
Thirty-three ministries and departments	16.0	55.9	28.1
Fuel and Power Complex	14.1	59.8	26.1
Metallurgical Complex	14.3	56.6	29.1
Machine-building Complex	19.9	54.1	26.0
Chemicals and Lumber Complex	16.0	53.1	30.9
Agro-industrial Complex	14.6	58.5	26.9
Construction Complex	10.7	50.5	38.8

Source: Goskomstat, *Material' no-technicheskoe obespechenie narodnogo khoziaistva SSSR* (Material Technical Supply of the National Economy of the USSR) (Moscow: Finansy i statistika, 1988), 223.

Note: Underlying data in Rubles

To start with, let us note that Soviet institutional arrangements divide the machine-building sector into a civilian and defense industry. The first, encompassing a number of ministries-directed branches, is coordinated like any other complex by an ad hoc interministerial collegium. The second is supervised and coordinated by a first-deputy primary minister and by the military-industrial committee (*voenno-promyshlennyi komitet*—VPK) under the Council of Ministers. While no direct information is available on the structure of the engineering facilities under VPK, and while VPK enjoys high priorities from many points of view, it is clear from what follows that many of the problems that beset the civilian MBC must also plague the military branches.

According to official Soviet claims in the 1980s, the Soviet Union had in use more machines than the United States, Japan, and West Germany put together. But the Soviet Union had some deep and intractable problems concerning the structure and use of this machinery. A large part of its inventory of machinery and equipment was technologically below world standards. As can be seen from table 4-2, only 10 to 20 percent of this equipment were up to desired standards, while between 26 and 39 percent were below even those that prevailed in the bulk of Soviet plants. In the machine-building industry, less than 20 percent of the inventory met world standards. More than half of the total inventory was in bad need of repair and reconditioning, if not complete overhauling. In his inaugural report of June 11, 1985 (*Kommunist*, no. 9 [1985]), in which he stressed the urgent need of retooling Soviet industry, Gorbachev complained that, up to then, "many operating enterprises were not technically reequipped for many years and, as they say, everything possible was squeezed out of them and very little was invested in them."

There are three categories of machinery-building facilities in the USSR.

The category most advanced from a technological point of view is constituted by the enterprises under the machine-building ministries. At a lower technical level are machine-building facilities that are not directed by All-Union ministries. Finally, the lowest category is constituted by a large number of workshops integrated into non–machine-building enterprises concentrating on repair and the production of spare parts for repair. According to data of the mid-1980s, 44 percent of the total amount of machinery was then concentrated in these workshops, which also employed roughly one-half (six million) of all workers in machine building. About a third of the total machinery inventory was concentrated in the upper category of the industry. Nevertheless, even this advanced part of the industry still had a long way to go before becoming a major producer of sophisticated machines of world standard, even though it had successes in developing universal machines.

As much as a quarter of the USSR's total industrial capital stock is in the MBC, which is comprised of some ten ministerial branches producing machines for: (1) power engineering; (2) heavy industry and transport; (3) electrical engineering; (4) chemical and oil industries; (5) machine tool and toolmaking industries; (6) instrument making for automation, electronics, and control; (7) the auto industry; (8) tractors and other agricultural machinery; (9) construction and road building; and (10) light and food industries. The pivot of the MBC and, therefore, much of the Gorbachev program was based on the machine tool and toolmaking branch—the primary equipment producer of the engineering industry. Its prospective development was tied inter alia to the ability to assimilate and amalgamate technologies developed by the instrument-making ministerial branch. Western studies of the Soviet machine tools industry point out that traditionally Soviet tooling has been a low priority and an inefficient part of overall industrial production. Demand for new machine tools has always exceeded supply and has had a detrimental rather than a spurring effect on the industry. New machine tools have been dispersed in all the parts of the economy, even where secondhand machines could have been used. A large part of the machine tools in use were made for more basic operations, and only a smaller part has been devoted to complex metal-forming operations. Due to supply problems, many factories have developed a self-contained cycle of production, specializing by end product, with most component parts made by the factory itself. A large stock of standard machine tools could have been needed in the USSR simply because of the low level of utilization of the machines available—as reflected in part in low average shift use, which, according to the guidelines, was scheduled to be doubled by 1990.

The great structural changes in the MBC required by perestroika, entailing transfers of equipment between the indicated machine-building classes, the breakup of certain giant enterprises and the creation of more efficient medium and small ones, and the accelerated growth output of sophisticated machine tools of world standard, faced, from its inception, enormous hindrances. Such changes were severely hampered, to start with, by the inertia of the apparatus—the ingrained customs of wasting resources, lags in scientific and technical updating in a number of directions, and, last but not least, severe scarcities of certain strategic inputs. Officially recognized shortages existed with respect to such critical inputs as control systems, microcircuits, electrical engineering steel sheets, bimetallic rolled pieces, and aluminum and aluminum alloys, among others. The 12th Five-Year Plan (1986–90) placed exceptional emphasis on the efficient use of steel and included specific targets for steel saving into the plans of every ministry of the MBC. Better utilization of steel and modernization of the steel industry were certainly of critical importance but constituted only one of the numerous problems facing the machine tools industry in regard to modern needs for precision, speed, and the handling of new materials. Indeed, during the 1980s enormous changes have taken place in the West in the design of machines that could deal with *new* metal alloys, plastics, and composites, such as blends of carbon fibers and epoxy used in aircraft. As usual, Soviet plans lagged technologically compared with Western developments, and planners placed far too many hopes on catching up, even with obsolete technologies. The planners selected no less than forty-four priority directions of improvement, concerning, in particular, fuel and power, metallurgy, machinery, chemicals, the construction complex, transportation, the food program, and even certain social needs. In short, much of what was projected was far too ambitious in relation to the means available.

Too much was also hoped for from a single, unified technological policy and better use of the country's high-powered scientific talent. Similar hopes were also expressed in the 1960s when the prevailing restructuring of the Soviet Research and Development (R&D) institutional setup took place. As in the 1960s, great reliance was placed on "enhancing" the level of the USSR State Committee on Science and Technology for determining the appropriate priorities on "research complexes" (such as the research city *Academgorodok* of Novosibirsk) and on "research corporations" (such as the B. I. Paton Institute of Welding and the Blagonravov Institute of Machines, run under the auspices of the USSR Academy of Sciences). But actual expenditures on R&D remained low in regard to the MBC—if one is to believe *Pravda* (May 13, 1987), which speculates in this connection that the machine-tool industry was, in fact, "the Cinderella rather than the alleged queen of the ball."

While in 1985 Gorbachev asserted that "we cannot permit our country to depend upon deliveries from the West, the experience of recent years has taught us a great deal," the Soviet Union would benefit immensely from the relaxation of selective embargoes applied by the West with respect to a number of critical, "strategic" electronic, control, and automation products. In 1988 and 1989 the Soviet Union imported about one billion dollars a year worth of machine tools from industrial countries. It is estimated that at the end of the 1980s, about 45 percent of West German machine tools exports ended up further East. Yet the Soviet Union was still not able to obtain either the total quantity or assortment of machinery that it would have liked to obtain. Clearly, the Soviet Union would have to reach a much higher level of machinery imports in the 1990s (particularly from Germany) if some of the hoped-for changes are to be implemented. In short, the ensemble of vast reallocations of Soviet machinery and the labor force among alternative uses, reorganization and technological advance of the machine tool and toolmaking industry, integration and amalgamation of critical changes in the instrument-making industries, solving of certain bottlenecks on the side of numerous inputs, expansion of R&D and spurring of innovation along with the need to expand strategic imports raise a host of complex problems for Soviet policymakers during the 1990s and beyond. These problems are wider, more sophisticated, and more demanding than those that confronted the Soviet Union at the turn of the 1920s, when it laid the foundations of its industrialization on the technology of iron and steel developed in the West a quarter of a century earlier.

Norms and Achievements

The great discrepancies between the planners' norms and the actual achievements do not suggest that the ambitious targets set by the perestroika program are within easy reach. Consider the technical aspects raised in the process of capital construction by: (1) the project making and prospecting phase; (2) delays in construction; (3) changes in the processes of expansion and renewal of the existing enterprises; (4) the scrapping of old equipment; and (5) the overall balance of the capital stock in use.

Project making and prospecting involves crucial technological and organizational problems and requires great technical knowledge as well as familiarity with the planned goals and recommendations concerning special technical characteristics of the projected enterprise, its scheduled specialization, input and output mixes, prospective suppliers and customers, and location. It is in the project phase that issues are decided that will bear heavily on the physical operative characteristics and effectiveness of a given plant and on its integration into a given branch and sector. The project maker, relying on up-to-date technology and on centrally established norms (standard measurements) for construction, utilization of materials, and every technical engineering aspect, will, according to the official rules, carefully document each project.

Actually, there are numerous and wide discrepancies between rules and reality. To start with, already at the preproject phase, many deficiencies handicap the Soviet project maker, such as a lack of knowledge of foreign technological innovations, poor planning forecasts, distorted prices, poor equipment, and the absence of the possibility of selecting clearcut alternatives. Further, numerous projects can be launched that bypass the project-designing bureaus. Thus, according to the belated recognition of *Stroibank*—the state Soviet bank of investments—close to three hundred projects (costing no less than fifty billion rubles) launched during the Tenth Five-Year Plan (1976–80) bypassed these bureaus. On the other hand, many "final" documented projects involving large designing costs remained on the shelf. The documented projects are not necessarily up-to-date, technologically speaking. As Gorbachev himself pointed out in his June 1985 speech quoted above, much of Soviet equipment is shoddy and obsolete *when new*: "already at the designing stage some newly created technical equipment is lagging behind the best models in its reliability, work capacity, and efficiency. Even the products that are placed in the highest categories at times cannot compare with the best world models." Exactly three years after Gorbachev's speech, the *Ekonomicheskaia gazeta* (July 29, 1988) noted under the signature of one A. Leshchevskii that "a sample check of the design of machine-building projects shows that only 17 percent of them meet the world standard. Which means that we are trying to rebuild 'yesterday.'"

The cumbersome bureaucracy makes haste slowly. Because of this, as Soviet sources point out, technological obsolescence increases continuously throughout the cycle of project making (construction, production, and delivery of equipment) and the mastering of the new techniques needed for the functioning of the given plant. The project-making phase takes two to three years; construction and equipment emplacement takes five to seven years; and mastering of the given techniques takes two to five additional years, and sometimes longer. This schedule means that the funds allocated for the mastering of techniques are spent nine to fifteen years after launching a given project, a fact that increases its actual aging and technological inefficiency. Dispersal of construction in too many directions and enormous delays in building form a particularly detrimental link in the Soviet process of capital formation, causing enormous handicaps in terms of integrating plans. And the situation seems to be getting worse rather than better. According to official data, from 85 to 90 percent of all capital funds earmarked for building are sunk each year into projects whose completion drags for years on end. Already in 1985, Gorbachev complained that the Saian-Sushenskoie Hydroelectric Plant (of Krasnoiarsk territory), for instance, had been under construction for more than twenty years—that is, it has been built twice as slowly as the Bratsk Hydroelectric Plant (the pride of the 1960s). A few years later, at the July 9, 1988, party Conference on Machine Building, the chairman of

TABLE 4-3.   Norms and Actual Expenditures, in Billions of Rubles and
Percentage Overruns, 1975, 1979, and 1982

	Project Design			Construction			Mastering New Techniques		
Year	Norms	Actual	Percent Increase	Norms	Actual	Percent Increase	Norms	Actual	Percent Increase
1975	117	212	81	212	372	75	94	188	100
1979	176	299	70	240	507	111	127	254	100
1982	180	310	72	280	560	100	145	288	98

Source: A. A. Malygin, *Planirovanie vosproizvodstva osnovykh fondov* (Planning the Growth of Basic Assets) (Moscow: Ekonomika, 1985), 12.

Gosstroi (Soviet Construction) remarked that the number of projects under construction has been slow to decline, and the volume of incomplete construction work is actually growing, not falling. Wide discrepancies tend to develop at each step between planned (norm) costs and actual expenditures in a system in which prices are supposed to be stable, norms reliable, and each stage carefully laid out. As can be seen from table 4-3, at each step actual expenditures exceed the estimates from 70 to 100 percent, making the notion of planning itself rather dubious.

A key policy of the 1970s aimed to limit the creation of new state enterprises and to direct investable resources toward the renovation (*rekonstruktsiia*) of existing ones. Gorbachev took over the same idea in the 1980s but put the emphasis on complete technical retooling (*techniheskoe perevooruzhenie*) of these enterprises. Neither policy succeeded in dampening the allocation of large sums to new construction or renovation, usually meaning expansion of building facilities rather than the modernization of equipment. The problem is not only that conservative managers are not in favor of technical innovations but also that the quantity, assortment, and quality of equipment are wanting. As Yu P. Batalin put it at the 1988 Conference on Machine Building, "currently there is perhaps not a single sector in the national economy whose needs for Soviet-made equipment are fully satisfied by the machine-building complex. The national economy continues to receive a lot of inefficient and unreliable equipment." As can be seen from table 4-4, new construction, expansion, plus a part of the investable resources allocated to reconstruction must still absorb two-thirds of capital investments: this figure marks an appreciable decrease in the sums allocated, particularly, to the expansion of facilities in relation to the 1970s but remains far below the hoped-for shift toward the modernization of equipment and broad retooling advocated by Gorbachev.

The discarding of wornout and long obsolete machinery and its replace-

TABLE 4-4. Structure of Capital Investments, in
Percentages, 1971–82 and 1986

Categories	1971–75	1976–82	1986
New Construction	42.1	41.8	35.1
Expansion	37.3	33.5	21.9
Reconstruction	11.5	10.7	43.0
Retooling	9.1	14.0	

Sources: A. A. Malygin, *Planirovanie*, 137, 160; and *Narodnoe khoziaistvo SSSR za 70 let.*, 104.

ment with new yet possibly inefficient and unreliable equipment is not a simple and easy matter. The continuous deterioration of Soviet industrial facilities is clearly mirrored in the following data. The yearly retirement rates of capital assets fell through the 1970s to the early 1980s from 1.8 percent to 1.2 percent, while the yearly rate of expansion of these assets contracted during the same period from 9.4 percent to 7.1 percent. Concomitantly the average years of service of fixed assets rose from 19.5 years to 27 years, while, paradoxically, the norms were "commanding" a decrease to 22.1 years (see table 4-5).

The rate of scrapping of machinery also fell during these years from some 2.3 to 2.5 percent per year to 1.8 percent. When considering the renovation coefficients, one must keep in mind that renovation refers mostly to new construction and, secondarily, to "renewal" and repair (rather than replacement) of available equipment. Renewal of Soviet equipment occurs usually after six years of service, which means that so-called reinvigorated equipment performs at best at its *original* technological level for some additional fifteen to sixteen years; the estimated years of service of the equipment were on the order of 21.5 years in the early 1980s. Soviet economists assert that the years of service of most machinery need to be reduced to five to seven years. As G. Sorokin rightly noted, renovation is often a screen for inertia and retarding technological change. In the early 1980s the amount earmarked for depreciation—thought unduly low—would have been sufficient to replace at least three times more obsolete equipment than that actually discarded. But much of these depreciation funds went for new construction. Being aware that the rates of depreciation need to reflect the rates of deterioration and obsolescence, Soviet economists urge higher rates of depreciation, shorter periods of amortization, and lower norm years of equipment utilization.

When, in conjunction with the data presented above, one considers that the capital-to-output ratio has risen continuously since the 1970s, one cannot but conclude that the deteriorating Soviet performance necessarily results from an increase in real costs as machinery and equipment ages and "decays."

TABLE 4-5.   Changes in Industrial Capital Assets, 1970, 1975, 1980, and 1982, in Percentages

Items	1970	1975	1980	1982
Renovation coefficient	11.9	8.8	8.1	7.3
Retirement coefficient	1.8	1.6	1.4	1.2
Pace of growth of capital assets	9.4	8.5	7.9	7.1
Average years of service of assets	19.5	21.3	23.5	27.0
Normative years of service	25.0	21.3	22.2	22.1

Source: A. A. Malygin, *Planirovanie,* 112.
Note: Percentages are of capital assets of the beginning of the year.

As the situation sets in and expands, the equipment yields less output, and, moreover, it absorbs more inputs of materials, labor, maintenance, and renewal costs. This is not only the penalty of a bad and shortsighted policy in the timing of replacement and the result of a refusal to recognize the economic demise of a large part of the country's productive facilities and unwillingness to accord it, as George Terborgh once put it, "a timely burial," but also a manifestation of a host of errors: the choice of the so-called national economic proportions; emphasis on heavy industry and military expenditures; cumbersome, ponderous, and inefficient project design; dispersal of construction projects around the country; the overall scale of building programs; the synchronization and the meshing of plans; the quality, assortment, and availability of equipment; and managerial incentives and the overall nature of the economic organization.

Concluding Comments

The enormous waste of the resources embodied in the giant, pyramidlike constructions of the past is best illustrated by the contemporary conditions of two of these celebrated achievements: one dating from the very First Five-Year Plan, namely Stalin's giant Magnitogorsk; the second immediately ante-dating Gorbachev's regime, namely, Brezhnev's project of the century, the Baikal-Amur Mainline.

Stalin's metallurgical combine and "iron city" built near the rich lode of iron ore of the Magnetic Mountain are now in a desolate state. As a *New York Times* reporter, Bill Keller, noted after visiting Magnitogorsk (August 16, 1988), "the local iron ore is depleted, the technology is outmoded, and the people [are] increasingly alarmed by the plant's malodorous and unhealthy fumes." Magnitogorsk now imports its iron ore from Kazakhstan, three hundred miles away. The output of the open-hearth furnaces that went into much of the Soviet armament in World War II is now considered suitable mostly for agricultural machinery. With its sixty thousand workers, Magnitogorsk turns out only as much steel as it would take fourteen thousand U.S. steelworkers to produce (and U.S. Steel is not notably productive). The open-hearth furnaces will be replaced by 1995, and perhaps by 2000 the decrepit, coughing giant will spew less malodorous fumes into the air. Pollution abatement facilities are very costly and not widespread, while environmental problems are acute in many parts of the country. The entire Soviet industry—its nuclear facilities, and many cities, lakes, and rivers—are far behind in pollution control (a situation aggravated by the great tragedy of Chernobyl).

The second albatross of Soviet gigantomania closer to us, the BAM, was proclaimed completed in 1984 with the laying of the so-called golden link joining it with the Trans-Siberian Railroad. As Victor Perevedentsev noted in *Sovetskaia kultura* (October 11, 1988), the original goal of the project was the creation of a powerful industrial belt, including what would be the fourth Soviet major coal and metallurgical complex and large new plants and towns all along its entire route. As it turned out, construction of most production facilities had to be postponed to the next century. It took ten years, at the turn of the last century, to build the Trans-Siberian Railroad, from Cheliabinsk to Vladivostok, a distance double that of the BAM. It took fifteen years to build the BAM, which was supposed to be the leading cargo carrier of oil and minerals, but the plans turned awry. The only remaining local cargo is timber, but for its transport the Trans-Siberian can do a better job. In short, there is nothing worthwhile to carry on the BAM, which has turned out to be an expensive and inefficient venture. As B. Selivanov, deputy director of an industrial administration, remarked in *Pravda* (May 2, 1988), "Grandiose 'projects' were designed, and billions of people's money were spent, but the effectiveness of these outlays, by the time they were embodied in actual construction, no longer interested anyone, since the next 'project of the century' was now ready."

As we noted, giant, pyramidlike constructions were used to mobilize the entire country at five-year intervals. Such projects are no longer in fashion in the USSR. But Gorbachev's central project of retooling the machine tool industry, and through it the machine-building complex and, thus, the entire country at an "accelerated pace," is not alien to the old-time illusion of a magic, rapid means of accelerating growth and curing all the country's problems. In other words, the USSR was engaged in yet another project of industrial restructuring, while simultaneously pursuing the goals of restructuring the economic mechanism. One was supposed to increase the pace of growth rapidly and push the economy onto a higher technological plateau, while the other was supposed to simultaneously weed out inefficiencies and yield quality products. These joint objectives—which, incidentally, were also supposed to be carried out jointly in Hungary since the 1960s (under the Kádár regime,

1956–88)—have meant only that, in practice, acceleration (that is, the green light for investment and quantitative output growth) rather than efficient production of marketable quality products had the real priority. As usual, the planned pursuit of simultaneous *quantitative growth* and *qualitative transformation* proved impossible.

CHAPTER 5

Manpower Management

Balances of Manpower

Like any other government, the Soviet government can affect the size, distribution, skills, and education characteristics of the population as well as of the labor force in a variety of ways. It can influence manpower demand with policies concerning investments and job creation and, with legislative measures, the formation of enterprises, wage levels, and incentive systems. It can further impact the distribution of labor via a variety of plans, rules, placement agencies, and, in the specific Soviet case, also via direct placement of vocational-technical graduates and organized manpower recruitment.

The formulation of any economic plan is preceded by the construction of a *preliminary balance of manpower resources*. In the Soviet acceptance of the term, manpower resources encompass the population of both sexes of working age—namely, men between the ages of sixteen and fifty-nine and women between the ages of sixteen and fifty-four, plus persons of nonworking age who are nevertheless working in the national economy. Labor has free access to the labor markets. The balance inventories the civilian employed manpower, its categories of employment (workers, employees, collective farmers, domestic workers, and subsidiary farmers), and its distribution by sphere of activity, industry, and service branch (see table 5-1).

Forecasting the availability and requirements of labor during the plan period rely on technical projections of the interrelations between growth and the changing distribution of the population and the labor force, on the one hand, and the output plans and opportunities for employment that they will engender, on the other. Population projections are made either with the help of so-called economic methods or various mathematical models. Extrapolations of past data follow standard procedures. A certain rate of change is assumed as a function of time for the total population, and/or for fertility rates, death rates, and interregional migrations with reference to the subclassification chosen. Cohort-type analysis, wherein the population is divided into particular groups, such as age categories, and the relevant rates determined for each cohort are also used to calculate overall rates. Forecasted changes in the size, age, and gender makeup of the population during a projected plan period,

TABLE 5-1. Schema of the Balance of Manpower Resources and Distribution

Row No.		Annual Average
	Manpower Resources	
01	Population of working age (excluding nonworking invalids and retirees)	
02	Youth under working age, but working	
03	Other persons still working	
04	Total manpower resources (01 + 02 + 03)	
	The Distribution of Manpower Resources	
05	Employed in the national economy (06 + 07)	
06	Workers and employees	
07	Collective farmers	
08	Full-time students, 16 and above	
09	Engaged in domestic work and subsidiary farming	
10	Total Distribution of Manpower Resources (05 + 08 + 09)	
	The Distribution of the Gainfully Employed by Sphere and Branch	
11	Engaged in the sphere of material production (12–19)	
12	Industry	
13	Construction	
14	Agriculture	
15	Forestry	
16	Transport	
17	Communication	
18	Trade	
19	Other material production sphere	
20	Engaged in the nonproductive sphere (21–24)	
21	Housing, public utilities	
22	Education, culture, and art	
23	Health services, social welfare, and sports	
24	Collective needs (including science, finance, credit and insurance, general government, and other needs of nonproductive sphere)	
25	Total gainfully employed in the national economy (11 + 20)	

Source: N. S. Koval' and B. P. Miroshnichenko, eds., *Planirovanie narodnogo khoziaistva SSSR* (Planning the National Economy of the USSR) (Moscow: Vyshaia shkola, 1968), 389; and U.N. Statistical Office, *Basic Principles of the System of Balances*, 104.

including changes due to migration, are then examined jointly with the baseline makeup of labor resources, intervening losses due to death, retirements, and transfers, and, finally, projected labor requirements resulting from plan requirements. The latter are determined on the basis of a *balance of working time* (defining the so-called socially necessary labor for the production of a given volume of output) and/or assumptions concerning changes in labor productivity. The balance of working time is drafted in man-hour units. It is based on calculations of "total labor consumption," that is, of labor outlays by industry and branch derived with the help of input-output tabulations and/or standard coefficients of labor inputs.

Traditionally, the Soviet policymakers and planners have payed close attention to the accounts of labor consumption in order to ascertain both patterns of capital-labor interrelations through the economy's branches, sectors, and spheres of activity, and the possible areas of labor saving. The basic planning indicator of labor productivity is the annual commodity output per average worker in the industrial work force computed in comparable prices. Projected increases in labor productivity are based on calculations on the impacts of technological changes (due to upgrading of equipment), managerial improvements (concerning wastage of time and resources), and structural production changes. The scheduled growth in labor productivity (ΔLp) can be computed with the formula $\Delta Lp = S_i/N_c - \Sigma S_i$, where S_i is the saving in numbers resulting from one of the indicated factors, and ΣS_i is the saving in numbers resulting from all the factors, while N_c is the number of industrial workers calculated for the volume of production in the planned period in output of the base period. The *final* overall balance of labor resources and distribution for the plan period rests, then, on the accuracy of the preliminary balance of manpower, balance of working time, plan targets, and scheduled productivity changes. What is the validity of this final balance? The enormous difficulties of the vast quantity of underlying computations—starting from the enterprises and associations up to branches and ministries, with consolidations at the levels of cities, districts, regions, and republics—combined with numerous factors distorting actual labor utilization and the managerial reporting of this utilization render discrepancies between planned and actual labor inputs unavoidable.

Yet the final balance of manpower is a critical element for all planning calculations. The *national wage fund* for the plan period is computed in relation to it, taking into account the key policy decisions concerning the ratio of consumption to accumulation, the division of consumption into the labor remuneration fund and the public consumption fund, the distribution of the labor remuneration fund into the wage bill of workers, employees, and collective farmers, as well as the contemplated changes of retail prices and public utilities and service rates. The calculation of the wage bill is based on estimates of the average weighted wage or salary rate depending on the type of work and the structure of the labor force. The state and its planning bodies still establish the conditions of pay, allocate expenditures on wages, and regulate their payment. Wage rates and scales are still fixed centrally, usually by the Council of Ministers of the USSR.

Over the balance of the century a number of important changes are to take place in regard to patterns of Soviet employment and labor rewards. To better understand and analyze the causes of these changes, the present chapter first examines characteristics of the Soviet labor market and shifts in Soviet approaches to the "limitless" growth of the numbers of the gainfully employed, wage equalization, and the relation of wages to productivity and output. It then considers the structure and range of salaries of employees, professionals, and executives, and the special privileges reserved for the leading members of the nomenklatura. After discussing Soviet measures concerning pensions, welfare, and public consumption, chapter 5 concludes with an analysis of Soviet ways of tackling the key issues of workers' attitudes toward work and public property as the Soviet society prepares itself to face the challenges of high unemployment.

Labor Market and Wages

Up to the 1980s the main thrust of Soviet manpower policy was the incessant expansion of the nonagricultural labor force and, within it, manufacturing employment. Permanent full employment was proclaimed the distinctive feature of the socialist system. The Soviet strategy for economic growth, elaborated in the 1920s, enshrined the principles of high capital accumulation rates and preferential allocation of investable resources to heavy industry, and it identified economic growth with the incessant growth of the industrial proletariat. The Soviet leadership's unbending commitment to full employment and the numerical growth of the industrial proletariat, as well as its satisfied acceptance of the latter's efficiency, discipline, and devotion to public property, started to give way to serious doubts as the overall performance of the economy continued to deteriorate more and more visibly from the late 1960s on.

Between 1940 and 1985, when Gorbachev took power, the total of the gainfully employed more than doubled, rising from 62.9 million to 130.3 million, compared to a population growth of 62 percent. Concomitantly, the activity rates in relation to the total population rose from 36.8 percent in 1940 to 39.4 percent in 1960, 44.1 percent in 1970, and 47.5 percent in 1980, increasingly drawing women into the labor force. Simultaneously, the gainfully employed in manufacturing rose from 13 million in 1940 to double that in the 1960s and almost treble in 1985 (38.2 million). The Soviet Union crossed over from a primarily agricultural country—when 51.4 percent of its manpower was engaged in agriculture—to a primarily nonagricultural one through the 1950s, with agricultural employment falling to 35 percent of the total in 1960. It crossed over from a primarily agricultural to a primarily industrial economy only in the 1960s, with full agricultural employment falling to 24 percent as compared to 29.6 percent in manufacturing (see table 5-2).

TABLE 5-2.   Gainfully Employed in the Soviet Economy, Selected Years, 1940–85, in Millions and Percentages

	1940	1960	1970	1980	1985
Manufacturing	20.7%	27.0%	29.6%	29.4%	29.3%
Agriculture					
State	3.2	7.8	8.3	9.2	9.2
Collectives	48.2	27.1	15.7	10.6	9.7
Construction	3.2	7.5	8.4	8.9	8.8
Transportation and communications	6.3	8.4	8.6	9.5	9.4
Trade and supply	5.2	5.4	7.0	7.7	7.7
Total material production	86.8	83.2	77.6	75.3	74.2
Health, education, arts, and science	7.1	12.2	14.3	16.1	16.6
State apparatus and housing and					
communications	6.1	4.6	5.8	7.2	7.5
Not specified	—	—	2.3	1.4	1.7
Total nonproductive sphere	13.2	16.8	22.4	24.7	25.8
Total labor force (in millions)	62.9	83.8	106.8	125.6	130.3

Source: Computed from *SSSR v tsifrakh v 1986 godu* (Moscow: Finansy i statistika, 1987), 141, 144, 171–75; and *Narodnoe khoziaistvo SSSR za 70 let.*, 411.

With high output targets—systematically built on the "already achieved levels"—and with taut allocation of scarce resources (but with increasingly aging and obsolete equipment requiring more inputs of all kinds, including labor above all, and yielding poorer and poorer results) the Soviet leadership became increasingly challenged by apparent labor shortages and more and more evident falling productivity rates. Soviet data for the 1970s, for instance, show that the number of workers and employees called for in the enterprises' plans consistently exceeded, year in and year out, the actual number of workers by some 2 to 2.5 million workers. Pointing to this and related data, some Soviet and Western demographers asserted that an increasing danger of Soviet labor shortages was throwing its shadow on the 1980s. Other analysts drew attention to the well-ingrained tendency of the managers of enterprises to "hoard" labor in order to insure the fulfillment of their plan targets. But the Soviet leadership itself became quite aware of the fact that the real problem it faced was not the specter of labor shortage, but rather the bloated-over employment in its economy, its retarding technology, declining productivity, and the massive dissatisfaction of workers and employees with the state's economy.

Concerning productivity, the Soviet data themselves have shown disastrous declines in the economy as a whole and for all its sectors from the late 1960s on. Many other labor problems have affected the economy since then. From the 1970s on, stress on the need to strengthen labor discipline became a leitmotif in the official press. Warnings against failures in organization and management, high rates of labor turnover and arhythmic work patterns engendering both overtime and idletime, chronic alcoholism resulting in high levels of industrial accidents, absenteeism, malutilization, and wastage of resources became current long before Gorbachev's passage to power. Gorbachev not only repeated these warnings—in a speech before the party's Central Committee (on January 27, 1987) and also before the Trade Unions' Congress (on February 25, 1987)—but added, for good measure, that the time had finally come to strengthen the link between work and rewards, liquidate "parasitic confidence in guaranteed work," put a stop to "warped attitudes toward work," step on the toes "of the slacker, the drunkard and the idler," and part with "wage leveling."

In theory the leading principle of socialism, its "principle of social justice" (which is supposed to reign only *below* the top levels of the nomenklatura), is distribution of income *proportional to the work supplied* by everyone. Inequality of rewards due to inequality of skills and conditions is not typical of capitalism only; it is characteristic of socialism as well. In the Soviet Union, however, a variety of correctives are also called into play with respect to the principle of social justice. Wages differ not only in regard to sex, training, skills, and hardship or intensity of work, but also between branches and sectors (according to policymakers' and planners' objectives concerning desired proportions among sectors) as well as among republics, regions, districts, and other areas, and, finally, among the enterprises themselves, depending on bonuses and other supplements added to the base pay because of a variety of managerial considerations or because of trade union pressure.

Soviet policymakers and planners have always perceived as key elements of planning the size and structure of the wage fund—the initial part of the net product created in material production—as well as its original distribution and subsequent "redistribution" for services. They have further seen crucial levers for furthering planned objectives and work stimulation in wage policies and the population's balances of income and spending, of wages and consumption. As might be expected, the ratio of the social surplus (profits) to the wage fund has tended to fall through the 1970s and early 1980s, as did the rate of return to total outlays on raw materials and the use of machinery (in Marxian terms, *surplus* [m] related to material inputs [c] plus wages [v]). This became one of the main preoccupations of the Gorbachev leadership.

Throughout the entire planning period from 1929 on, two tendencies interacted in setting wage rates. One tendency pushed toward higher wages via upgrading and an increase in pay rates for various categories of workers (depending on the ways managers perceived their needs for manpower and whether the unions were either complacent or felt forced to show "activism") and also, in certain conditions, via an increase in the dismally low pay of the lowest paid workers and farmers. Another tendency pushed in the opposite direction, namely, toward larger wage differentials in order to increase incentives and productivity. Wage differentials increased sharply in the critical planning years 1931–33, when Stalin stepped up the pace of industrialization. Then the wage span decreased somewhat, until 1937, due to increases in the lowest wages in relation to the average wage. After 1937 and in the early postwar years, the spread between the unskilled and skilled increased, ranging from 1:3.5 and even up to 1:4 to 1:8 in certain key industries—still less wide a margin, however, than in the early 1930s. Toward the second half of the 1950s, however, the ratio again decreased significantly, from 1:3.5 to 1:2. The process of wage readjustment in favor of the lowest paid workers and decreasing wage differentials continued during the 1960s until the mid-1980s. Before its increase in 1955, the minimum wage was at the abysmal low level of twenty to twenty-two rubles per month, that is, on the order of 28–30 percent of the average wage (71.8 rubles). By 1977 the minimum rose to 45 percent of the average (70 rubles as against 155.2 rubles). Interesting changes occurred also between the collective farmers' pay from collective funds and the industrial workers' average wage. The collective farmers' pay rose sharply from the 1960s on, from a level equal to less than 31 percent of the average wage of an industrial worker to 57 percent in 1970, 64 percent in 1980, and 73 percent in 1985.

In the official wage scale prevailing in the early 1980s, there were six skill categories within each industrial branch (except in ferrous metallurgy where there were eight categories) with a pay scale spread varying between 1:1.58 (in agriculture, the food industry, and clothing) to 1:1.86 (in lumber, oil extraction, and underground work). On the other hand, the spread between the interindustry relative basic rate—which is the rate of an unskilled (first skilled group) pieceworker performing a job under normal conditions—varied between 1:1.72 (between 74.9 rubles and 129.5 rubles) (see fig. 5-1). In the discussions on wage norms at the Supreme Soviet in the late 1980s, it was suggested that the traditional differentiation of wages by branches be discarded and replaced by norms based uniquely on skills differentiation (*Ekonomicheskaia gazeta*, no. 43, October, 1989). Finally, the "Law on Enterprises in the USSR" of June 4, 1990, authorized the managers of all enterprises to disregard, if they so desire, the official wage scale. But such decisions are not likely to be applied throughout the whole economy.

It is important to note that, while in Soviet theory socialism is alleged to oppose gender discrimination, there has always been widespread occupational segregation in the USSR based on gender differences. As a detailed study by Alastair McAuley makes abundantly clear, women have been confined to subordinate, lower-paying jobs in the main branches of manufacturing and

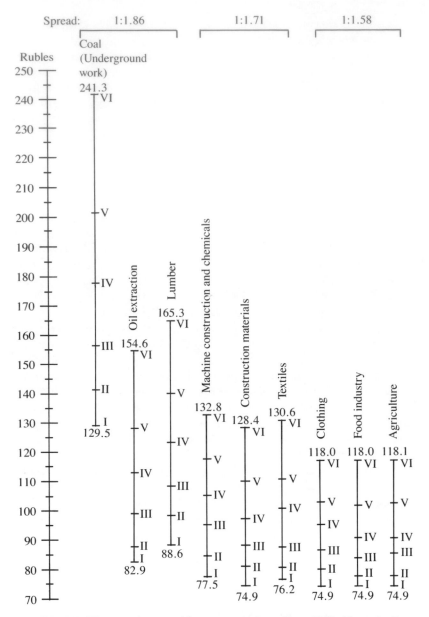

Fig. 5-1. Wage scale, monthly payments in rubles, 1980. (From L. E. Kunelskii, *Zarabotnaia plata i stimulirovanie truda* [Wages and Work Incentives] [Moscow: Ekonomika, 1981], 148.)

have acquired less training than men in industry in general and in all branches of material production. They have been confined to occupations regarded as "women's work" (notably, textiles and clothing). They are more likely than men to have suffered seasonal unemployment in agriculture and have been more prone to work overtime or to have second jobs. (Women have made significant gains, however, in services.)

With the centrally fixed rates and scales (which, up to the late 1980s, determined roughly 60–66 percent of the actual wage bills) have always been intertwined an array of additional payments, increments, bonuses, regional coefficients, as well as arbitrary classifications tending to jack up or decrease the differentials within and between categories. In the early 1930s, when Stalin wanted to step up industrialization, accelerate increases in productivity rates, discard the prevailing work norms, and break up the old work habits, he pointedly denounced wage equalization as harmful and "un-Marxist": "In order to put an end to this evil [of wage equalization] we must draw up wage scales that will take into account the difference between skilled and unskilled labor, between heavy and light work . . . . Marx and Lenin said that the difference between skilled and unskilled labor would exist even under socialism, even after classes had been abolished . . . consequently, even under socialism, 'wages' must be paid according to work performed and not according to needs . . . . But the egalitarians among our business executives and trade-union officials do not agree with this . . . . Who is right, Marx and Lenin or the egalitarians? It must be supposed that it is Marx and Lenin who are right" ("New Conditions—New Tasks in Economic Conditions," June 23, 1931, *Collected Works,* vol. 13). Gorbachev, who also aims to increase the faltering productivity rates, liquidate the ingrained poor working habits, eliminate the superfluous worker, punish the idle and the drunkard, reward the diligent "norm breaker," and end the tendency toward wage equalization, would have liked to proceed as forcefully as Stalin did in these respects at the beginnings of the industrialization drive. Gorbachev has also launched a campaign for a comprehensive restructuring of labor payments, aiming to revise work norms, introduce new wage rates and increase the wages' share in total labor payments, and expand wage differentials in favor of skilled workers and modify the mechanisms of additional pay increments and bonuses. But, unlike Stalin, Gorbachev cannot enforce his objectives with the use of terror and the menace of concentration camps. His reform has to proceed at a slower pace and not always in the hoped-for directions.

The new wage reform began in some respects in 1985 and in other respects in 1987 (the previous labor payment reform unfolded in 1972–75). But the reform is not moving at the same speed in all directions. The change in norms—that is, the redefinition of the conditions and "intensiveness" (quality) of each type of work—is by its very nature a contentious and long drawn-out process. The first measures of the new reform aimed at increasing the wages of the highly skilled employed in the state enterprises. On the other hand, they expanded the six-grade system to an eight-grade system in a number of branches (for example, in the machine-building industries) and raised wages in the upper brackets. But while the enterprises have been given broad rights to differentiate the size of additional payments for differing working conditions, the managers of state enterprises have tended to assign the *same* additional payments to all workers. Finally, and most importantly, the managers of these enterprises have responded well to the incentive of firing workers in order to increase additional payments for work performed with a smaller work force financed by in-house resources. By the end of the 1980s some five million workers were discharged from their jobs. But, when the size of the work force drops and resources accumulate, the growth of wages lags for a variety of reasons, including interference by higher supervisory organs.

Many other factors tend to block the effectiveness and the full play of reform. As Gorbachev himself noted in his February 1987 speech at the Congress of the Trade Unions, "you know even better than I do that certain enterprises are still reluctant to part with wage leveling. Their managements are reluctant because it is a bothersome matter, [and] the trade union locals . . . often want to go on living with this kind of 'timidity.'" Above all, what matters even for the best paid workers, is what one can actually *obtain* with the increased pay. Value depends not only on the prices of goods and services but also on the timing and extent of their availability, their appearance, assortment, and quality, the extent of access to and schedule of delivery of various durable goods, the nature and effectiveness of retail trade and repair and personal care services, and the possibility of acquiring decent living conditions. All of these things, as it has been noted, are seriously wanting.

Salaries of Employees, Professionals, and Executives

The industrial workers' average wage has been consistently much higher than the salaries of employees in both material production and services. Typically, in 1986, an employee in industry made 172.2 rubles, in trade 152.9 rubles, in the commercial services 149.3 rubles, and in health care 134.9 rubles, as against the monthly average of the industrial worker of 216.4 rubles. In the national education system the average monthly pay was 155.7 rubles. The salary revisions of the late 1980s did not significantly modify these differentials except in education and health care.

Quite different is the situation of state managers, designers, technologists, scientific personnel, and quality control employees in material production as well as the nonproductive sphere. The staffs of state enterprises and

TABLE 5-3. Social-Professional Classification of Employees in the Branches of the National Economy

Social-Professional Classification	Grades	Job Descriptions
Executives of enterprises and establishments, and jobs and sections executives within enterprises and establishments	10	200
Specialists employed in the engineering, technical, and economic work, and specialists employed in agriculture and forestry	10	224
Technicians employed in accounting and control, document preparation, and maintenance	10	81
Total	30	505

Source: Trud i zarabotnaia plata v SSSR (Labor and Wages in the USSR), ed. by L. S. Bogatyrenko (Moscow: Ekonomika, 1984), 101, 119–20.

establishments comprise three categories of employees divided into thirty echelons or grades covering 505 types of jobs (see table 5-3). The official data for 1987 indicate that the total of executives, specialists, and technicians in manufacturing, agriculture, and construction comprised over 9.5 million persons out of forty-eight million workers, a ratio of one to five. A wide range of salaries exists within and between these categories, depending on grade skill within the category, industrial branch, and size of the enterprise. Before the 1987 reform the highest director's salary was 450 rubles in the coal mining trusts. After reform the new salary scale for directors in the productive branches is supposed to range from 350 rubles in the food industry to 500 rubles in ferrous metallurgy and 480–520 rubles in the large association of enterprises. For chiefs of shops and departments the salary range was set to rise from 220 60 rubles in the clothing industry to 400 rubles in the machine-building industries. The salaries of chiefs of shops and departments were set at 60 to 90 percent higher than the rates of workers in the highest wage skill rates. Restructuring of remunerations was also carried out in the nonproductive sphere involving increases in the pay of personnel of institutions of higher learning, scientific establishments, and in health care. As noted, female employment is particularly high in education and health care (doctors, nurses, and paramedics) where salaries have been traditionally very low. The standard thirty grades in the economy—of executives-specialists-technicians—likely are standard grades also in the other branch of the state.

Since Stalin's time, appointments in the leading positions of the party, the state, and the economy have been made by cooptation rather than by election, competition, training, or merit. The selections and assignments of cadres—starting from the locus of supreme power down through the various echelons of the party and its satellite organizations, the top positions in the state's administration, and the economy—have been made as a *gift* of the party's ruler(s). Anybody could be dismissed and replaced by the appropriate party committee if the party withdrew its confidence. Because of this, the Soviet civil service became in practice "an extension of the party in composition and training." Stalin's 1923 declaration at the Twelfth Congress of the Communist Party of the Soviet Union explained the logic of the system he was putting in place as follows: "We must select the officials in such a way that the positions should be held by people who will know how to apply the [central] directives, will understand the directives, and will transform these directives into realities." Only after Gorbachev's rise to power did the Politburo accept, reluctantly, the possibilities of trimming the party, state, and management hierarchies, and, up to a point, allowing training, merit, and ability to count in the selection and promotion of cadres.

The official salary figures for the so-called nomenklatura do not conform to the real situation. Recall that, as of 1988, the total of the executive-administration-managerial state apparatus comprised some 15 million persons, 13.1 million of whom represented the managerial personnel and 1.8 million the top layer of state administrators (see table 1-1). We do not know the exact number of directors, but for many of them their monthly salaries have exceeded by far the official norm of 350 to 520 rubles. As V. S. Pavlov, then USSR Minister of Finance, disclosed in his report on the 1990 budget (*Izvestia*, September 26, 1989), associations of enterprises have frequently been formed in order to increase the earnings of the managerial personnel, circumventing the control of labor collectives. The associations have been turned into "feeding troughs" for the management. A typical example, according to Pavlov, was the case of the Association of Enterprises of the USSR Ministry of Power and Electrification, *Gradostroitsel'* (Urbaп Planner), which paid monthly salaries of fifteen hundred rubles to its president, one thousand rubles to his assistant, fourteen hundred rubles to the general director, five hundred rubles to a driver, and three hundred rubles to a secretary typist.

In the traditional system of Soviet rewards, the monthly pay of a member of the state apparatus was set deliberately at a low level; according to Soviet statistics, in 1986 the average monthly pay of a member of this apparatus was 170.5 rubles, as compared to 195 rubles for the average gainfully employed, and 216.4 for a worker. But, beside a low salary, the party and state nomenklaturist enjoyed various perquisites, which increased with rank as one went up the ladder. These privileges, carefully hidden from the vulgum pecus, involved access to a world of luxury, all types of goods at special low prices in special stores off limits to the rest of the population, and included luxuriously appointed houses with rich furniture and works of art, summer homes, resorts, sanatoria, special hospitals and special care, entertainment, and domestic and foreign travel. Many of these perks were administered and handed out directly from the "party's household economy" and were not included in the official budgetary costs of public administration. The nomenklaturist's rubles were of a special kind, since they could buy an assortment of quality goods unavailable to the holders of "ordinary" rubles. All rubles looked alike, but some rubles were worth more than others—depending on who held them. As a well-known sociologist, Tat'iana Zaslavskaia, put it in 1986 in the theoretical and ideological journal of the Central Committee, *Kommunist,* "the fact that different social groups have unequal access to different channels of trade creates a specific form of social inequality, and essentially means the formation of consumer markets in which the ruble has varying purchase power. However, the 'equality of all rubles' as the measure of consumption is the basic premise of the wage system."

Mikhail Gorbachev avoided challenging this well-entrenched system. At the end of the 1980s, G. Kh. Popov, the editor-in-chief of the crucial Soviet journal *Voprosy Ekonomiki,* angrily pointed out in a speech at the Second Congress of USSR People's Deputies (*Izvestia,* December 15, 1989) that, at a time of "worsening of the situation of all working people, especially of employees on fixed salaries . . . , executives privileges are being retained, and an astonishing attempt is being made to begin solving our country's problems by raising pay for the apparatus of party agencies and employees of ministries." Yet the traditional system of nomenklatura rewards is being slowly but surely undermined by a number of factors and is bound to change significantly in the 1990s. As the locus of power is shifting from the party apparatus to the hierarchy of Soviets, it is the latter that will ultimately determine the scale of rewards of its own members and of those of the Soviet bureaucracy in general. On May 21, 1990, the Supreme Soviet enacted a law setting the USSR president's monthly salary at four thousand rubles and providing him, in addition, with a Moscow apartment, a country house outside the city, and another one in Crimea. The law also established that the president will be provided with transport by specially equipped planes, helicopters, and special cars. Upon his retirement, he will be entitled to a monthly pension of fifteen hundred rubles and a state-owned country house with servants, guards, and transport. Thus, an important legal precedent has been created, and, henceforth, privileges will be codified. Increasingly, the elected Soviet hierarchy will determine *who gets what, when, and how*. The hierarchy will bestow openly on the state apparatus' members privileges previously determined and distributed under the table by the party machine.

Inequality and Economic Welfare

The social stratification of Soviet society can be visualized in a number of ways. On the basis of the pay scale, the top layers are represented in descending order by members of the executive organs of the state and the economy, the engineering-technical personnel, and the scientific and cultural personnel—some of whose salaries barely exceed or do not exceed an industrial worker's average wage. These layers are followed, again in descending order, by workers, collective farmers, employees, and, finally, at the bottom the pensioners. The latter, counting in 1986 no less than fifty-seven million persons (of whom about ten million were in agriculture) had an abysmal average monthly pension of some seventy-five rubles, or about one-third of the average monthly pay of an industrial worker. The situation of the pensioners has continuously deteriorated since 1956, when the minimum and maximum pensions were established by the USSR Law on State Pensions. In 1956 the minimum pension was equal to 62 percent of average earnings; the maximum was 164 percent of the average. In 1985 the minimum pension dropped to 32 percent—by almost one-half—while the maximum dropped to 69 percent, a decrease, in relative terms, of 60 percent. At the same time—namely, from 1960 to 1985—state retail prices increased by 20 percent, while the collective farm market prices rose to a much higher degree, as did the cost of domestic and imported medicine. This situation has continued to deteriorate ever since. The *Ekonomicheskaia gazeta* of October, 1989 (no. 42), pointed out in an article entitled "The Difficult Road to the Market," that forty-one million Soviet citizens lived on an income below the official poverty line of seventy-eight rubles per month.

Soviet social stratification can also be observed from a different angle. According to official data, a three-way division of the work force exists, consisting of specialists with higher education, specialists with secondary and vocational education, and the rest of the work force. In 1960 the first and second groups accounted for 4.2 and 6.2 percent of the total, and the rest of the work force for 89.6 percent. In 1985 the percentages were 11, 14.7, and 74.3 percent, respectively. In 1960 and 1985 specialists with higher education—some 3.5 million in 1960 and 14.3 million in 1985—must have supplied the bulk of the privileged nomenklatura positions open to factory executives and engineering-technical and scientific personnel.

Soviet economic texts written before the changes initiated during perestroika always claimed that socialism had "abolished the inequality of income," since the latter could be engendered only by a "different relation of classes to the means of production." *The Teaching of Political Economy* (1984), edited by A. D. Smirnov, V. V. Golosov, and V. F. Maximova, also claimed that it was a mistake to speak of an increase in the spread of incomes in the USSR, since, on the contrary, socialism created the conditions for "a convergence of the incomes of the members of the society." Clearly, such claims do not square with the reality.

In this connection, it is interesting to recall that the old and new Soviet economic textbooks put strong emphasis on the supplements to personal income represented by transfers and public goods, that is, by the expenditures from the "social consumption fund" (SCF). In Soviet income accounting, the national income, created in material production, is divided into accumulation and consumption, with the latter divided into the wage fund (the "labor remuneration fund") and the SCF divided into all kinds of public expenditures, including stipends, grants, and subsidies, as well as pensions (which, in fact, should be included in individual consumption). A closer look at the official data on the SCF for 1986, for instance, shows that 42.4 percent of these funds went to social security and social insurance (of which 32 percent were accounted for by pensions), 25.4 percent were allocated to education, 13.4 went for health care, and 6.3 percent were earmarked for housing funds. Besides pensions, the social security expenditures encompassed outlays for temporary disability, allowances for various services for the aged and the disabled, grants for maternity leaves, and allowances for poor families and child maintenance. Until the late 1980s no thought was given to the question of unemployment compensation. No explanation was given for the remaining 12.5 percent of the total SCF (that is, for over nineteen billion rubles), which probably represented the hidden costs of administration.

The state subsidy for the maintenance of housing, while viewed as acceptable for the relatively low-income strata or large families of workers and employees, has been increasingly denounced as unjustified for other families. In the past, Soviet economists used to take pride in the low payments for rent that accounted for less than 3 percent of workers' and employees' outlays and, allegedly, provided "a firm basis for an increase in the material welfare of all the working people." But since the accession of Gorbachev to office, the general question of subsidies and grants is no longer regarded as a way of increasing material welfare but as one of the principal contributors to the distortion of the price system and the misallocation of welfare benefits. It is pointed out that the distribution, free of charge or at a nominal price, of the scarcest Soviet goods—namely, dwellings and educational and health care services—actually favored high- rather than low-income groups. Instead of expanding the sphere of housing for a fee, including the raising of rents, and just differentiating between them with due regard to the quality and location of apartments, the prevailing system instead encourages speculation in state housing, subletting at high surcharges, and other shady deals in apartment swapping. As Tat'iana Zaslavskaia pointed out in "Social Justice and the Human Factor in Economic Development" in 1986 (*Kommunist*, no. 13), the alleged contribution of SCF to supplementing the distribution according to one's labor to a certain degree and to equalizing the injustice imposed on those who, despite their desire, are not able to work effectively is, thus, completely thwarted. Obtaining decent housing is an elusive goal for a large part of the urban population, while investment in housing has, in relative terms, steadily decreased from the 1960s on. This decrease and misallocation of public funds have led to the paradoxical result also noted by Zaslavskaia that "a well-paid worker can buy furniture, a refrigerator and television set, but must wait years to get an apartment to put them in."

It should be noted that the SCF includes the expenditures on material goods and services provided free or at discount prices from *all* kinds of sources: the state budget, state and cooperative enterprises, collective farms, trade unions, and social organizations. The social security management system is discharged by the state organs but under the supervision of the trade unions, who are empowered to participate in the activities of the state social security organizations and exercise control over their work. Since the 1930s the trade unions have fully managed the social insurance system and have controlled the budget for state social security. Within enterprises and institutions the factory trade union committee alone decides how social insurance money is to be spent. The union leaders indeed wield the power to decide who will get benefits for temporary disability, allowances for children of low-income families, maternity grants, holidays, and sanatoria care.

The interrelations between various types of incomes and various types of outlays used for compiling the financial plan of the state budget, the State Bank's currency and credit plans, and the plans of retail trade, are itemized in the *balance of money incomes and expenditures* of the population. The balance is not published. Instead, the statistical office issues three summary tabulations concerning: the money incomes and expenditures of a "worker's and employee's family," an "industrial worker's family," and a "collective farmer's family." (Chapter 8 examines the structure of these balances in their relation to total consumption and national income in the context of measuring the overall performance of the Soviet economy).

Concluding Comments

Since the 1970s Soviet manpower management has been increasingly plagued by the slowing down of productivity rates and workers' faltering motivation and discipline in the face of deteriorating food supplies and standards of living. Recoiling from Stalin's barbarous and inefficient methods of mass terror and ever-expanding concentration camps (gulags) but unable to develop adequate incentives and rewards for spurring higher levels of productivity, Soviet policymakers, planners, and managers have been at a loss for how to cope with increasing worker indifference toward work, socialist property, and officially established norms, rules, regulations, and interdicts.

Actually, workers' behavior is part and parcel of a broad set of phenomena gnawing at the vitals of the centrally guided system. Under the protection of Gorbachev's *glasnost* ("openness"), some Soviet economists, such as O. Osipenko, have tried to catalog these widely ramified phenomena under the general heading of "unlawful" income sources, that is, of improperly earned income in production, labor activity, or trade. According to Osipenko's study (in *Ekonomicheskie nauki,* no. 11, 1986), this type of income results from theft, bribery, extortion, fraud, illicit entrepreneurial activity, brokerage, and distortion and falsification of enterprises' reports on plan fulfillment. It results also from defective and substandard production, deviations from approved designs and violations of construction rules, unlawful utilization of state machinery for personal gain, incorrect application of bonuses and additional wage payments, jacked up wholesale, retail, and purchase prices, and illegal markups of transport rates and other similar distortions. In fact, "the possibility of converting part of public property into private property"—to use Osipenko's formula—arises from the vast scope for fraudulent manipulation of any one of the vast array of Soviet norms monitoring labor expenditure and productivity, utilization of materials and input-output coefficients, productivity of the means of production, design and construction, and transport and trade. The innumerable threads sorted out by Osipenko connect the stagnant surface economy with its teeming "shadows," the barter and/or black market economy—the first chasing after an often elusive double coincidence of opposite wants, the second brimming with stolen state property, clandestine private production, and all kinds of illicit diversions of public goods. Yet, the editors of a standard 1984 Soviet book, *Teaching of Political Economy,* pretend that "speculative prices and incomes, graft, and embezzlement of socialist property . . . are anti-social phenomena that contradict the very essence of socialism," and, consequently, they refuse to inquire whether such antisocial phenomena do not flow in fact from this very essence itself.

Be that as it may, much of the hope of disciplining labor and improving its productivity rests with the state enterprises' rights to differentiate the size of additional workers' payments, reorganize wages and bonuses to make them more directly dependent on performance, and release a substantial number of "superfluous" workers. The specter of unemployment, which, allegedly, had only the capitalist economies as haunting grounds, is now roaming freely in the Soviet land. Indeed, the question of job placement, retraining, and relocation of the expanding number of released workers and employees has become one of the key preoccupations of the USSR Council of Ministers and the All-Union Central Council of Trade Unions. The right to work is still "guaranteed" for all, but, as *Pravda* and *Izvestiia* put it (January 19–20, 1988), the system of manpower placement must be developed, and close attention must be paid to new uses of the freed manpower. What the top Soviet leaders have finally come up with is to orient the new unemployed toward "do-it-yourself" construction and cooperatives and subsidiary farming and to relocate as many of these people as feasible to the North, Siberia, the Far East, and the abandoned Russian Non–Black Earth zone.

In short, to cope with a new and increasingly important problem Soviet policymakers have fallen back on old methods of organized labor recruitment, public appeals and exhortations, and agricultural resettlement. The only thing that released state workers and employees can legally expect is to be paid severance pay on the amount of one month's average earnings and an additional one-month pay while searching for work. Clearly, the Soviet Union is far from ready to confront the serious question of unemployment, which, according to Soviet estimates, should involve no less than sixteen million superfluous personnel by the end of the century.

CHAPTER 6

Fiscal Management

Nature and Scope of the State Budget

To what extent and in what ways do the central decisions about income, capacity expansion, and manpower shape the state's financial plan, its budget, and the control of money and credit? Consider first the financial plan. This plan is a working document compiled by the central planning organ and the Ministry of Finance, coordinating *all* financial aspects of the country's activity and mapping the financial interdependencies of its production process. On the one hand, it takes into consideration the scheduled expansion of the gross value of output and its components (that is, interindustry demands and factor payments—in Marxian notation $c + [v + m]$) and the "financial resources" that these expansions will generate. On the other hand, it surveys the obligations that these resources must cover, obligations embodied in the capital construction plan, manpower plan, Control Figures, plans of associations (enterprises), and plans of the State Bank. (A number of special balances—by industrial branches, including balances by ministries and administrations, regions, organizations, and the balance of foreign trade—are connected with the overall financial plan.) The resources of the plan comprise all public funds (the state budget), the finances of the state insurance, the associations (enterprises) and organizations, and their supervisory organs, foreign trade, and the State Bank. The specific relations of these resources to the components of the gross value of output are detailed in fig. 6-1. The state's outlays include, for their part, all the expenditures for capital construction (for capital renewal, capacity expansion, and productive equipment), increases in working capital, subsidies (price supports, municipal economy, and housing), state administration and defense, and social and cultural measures. Also specified in this connection are the funds allocated to the banking system for extending short- and long-term credit and the amount of surpluses expected to accumulate at the State Bank. All Soviet financial plans are classified into centralized and decentralized funds. The centralized plans (and funds) managed by the Ministry of Finance are the state budget, budget of the social security system, state insurance budget, currency and credit plans of the State Bank, and the balance of income and expenditure of the population. The decentralized funds, man-

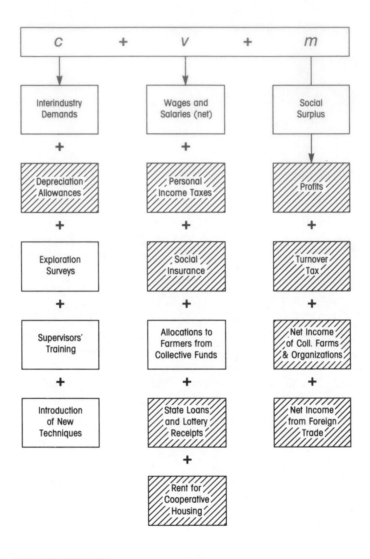

*The shaded boxes indicate the "Resources" of the Financial Plan.
   Based on V. N. Senchagov, *Finansovye resursy narodnogo khoziaistva*
   (Financial Resources of the National Economy I, Moscow, Finansy i statistika,
   1982, p. 50.

Fig. 6-1. Gross value of output ($c + v + m$) and the resources of the financial plan. The shaded areas indicate the "resources" of the financial plan. (Based on V. N. Senchagov, *Finansovye resursy narodnogo khoziaistva* [Financial Resources of the National Economy 1] [Moscow: Finansy i statistika, 1982], 50.)

aged by the associations (enterprises), collective farms, cooperative enterprises, and their supervisory organs, concern their respective activities and obligations.

The state budget constitutes the center of the Soviet financial system and Soviet financial planning. It disposes of different resources than those of the government budgets in market-directed economies and spends these resources for different purposes. In the market-directed economies, besides the provision of the funds needed for discharging the recognized collective needs such as defense, public order, and education, the uses of fiscal and monetary instruments tend also to have as objectives the securing of economic stability (that is, the prevention of significant unemployment and heightened-demand inflation), various kinds of redistributions of income (via differentiation of taxation between income classes), and the provision of social security and welfare (because of ethical considerations concerning the underprivileged, unemployed, sick, and aged). In addition, the government of market-directed economies also discharges regulatory functions concerning market structures and certain industries (in order to increase competitiveness and protect the consumer) as well as other types of regulation affecting, notably, the health of the population, the safety of the work force, and the general quality of the environment. In the developed market-directed economies, the government does not dispose of significant ownership (if not in land and other natural resources), and its capital expenditures might be small except at state and local levels. The government does extend out of the allocation of some resources a variety of explicit or implicit subsidies in favor of certain private industries and economic sectors. The Soviet state budget, like those discussed above, also provides the funds needed for discharging the same collective needs concerning defense, public order, education, and the like. But, over and above these provisions, the Soviet state budget is still an instrument of the state as *owner and manager* of vast sectors of the economy, an instrument for coordinating the material and the financial plans, correlating the centralized and the decentralized funds, controlling (directly or indirectly) the activities of associations and enterprises, and channeling a large part of its resources toward the selected branches of the economy and various kinds of subsidies.

In a country like the United States, say in the late 1980s, roughly one-quarter of the consolidated budget (federal, state, and local) covered capital expenditures (that is, gross purchases of capital goods), which were incurred mostly by state and local governments in areas such as transportation, sanitation, and education facilities. Direct or indirect subsidies were insubstantial except in agriculture. Contrariwise, in the Soviet Union the state budget (consolidating the All-Union, republic, and local budgets) directed almost two-thirds of its resources toward the national economy. Some 25 percent of the total state budget was earmarked for capital formation and about as much for all kinds of subsidies. In the United States, roughly one-third of the national income was cleared at the time through all levels of government; it follows that some 8 percent of the gross national product (GNP) was returned to the economy as capital expenditures. Even if we added to this total some covert subsidies for capital construction and implicit tax advantages extended by government, the figure could certainly not be much larger. In the Soviet Union roughly 73 percent of the net material product (NMP), excluding nonmaterial services, was cleared at the time through the government. It follows that some 18 percent of the NMP was reallocated through the budget for capital expansion and renewal and about as much toward all kinds of subsidies. The sharp difference between the scope of the two budgets could not be significantly attenuated even if we keep in mind that there are all sorts of caveats concerning hidden allocations on both sides that cannot be properly measured in either of the standard frameworks.

The Soviet budget system is still a hierarchically consolidated one; that is, the budget of any territorial unit includes both the individual budget of the top-level government of that unit as well as the budgets of all lower-level governments within the given territory. Until the eventual transformation of the USSR into a loose confederation, the USSR state budget will continue to include the All-Union budget as well as the budgets of the fifteen Union republics and that of state social insurance. The budget of each individual Union republic includes its own and those of the state and republic autonomous regions as well as the local budgets. The latter include the budgets of territories, *oblasts*, districts, cities, raions, and rural settlements. In keeping with the principle of All-Union centralization—which, undoubtedly, will be modified in the 1990s—only the budget of the USSR has the right to levy taxes, whether All-Union, republic, or local; the budgets of the lower level have the right to their "own" revenues, but these are designated from above. In the system that prevailed through the 1980s, there were no clear-cut answers as to which specific budget collected which revenue and which specific expenditures were made by each budget. Data on the structure of budget revenues and expenditures indicated only their *total* distribution by levels. Thus, data on the structure of budgetary expenditures for 1981–85 indicate that 54.5 percent of expenditures were made by the All-Union budget and 45.5 percent by the budgets of the fifteen republics—29.8 percent through the republics' budgets themselves, and 15.7 percent through the autonomous regions and local budgets.

Traditionally, the budgets for the whole USSR—both plan and budget—were presented for approval to the two Councils of the Supreme Soviet. Year in and year out, all these budgets were proclaimed to yield a small surplus, and there was never a state deficit. There was no public discussion of defense expenditures, and most other key issues of the budget were not even mentioned before the Supreme Soviet. The one-day "debate" of the Supreme Council, usually praising the economy's performance, was followed by a summing up by the Minister of Finance, and then the final budget version was published as "law" in the daily press. The first signs of change appeared in 1988. On October 28, 1988, the report of Boris I. Gostev (then USSR minister of finance) on the state budget for 1989 and the fulfillment of the USSR state budget for 1987 recognized explicitly—for the first time since 1944—not only that the state budget was in deficit but, moreover, that "the state expenditures have run ahead of its revenues *for many years*." And, Gostev added, "the budget deficit [for 1989] is not a problem that arose just today, it is the consequence of imbalance in the economy, large subsidies, enormous losses—all things that were caused by extensive methods of economic management, dependence, and a passive financial policy." The changes introduced in 1989 in regard to the responsibilities of the Supreme Soviet will bring significant changes both in the debate on the state budget, in its final version, and in all the budgets dependent on it.

What follows is an analysis of the principles and structure of taxation and an examination of the structure of outlays, the question of the deficit, and the historical trends in the evolution of the state budget with respect to the interrelations between receipts and expenditures and between the All-Union, republic, and local budgets. The chapter concludes with a short summary and an evaluation of future prospects.

Principles and Structure of Soviet Taxation

As indicated above, the Soviet state budget is still at the center of the country's financial system. Besides assuming and discharging the functions of any other state budget, the Soviet budget is a crucial instrument in the management of the economy and the reallocation of resources. It centralizes an enormous share of the country's net income and redistributes it via grants to specific economic branches. The state budget's receipts and expenditures by main entries are usually aggregated in the ways presented in table 6-1. The revenues are broken down into two main groups: revenues from the economy and receipts from the population. Consider first the payments from profits and the turnover tax, which are the revenues from the state-owned sector (excluding collective farms and cooperatives). Are both the payments from profits and the turnover tax indirect taxes on commodities purchased by consumers whose incidence is on the consumer? Why the distinction between the two? Could the payment from profits and the turnover tax be replaced by a single instrument of taxation?

In his classic work, *Soviet Taxation*, written in the 1950s, Frank D. Holzman suggested that there was *no difference whatsoever* between deductions from profits and the turnover tax, since both must be "borne by the consumer." His assertion has been repeated since then by many other students of Soviet taxes. According to Holzman, in the United States a profit tax can be shifted backward and thus reduce factor prices paid by the enterprise, or it can go forward, raising prices paid by the consumer. In the USSR, where the producing enterprises are state-owned, a profit tax levied on them must be borne entirely by the consumer. Actually, the answer to this problem hinges on whether prices are set in the Soviet Union (or authorized to be set by the enterprises or other higher administrations) so as to yield a certain profit before or after "deductions" transferred to the budget. In the former case, the size of the deduction is unrelated to the level of prices. In the latter case, however, the deduction would be somewhat analogous to a sales tax paid mainly by the consumer. In the Soviet Union, centrally administered prices are clearly set, relative to cost, so as to yield a given profit *before* deductions, thus they cannot be said to be borne by the consumer—except, of course, in the sense that all enterprise receipts ultimately flow from the buyer. Deductions from profits transferred to the state budget can, in fact, be large or small, according to a policy seeking to centralize a large share of profits and re-distribute them among various branches or, for incentive purposes, leave most investable resources directly in the hands of the enterprises themselves. The fluctuations in the size of these deductions do not ordinarily affect the con-sumer; the amount of the transfer in each particular branch does not determine the amount of total gross profits, which is set at the level of planned capital formation. On the other hand, whatever the *size* of the deductions from profits might be, the enterprise cannot usually compensate for it by way of increased prices. The situation would change if the enterprises were granted more freedom with respect to input and output mixes. But, even under the 1987 Law on the State Enterprise, prices remain subject to the central authorities' supervision and approval.

In principle, total state receipts can be so planned that total volume of profits—not only the part transferred to the budget—and total turnover tax receipts move in a complementary way. Furthermore, it is also clear that, under their institutional arrangement, the Soviets could dispense with the profit category, equate prices to labor cost within the state sphere, and then increase taxes so that aggregate turnover tax receipts would equal aggregate accumulation. Conversely, they could dispense with the turnover tax and plan profit margins so that aggregate profit income would equal the accumulation targets; the profits could either be left largely in the hands of the enterprises or they could be centralized and redistributed by the state.

Soviet policymakers and planners have not chosen either of these solu-tions because the payments from profits and the turnover tax have acquired increasingly well-defined, different roles and have exercised different impacts. Planned or authorized profits are split between the enterprise, its higher-level agency, and the state budget. The division is meant not only to provide the budget with the investment funds and the higher-level agencies with centralized funds and reserves, but also to provide the managers of the enterprises with various funds to be used for incentives and development. The turnover tax (indirect commodity tax) has different functions; besides the provision of investable resources to the state budget—at a different pace and with a different predictability than that guaranteed by profit deductions—the turnover tax is also functioning as an anti-inflationary tool in the poorly supplied consumer goods market.

Under the legislation adopted during Stalin's tax reform of 1930, the state enterprises were obliged to transfer to the state budget 85 percent of their planned profits. The accounting of the actual transfers was made at the end of the year. Eventually, the deductions from profits were adjusted to take account of the different needs of each enterprise, and the range of payments was differentiated to between 10 and 80 percent of the profits. Until the mid–1960s the set deductions from planned profits and above-plan profits were transferred to the budget independent of which funds the enterprises actually used for discharging their obligations. Following the 1965 reforms, the deductions were set on the basis of new criteria, and their managerial incentive functions were strengthened. Other reforms determined that the transfer to the budget of the deductions from profits was to be made not on the basis of the enterprise but rather its respective higher-level authority. After the adoption of the Law on the State Enterprise in 1987, the deductions from profit were to comprise a charge for productive assets (paid on the basis of a similar norm for all enterprises); reimbursement for the training of the work force and various other services; differential rents (for special natural and locational advantages), and an additional charge levied on the residual profits left after the payment of the indicated charges plus the repayment of bank credits and interests. Various changes have been contemplated in this respect since then (see chap. 9).

The turnover tax has evolved since its creation in 1930 into a highly differentiated kind of tax—differentiated by type of product, type of enterprise producing it, and the jurisdiction to which that enterprise is subordinated. When it was created, the turnover tax was applied with different rates to the products of some forty industrial administrations (including certain branches of heavy industry). By 1933, 448 tax rates were in existence; by 1938 there were 2,444 rates, differentiated by the quality of the taxed products and applied by groups of products. In 1939 the turnover tax in the textile industry started to be levied at the wholesale stage, and by 1948 the application of this method was extended to almost all of the products of the food and light industry and other products of mass consumption. By the mid-1960s the

Ministry of Finance of the USSR was authorized to add turnover tax rates at the level of Union republics by type of goods, taking into account the specific technical-economic conditions of each enterprise. Turnover tax receipts are transferred to the state budget daily or at most within two weeks by the state banks, and are paid by the industrial administrations, associations, supply-wholesale organizations, as well as by the cooperatives (excluding collective farms). Over 85 percent of the tax yield is obtained at the wholesale stage as a tax ad valorem; the balance of 15 percent is accounted by taxes ad rem. While the tax is applied to producer goods (at very low rates) and consumer goods (excluding staples and a few other subsidized products), its major yields are due, as in the 1930s, to its imposition first of all on alcoholic beverages, and then on sugar, tobacco, and textile products.

The magnitude of the contribution of the tax on alcohol is staggering indeed. Gorbachev's anti-alcohol campaign, launched in 1985, created a big hole in public finance, led to the rapid expansion of moonshine production, and, eventually, brought about the rationing of sugar (the principal input of this kind of product). In his speech at the plenary session of the Central Committee of the Communist party, on February 18, 1988, Gorbachev stated (as reported the next day in *Pravda* and *Izvestia*) that the country's rates of economic growth had been achieved "in large measure on an unhealthy basis"—namely, thanks "to the trading of petroleum on the world market at high prices . . . and to a totally unjustified step-up in the sale of alcoholic beverages. If we remove the influence of these factors from the economic growth indices, the result is that we had no increase in the absolute growth of the national income over four five-year plans." In his October 28, 1988, report on the 1989 state budget, Boris I. Gostev, then USSR minister of finance, indicated that the projected turnover tax losses due to the production and sales of wine and vodka "in volumes lower than those envisaged by the relevant decisions" will amount in 1989 to more than thirty-six billion rubles, that is, exactly equal to the total budget deficit projected for that year. Actually, the budget deficit turned out to be about three times larger than that figure. The projected deficit for 1990 was set at sixty billion rubles (see table 6-1).

Individual enterprises (authorized since 1987), cooperatives, public organizations, and collective farms pay various taxes, including taxes on personal incomes. The collective farms have paid taxes in a variety of forms since the 1920s. These taxes now have two components: an imposition on the collectives' taxable net income (after allowance of a certain profitability rate) and a tax on the wage fund, that is, on the collective funds used for the payment of the labor of collective farmers. The tax on cooperatives is assessed on the value added as well as on individual earnings (see chap. 9).

Traditionally, direct personal income taxation has played a limited role in

TABLE 6-1.   USSR State Budget Law for 1990 Main Entries: Schematic Presentation

	Billion Rubles	Percentages
Total Receipts	429.9	
From the national economy	384.4	89.4
Payments from profits	64.9	14.4
Turnover tax	28.6	6.6
Deduction for social security	28.9	6.7
Taxes on cooperatives	0.2	0.4
From foreign economic activities	58.9	13.7
From the population	19.9	4.6
From state loans	26.0	6.0
Total Outlays	489.9	
For the national economy	366.9	74.9
For current expenditures	200.9	41.0
Centralized capital construction	19.3	3.9
For science	9.1	1.9
Foreign economic activities	26.4	5.4
Debt repayment	8.8	1.8
Social cultural measures	35.9	7.3
State administration	87.1	17.8
Defense	70.9	14.5
State apparatus	1.0	0.2
Public order	9.2	1.9
Other	6.0	1.2

Source: Ekonomicheskaia gazeta, no. 47 (November 1989).

Soviet budget receipts, even though the personal income tax—by far the principal tax in the group of receipts officially conceded to be taxes on the population—was imposed on all factory and office workers, writers and artists, and professionals and artisans. Separate tax scales were established for each group with a *slightly* more favorable scale for the first two groups. In practice, given the ways in which tax rates were established in relation to wage levels, the majority of workers paid the maximum rate (namely, 13 percent) imposed monthly on incomes in excess of one hundred rubles. The income tax on workers' incomes was never progressive. The tax was constructed to minimize disturbances to the resource allocation function of the wage differentials. The other "taxes on the population" were a personal income tax on bachelors, single citizens, and citizens with small families, and the agricultural tax paid by persons having an income from private subsidiary farming. Finally, a number of taxes were applied both on enterprises and organizations and on individuals. (Among these taxes were local taxes on buildings, land, the ownership of vehicles, various state duties, and taxes on foreign legal entities and persons.) This system is scheduled to change; the importance of personal income taxes will increase sharply in the 1990s.

As the structure of budgetary receipts shows, the Soviet Union traditionally had a strong preference for indirect rather than direct taxation. What were the rationale and the impact of this preference in relation to equity, incentives, inflation, and the allocation of resources?

Western economists tend to believe that equity is an essential element in a tax. *Equity* might be defined as equalizing the tax burden on all citizens by taxing each according to his or her ability to pay. Since it is assumed that, after a certain point, money income has a diminishing marginal utility and since all taxes are presumably paid from net income, equity is in practice achieved by a progressive net income tax. At the same time, concern with business cycles has spurred Western interest in the use of taxes as anticyclical measures. Indirect taxes qualify as an automatic fiscal stabilizer but do not recommend themselves as a main source of revenue, given a government's concern with tax equity. On the other hand, personal taxes and corporate taxes meet both criteria in varying measure. Finally, indirect taxes are used for allocative purposes in only a limited way. (To some extent, such taxes are applied as the modern counterpart of the older sumptuary laws.)

In the Soviet economy, progressive taxation has been traditionally regarded as interfering with established incentives, whereas the impact of turnover taxes was taken to be neutral with respect to these incentives. The tax system was devoid of equity—if equity is taken to imply equal burden regarding each person's ability to pay. If equity (and "social justice") is taken to mean, simply, to each according to the quantity and quality of his or her work, then the Soviet system indeed had equity. Yet, it may seem paradoxical that modern capitalism attempts, up to a point at least, to redistribute income through progressive taxation, whereas the Soviets systematically shied away from such measures.

In the traditional Soviet framework, the turnover tax qualified to some extent under the anticyclical criterion because it played an anti-inflationary role akin to that played in the West by high taxation during an inflationary period. It is the resource allocation element that was of paramount importance in the USSR, whereas in the West, under normal conditions, this factor plays only a minor role.

Structure of Outlays and the Budget Deficit

The Soviet budgetary data are presented yearly in speeches of the minister of finance to the Supreme Soviet, the annual statistical handbooks on the national economy (and in ad hoc commemorative issues of these handbooks), as well as in five-year statistical compendia on the state budget. Throughout these documents the budgetary data are presented in highly aggregated forms, frequently amalgamate ill-assorted information, and are time and again ambiguous, incomplete, and not fully reliable. Yet these data convey the basic budgetary policies and elucidate the multiple functions assigned to the budget and its components in the Soviet system.

The Soviet budgetary outlays can be grouped into two major subdivisions: *operative* (or functional) expenditures concerning the customary state expenditures included everywhere in the ordinary state budgets; and *economic* expenditures, akin to capital budgets but with a much broader coverage. The first outlays concern institutions that are *entirely* dependent on the budget, such as the state's agencies, military installations, schools, and hospitals. These institutions are financed through outlays on the state administration, defense, and on so-called sociocultural measures. The second type of outlays concern enterprises that are independent accounting units functioning on the basis of economic accountability (somewhat incorrectly defined as "self-financing"), which depend on the state for a whole range of appropriations.

The largest bloc of independent accounting units, meant to supplement the economic accountability monies, are allocations to economic branches and sectors and subsidies (see table 6-1). Besides capital investments, these outlays include working capital advances and bank credit allowances, certain operational expenses for geological surveys and for the introduction of new techniques, subsidies for the sale of agricultural and other products, as well as outlays for reserves (inventories) and for foreign economic activities (including noncommercial operations). The capital investments alone—with priorities for defense, and from 1985, particularly, for the machine-building industries—amount to roughly a quarter of the total budget outlays, followed by subsidies reaching over 20 percent in 1989. For that year the planning operative expenditures were set to attain close to 38 percent of total appropriations (cf. table 6-1).

The outlays on the state administration, namely 0.6 percent of total outlays, are extremely low; in fact, state administrators benefit from many extra budgetary advantages. But the most deceptive data have traditionally been those concerning defense. Already in 1981, Igor Birman pointed out in his detailed study, *The Secret Incomes of the Soviet State Budget,* that the published figure for defense outlays covers only the expenditures of the Ministry of Defense itself, excluding the other more considerable outlays. U.S. intelligence sources have long asserted that the Soviet budget data on defense were inconsistent with the observed expansion, size, and maintenance of Soviet strategies, theaters of operation, and land, aerial, and naval strength. The CIA usually estimated Soviet defense expenditures as being on the order of 13–15 percent of the Soviet GNP, expenditures financed from other budget categories (for example, expenditures on the national economy) and perhaps also from nonbudget resources (concerning military-related outlays on science and research). Finally, on May 29, 1988, Gorbachev himself asserted that the 1989 projected data for defense were on the order of 77.3 billion rubles—not 20.2 billion, as indicated by the Ministry of Finance—and that the difference between the two was due to the inclusion in the Gorbachev figure of defense contracts with industry. The data for the 1990 budget placed defense outlays at 14.5 percent of total outlays (cf. table 6-1), a significant recognition of the validity of Western intelligence's evaluations.

The manner in which Soviet budget outlays and receipts interact, and the ways in which both the uses and sources of funds of the state budget and of those of the associations are interrelated to the changes in the cash balances of the households, can be visualized as follows.

Let P_d stand for the deductions from enterprises' profits transferred to the budget, R_{np} stand for state receipts other than profit deductions, and ΔB_g indicate changes in State Bank advances to the government (through purchases of government bonds). With E_{ca} denoting government expenditures on current account including transfers, G_g government grants to the enterprises, and ΔM_g changes in the government's balances at the disposal of the State Bank, sources and uses of funds by the government can be expressed as follows:

$$P_d + R_{np} + \Delta B_g = E_{ca} + G_g + \Delta M_g \tag{1}$$

Let P_r stand for the profits retained by the enterprises, D for depreciation allowances, ΔB_e for changes in the value of outstanding bank loans to the enterprises. With I_e designating gross investment by the enterprises (that is, total investment in the economy other than households) and ΔM_e changes in the enterprises' money balances, the sources and uses of funds by the enterprises will be:

$$P_r + D + G_g + \Delta B_e = I_e + \Delta M_e \tag{2}$$

The sources and use of funds by households can be expressed as

$$S_h = I_h + \Delta M_h \tag{3}$$

where S_h is household savings, I_h is private capital formation (housing), and ΔM_h stands for changes in households' cash balances (assuming that household borrowing from the other sectors is negligible).

Replacing the balance on current account in equation 1 ($P_d + R_{np} - E_{ca}$) with the symbol S_{ca}, savings on the current account, and consolidating equations 1, 2, 3, we get

$$S_h + S_{ca} + (P_r + D) + (\Delta B_g + \Delta B_e) - (\Delta M_g + \Delta M_e + \Delta M_h)$$
$$= I_e + I_h \tag{4}$$

Expression 4 states that savings by households, government, and enterprises, plus net changes of bank indebtedness and minus the changes of cash balances, must equal gross investment by enterprises and households. If there were no net foreign investments, the change of indebtedness to the banking system would equal the changes in cash balances, and the differences between the two would be equal to the negative of foreign investment, reducing equation 4 to the familiar form:

$$S_h + C_{ca} + (P_r + D) = I_e + I_h + F \tag{5}$$

Actually, these theoretical equilibria are not exactly those that obtain in the Soviet economy. Part of the state budget receipts are fictitious, since receipts from enterprises are accounted for before the products are sold and regardless of whether the goods will be sold. Further, the State Bank extends above-plan credits to the budget and to enterprises—credits that are often nonreturnable. Most likely, the budget accounts (minus bank advances) have never been in equilibrium, since such balance requires the conjunction of innumerable plan elements. To understand the magnitude and complexity of the factors involved in such equilibria it is interesting to recall that in October, 1988, Minister of Finance Gostev indicated that "still" one out of five enterprises in industry and construction (and one out of four enterprises in machine building) had not fulfilled their yearly financial obligations toward the budget; specifically, twelve thousand enterprises and organizations and twenty-three ministries had not fulfilled the planned obligations. The same deficiencies were shown by branches and republics (concerning the turnover tax). The biggest failures were registered in respect to foreign trade operations, where exports toward hard currency areas were only 43 percent fulfilled.

In his 1981 study, Igor Birman rightly remarked before anyone else that the Soviet state budget was a *deficit budget,* covertly but systematically covered by State Bank grants. Now, Soviet proreform writers such as Nikolai Shmelev state openly (in *Novyi mir,* May, 1988) that the entire Soviet financial system "is based on methods that are largely inflationary"; it is so because state revenues and expenditures are often merely "thin air," the first being based on taxes on unsold products and the second on the pumping of nonreturnable credits into the economy.

The State Budget in Historical Perspective

Until 1988 the official data on the state budget showed a budget surplus of 0.5 to 6 billion rubles for each year since 1944. In fact, the outlays must have exceeded the receipts in many of these years, with deficits as yet undisclosed. Given this situation, what kind of indications do we get concerning the *planned* (rather than the actually fully achieved) objectives of policymakers with respect to the role of the budget in redistributing net material products, structural shifts in budgetary receipts and expenditures, and interrelations between the union, republics, and local budgets?

Over time the share of NMP cleared through the budget has steadily increased. From the 1950s to the 1970s the state budget redistributed some 55 percent of NMP; during the 1970s this share rose to between 60 and 65 percent, and then, in the 1980s, to 67 to 72 percent (1989). In other words, the role of the central state organs has continuously increased until the end of the 1980s, a tendency that eventually should be held in check as the effective autonomy of the enterprises is scheduled to increase.

Some significant changes have occurred over time in the structuring of receipts and outlays (see fig. 6-2). We can look upon the state revenues as consisting of two broad "composites" fluctuating around a relatively stable axis: constituted by the personal income taxes consistently amounting to 7.5–8.5 of state receipts. The two composites are, on the one hand, the budgetary receipts from the enterprises (turnover tax, profit deductions, and social insurance), and, on the other, receipts from all other sources (mainly state loans and receipts from foreign economic activities). The combined share of receipts from the enterprises has tended to fall from 1965 on—that is, from 73 percent of total budgetary receipts to less than 60 percent by 1989. Within this group the share of the turnover tax has tended to fall, while that of profit deductions has tended to increase at least until the 1980s. The decreasing share of the profits—in relation to the 1970s—should further decrease as a large share of profits should be left, in principle, at the disposal of the associations as the consequences of the 1987 Law on the Soviet State Enterprise unfold in the 1990s.

The outlays can be grouped into the aggregates mentioned previously— namely, the operative expenditures on state administration, defense, education, health, and social security and welfare, on the one hand, and the expenditures on the national economy, including subsidies, on the other. Over time the operative expenditures have tended to decrease from roughly 52 percent of total outlays in 1950 to roughly 43 percent in 1989. One of the major components of this bloc, the so-called defense outlays, have decreased, in principle, but, as noted, these figures refer only to a specific *part* of the defense expenditures and not to their actual total. Since the comprehensive data concerning defense expenditures that included contracts with industry have not been available, the available data will suffice, as they refer over time to the same, limited, defense-type outlays. The second bloc of outlays, comprised of the expenditures on the economic branches (a large part of which are capital

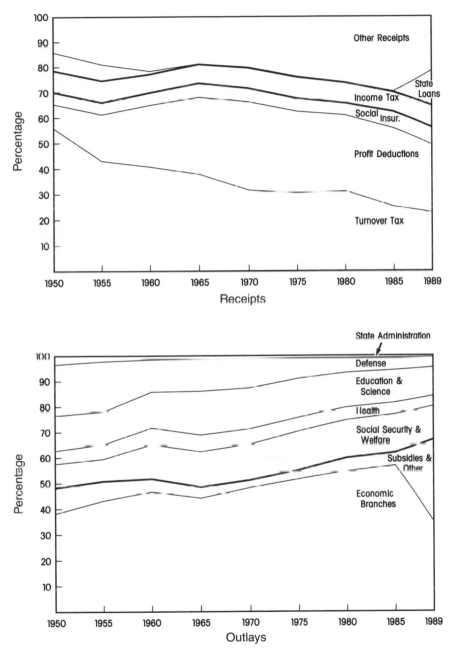

Fig. 6-2. The Soviet state budget, receipts and outlays, 1950–89

grants directed toward both the defense and nondefense industries) and subsidies, has risen continuously, with subsidies increasing at an accelerated pace
from the mid-1980s and depressing the other standard budget allocations.

Both receipts and outlays display two major interrelated components: on
the side of receipts, revenues from the enterprises; on the side of outlays,
expenditures on the enterprises. As a rule, revenues from the enterprises have
exceeded budgetary allocations to the enterprises—amounting, respectively,
to 73 percent of total revenues as against 48 percent of total outlays—except
for 1989 when the respective planned figures were (in round figures) 56
percent of receipts compared to 67 percent of total outlays. As the centralized
revenues from the enterprises may decrease eventually, the respective shares
of budgetary receipts and outlays from and to the economy should, in principle, be brought into balance, as subsidies are also scheduled to diminish in the
1990s. A closer look at the budgetary receipts from and to the economy for
1985 reveals that state budget outlays for industry, agriculture, and housing
tend to exceed the corresponding receipts from these activities; by contrast,
the receipts exceed the outlays in the case of transportation, communications,
and trade.

The budgetary relations between the Union, republics, and localities
(including the autonomous regions) reveal some remarkable indications concerning the interactions between the Soviet center of policymaking and planning and the Soviet republics. As Donna Bahri has pointed out in a remarkable 1987 study on budgetary policy in the Soviet republics, the Soviet Union
has been confronted by a variety of dilemmas in its efforts to establish an
appropriate mix of center-regional authority and "optimal" regional borders.
Programs have been shifted from central to republic jurisdiction and back;
regionalization schemes have been devised, applied, and then discarded; reforms have been introduced in order to adjust and readjust the connections
between central planning agencies, industrial associations, and variously determined "territorial-production complexes." The degree of centralization and
the role of each specific republic has varied depending on the level of subordination of a given program and a given industry and sector, the issues to be
decided, and the ability and possibility to muster both central support and
regional power coalitions within the institutional setup.

The All-Union budget consistently has represented from 52 to 53 percent
of total state budget outlays, and the republics' budgets made up the balance
of 47 to 48 percent. The republics' budgets, which include the local budgets,
have increased slowly within this 47–48 percent to 28–31 points of the total,
while the share of local budgets has fallen from some 20 percent of the total
state budget to less than 16 percent. The major underlying factors accounting
for these allocation shifts are the *patterns of control* of the economy's

branches and sectors; manufacturing is almost entirely under Union jurisdiction, while mining, utilities, the light and construction materials industries are under republics and local control. Main food-processing facilities are also under Union authority, while agriculture, agricultural procurement, and smaller food-processing installations are under republics' commands. Notwithstanding repeated campaigns for initiative at the local level, budgetary expenditures and, hence, administrative power has tended to decline at the local level. Gorbachev promises to reverse the trend, but many such promises have been made in the past.

A detailed examination of the receipts and outlays at the Union, republic, and local levels reveal that profit deductions play the major role in the receipts at the All-Union level, while the turnover tax plays the major role in the receipts at the republic and local levels. Personal income taxes play a much larger role in the republics' and local budgets than in the All-Union one. On the side of expenditures, allocation to economic branches plays the highest role in the All-Union budget, the lowest in local budgets. In the latter, the so-called sociocultural expenditures (on education and public health) play a major role.

An interesting perception of the ranking of the Soviet republics by levels of economic development is furnished by the tabulation of per capita budgetary outlays (see table 6-2). On the left the republics are arranged in the standard way in which they are presented in Soviet handbooks—an arrangement that is not correct either historically, geographically, or by size of population. On the right is the ranking by per capita outlays. As can be seen from the table, the Baltic republics (Estonia, Lithuania, and Latvia) are still at the top of the list; the Tadzhik, Azerbaijan, and the Uzbek republics are at the bottom. As we will see, similar rankings are obtained with the help of other indicators. It is noteworthy, however, that the ranking of Russia (RSFSR) in sixth place should not be construed to imply that the latter does not play the *central* role in all interrepublic relations. As the Soviet author A. G. Granberg put it in the early 1980s, using official Soviet jargon, "the RSFSR, around which all Soviet republics have united on a voluntary basis" plays "a decisive role in the creation of an integral union state." In fact, the RSFSR concentrates approximately 60 percent of the Soviet Union's economic potentials and commands large human and material resources, including key branches of the Union's manufacturing, though it remains, like the rest of the USSR, poorly developed outside its main urban centers. Notwithstanding the interplay between interrepublic *specialization* (to take advantage of both natural conditions and large-scale production) and regional *diversification* (to promote all-around development in each area), the dependency of the republics on the RSFSR continues to be decisive.

TABLE 6-2. Budgetary Outlay per Capita and Ranking of the Republics in 1985

Republics	Outlays (in rubles)	Rankings
Russian	703.9	6
Ukrainian	621.2	9
Belorussian	775.0	4
Uzbek	451.1	13
Kazakh	720.9	5
Georgian	620.7	10
Azerbaijan	449.8	14
Lithuanian	1,072.9	2
Moldavian	632.0	7
Latvian	994.6	3
Kirghiz	541.7	11
Tadzhik	380.6	15
Armenian	624.0	8
Turkmen	490.7	12
Estonian	1,124.5	1

Source: Computed from *Gosudarstvennyi biudzhet SSSR 1981–1985* (The USSR State Budget 1981–1985) (Moscow: Finansy i statistika, 1987).

Concluding Comments

In traditional Soviet budget theory, the operative budget outlays—on state administration, education, and public health (but excluding defense)—were viewed as allocations for the system's nonproductive sectors, appropriations to be minimized in favor of larger expenditures for the productive branches of the economy—above all, for the heavy industry branches. The military outlays per se were viewed as losses, incurred to the detriment of the national economy. Since the 1980s these views have been somewhat altered. The term *nonproductive sectors* is increasingly shunned, while attention is drawn to the managerial role of the state administration and the importance of education and science in technological development. The nature and content of the state budget, however, continues to be shaped both by the traditional rationale and methods for allocating resources and by a host of changing factors concerning various aspects of the management of the economy and its modus operandi, new institutional arrangements and sectoral emphases, price policies, and pricing behavior.

Over the years the state budget has exhibited an enormous expansion, as illustrated by the increasing share of NMP cleared through it. This expansion has been due both to the growth of the economy and, as we now know, to expanding deficits, inflated currency emissions, and the upward drift of prices. Predicated on the broad basis of the financial plan, the state budget determines the volume and distribution of financial resources and estimates what is to be allocated to the banking system and what the latter would accumulate as surplus resources in order to carry out the appropriate credit policies. If the budget receipts exceed budget expenditures, the State Bank can use the surplus to offset its short-term credit operations, or it can retire currency from circulation. If budget expenditures exceed receipts (and short-term credits exceed bank receipts), new currency must be injected into circulation. The Soviet leaders have now become actuely aware that the incessant growth of the deficit and injections of new currency cannot go on indefinitely. As Gorbachev put it "for many years, the state budget's expenditures grew more rapidly than revenues. The budget deficit presses on the market, undermines the stability of the state and the monetary circulation in general, and gives rise to inflationary pressures" (*Pravda,* June 29, 1988).

The Soviet tax system has not been construed with the aim of doing justice to both incentives and equity. Indeed, the greater the tax requirements of the state, the more difficult it becomes to satisfy both incentives and equity criteria. As Frank Holzman rightly noted in the 1950s in his study, *Soviet Taxation,* "no other nation has levied as high a rate of taxation as the Soviet Union, and it may be that the cause of equity cannot be served when the financial requirements of the state are so enormous; taxes must reach down into the last person's pocket if the program is to be successful." So far, things have not changed. The failure of the Soviet system to exempt the lowest income strata from personal income taxation implies terrible strains for the lowest-paid workers, pensioners, and other disadvantaged taxpayers. The turnover tax weighs heavily on these strata, and its impact is offset only partially by the distribution of free social services and various subsidies. (Moreover, many of the subsidies are scheduled to be removed in the 1990s.)

The state budget has been a powerful instrument in the hands of policymakers for centralizing financial resources and redistributing them according to the central plan. As noted, each lower-level budget is included within that of the higher-level one (namely, local budgets are included in the republic budgets, which are included in the state budget of the USSR). In principle, the center alone has been empowered to levy taxes, whether these be All-Union, republic, or local. In practice, the allocation of funds has always involved complex and other hidden apportionments between consumption and accumulation, between various economic sectors and branches, and between the center, the republics, and the lower levels. As Igor Birman pointed out in his study on the Soviet budget, *Secret Incomes of the Soviet Budget* (1981), there are no simple answers to the questions of which expenditures are made by each budget, and how and which budget exactly collects which revenues.

There are many exceptions even to the cardinal rule that the appropriations of each budget follow the administrative subordination of organizations. What is clear is that budget allocations have implemented planned choices concerning basic proportions and that they have aimed to develop first of all the Russian heartland—the seat of heavy industry—rather than to equalize the living standard. While asserting that the strength of the USSR must be grounded "in the strength of the republics," Gorbachev has also added that, allegedly, "all republics have a vital stake in a strong center that is capable of insuring the accomplishment of nationwide tasks" (*Pravda,* November 30, 1988).

The partisans of perestroika have directed some virulent criticisms against the ways in which financial authorities credit the budget with fictitious receipts and then "recirculate" these fictitious revenues as outlays for various purposes. In a study published in 1988 by the Soviet Academy of Sciences, Leonid I. Abalkin noted that the crediting of the budget with the turnover tax at the wholesale level, and before the products are sold (or whether or not they are sold), had no connection with either cost accounting, the results of the enterprises' performance, or actual sales. In *Novyi mir* (1988), Nikolai Shmelev affirmed that what was indispensable in the scheduled pricing reform was that the turnover tax cede its place as a basic budgetary revenue source to the taxing of the incomes of industrial and agricultural enterprises, that, moreover, the center of gravity in investment financing must shift from the state budget to the associations with financing achieved on the basis of their income, and, finally, that all forms of nonreturnable credits must be ended if inflationary pressures are to subside. Gorbachev himself put all this in a more direct way (in *Pravda,* June 29, 1988): "pricing reform . . . will not improve anything" unless "questions of financial balance and bringing order into the credit and financial system, the activity of the banks, the budget, etc., are solved at the same time"—a tall order and a daunting task, indeed.

As noted above, slowly and hesitantly, significant data have started to be released by the authorities concerning many budgetary operations, including expenditures for defense as well as those for law enforcement agencies, state credits and "nonrepayable assistance to foreign states," and other items long kept under wraps. In statistics, much remains to be done in respect to glasnost, however—not only in the estimates on defense but also in a host of other statistical data and historical series involving, to start with, all the relevant financial data concerning the budget, money and credit, and the national income and product series.

CHAPTER 7

Money and Credit Management

The Rules of the Game

To better understand the specific elements involved in the control of the money supply and credit in the Soviet-type economy of the Stalin or Gorbachev variety, it is useful to recall briefly the factors called into play in the money supply in market-directed economies. Consider the relation between money (M), velocity (V), and total output (price, P, times transactions, T). The famous "quantity equation"—actually, an identity—requires $MV = PT$. In market-directed economies the supply of M (currency and demand deposits) is determined more or less independently by a central bank. In our own economy this supply is determined by adjusting the reserves of the member banks of the federal reserve system. The input of reserves into member banks enables commercial banks to produce an expanded supply of M that affects M's velocity and the interest rate and has important effects on output. Economic schools are divided regarding the specific effects of money supply changes. In classical and new classical models, money primarily affects the price level, with, at most, short-lived effects on real output. Fiscal policy (taxes, government spending, and magnitude of the budget deficit) can have only a small, if not negligible, effect on V and, therefore, a negligible effect on the relationship between money and prices. In modified Keynesian and post-Keynesian theory, money supply changes have clear, possibly long-lasting real effects, and fiscal policy can produce price effects. In either theory, of course, government spending will impact the supply of M if this supply provided by the Central Bank finances a budget deficit.

Consider now the conditions prevailing in the Soviet-type economy. Take as the starting point the identity $MV = PT$. In the formulation of the financial plan Soviet policymakers and planners focus their attention on T—the scheduled output quantity and structure—and assume that prices, set administratively, will remain fixed by and large during the plan period of five years or more. Assuming that V is constant or predictable, a decision on the growth rate of T (or of quantity Q) will imply a planned growth rate of M consistent with the desired constancy of the price level. If V is not stable, then the planned target for M will not be compatible with the selected growth rate of Q, bringing about pressures on P that planners will tend to suppress.

The government budget, which is the main instrument for implementing the financial plan—that is, the principal tool for centralizing and disbursing the country's financial resources—in addition to the volume and distribution of the centrally allocated investment funds, determines the resources to be allocated to the state banking system for extending credit and estimates the surpluses expected to accumulate at the State Bank. The latter, in turn, draws up two plans: the *credit* and the *cash* plans, destined to guide its activities concerning the extension of credit and the management of currency circulation to maintain price stability. The bank plans concern two interrelated but clearly distinct spheres of activity: the state's interfirm transactions and the relations of the firms with households as well as interhousehold transactions. Since the state firms' transactions and those of the households are segregated, the supply and holdings of money are *bifurcated*. Only the firms and government agencies can have settlement and checkable deposits (diversified by purpose). The holding of monetary assets by households is restricted by convention to currency and saving deposits; wages, salaries, and transfers are paid in currency. In the management of credit the rule is that the State Bank centralizes the temporarily redundant balances of the government budget, the enterprises, and households' savings, and it "redistributes" them according to the planned output requirements of the ministries, departments, and associations. In the management of currency, the State Bank focuses on the wage fund (planned wage bill) to be released in material production, as well as on the state budget's needs.

These two rules of money management—credit limited to the "idle" resources available and currency released in function of the wage bill and budget demands—are neither rigid nor anti-inflationary. The underlying rationale of the rules is questionable. In the Marxian and Soviet monetary theory, currency and checkable deposits are supposed to be "tokens of gold." Gold backs the currency up to 25 percent. Money is a measure of value, a unit of account, because it embodies, or stands for, a use value and an exchange value. Variations in the "value" of gold itself do not impair its role as a standard of price, since, as Marx put in *Capital*, no matter how gold's own value might vary, "twelve ounces of gold still have twelve times the value of one ounce; and in prices the only thing considered is the relation between different quantities of gold." In practice, deposits or currency will be increased by procurement decisions of the Ministry of Finance or the issue of Treasury bonds that need no gold coverage. The bank itself can create money without a specific decision of the Ministry of Finance by opening a deposit (say, for paying procurement of agricultural produce), which, if it is not used immediately, becomes an idle resource against which other deposits can be expanded. Further, in the future newly created commercial banks will be authorized to extend certain types of loans to firms purchasing or selling goods under certain conditions. Thus, at least two, if not more, banks may be engaged in the process of monetary expansion—an expansion that will necessarily come into conflict with the assumption that the ceiling on credit is constituted by the volume of idle resources. The Soviet Ministry of Finance and the State Bank thus dispose of channels through which they can modify the initially planned money supply. As the plan unfolds, of course, such limits put an additional pressure on the desired price level.

For all practical purposes, the stated connection of currency and credit with gold is only a fetish. Consider the actual characteristics of this currency. It cannot be converted into gold, and it is not affected by changes in Soviet gold reserves. Since the 1920s it has been impervious to international price fluctuations and has been severed from other currencies—a situation that is scheduled to change in the 1990s. Since the 1920s the purchasing power of the ruble has depended not on its stated fetishistic relation to gold, but on the government's price fixing, its attempts to balance the budget and equilibrate various plan balances (above all, the households' purchasing power [dependent on wage regulations] and the consumer goods supply), and various other covert or overt regulations concerning each specific consumer category. Indeed, until many institutional changes are carried out, a ruble will still buy different types of goods according to whom it belongs—say, to a nomenklaturist or an ordinary worker or peasant. Moreover, not all rubles are domestically convertible into certain goods, for instance, into rationed producer goods such as building materials. Only recently, changes have been recommended in these respects by such pro-Gorbachev supporters as the academician Tat'iana Zaslavskaia.

The severance of interfirm transactions—involving the bulk of producer goods and requiring clearing transfers in the central State Bank—and the payment of wages destined for the purchase primarily (if not exclusively) of consumer goods and services originated in the idea that interfirm transactions did not reflect "commodity-monetary relations" but, rather, relations of a new type among firms belonging to the same owner (the state). Eventually, in the 1960s, this idea was discarded, but the dichotomy between "noncash and cash flows" (as the Russians call them) has remained. In interfirm relations the bookkeeping (or clearing) ruble serves as a medium of exchange only in a prescribed way, namely, for accounting for the movement of specified goods at predetermined prices. The assumption that the interfirm movement of real goods is correlated with the judicious injection by the bank of currency or loans is based on an old theory, the fallaciousness of which is well known— that is, that money requirements and capital requirements are identical. Actually, if the loans provided for inventory buildup remained fixed to these inventories until their emergence as final products, the impact of the bank's lending policy might be neutral; the increment in the quantity of money would be matched by an increment in final product. But the money credited does not sit and wait for the completion of a single, specific transaction, but goes off on its own. In other words, if the plans of associations were entirely consistent with each other and the total of resources, extending the enterprises just enough credit to carry out the specified planned transactions would be consistent with stability. But the plans are not fully consistent, and credits are not used only for the specified purpose for which they are extended but for a set of both planned and unplanned transactions.

The Soviet financial system relies not only on the separation of money management of the state firms and of the households but also on the separation of foreign exchange management. The Soviet currency, besides the characteristics already indicated, also has the special feature that it cannot be either exported nor reintroduced into the Soviet Union. The ruble lost its international standing during the mid-1920s. Since June 1987 the highest echelons of the party-state have repeatedly affirmed that the convertibility of the ruble (that is, its free exchange on the international market) has to be seriously envisaged. Interrelations have been established (beginning in 1989) between certain Soviet enterprises, production cooperatives, and other organizations and various foreign firms. In addition to joint enterprises created in conjunction with foreign firms, thousands of Soviet firms have been given the rights to sell (only) their own products and to buy (only) for their own uses in foreign markets. Following Hungary's experience, the USSR Bank for Foreign Economic Activity has provided for the free exchange of foreign monies and the sale and purchase of such monies for Soviet rubles at contractual prices at currency auctions. The process is still only an imperfect guide for determining what is the real "worth" of the ruble. What such actions can indeed reveal are the prices that enterprises are willing to pay for limited amounts of foreign currency available for open tender after the rest of that currency has been rationed by the bank. The goal of providing one or a number of exchange rates for the ruble is far from settled. By the end of the 1980s there were thousands of "currency coefficients" setting different exchange rates for just about every product and reflecting the consequences of old, traditional inward-looking Soviet policies. With the objective of providing more realistic assessments of the effectiveness of exports and imports, a new currency exchange rate in the settling of accounts in foreign economic operations is to be established in the 1990s. But, as pointed out by both Western and Soviet economists, the planned move toward a single commercial rate applied to importers and exporters would necessarily involve changes in economic policy orientations, reforms in prices and financial arrangements, and a series of devaluations of the ruble. The first historic step in this direction was taken on October 25, 1989, when the Soviet Union reduced the exchange value of the ruble for Soviet citizens traveling abroad from the rate of 1.6 to the dollar to sixteen cents. Further sweeping changes will have to be made in the exchange rate for virtually all export transactions. Convertibility, however, is the stated direction of perestroika, which has as its goals expanding the country's overall foreign operations, eliminating obstacles to the organization of joint enterprises, and improving the price signals within the Soviet economy as a whole.

Money Bifurcation and Circular Flows

As indicated above, noncash transactions concern the movement of goods and services within the entire state-owned system of production and distribution; cash transactions concern the relations of the state-owned system with the households and interhousehold transactions. The resulting circular flows can be visualized as follows (see fig. 7-1). Households provide productive services to the consumer goods industries and trade, the producer goods industries, and the government and, in exchange, receive wages and salaries paid in currency. Additional currency receipts are provided to them by government transfers (primarily, pensions and subsidies). The consumer goods industries and trade and the producer goods industries provide each other with the goods they need; these transactions involve deposit transfers. Further, all the industries and the related organizations involved in the movement of goods (trade and transport) transfer certain payments out of profits and the turnover (sales) tax through the banks to the government budget. They receive deposits as well as the cash needed for paying out wages and salaries from the banks. The state budget, finally, allocates investments in fixed and working capital (via bank deposits) to the industries and pays out administrative outlays on wages and salaries and transfers to the households in currency.

The central bank's All-Union currency (cash) and credit plans are centralized state plans reflecting both production relations and production objectives. The cash plan aims to bring receipts of currency into balance—mainly from state retail trade and transport, taxes, social security, and loans—and disbursements of currency—mainly in the form of wages, salaries, transfers, and advances for state agricultural purchases. Thus, the plan deals with gross flows of currency to and from the socialist sector, excluding transactions among households. Generally, receipts from trade represent up to 80 percent of the currency inflow, and payroll payments account for as much of the outflow. The State Bank's currency plan is drawn up on the basis of the observed trends in currency turnover in the country as a whole and its branches, which have their own plans based on the general trends in their respective spheres of operation. The branch plans are closely tied both to fulfillment of consumer goods output plans and retail trade and movement of the wage bill in all enterprises. If wage bill requirements are estimated correctly (and the budgetary outlays are in balance), any currency surplus or

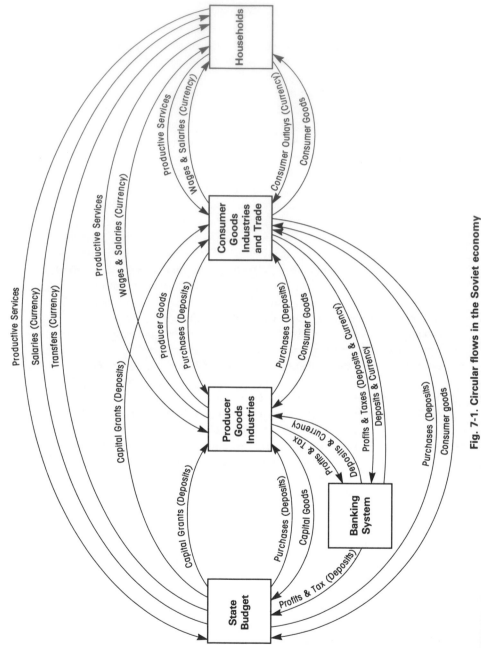

Fig. 7-1. Circular flows in the Soviet economy

deficit at the end of a planning period will obviously arise only from shifts in the pattern of household expenditures. It follows that the transaction velocity of currency can be estimated within narrow margins during any short-term period (say, from fifteen to thirty days). The parameters of currency plans are relatively few in number because of the discretion exercised by the state over the amount and timing of the wage bill.

The credit plan is closely related with the cash plan: both embody in specific ways the money supply's structure and fluctuations. In practice, the credit plan has systematically aimed to siphon off resources from the efficient state companies and shift them to the inefficient ones in order to keep them afloat and fulfill their output plans. The credit plan is drawn quarterly by the State Bank on the basis of forecasts of receipts and expenditures of each of its offices, branches, and agencies, each of the specialized sectoral banks and their branches, and each of their respective customers. After approval by the Council of Ministers, the plan is broken down by republic, regional, and district bank offices, which, in turn, establish limits to the credits to be granted to their clients for the end of each given plan period. But the policy of lending on "real bills" does not insure that the quantity of money thus created matches the actual transactions requirements, though the credit plan might perfectly equate the two sides of its balance.

In order to keep the quantity of currency at a minimum and enforce controls over its circulation, each state enterprise is ordered to hold as little currency as possible, and each socialized retail shop is required to deposit its daily receipts with the respective state bank. Any imbalance between inflow and outflow of currency is made up by issuing or withdrawing currency with the express approval of the Council of Ministers. In order to cope with urgent currency needs, each main bank office is provided with a certain amount of special reserves of paper money and coins, which it can inject into circulation at the appropriate moment upon approval of the head office. The impact of such factors as the time element in income formation, redistribution of income through transactions among persons, and propensities to save and consume can, in principle, be ascertained both through the variation in the fulfillment of the bank's currency plans and through correlation of other data grouped in the closely related *balance of money income and expenditures of the population*. This balance, part of the general economic plan, derives its data from the basic proportions between scheduled outputs of producer and consumer goods and the planned income distribution.

From Monobank to Complex Banking

Since the beginning of 1988, a number of measures, patterned more or less on the Hungarian reforms of the late 1960s, have been set in motion in the Soviet

Union with respect to the structuring and functioning of the banking system. While these modifications have cracked the "eggshell" of the academic system many obstacles are still in the way toward a true commercialization of banking operations.

Until mid-1988, the State Bank serviced all the currency, credit, and payments needs of the economy. It acted as the fiscal agency of the government and constituted an all-encompassing center for the settlement and clearing transactions of all associations and organizations. After a number of reforms, the State Bank had become, as Lenin had willed it in 1917, the country's *monobank*. It was "a single giant state bank with branches in every rural district and in every factory," achieving, as Lenin had envisioned, "countrywide bookkeeping and general state accounting of the production and distribution of goods."

Consider first the concentration of powers in the State Bank and then the process of its transformation, which started in mid-1988. The USSR State Bank was constituted in July, 1923, on the basis of the RSFSR State Bank, founded two years earlier. Besides the State Bank, the banking system of the mid-1920s comprised a host of interbranch and territorial joint-stock banks, cooperative, commercial, and agricultural banks, savings banks, and credit unions. A decision of the party's leadership in June, 1927, published as "On the Principles of Constructing the Credit System," set the stage for a deep transformation of Soviet banking. During the early 1930s a thoroughgoing reform brought about the liquidation of all the banks except for the State Bank and four newly constituted All-Union *sectoral* banks for financing long-term capital construction: in industry (*Prombank*), agriculture (*Sel'khozbank*), trade (*Torgbank*), and building (*Tsekombank*). Moreover, the reform consolidated a system of saving depositories (*Gostrudsberkassy*) and maintained a bank for foreign trade and foreign economic relations (*Vneshtorgbank*) under the control of the State Bank. The State Bank thus became not only the bank of issue but also the center for crediting and accounting the production and distribution of all state-owned firms—with a vast network of branches throughout the country. Another reform was carried out in 1959 expanding the roles of the regional State Banks. The State Bank also absorbed the *Sel'khozbank* and extended its control over the saving depositories. Simultaneously, a single bank for capital investment in the economy as a whole, *Stroibank*, was constituted on the basis of the bank of industry (Prombank) and replaced all other investment banks.

By 1988 the giant State Bank operated some 4,500 branches manned by 194,000 employees. It was handling the business operations of over 825,000 enterprises and organizations and was managing over four million accounts (besides some 178 million savings deposits). Each enterprise had its basic *settlement* account in the State Bank and, if needed, special *subsidiary* accounts, for example, for important repairs. Payments were made through the "acceptance" method, letter of credit, through special accounts, or by check. The acceptance method was most widely used. The seller dispatched the goods to the buyer and presented the invoice to his own State Bank office, which in turn forwarded it to the bank office of the buyer so that it could be submitted for approval. In case of acceptance, which had to be given within a certain number of days, the bank debited the buyer in his account and credited the seller; in case of conflicts about pricing, or in case of outright refusal, the goods remained under the care and responsibility of the buyer until new instructions were sent by the seller. In the letter of credit and special account systems, the buyer established beforehand an account to the order of the seller, who was thus assured of payment as soon as the goods were dispatched.

In time, the vast multiplication of mutually compensatory transactions led to the establishment of various interbranch, interindustry, or regional mutual-offset clearing schemes within the State Bank. About half of all inter-firm transactions were cleared in this way in order to reduce the volume of control needed and increase consolidation of operations at the higher levels of the State Bank. In a so-called decentralized accounts system, each participant in a given scheme had a special account segregated from the basic account at his or her usual bank branch. Only dealings with the participants in the given mutual-offset group were entered in the segregated account; the account was netted and audited at intervals adapted to the specific production conditions of the given enterprise. The nets were then entered in the regular account of the firm at the dates of auditing. In practice, the system gave the firm somewhat more freedom to maneuver its total funds, while, through the periodic control of end results, it also freed the bank from the need to control each of the mutual-offsetting operations. For speeding up clearing operations, the partici-pants in a mutual-offset scheme were credited automatically without waiting for the buyer's official acceptance (in any given period, the final result of the procedure might have produced an expansion rather than contraction of the total volume of credits outstanding). The State Bank alone was presumed to be the source of legitimate short-term loans. No enterprise could extend credit to another, although in practice numerous cases of mutual indebtedness occurred between enterprises and amounted to significant sums.

Following a Western-type accounting form, the State Bank's balance sheet consisted of, schematically, on the side of assets, gold holdings, Trea-sury notes, foreign exchange, and loans; on the side of liabilities, of currency and deposits; finally, its net worth included its charter capital and its reserves (see table 7-1). The State Bank charged and paid interest, except on budgetary accounts; the difference between charges and payments represented its in-come. Rates charged were differentiated according to type of credit and cost

TABLE 7-1.   Schema of the Balance Sheet of the State Bank

Assets	Liabilities
Gold stock	Currency
Treasury notes	Deposits
Foreign exchange (credits)	Settlement accounts of associations loans (enterprises)
Planned (on basis of	Subsidiary accounts of associations (enterprises)
output programs)	Current accounts
	Government
	Institutions and other organizations
	Saving depositories
	Collective farms
	Cooperatives
	Individuals
	Net worth
	Charter capital
	Reserves

of handling. The bank charged 1 percent for loans on "goods in transit," 2 percent for all other short-term credit, and 3–5 percent for loans overdue. For its part, the bank paid 0.5 percent on the deposits of enterprises and 1.5 percent on the deposits of collective farms. Finally, as the government's fiscal agent, the State Bank discharged numerous duties, including collection of taxes, disbursement of expenditures, and control of the execution of specified budgetary tasks for the All-Union or republic ministries of finance. Due to the custom of sharply differentiating each account according to its purpose and because of the variety and complexity of operations connected with the budget, more than one-quarter of the State Bank's total accounts were budgetary accounts.

The second key element of the Soviet banking system was the bank for capital construction, Stroibank. Its assets were augmented periodically by budget appropriations, specific parts of depreciation allowances (excluding the shares earmarked for important repairs), and shares in the profits of enterprises. The budget grants represented the most important part of this funding and accounted for some three-quarters of yearly disbursements. The bank extended both non–interest-bearing grants and long-term credits (at 1 percent interest), which together with the State Bank's credits amounted to close to 79 percent of the country's net material product (see table 7-2). Grants went to state enterprises; credits went to collective farms, cooperatives, and local industries, as well as to individuals for building houses. The bank made direct payments to the contractors for materials, transportation, and related charges on the basis of orders from the recipients of grants or loans.

Along with these banks the Soviet Union maintained the Bank for For-

TABLE 7-2. The Allocation of Credit as of 1986, in Billion Rubles

Total Credits	452.6
State Bank (*Gosbank* SSSR)	398.5
Construction Bank (*Stroibank* SSSR)	54.1
Short-Term Credits	356.6[a]
State Bank	325.7
Construction Bank	30.9
Long-Term Credits	96.0[b]
State Bank	72.8
Construction Bank	23.2

Sources: Narodnoe Knoziaistvo za 70 let., 635; and *Den'gi i Kredit* (Money and Credit), no. 11 (November 1987): 55.

[a] Loans to enterprises for raw materials, goods in process, finished goods, construction equipment, trade inventories, and other purposes.

[b] Loans, in particular, to state and collective farms and house construction cooperatives.

eign Trade (*Vneshtorgbank*), a subsidiary of the State Bank, and a number of banks abroad, namely the *Banque Commerciale pour l'Europe du Nord, S.A.* (*Eurobank*) in Paris; the *Moscow Narodnyi Bank, Ltd.*, in London; the *Voskhod Handelsbank A.G.* in Zurich; the *East-West United Bank* in Luxembourg; the *Ost-West Handelsbank* in Frankfurt; the *Donau Bank* in Vienna; and the intersocialist ("international") banks for economic cooperation (Mezhdunarodnyi Bank Ekonomicheskogo Sotrudnichestva—MBES) and investment (Mezhdunarodnyi Investitsionnyi Bank—MIB), participating in the financing of Soviet foreign trade, exchange activities, and international payments.

Following the decisions of the 27th Plenum of the Central Committee of the Communist party of July 1987, the USSR Council of Ministers established the framework for a broad reform of the Soviet banking system. The importance of this reform lies perhaps less in what it set out to achieve immediately and more in what it promises for the future. The reform brought about the formation of a *two-tier* All-Union banking system, and, secondly, it authorized the development of a distinct network of *commercial banks*. (The reform did not affect in any way the Soviet banks abroad and Soviet participation in the intersocialist MBES and MIB.)

However, in the framework of this reorganization, the USSR Council of Ministers still retains in its hands the direction of the banking system. It defines its structure and confirms the credit and the settlements plans of the economy as a whole. The State Bank continues to be the country's central bank and, in this role, participates at the highest level in the formulation of the planned direction of the country's development, the framing of the government budget, the planning of the balance of incomes and outlay of the population, and the drawing of the overall financial plan. The State Bank continues to be the country's bank of issue, coordinator of the monetary circulation, and primary decision maker concerning the conduct of credit operations. But it is no more the all-encompassing center of the economy's accounts, and it no longer has *direct* credit deposits and accounting relations with the associations (enterprises). These functions are transferred to new, specialized All-Union banks (superseding also the former Construction Bank), namely: the Industrial Construction Bank (*Promstroibank*), the Agro-industrial Bank (*Agroprombank*), the Bank of Housing and Municipal Services (*Zhilsotsbank*), the Bank for Foreign Economic Activity (*Vneshekonombank*), and, finally, the Bank of Savings and lending to the population (*Sberegatel'nyi bank*). A Council of Soviet Banks (*Sovet bankov SSSR*) has been created under the leadership of the president of Gosbank.

The restructured State Bank organizes and implements the fulfillment of government budget transactions both through its republican and local branches and branches of the specialized banks. Further, it draws the overall credit plan of the system and concentrates in its hands the country's credit resources, which are derived from the budget receipts, state social insurance funds, and resources existing in the accounts of the specialized banks. They are then redistributed to the same specialized banks and to their regional branches in conformity with the state's objectives. The transformation of the monobank into a two-tier banking system does not necessarily enhance the efficiency of capital allocation. The creation of the specialized banks has not been the outcome of a competitive process but the result of an administrative decision. The range of clientele of each of these banks is not due to free choice but flows directly from each bank's specific assignment. The size of each bank is determined by its assigned scope and is not intended to yield differences in profitability levels related to the particular effectiveness of its activity. The banks cannot increase the claims against themselves on the basis of the yield they offer and cannot persuade clients to increase deposits because of their characteristics in terms of safety, liquidity, or other such features. The yields on assets do not influence what the banks can pay on their liabilities. There are no incentives to raise funds via liabilities. In fact, the unlimited power of the State Bank to centralize all their net income stimulates these banks to maximize cost rather than profits. The banks do not face uncertainties as to their future income and prices. They do not face default risk or market risk due to fluctuations in the market rates of interest. All the banks remain subject to the objectives of the central plan, aiming to secure first the selected basic proportions and, secondly, if possible, financial equilibria.

In the aggregate, the credit deposits and settlement accounts of all the sectoral banks necessarily cover the main transactions taking place in the economy at large. The consolidated Balance Sheet of these banks and the pre-

**TABLE 7-3. Aggregate Balance Sheet of the Specialized
Soviet State Banks**

Assets	Liabilities and Capital Account
Cash on hand	Deposits
	Settlement accounts of associations
Loans	(enterprises)
Raw materials	Subsidiary accounts of associations
Goods in process	(enterprises)
Finished goods	Current accounts
Construction equipment	Government
Trade inventories	Institutions and organizations
Wage payments	Saving banks
Other	Collective farms
	Cooperatives
	Individuals
	Foreign Transactions accounts
	State Bank accounts

vious Balance Sheet of the State Bank will therefore necessarily have a similar structure (compare tables 7-3, 7-1, and 7-2). The consolidated Income Statement of these banks, summarizing all the gross income accruing to the banks against all their debts, will necessarily include, in the first case, income transfers *from* the State Bank and, in the second, income transfers *to* the State Bank (see table 7-4).

This setup will probably yield some advantages from specialization—for instance, better direct supervision of the deposits and withdrawals of each bank's client. But more significant changes are in store concerning the expansion of the financial role of the republics, the autonomy of enterprises, the direct wholesale and purchase of inputs replacing the centralized material-technical supply system.

As of the end of 1990, commercial banks accounted for less than 2 percent of the volume of loans in the USSR. These banks can take the form of joint-stock companies set up by industrial branches (for example, an Automotive-Industry Bank), interbranch arrangements, territorial organizations, and cooperatives (the latter alone could reach several hundreds). The operation of the banks is regulated by the State Bank with the view of preventing conflict between the flexibility imparted to credit and basic plan choices. Further, one must keep in mind that the interest of the indicated shareholders (except in the case of the cooperatives) remains primarily in maintaining the practice of revolving credits rather than the profitable placement of credits. Nevertheless, many uncharted ways could open because of the creation of such banks. The main forms commercial credit likely will take are *seller-creditor operations* (sales of goods on an installment basis) and *buyer-creditor operations* (advances by customers to the producer for the speedier delivery of

TABLE 7-4. Aggregate Income Statement of the Specialized Soviet State Banks

Credits[a]	Debits (according to purpose)[b]
Profit taxes	Procurement of nonfarm products
Turnover taxes	Procurement of farm products
Trade receipts	Collective farms payments
Transport earnings	Individual housing construction
Rent and communal services	Other housing-related operations
Savings banks receipts	Savings Banks expenditures
Cooperative earnings	Transport enterprises outlays
Other receipts	Communal expenses
Income transfers from the State Bank	Pensions, stipends, and insurance
	Other outlays
	Net income transfers to the State Bank

[a] Increases in deposits
[b] Decreases in deposits

better goods). Indeed, the 1987 Law of the State Enterprise gives enterprises the right to transfer materials and monetary resources (including money from their incentives fund) to other enterprises for services performed by the latter for the former. The discount papers created, moving from bank to bank, will expand the scope, rapidity, and flexibility of credit, as well as the financial maneuverability of both the banks and the enterprises.

The partisans of commercial credit stress that all these activities will allow the All-Union banks to concentrate on major transactions, while increasing the self-control of associations over their own financial resources. Thanks to commercial credit, the seller-creditor will expand his sales, while the buyer-creditor will better select his suppliers and their products. The commercial credit operations will provide competition for certain All-Union bank credits, and the commercial banks' interest rates, determined by competition, will exercise a useful influence on the structure of interests rates charged by the All-Union banks.

The critics of the reform fear that the expanding scope, rapidity, and flexibility of credit will hamper the All-Union bank activities, increase credit beyond control, and multiply bank bureaucracy and accounting procedures. In a discussion in *Deng'i i Kredit* (November, 1988), O. I. Larushin, for instance, points out that, in the 1920s, promissory notes accounted for a large part of the volume of credit and that many of these notes were not honored. (In 1925–27 the promissory notes in circulation accounted for 60–65 percent of the volume of credit; this percentage was still on the order of 35–40 percent of that total in 1929, the last year before the great banking reform of the 1930s.) And a member of the board of the State Bank, V. S. Zakharov, remarked in *Ekonomika i organizatsia promyshlennogo proizvodstva,* no. 3 of 1988, that the eventual curtailment of (state) bank credit and its replacement by commercial credit would "weaken bank oversight by the ruble," make difficult "the observance of self-financing principles," and allow enterprises, by drawing suppliers' funds into circulation, "to veil the real state of affairs and the actual self-recoupment which is an integral part of self-financing."

Clearly, the launching of commercial credit portends significant changes in the interrelations between the associations and the All-Union banks. The controversy about their eventual activities is certainly not going to die out soon.

The Unplanned Financial Disequilibria

As the monobank did before 1988, the specialized All-Union bank offices are now supposed to exercise detailed control over the financial activity of each of the state enterprises belonging to their respective spheres of operation. In particular, these banks must watch closely the movement of the state enterprises' wage and their fulfillment of the cost and output plans in the quantitative as well as qualitative terms prescribed. The segregation of settlement and current accounts and currency and credit flows and the specificity of each account and each operation are all devices for the establishment of a comprehensive financial control, or, as the Russians call it, "control by the ruble." The banks are supposed to treat enterprises that carry out their obligations leniently and delinquent enterprises severely—and all the state managers are supposed to willingly conform to these decisions. To the former, the banks can grant longer periods for credit repayments, while to the latter the banks can refuse any credit unless their superior administrative organs—ministry or branch administrations—endorse the loan. The banks can further require the delinquent enterprise to use the acceptance payment form only for in-town transactions and letters of credit, special accounts, or special checks for all out-of-town payments. The banks can also prevent the lagging enterprise from using credits for unpaid shipments until payment is made in full. Under certain conditions, the banks can ultimately proclaim the deficient enterprise insolvent—no enterprise could take such an action itself—and thus provoke a full-scale inquiry into the affairs of the negligent client by some ad hoc state organ.

In practice, the economic managers of the state enterprises have always operated under a "soft budget constraint"—to use an expression coined by the Hungarian economist Janos Kornai—that is, they have not been held responsible for the financial consequences of their decisions. In 1988, four years after the beginning of perestroika, Boris I. Gostev of the Ministry of Finance reiterated in his report on the budget the oft-repeated recommendation: "it is necessary to resolutely repudiate the existing practice of mechanically covering losses . . . . About 24,000 enterprises in various branches are operating at a loss." Yet the bickering between managers of the state enterprises and the banks is unstoppable. The managers are dissatisfied with what they consider to be nagging intrusions of the state banking system in their affairs. And the banks' economists just as often point to breaches of credit and payment, the lax financial discipline of the enterprises, and their "irresponsibility" in regard to the use of their own resources and the banks' loans. As a rule, the state enterprises tend to systematically understate anticipated inventories at the beginning of the year, overstate carryover of inventories at the end of the year, and accumulate debts to suppliers before the scheduling of accounts, which usually takes place at the end of the year. "There seems to be no end to the claims of one enterprise on another," affirmed *Pravda* on October 8, 1988, and added, "every association (enterprise) owes, and every one is owed." A kind of chain reaction of nonpayment is growing in the Soviet economy. Mutual nonpayments have indeed snowballed since the mid-1960s, when the volume of *sold output* replaced *gross value of output* as the basic performance evaluation index. Following that reform, the plan was proclaimed fulfilled when output had been shipped and accepted by the client; but often after acceptance, "wrangling" set in between sellers and buyers about the timing of the full payment.

Following the 1987 Law on the State Enterprise, the collective of state plants and factories have an interest in working according to contracts and observing strict discipline of deliveries. But again, as *Pravda* points out in the article cited above, "the absence of a proper guarantee of 100 percent payment for 100 percent deliveries is a serious obstacle." The lion's share of credit resources is still used to cover unproductive outlays connected with above-norm stocks of goods that are not in wide demand. Further, as noted, the banks readily credit the budget with the tax on nonexisting turnover, that is, on goods unsold or goods sold but not fully paid for, with fallacious consequences for the budget and the financial plans in general (for example, with respect to the redistribution of income). Major discrepancies occur also when banks credit the consumer goods industries and state retail trade for various goods unsold to the population, while the latter increases its "unplanned" savings in the Savings Bank.

Inflation—that is, increases in "unplanned liquidities"—is endemic. Faulty planning and faulty plan implementation, in respect to the state budget, the volume of wages, working capital requirements, bank credits, and the actual discrepancies between supply and demand in regard to consumer goods, are chief culprits. Other things being equal, increases in the volume of wages (due, for instance, to illicit or even licit bonuses and over-norms employment) immediately affect the liquidity of households; increases in working capital and bank credit affect the liquidity of enterprises and also, ultimately, that of households. Increases in the wage fund and shortages in certain basic consumer goods outputs push the collective farm market prices upward, stimulate the development of the shadow economy, and increase the spread between all these prices and the state retail prices (more so since the latter do not respond readily to changes in supply and demand). Prices of raw materials and intermediate goods within the state sector, though sluggish, react to the upward price push of the indicated consumer goods via cost-wage increases, that is, through pressures on planned profit margins.

The discrepancies between the banks' plans and actual results can be illustrated as follows. Between 1970 and 1987 real output doubled, while money in circulation increased 3.5 times and household's savings 5.7 times. In *Literaturnaia gazeta* (September, 1987), academician Oleg Bogomolov remarked that the "basket" of goods consumed by the average Soviet urban resident in a year "has become more than twice as expensive since the late 1950s." According to the official retail price index of goods of mass consumption sold in the state and cooperative stores—an index that "does not completely reflect reality," as Bogomolov puts it—prices increased between 1980 and 1987 by 27 percent (with ranges from 25 percent for milk to 39 percent for meat and 59 percent for tea) and by 34 percent for nonfood products (with ranges from a 10 percent increase for linen goods to 39 percent for knitted goods and 70 percent for fur products). Other computations by A. Shmarov and N. Kirichenko, published by the authoritative *Ekonomicheskaia gazeta* (1989), suggest that inflation was on the order of 5.7 percent per year between 1981 and 1985 and 7 percent per year during 1986–88, with billions of rubles lost in the purchasing power of the population, arising from both price increases and declines in the quality of products. Inflationary pressures continue unabated due to consumers' fears of future accelerated price increases fueled by the announced price revisions (first scheduled for the early 1990s and then postponed to the mid-1990s) and by rumors of currency reforms. Other factors increasing the dangers of inflation are the "overhang" of unusually large ruble holdings by the population (in the saving bank and in "strongboxes")—exceeding 45 percent of the net material product in 1988, the officially recognized large government budget deficit, and, last but not least, the push on prices exercised by the increasingly autonomous and self-financing enterprises, which must cover their rising costs. Particular attention is paid to the danger that consumers will feel tempted to throw much of their cash balances onto the market in order to purchase anything available in the shops, thus increasing the dearth of basic goods and imperiling the credibility and prospects of perestroika.

Soviet economists seem to suggest that there are only two solutions to this situation. Either one freezes prices (that is, indefinitely postpone the scheduled price revisions), distributes ration cards and continues central allocation of goods, or, as Bogomolov suggests, lets prices rise in a "regulated" fashion, increases outputs, and accepts that this process will necessarily further expand income. Presumably, however, the increased output will absorb the increased income and some of the savings as well, while the increased efficiency brought about in the economy at large will in turn lead to increased budgetary revenues and so, hopefully, to budgetary balance. In the *Wall Street Journal* on April 21, 1989, Martin Feldstein of Harvard University, former chairman of the Council of Economic Advisers under President Reagan, offered the Russians more cogent advice. He pointed out that there was no practical alternative to the current Soviet stagnation but the painful *decontrol of prices* and the expansion of the freedom of the enterprises to set prices for their own products. If the Soviet government cannot or does not want to decontrol and let prices rise, it must either run a budget surplus—the contrary of what it feels now able or compelled to do—or get the population to hold on to its wealth, perhaps under the form of government bonds, a highly problematical solution, since the population has no confidence in the government.

Concluding Comments

The perestroika is thus stymied; price reform, the crucial ingredient needed for the expansion of the financial autonomy of the enterprises, is postponed to the mid-1990s or beyond, while the Bogomolov "solution" is pushed timidly forward. In fact, even after the restructuring of the banking system, the Gorbachev system remains enmeshed in the absurdities, inefficiencies, and fallacies of Soviet money and banking theory. The old misconceptions and methods that unduly complicate Soviet banking—such as the confinement of households essentially to cash transactions only—remain indeed unchallenged and operate as haphazard, unpredictable constraints.

As indicated, the dogmatic assertion that Soviet currency is but "gold tokens" could be dismissed more often than not as inconsequential. (Its actual application is difficult to assess by an outsider.) In practice, the actual purchasing power of the ruble and the constancy of its value depend not on the application of this rule but on the equilibrium or lack of equilibrium in the planned money balances in the course of the implementation of the basic proportions set out centrally.

Again, the contention that the increase in the liabilities of the banks is backed by some special idle resources cannot be consistently applied in practice. The assertion that Gosbank extends credit only up to the limit of idle resources—since its sole function is allegedly only to redistribute the available funds, without creation of new money—is false and does not yield a consistent anti-inflationary discipline. The banks expand credit as needed by the plan, that is, by the need to keep all state firms in operation. The movement of money among firms is not influenced by prices nor interest rates.

The theory that state banks' loans must be secured against material values so as to ensure a "direct connection between credit and the process of production" rests on the fallacious assumption that the money released remains fixed to the intermediate goods that it first purchases. The alleged connection of credit to the real movement of goods is illusory, however, and does not guarantee economic stability in any way.

Inflationary pressures and hidden inflation are endemic in the Soviet economy given the absence of consistency and accuracy of the planned goals and the actual divisions of income between enterprises, banks, and the budget and of the actual relation between wages, savings, and consumer spending versus the assortment, quality, and quantity of the goods produced. Bogomolov is right when he chides those who still think "that a planned socialist economy has a reliable antidote for inflation" and when he points out that, in such an economy, inflation manifests itself both in the form of shortages in retail trade and in a buildup of excessive deferred demand and the rising of certain prices such as raw materials and equipment. Even the mention of eventual price reforms exacerbates the fears of more virulent inflation. The Soviet population rightly expects that the price reforms officially postponed until the mid-1990s will further increase the inflationary pressures resulting from the policies that preceded reform, the scheduled reduction in subsidies, and, finally, the various imbalances generated by all the reforms.

CHAPTER 8

Measuring the Economy's Performance

Soviet Accounts of Income and Product

The traditional Soviet measures of Soviet economic growth, like the data on Soviet defense expenditures, are scanty, devoid of indispensable details, inconsistent, and not fully reliable. Soviet measures are conceptually different from those commonly used in the West and diverge also in relation to the latter in regard to statistical practices. Conceptually, the differences cluster around the Marxian definition of the boundaries of production and the definitions of consumption (both intermediate and final), investment (accumulation), the redistribution of income, and the contents of imports and exports. Statistical practices differ in regard to the inclusion or exclusion of many types of outlays concerning, for instance, work in progress in construction and expenditures on military purposes, the scope of consumption of fixed assets, outlays on services and travel and other items. Since the end of the 1980s, the Soviet Statistical Office has released national income data computed, as usual, on the basis of Marxian concepts, as well as some aggregative data based on United Nations' conversion methods, which will be examined further on.

In Marxian growth theory, production is confined to the sphere of physical goods. In keeping with the labor theory of value, the aggregate net product is equated to $v + m$—that is, wages and salaries, plus the social surplus in material production excluding services not directly connected to material production. Incomes outside material production are treated as transfers from the "primary" fund, $v + m$, since, in accordance with Marx's basic assumption, no new value can be created outside the boundary of material production. The social surplus—that is, profit, rent, and interest charges—is assumed to be engendered exclusively by labor (engaged in material production; the surplus consists of a difference between the product of labor and the cost of labor).

Following Marx, Soviet economists have traditionally started the accounting of the national product from costs of production and the gross value of output of physical products. They have excluded from the aggregate product all personal and domestic services and government (including defense), health, education, scientific research, welfare, and housing and municipal

149

services. They have adjusted the boundaries of the sphere of material production, however, to include in it not only "the acquiring of the products of nature and their processing" but also their distribution and transportation. Product, *genus sovieticus,* thus includes certain services, namely, those directly connected with production, transportation, and distribution.

In the traditional Soviet social accounting system, net product is computed from gross output by either the enterprise or the sector method. Gross output of each enterprise (*valovaia produktsia*) is defined as production at its selling prices; it excludes internal turnover of the enterprise so that the total depends on the organizational structure of the given industry. This computation method is used for industry and agriculture. For construction, transportation, and trade, the so-called sector method of computation is used, which excludes the internal turnover in the given sector as a whole. Material production is divided into the following branches: industry, agriculture, forestry, building, transport of commodities, communications serving production, material-technical supply, agricultural procurement, trade, and other material services. Industry includes mining and manufacturing. Agriculture includes both crop and livestock output, computed at the respective selling prices, the nonmarketed share being estimated at average prices of all agricultural sales. Since the early 1980s, agriculture includes also the net product of the industries processing agricultural products, namely, the food and some light industries. Forestry is accounted for separately and includes various subbranches (culture of trees and grafting, for example). Building covers construction work, installation of equipment, and design connected with construction. Transport includes all types of freight but excludes passenger transportation. Material-technical supply, agricultural procurement, and trade are all computed at selling prices—trade, therefore, includes the turnover tax. Foreign trade surplus or deficit in foreign currency converted at domestic prices is added to, or subtracted from, total trade.

Gross value of output of each enterprise or branch, consolidated for the economy as a whole as the "global social product" (*sovokupnyi obshchestvennyi produkt*), reveals broad interenterprise and interbranch connections. From the same data, value added is obtainable by deduction of depreciation and interfirm transactions (*c*) for each unit or for an industrial branch as a whole—that is, the total of raw materials, fuels, electricity, and other materials used, and capital consumption. Similarly, for agriculture, value added can be obtained after deduction of the value of seed, animal feed, fertilizers, and insecticides.

Income generated in material production can also be computed by factor payments through summation of the incomes of workers and employees in enterprises of material production (including state farms), incomes of peasants (in money and kind) from collective farms and their own plots, incomes of

TABLE 8-1. Soviet Income and Product, in Billion Rubles and Percentages, 1985

Social Product	Billion Rubles	Percentage	Product by Use	Billion Rubles	Percentage
Material inputs (c)	804.8	58.2	Consumption	418.4	72.4
Wages and salaries (v)	293.8	21.3	Personal	330.8	57.3
Surplus (m)	283.9	20.5	Public	87.6	15.1
Total	1,382.5	100.0			
			Investment	150.3	26.0
Total outlays (c + v)	1,098.6	79.5	Productive	89.0	15.4
Surplus (m)	283.9	20.5	Nonproductive	61.2	10.6
Total	1,382.5	100.0			
			Reserves and other	9.0	1.6
Wages and salaries (v)	293.8	30.8			
Surplus (m)	283.9	49.2	Total net product	577.7	100.0
Total net product	577.7	100.0			
Net product produced in:					
Industry	263.6	45.6			
Agriculture	112.2	19.4			
Construction	61.7	10.7			
Transportation and Communications	35.1	6.1			
Trade and other	105.1	18.2			
Total	577.7	100.0			

Source: Computed from *Narodnoe Khoziaistvo v 1985 godu* (The National Economy in 1985) (Moscow: Finansy i Statistika, 1986), 45, 46, 52, 409, 412, and *SSSR v tsifrakh v 1987 godu* (The USSR in Figures in 1987) (Moscow: Finansy i statistika, 1988), 187, 195, 202.

workers and employees of producers' cooperatives, profits retained by enterprises, deductions from profits, transfers to the budget, and the turnover tax.

The net product can be either consumed or invested. Consumption is divided into personal and collective consumption. Personal consumption consists of goods and services consumed by individuals plus depreciation of dwellings, but excluding actual and imputed rent. Collective consumption is equated to the value of raw materials and fuels and material services used up in institutions and organizations in the nonproductive sphere, as well as the depreciation of fixed assets other than dwellings. Accumulation is income minus consumption and consists of net investment and increases in stocks and reserves. The value of net investment is derived from the sum of gross investment plus capital repairs minus depreciation charges fixed according to given rules. Changes in reserves probably include strategic stocks and gold. (See the illustrative data for 1985 in table 8-1.) As shown further on, serious deficiencies affect the calculation of the shares of consumption and accumulation in the national income.

The primary incomes received by labor and enterprises in material production are not completely utilized by them but are routed in part to further

Sectors and Branches	Production and Primary Distribution		Redistribution of Incomes Paid Out				Redistribution of Incomes Received				Final Use		
	Global Social Product	National Income	Through the Financial and Credit System		Outside the Financial and Credit System		Through the Financial and Credit System		Outside the Financial and Credit System		Balance of Redistribution	National Income	
	$c + v + m$	Primary Incomes $(v + m)$	Payments Into the State Budget	Payments Into the Credit System	Payments for Nonmaterial Services	Transfers and Other Payments	Receipts from the State Budget	Payments from the Credit System and Other	Receipts for Nonmaterial Services	Other Receipts	Balance of Redistribution	Consumption	Accumulation
	1	2	3	4	5	6	7	8	9	10	11	12	13
Material Sphere by social sectors by branches													
Private Sector by branches													
Nonmaterial Sphere by social sectors by branches													
Population by social categories													
Foreign Trade													
Totals													

Fig. 8-1. Schema of the balance of production, distribution, and redistribution of the global social product and of the national income. (Based on *Comparisons of the System of National Accounts and the System of Balances of the National Economy* [New York: United Nations Department of International Economy and Society Affairs, Studies in Methods, 1981], ser. F, no. 20, pt. 2.)

distribution. As a result, incomes of the nonmaterial sphere and households are generated, as well as transfers between the budget, the credit system, branches, enterprises, households, and foreign countries. The division of the global social product and its distribution and redistribution are consolidated in the balance schematically presented in figure 8-1. The redistributions *through* the financial and credit system involve, on the one hand (cols. 3 and 4), payments into the budget (deductions from profits, turnover tax, and other taxes) and payments into the credit system (loans repayment and increases in deposits); and, on the other hand (cols. 7 and 8), budget outflows (capital construction, grants, and current expenditures) and bank payments (decreases in deposits and currency). The redistributions *outside* the financial and the credit systems involve budget and other payments to the economic units and the gainfully employed of the nonmaterial sphere (cols. 5 and 6), and, correspondingly, the receipts of the incomes for services provided (cols. 9 and 10). The transfers of income to the financial and credit system is balanced by the receipts of incomes from the system. Since the sphere of material production redistributes part of its income to the nonmaterial sphere, the population, and abroad, its net balance is negative. On the contrary, for the nonmaterial sphere the net balance is positive. For the economy as a whole the net balance of redistribution is zero. Finally, the total of primary incomes $(v + m)$ is equal to the national income (net material product) consumed and invested $(C + A)$ (col. 2 is equal to cols. $12 + 13$).

Can the conceptual divergences and the statistical differences between the Soviet and Western methods of national income accounting be adjusted to allow the conversion of the data from one system to the other? If such adjustments are feasible, do they yield conceptually and statistically acceptable results, and do they allow meaningful comparability at the levels of each industry and each category of final demand? If such adjustments are possible but do not yield satisfactory results, can alternative Western methods be used in order to ascertain the Soviet economy's performance?

Western Alternatives to Soviet Measures

In a "Study in Methods" of the Soviet Material Product System (MPS) and the Western System of National Accounts (SNA), the statistical office of the United Nations Department of International Economic and Social Affairs developed three *conversion procedures* for bridging the statistical differences between the two systems at the level of gross domestic product (GDP) and net material product (NMP). The first of these procedures relies on value added data, the second on final demand data, and the third on gross output and intermediate consumption data. The first conversion indicates that:

$$G - D - V + P + E + I = N \qquad (1)$$

where G stands for GDP; D for depreciation; V for value added in the nonmaterial sphere; P for purchases of nonmaterial services; E for business travel expenditures; I for expenditures on cultural, recreational, and other services provided to employees by enterprises of the material sphere; and N for NMP.

The second conversion requires the following adjustments:

$$G - D + F + L + D_2 + E_m + I_m = N \tag{2}$$

where G, D, and N are as in equation 1; F is final consumption of nonmaterial services; L, material input by the nonmaterial sphere; D_2, consumption of fixed assets in the nonmaterial sphere; E_m, travel expenditures in both spheres; and I_m, material expenditures on certain services provided by the enterprises in both spheres. The third conversion involves the following variables: Q, gross output of material goods and nonmaterial services; Q_1, gross output of material goods; Q_2, gross output of nonmaterial services (that is, $Q - Q_2 = Q_1$); M, total intermediate consumption; M_1, intermediate consumption on the material sphere including depreciation; M_2, intermediate consumption in the nonmaterial sphere; D_1, consumption of fixed assets in the material sphere; and P, E, I, and N defined as before. With

$$M - M_2 + D_1 - P - E - I = M_1 \tag{3}$$

$$Q_1 - M_1 = N \tag{4}$$

Soviet statisticians, while continuing to compute the national income data following the Material Product System, have begun since the late 1980s, to compute along with NMP the gross national product (*valovoi natsional'nyi produkt*—VNP) according to the United Nations (UN) method. That is, on the pattern of equation 1, the VNP, unlike the traditional net material product, includes—besides the net output of material production (the value added in the branches of material production)—depreciation of fixed assets in the material and nonmaterial spheres, and the incomes received in the nonmaterial sphere as well as from foreign economic activities. According to these computations, the Soviet net material product amounted to 600 billion rubles at current prices in 1987, while the GNP amounted to 825 billion rubles.

The UN suggested adjustment can facilitate transpositions of the two systems of national accounts into each other, but it does not solve in any way the question of the validity of the Soviet data nor does it cope with their underlying flaws concerning, in particular, the inflation of Soviet value series. From the 1950s on, a number of American economists have noted that Soviet income data were not only far too scanty but that, moreover, they exhibited far too many gaps, inconsistencies, inadequacies, and inaccuracies to be used in any meaningful way either for ascertaining Soviet performance or making certain comparisons with corresponding Western data. They pointed out that in the West GNP defined the *market value* of the final goods and services produced by any country, and that the Soviet Union's administered and highly distorted prices could not reflect real resource costs of each product as market prices could. In *Soviet National Income and Product in 1937,* a pioneering work written in 1953, Abram Bergson, then at Columbia University, argued that, in order to avoid the distortions caused by the Soviet price system, the Soviet GNP had to be computed in a set of *alternative prices*, namely *factor cost prices* determined by imputing a uniform capital charge in place of the officially determined profits and turnover taxes. In order to compute the real growth of Soviet GNP, Bergson developed price indexes to deflate the current price value of each end-use component of GNP.

Bergson's calculation of the Soviet national income and product in 1937 was followed by numerous studies by other scholars who refined what came to be known as the Adjusted Factor Cost Standard. Eventually, economists of the U.S. Central Intelligence Agency computed extremely detailed accounts for certain years on this basis and moved each component over time in order to construct estimates for the growth of Soviet GNP from the beginning of the plan era (1928–29) to the present. These series throw new lights on the growth rates of the Soviet economy as well as on the performance of each of its sectors and of the changing levels of the final demand categories. The configuration of the Soviet economy and its components and their changes over time became thus comparable in detail to similar elements of structural change in the Western economies. A whole set of series of the yearly Soviet GNP by sector of origin, the growth of GNP and factor productivity, the growth of industrial output and factor productivity, agricultural output, gross fixed capital investment, consumption, and many other aspects of the Soviet economy were thus carefully recomputed.

Before examining the implications of these series in regard to the hotly debated issue of the trend in growth rates of the Soviet economy, it is useful to examine an example of the ways in which the Soviet data and Western estimates diverge in regard to both the assessment of the size of the Soviet national product and its structure by sector of origin. As can be seen from table 8-2, for 1970–85 the Soviet and Western figures diverge widely with respect to the sectoral contributions and their related changes over time, even though they might at times come closer with regard to total NMP. The Soviet data are indeed affected by the way in which prices in general and consumer prices in particular are constructed, the impact of the turnover tax, and the ways in which agricultural output is distributed among other sectors.

TABLE 8-2. Soviet and Western Estimates of NMP and Its Structural Changes by Sector of Origin, 1970–85, in Billion Rubles and Percentages

	Official Statistics				CIA Estimates			
	1970	1975	1980	1985	1970	1975	1980	1985
NMP	289.9	363.3	462.2	577.7	382.9	446.0	492.5	538.9
Industry	51.1	52.6	51.5	45.6	37.2	42.0	42.8	43.2
Agriculture	21.9	16.9	14.9	19.4	35.9	27.5	25.1	24.2
Construction	10.3	11.4	10.3	10.7	8.8	9.9	10.1	10.3
Transportation and Communications	5.6	6.3	5.8	6.1	10.6	12.5	13.5	13.9
Trade	11.1	12.8	17.5	18.2	7.5	8.1	8.5	8.4
Total Percent	100.0	100.0	100.0	100.0	100.0	100.0	100.0	100.0

Source: Computed from *Narodnoe khoziaistvo 1985,* 409; and *The Soviet Economy in 1988: Gorbachev Changes Course.* A Report by the CIA (Washington, D.C.: GPO, April 14, 1989), 40.

From Slowdown to "Acceleration"?

The contention that the Soviet Union could achieve sustained high rates of growth, higher than those of any market-directed economy, has over time lost all credibility. But the myth flourished for many years. It germinated and bloomed in the fertile soil of the Marxian utopian theory that a fully socialized, consciously planned, rationally directed, technologically advancing economy would be superior to any other. In a famous article, "Industrialization of the Country and the Right Deviation," published in November, 1928, in *Pravda,* Stalin asserted that the USSR could indeed have a very fast rate of economic growth and that, in fact, such a rate was both "necessary and imperative." The high rate could be achieved because the regime could provide for "maximum capital investment in industry," and it had to be achieved not only to overcome backwardness and "build an adequate basis for defense" but also, as Lenin had warned already in October 1917, because the country was confronted by the inexorable dilemma: "either perish or overtake and outstrip [economically] the advanced countries." "Full steam ahead" became a favorite Bolshevik formula that no one dared to call into question even after the death of Stalin.

The most extreme position concerning full steam ahead was embodied perhaps in the planning model devised by G. A. Fel'dman. On the threshold of the all around planning era in 1928, in a celebrated study, "On the Growth Rates of the National Economy," published in the central planning organ *Planovoe khoziaistvo,* Fel'dman indicated how the highest rates of growth could be achieved under given conditions. Following Marx, Fel'dman asserted that, since the rate of growth of production depends on the rate of growth of equipment, the producer goods sector (sector I, or Group A) must "necessarily" have a higher rate of growth than the consumer goods sector (sector II, or Group B). Fel'dman then suggested ingeniously that to achieve the highest rate of growth the two sectors could be severed; in his model, investment is directed to sector A, in which Fel'dman retains the capacity-increasing activities of the economy, while B is set to provide both the needed consumer goods and to compensate for the wear and tear of its own equipment. In essence, what he proposed was that growth be confined to A, while sector B would be maintained at its given level. Fel'dman's model was not entirely applied by the central planners, but the postulates that the output of sector A must exceed that of sector B and that A must absorb most of its own output remained unchallenged for decades to come.

The myth of the capacity of the Soviet economy to achieve sustained high rates of economic growth was further nourished by the ambiguities and exaggerations compounded in the Soviet computation of real national income. For the decisive years 1929–50, national income was computed at 1926–27 prices, that is, in a preindustrial price structure at increasing variance with the scarcity relationships that arose as industrialization developed. Numerous changes in underlying definitions, inconsistencies in assessing the sectoral contributions to net output, and deficiencies in valuations imparted a serious upward bias to the series. Thus, crop output was assessed first on the basis of crops stored, then of crops harvested, and finally of standing crops, although the latter, if not reduced by losses in the fields, might be larger than the barn crops by as much as 30 percent. Further, some sectoral contributions, which are usually troublesome to assess, such as the net output of construction, were simply included in the real income totals on the basis of computations at current prices. In a period of both rapid inflation and sharp increases in new industrial products, 1926–27 prices assigned to these products were simply the current prices of their first year in production. Assigning such weights meant inflating total output and overestimating the contribution of new outputs in relation to old ones.

The related Soviet computations of gross industrial output suffered, moreover, from the fact that any gross measure is sensitive to changes both in structural organization and volume of production. Inclusion in industry of the previously omitted private and small-scale industries, on the one hand, and increases in independently reporting units of the state industry, on the other— due both to reorganizations and accounting window dressing—further accentuated the upward bias of these indices.

Although various Soviet economists complained about the upward distortion of these indices, the official data were not revised. The Soviet Union still claims phenomenal increases in income and output for 1928 to 1950. According to official sources, income increased by 840 percent, gross value of industrial output by 1,110 percent, and gross value of large industry output by 1,350 percent. Since 1950, the 1926–27 weights have been discarded and

TABLE 8-3. Soviet Economic Growth Rates, 1951–87, Soviet Official Data and
Central Intelligence Agency (CIA) Estimates

Periods	National Product[a]		Industry		Machine Building and Metalworking	
	Soviet Data	CIA Estimate	Soviet Data	CIA Estimate	Soviet Data	CIA Estimate
1951–60	10.3	6.7	11.7	8.7	15.4	7.5
1961–65	6.5	4.9	8.6	6.5	12.4	7.0
1966–70	7.8	5.3	8.5	6.3	11.8	7.1
1971–75	5.7	3.3	7.4	5.4	11.6	6.6
1978–80	4.3	2.2	4.4	2.6	8.2	3.7
1981–85	3.6	1.7	3.7	1.8	6.2	1.3
1986–87	3.2	3.0	3.2	2.1	5.9	1.4

Source: Revisiting Soviet Economic Performance Under Glasnost: Implications for CIA Estimates (Washington, D.C.: Directorate of Intelligence, September 1988), 9.

[a] Soviet data for national income produced (sum of value added in all branches of material production, excluding depreciation); CIA estimates of GMP adjusted to make them roughly comparable in coverage, but including depreciation.

have been replaced by moving weights for quinquennial periods. Again, however, the industry indices are computed for gross rather than net output, and, furthermore, the new data have been welded to the old discredited series without any attempt at correction.

The official post-1950s series display a marked upward bias in relation to the estimates made in the West. As can be seen from table 8-3, the official Soviet data claim a yearly rate of increase of 10.3 percent during the 1950s as against a rate of 6 percent suggested by CIA calculations on the basis of the work of its own economists. Yet, as we shall see further below, many Soviet economists—Abel Aganbegyan, for instance—now consider CIA estimates "too optimistic." Be that as it may, it is worth noting that discrepancies between the official series and the CIA estimates concerning the growth rates of industry as a whole and of the key machine-building and metalworking industries are equally very large throughout the period 1951–87. What is important, however, is that no matter what series one considers, the Soviet economy has been unmistakenly losing its dynamism *since the end of the 1950s,* that is, in relation to the reconstruction years and the high investment rates of the late 1940s and 1950s. The slowdown deepened after a spurt in 1966–70, but by then the contractions had become increasingly alarming, reaching bottom in the early 1980s—an annual rate of 1.7 percent per year in 1981–85, according to the official figures; 1.3 percent, according to Western estimates; and less than 0.6 percent, according to subsequent estimates made by various Soviet analysts, such as Vasilii Seliunin and Gregorii Khanin (in

Znamia, 1986). The continuous contraction in the pace of growth was accompanied by increasingly deteriorating results in respect to actual volumes of investable resources, outputs, construction, and productivity (see fig. 8-2). The Soviet party leadership, alarmed by the prospects facing the economy, decided to reverse course and pass the reins of command to new leaders in April 1985. The new general-secretary, Mikhail Gorbachev, affirmed in his reports to plenary party conventions and to the party's Central Committee that the post-1970 decline—baptized "the period of stagnation"—was due to "subjective factors," namely, to the incapacity of previous leaders, in particular, Leonid Brezhnev, to properly assess "the changes in the objective conditions of the development of production," to shift in time from extensive to intensive uses of materials and equipment, to hitch onto advancing technologies, and to discard inefficient methods of management (reports of April 23, 1985, and February 25, 1986).

Actually, the sharper and sharper contractions in growth rates involve the entire legacy of assumptions, concepts, methods, and results of the administrative command system shaped by Stalin. As pointed out, for instance, in

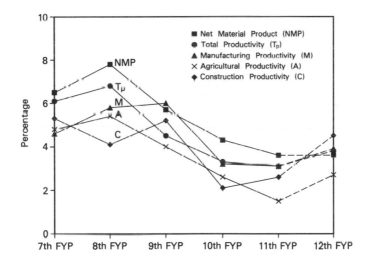

Fig. 8-2. NMP and productivity, annual rates of growth 1961–85 and 1986–90 (planned). (From *Narodnoe khoziaistvo za 70 let.* [The National Economy during Seventy Years] [Moscow: Finansy i statistika, 1987], 5, 107; and Plan figures, 1986–90.)

an overview of "Soviet Growth Retardation," published by Padma Desai in the *American Economic Review* (May, 1986), a combination of old and new ills are at work in the process of declining growth rates, including diminishing returns to new investment, declining rates of innovation, a poor incentive system, soft budget constraints, increasing bottlenecks and rigidities throughout the economy, increases in the real cost of output, and, last but not least, the alarming expansion of illegal markets.

In contrast to the so-called years of stagnation, Gorbachev stressed the allegedly glowing results that preceded the 1970s and the "accelerated" pace to be achieved in the late 1980s and, particularly, through the 1990s. By now, however, the alleged pre-1970s achievements—namely, according to Gorbachev's reports on the 1986–90 five-year plan (June 16, 1986), the surging of Soviet industrial output from the 1950s to 1970 "from 30 percent of the U.S. level to 75 percent" and of the Soviet national income "to two thirds of the U.S. level"—are not taken at face value even by pro-Gorbachev analysts. Seliunin and Khanin, for instance, noted that the official claim that Soviet national income increased "ninety fold" between 1928 and 1985 must be scaled down to, at best, an increase of six- to sevenfold. Moreover, the basic tenets of the early Gorbachev program, positing *both* the acceleration of the pace of growth and the transition to a "new quality of growth" (involving the overhauling of equipment, reaching of higher technological levels, and efficient reorganization of management and incentives), have proven invalid. Gorbachev's economic adviser, Aganbegyan, remarked in his 1986 book, *The Economic Challenge of Perestroika,* that, if one proceeds from the official Soviet statistics of 1981–85 (which, incidentally, he considers seriously upward biased), the rate of growth of national income "should rise on average by an annual 3 percent from 1981–85 to 4 percent in 1986–90 and to 5 percent or more in 1990." "3–4–5 percent is the *quantitative* formula of acceleration" to which one must add the "qualitative" dimensions. Is it feasible? In a 1987 article, "Acceleration, a Turning Point" (published in a collection edited by the USSR Academy of Sciences), Aganbegyan himself noted that the indicated growth rates were supposed to be achieved in conditions of declining capital inputs, declining fuels and raw materials, and declining gainfully employed, to be offset by rapid rises in productivity. This, however, turned out to be "a tall order," since its fulfillment was "obstructed by deeply ingrained inertia and by the prevalent mood 'to take it easy' and raise efficiency at moderate annual rates."

Another outstanding Soviet economist, R. R. Simonian, remarked in an interview published in *Izvestia* (July 8, 1988) that, "given the existing structure of our economy and its imbalances, setting our sights on increased rates is not always justified." The need to maintain a high rate of growth with a "full load on worn out equipment . . . is fraught with the danger of major accidents. As a matter of fact, such accidents are already occurring." Still another pro-Gorbachev economist, Leonid I. Abalkin, referring to the 1986–90 plan, remarked that "a choice should have been made between quantity and quality," but then, given "our traditions and experience it is obvious what was given preference" (that is, quantity). And, in a speech published in *Pravda* (June 30, 1988), he warned that, if the orientation toward volume and purely quantitative growth is pursued, "*we cannot* solve the problems of a cardinal improvement in output quality, the technical reequipment of the national economy and an increase in efficiency, and we cannot regear the economy to the consumer."

In fact, the state enterprises' managers are buffeted by a variety of disruptions engendered by the inconsistencies and timing of the perestroika requirements. These managers are pushed hither and thither by the pressure for acceleration and a shortfall of materials and equipment; the organizational problems posed by self-financing, wage reform, and encouragement to cut personnel; the exigencies of quality control programs (*gospriemka*); and the backsliding discipline of an increasingly dispirited work force.

Consumption and Its Relation to Income

Official data on individual and collective consumption and the share of consumption in income are truncated, ambiguous, and in some respects outright deceptive. According to these data, between 1970 and 1987 personal consumption varied between 56 to 60 percent of the national income used (which is smaller than the national income produced by losses, net exports, and reserves), while public consumption has been on the order of 15 to 16 percent. Per capita consumption has increased during the period considered but at a decreasing rate from one quinquennium to another following the general declining trend of the pace of growth of the national income (see table 8-4).

In the Soviet system of plan balances, the *balance of money incomes and expenditures of the population* analyzes the magnitude, structure, and source of all the money receipts of the population and all of its expenditures (both by cash transactions and transfers without actual cash payments). The income and expenditure sides of the balance attempt to map the interrelations of the population with the state, cooperatives, institutions, and organizations and the relationships between the individual groups of the population. The balance links the State Bank's cash and credit plans and the plans of retail trade (see fig. 8-3). Unfortunately, the actual data are not released to the public. The statistical annuals release instead various tabulations that raise more questions than they answer. According to official data issued in the 1988 statistical annual, roughly 79 percent of a worker's family income in 1987 was made up of wages, with the rest accounted for by pensions and subsidies (9 percent),

TABLE 8-4. Shares of Personal and Public Consumption in "National Income Used," 1970–87, Illustrative Data in Absolute Figures and Percentages

	1970		1975		1980		1985		1987	
	Rubles	Percentage	Rubles	Percentage	Rubles	Percentage	Rubles	Percentage	Rubles	Percentage
National income used (billion rubles)	285.5	100.0	363.0	100.0	454.1	100.0	576.0	100.0	585.9	100.0
Personal consumption (billion rubles)	159.7	56.0	209.9	57.8	272.8	60.0	330.8	57.4	347.3	59.3
Public consumption (billion rubles)	41.6	14.6	56.5	15.6	72.7	16.0	87.6	15.2	94.0	16.0
Total consumption (billion rubles)	201.3	70.6	266.4	73.4	345.5	76.0	418.4	72.6	441.3	75.3
Per capita consumption (rubles)	832.0		1052		1306		1514		1566	
Increase in per capita consumption				26.4		24.1		15.9		3.4

Source: Computed from Narodnoe khoziaistvo SSSR v 1985 godu, 409, 412 (with pensions and subsidies included in personal consumption); and SSR v tsifrakh v 1987 godu, 195.

Money Incomes	*Expenditures*

Money Incomes	**Expenditures**
From state and cooperative institutions and organizations	In state shops
—Wages	In cooperative shops
—Nonwage income (bonuses, for example)	
—Collective farm guaranteed payments and money income distributed as dividends for labor	For farm goods on commission
	In collective farm markets
—Income from sales of agricultural and other produce to state and on commission	Services and other
—Pensions	—Rent
—Stipends and allowances	—Private urban house building
—Loan service and redemption	—Private rural house building
—Pay and pensions of armed forces, dividends of members of cooperatives, other incomes	—Entertainment
	—Payments for personal services
	—Transport and communication services
From the population	—Obligatory payments (taxes, state insurance, repayment of loans)
—Sales in collective farm markets	
—Sale of other goods and services	
	Savings
	—Purchase of state bonds
	—New savings deposits
	—Changes in cash balances
Total	Total

Fig. 8-3. Schema of a balance of monetary income and expenditures of the population

subsidiary household economy (3 percent), and the balance by income from other sources. (This balance does not mention incomes made in nonformal ways, which constitute a significant part of the daily life of a Soviet household, nor nonmonetary incomes such as consumption out of the income in kind from personal plots.) On the side of expenditures, the outlays for foodstuffs and alcoholic beverages accounted for some 36 percent (2.6 percent for alcohol), 17 percent for clothing and footwear, 7 percent for furniture and appliances, 10 percent for social and cultural services (education, medical care, and other), 3 percent for rent, and the rest for savings, taxes, and other payments. In the collective farmer's family income, 52 percent of the total came from the collective farm, while 10 percent was contributed by wages of the members of the family, 10 percent by pensions and stipends, 24 percent by the subsidiary household economy, and the balance from other sources. On the side of outlays, some 40 percent went for foodstuffs and alcoholic beverages (3.3 percent for the latter), 16 percent for clothing and footwear, 5 percent for furniture and other household needs, 10 percent for social and cultural services, and the rest for savings, taxes, and other payments. Most of the data are flawed, however, and, indeed, both the figures on total consumption and those on its pattern have been questioned inside as well as outside the USSR.

Concerning the data on the distribution of the Soviet GNP by end use, CIA computations for 1982 (compare to tables 8–3 and 8–4), using the GNP by origin as a base, evaluated the share of consumption at 52.7 percent at established prices (namely, over 41 percent for consumer goods and 11 percent for consumer services), investment at 28 percent, and government expenditures (with most of it for defense spending) at over 19 percent. Using a totally different procedure, Vasilii Seliunin pointed out in a July 1988 article in *Znamia* that the Soviet computations of the material product by end use measured consumption and accumulation with *different rubles*. The value of consumption goods is calculated in retail prices, that of accumulation at wholesale prices. The difference between the two falls to the turnover tax, which for 1985, for instance, accounted for 97.7 billion rubles. Subtracting this total from the figure on total consumption in table 8-4 (418.4 billion minus 97.7 billion), gives a total of 320.7 billion, that is, 55.6 percent for consumption (instead of 72.6 percent) of the national income used and 44.4 percent for accumulation, including investment and other government spending. Another Soviet economist, R. R. Simonian, points out that the official data leave us in the dark in regard to the relation between consumption and living standards (*Izvestia*, July 8, 1988). Simonian notes that the data do not shed much light on the cost of living of various social groups nor the evolving costs of consumer goods baskets, not because of methodological difficulties but "because we are ashamed of these 'awkward' statistics." Simonian, who holds the high position of a department head of the USSR Academy of Sciences' Institute of World Economics, adds that the Soviet per capita consumption is "only about one third of what it is in the U.S.," while per capita housing "is only 28 percent of what it is in the U.S."

The prospects for increasing consumption are not favorable and, if one is to believe the statements of Vladimir Tikhonov at a seminar of the economists elected at the 1989 Congress of People's Deputies, "famine in the very near future" is possible unless radical changes are effected (for example, in respect to the importation of consumer goods) (cf. *New York Times*, June 18, 1989). It is interesting to recall in this connection that, given the increasing discrepancy between the supply and demand for consumer goods, Abel Aganbegyan has indeed suggested the need to sharply increase the share of consumer goods in total imports (from 13 to 25 percent of the total, through reductions in the purchase of certain types of equipment and metal products). Aganbegyan has further pointed out that, even at the rates of growth of income embodied in Gorbachev's acceleration formula, consumption would grow at a rate *not* significantly above that of the rates of growth of the total population. Vasilii Seliunin, who notes in *Znamia* that these calculations have gained "immediate renown" in the USSR, adds that what is really needed in order to end a situation in which "accelerated growth has only a weak influence on the standard of living" is to discard the paradoxical and unacceptable economic policy that ensures that, "in each successive cycle, the share of production of consumer goods is lower than in the preceding cycle."

Concluding Comments

Innumerable party documents have enshrined the idea that all that was needed for the Soviet Union to "overtake and outstrip" the most advanced capitalist countries was to concentrate the economy's resources on "all-out industrialization." By the time of the launching of the First Five-Year Plan in 1929, some ten–fifteen–eighteen–twenty years seemed all that was needed to catch up with and surpass the United States. L. M. Sabsovich, in his then well-known "Hypothesis concerning the production scale of the main branches of the USSR economy during the period of the General Plan" (published in 1929 in *Planovoe khoziaistvo*, the organ of Gosplan), asserted that planning had necessarily to be based on "accelerating growth rates," since the introduction of new technology will necessarily lead to massive increases in production. "With respect to the scale of industrial production," added Sabsovich, "we shall considerably exceed, within fifteen years, the present level of development of the most advanced capitalist country, the U.S.A., and leave far behind in eighteen to twenty years the level which it will be able to reach at that time, if it continues to develop under capitalist conditions." Another economist, N. K. Kovalevskii, affirmed in "On the Construction of the General Plan" (*Planovoe khoziaistvo*) in 1930 that *his* sectoral projections "guaranteed" that the USSR would attain "the American consumption levels in ten years, and a threefold increase over American consumption in fifteen years."

In the meantime, Stalin was rejecting the rates of growth of income and output suggested by Gosplan's more sober experts and was requesting ever higher targets. The first draft of the five-year plan drawn up by Gosplan early in 1927 scheduled an increase in the gross value of output of between 67.9 and 87 percent (maximum). By December, 1927, successive drafts requested by Stalin's Politburo had pushed the scheduled rates of growth of industrial output upward to 108, 122, 140, and, finally, 167.7 percent for the five-year period. The final December draft, which became the plan, scheduled an increase of 221 percent for Group A (heavy industry) and 109.6 percent for Group B (light industry). The First Five-Year Plan was proclaimed completed in four years instead of five; allegedly, it had yielded an increase of 290 percent for Group A and 163 percent for Group B. Then, after another strenuous stretch of five years, at the end of the Second Five-Year Plan in 1937, Stalin affirmed that socialism had been completed in the USSR.

After World War II, notwithstanding the enormous destructions inflicted by the Nazis, Stalin and the Soviet leaders continued to assert that the Soviet Union would soon "reach and surpass" the highest levels of capitalism. The idea that the Soviet Union was indeed "bridging the gap" with the United States was particularly popular in Europe, at least by the end of the 1950s and the beginning of the 1960s. Currently, the Soviet official data assert—as does, for instance, the statistical compendium *SSSR v tsifrakh v 1987 g.* (*The USSR in Figures in 1987*, released in 1988)—that the Soviet Union had reached 58 percent of the U.S. income in 1960, 65 percent in 1970, and 67 percent in 1980, but that this ratio had fallen to 64 percent after the period of stagnation (which, incidentally, had started long before). Such figures are not very meaningful, however; we are not told at what prices these calculations have been made and in which specific ways.

According to a study by Gur Offer of the Hebrew University of Jerusalem on "Soviet Economic Growth: 1928–1985," published in the *Journal of Economic Literature* (December, 1987), the Soviet Union "has been closing the gap" with the United States as follows: "from about one quarter of the size of the U.S. economy in 1928, the Soviet Union climbed to about 40 percent in 1955, 50 percent in 1965, and about 60 percent in 1977." But these figures also are not acceptable, and for the same reasons. Other current estimates from Soviet or Western sources are equally unconvincing. Certain Soviet economists, such as Viktor Belkin, for instance, the prominent economist of the Soviet Academy of Sciences, now states that the Soviet output is "not more than 28 percent of the American GNP and might be substantially less" (*New York Times*, April 14, 1990)—confirming a figure advanced by the influential Western columnist, William Safire, who asserted earlier that the Soviet product was indeed "less than a third our size" (*New York Times*, June 8, 1989).

These kind of guesstimates are not very helpful. It is interesting to recall in this connection the important and detailed study by Morris Bornstein of the University of Michigan, *The Soviet National Income Accounts for 1955* (1962). According to his computations, Soviet and American GNPs, measured in Soviet prices, were, in 1955, 1,285 and 4,802 billion rubles, respectively, and the ratio between them was thus only 26.8. Measured in United States prices, Soviet income was of the order of $212 billion as against $397 billion for the United States, and the ratio stood at 53.4. These large differences occurred because goods with relatively lower (higher) prices in either the United States or the USSR are produced in the respective countries in larger (smaller) quantities so that, in comparing the two GNPs, a greater price weight is given to goods more abundantly produced in the USSR when dollars are used, and, conversely, a greater price weight is given to goods produced more abundantly in the United States when rubles are used. Since the question of the respective sizes of the contrasted GNPs eludes a single answer, one can perhaps consider the implications of the dollar valuation, since it is cast in more familiar, though no more meaningful, terms than the ruble valuation. Again, according to Bornstein, whereas the ratios between the two GNPs were 53.4, the ratios of consumption were only 39.0, investments 68.3, defense 94.3, and government administration 152.1. Although Soviet GNP per capita was of the order of 44 percent of that of the United States, Soviet consumption per capita was less than one-third that of the United States. Thus, in 1955, from an income half as large as the American income for that year, the USSR invested an amount equivalent to over two-thirds of United States total investment and spent a sum almost equal to United States' expenditures on defense.

Only carefully detailed computations of this kind, still to be made for the years after the 1950s, can convey some useful approximations about where the ratios of the products of the two economies might presently be.

Part 3
Reforming the Sectoral Arrangements

While the president of the Russian republic, Boris Yeltsin, asserts erroneously that it is possible to transit to market relations at a lightning speed, the central Soviet policymakers labor cautiously, hesitantly, and undecidedly at the replacement of the primarily administrative methods of command planning and management with economic guidance at all levels of the economy. How is replacement supposed to take place in manufacturing, agriculture, supply and trade, and foreign trade? Replacement does not entail abandonment of the central plan of macroeconomic policy or ending central microeconomic controls. Restructuring attempts to ensure supremacy of decisions while avoiding interference in the details of firms. It aims to increase the options of firm managers, put their operations on a real cost-accounting and self-financing basis, and involve firms in an expanded network of contracts. It seeks to expand, but at a "controlled pace," the private sectors in industry, agriculture, and retail trade and increase relations of domestic enterprises with foreign firms.

How are new powers of the center supposed to combine with the proposed autonomy for enterprises? In his effort to reduce the state's administration and increase efficiency, Gorbachev has initiated personnel reductions at the top of planning and management and the concentration of power in fewer hands. But statutes of umbrella economic agencies hastily created or modified are still under discussion, as is the General Statute of the Council of Ministers and of state committees. Definitions of functions under perestroika of branch ministries and departments, which raise questions, are not yet solved. But the state enterprises are already operating on the basis of new laws that are supposed to grant them autonomy, an autonomy to which are connected all kind of normative documents on the ownership of assets, reorganization and liquidation, contracts, wholesale trade in means of production, and measures concerning state budget and credit.

The 1987 Law on the State Enterprise indicates how architects of perestroika intend both to maintain centralization and expand the freedom of choice of the state enterprises. According to the law, each of these enterprises (and associations of enterprises) must function according to a two-level system, that is, subordination to a ministry, state committee, or department. The higher-level agency monitors activity, audits production and financial operations, determines technical policies, counteracts monopoly propensities, overcomes tendencies for unit cost and price overstating, and ascertains safekeeping of socialist property. But the state enterprise, just like the private ones (individual, cooperative, communal), is supposed to form its plans within the framework determined by indices of the Basic Lines of Development of the USSR, of centrally set, long-term financial norms concerning distribution of profits (income) and ceilings set by state construction and supply needs. In addition the state enterprises must take account of direct state orders and of those from other enterprises, all confirmed by contracts. Further, the law stresses self-management of the state enterprise by "labor collective" (its entire personnel), which elects executives (from head of the enterprise to foremen) and sanctions policies. To what extent could extensive powers of the titulary agency shape decisions—allegedly autonomous—of enterprises? To what extent could conflicts between the agency and enterprise lead to bargaining and joint accommodations, thwarting the central planners? Is self-management a guarantee of independence or rather a formality that might lead only to the promotion of undemanding executives put forward by inefficient, overzealous employees? The law states that, regardless of particular specialty, "the enterprise carries out the production of consumer goods and provides paid services to the population." How is this activity to be implemented by enterprises diverse by definition? To what extent and how is all this tied to cooperatives? Chapter 9 focuses on these issues.

In regard to agriculture, restructuring tries to embody a second New Economic Policy patterned on Lenin's NEP of 1921. As Gorbachev recalled in a report to the Central Committee on March 15, 1989, Lenin replaced requisition of grain from peasants with a tax in kind, allowed free trade and cooperatives, authorized land leasing and use of hired labor, promoted a forward-contracting system, and increased agricultural prices. Gorbachev added that, after Lenin's death, the country's leaders—Stalin and Trotsky—took an opposite path in economic methods. They curtailed commodity-monetary relations, belittled incentives, and introduced command-administrative methods. This "deviation from Marxist views" is to be redressed. Land ownership is to be reconsidered. Along with a "large changeover to leasing," a diversity of transformations is to be encouraged, including the change of each collective farm into a "cooperative of cooperatives," combination of agricultural, industrial, construction, and other enterprises, and the development of personal subsidiary farming. Forward contracting should guarantee the producer state supplies and should allow the producer to sell produce as he or she chooses after having fulfilled obligations to the state. Cost recovery, self-financing, and self-management should prevail after the price system becomes "an effective instrument of shaping progresive proportions and structural changes for better final results." The drawback of this second NEP is that the scheme, including terms of leasing, is to operate within the existing framework of collectivized agriculture. Peasants remain uncooperative, while Gorbachev insists that it would be "unjustifiable" to assume that the traditional organization of the countryside is inefficient and that it necessarily yields poor results. Chapter 10 examines these issues.

The process of creating a vast free network of private enterprises, of purchase, wholesale and retail, looking to more industrial and agricultural production, toward solving the food problem and consumer goods shortages, as well as expansion of markets, is stymied. Policymakers fear that the dismantling of the system of allocation of scarce supplies would lead to explosive inflation at a time when the economy has both innumerable shortages and an enormous "overhang" of currency holdings. But the alternative of continuing the same system is not promising. Chapter 11 focuses on the material-technical supply system, its structure and ramifications, as well as on the characteristics of the retail trade network and the growth of black markets. Chapters 9, 10, and 11 give attention both to the global problems of each of these sectors as well as to the development of the "second economy"—private and semi-private, legal and illegal—and to its relation with the "first economy" (state-owned firms).

The final chapter of part 3 focuses on foreign trade. While maintaining the principle of monopoly of foreign trade—that is, that foreign economic activities are part of the overall national economic plan—the architects of restructuring have initiated a vast modification of the old system of centralized management of foreign trade. A whole new set of institutions has been created under a new supervising State Foreign Economic Commission, and broad rights have been granted to ministries, departments, associations, and enterprises to engage in foreign trade. The changes in this sector are perhaps the deepest changes carried out under perestroika policies and express the clear decision of Soviet policymakers to break the country's economic isolation.

The four chapters of part 3 are organized along similar lines, each presenting, first, the sector's structural patterns of organization. Next, they show how the firms' autonomy and options, expanded by the new policies, interact with various unchanged elements of the traditional hierarchical system. They then focus on the growth of private, semi-private, legal, or illegal economies of all kinds (individual and cooperative establishments, subsidiary farms, black markets, and joint ventures) and examine the drawbacks of certain reforms and sketch possible ways for overcoming these handicaps.

CHAPTER 9

Manufacturing

State Enterprises, Associations, and Complexes

Soviet leaders have always assumed that large-scale production was synonymous with scientific-technological progress and that integration of production processes into higher and higher complexes was the sine qua non of efficiency. From the earliest years of the Soviet regime, innumerable documents have extolled large-scale production. Concentration of manufacturing and agricultural production as well as organization of supply and trade have been viewed as the means of economies of scale and the way to compress upper ranges of the managerial hierarchy while streamlining control over production units.

The pace of concentration accelerated in the late 1950s. According to a statistical compendium published in 1957, *Achievements of the Soviet Power in Forty Years*, Soviet industry was already the "most concentrated industry in the world." Actually, as indicated by the first Soviet statistical yearbook published after Stalin's death—*National Economy of the USSR in 1956*, also published in 1957—in addition to 206,000 "large and small industrial enterprises" owned by the state, there were 107,000 small-scale industrial cooperatives and 28,000 industrial consumer cooperatives. Cooperative industries accounted for 7 percent of industrial output, to which was added a 1 percent contribution of 350,000 blacksmiths and other small workshops in the agricultural sector. The situation led to change by the end of the 1950s. Industrial cooperatives were disbanded, their property handed over to the state, and the industry was reorganized. By the beginning of the 1960s the number of enterprises—now state enterprises—was boiled down to 46,500. During ensuing years the number has not varied. During the entire post–World War II period, the industrial work force increased three times in relation to 1940, from 13 million in 1940 to 15.3 million in 1950, 22.6 million in 1960, and stabilizing around the 38 million mark since 1987.

A look at the size of Soviet manufacturing enterprises for 1960, 1975, and 1987 shows a shift toward enterprises with more than one thousand employees (see table 9-1). In 1960, 7.2 percent of enterprises had one thousand or more employees. By 1975 this percentage had doubled, and by 1987 it

TABLE 9-1. Size Distribution of Soviet Manufacturing Enterprises, 1960, 1975, and 1987, in percentages

Size Distribution by Employment	Total Number of Enterprises			Share in Total Personnel			Share in Total Output		
	1960	1975	1987	1960	1975	1987	1960	1975	1987
up to 100	43.6	28.7	27.2	5.6	2.2	1.7	7.0	2.7	1.8
101–500	40.7	41.3	43.3	25.3	15.3	13.2	25.3	16.9	12.9
501–1000	8.6	12.5	13.1	15.8	12.5	11.7	14.9	11.2	11.4
1001–5000	5.5	12.1	13.8	24.2	35.6	36.2	24.0	35.3	38.0
5001–10,000	1.4	1.6	1.7	18.9	15.4	15.6	19.4	16.1	15.7
10,000 +	0.2	0.8	0.9	10.2	19.0	21.6	9.4	17.8	20.2

Sources: Narodnoe khoziaistvo SSSR (National Economy of the USSR) for 1973 and 1984 (Moscow: Finansy i statistika, 1974 and 1985), 244–45 and 159, respectively; and Goskomstat, *Promyshlenost' SSSR* (The USSR Industry) (Moscow: Finansy i statistika, 1988), 14.

Note: Excluding the power stations and their personnel. For 1960 the range was 1001–3000 and 3001–10,000.

stood at 16.4. Corresponding shares of these enterprises in total manufacturing personnel rose from 53.3 percent in 1960 to 70 in 1975 to 73.4 in 1987. But these changes were not accompanied by large increases in output, as might have been expected; concentration did not yield increase. Discrepancy between the shares in total personnel and output remained just as narrow in the case of enterprises with more than ten thousand workers. The share of these enterprises in the labor force rose from 10.2 percent in 1960 to 21.6 in 1987, that is, more than double, and, correspondingly, the share in output rose from 9.4 percent to 20.2 percent, also more than double. But in both cases these shares were smaller than those in the total employees in manufacturing. Changes again did not yield any apparent increases in productivity in relation to average productivity in all other manufacturing enterprises.

To reduce further the objects of top-management control and amalgamate enterprises, Gorbachev emphasized the need for a vast overhaul of ministerial management procedures and for even higher concentrations in the state's industrial branches and subbranches. In the early 1970s Soviet policymakers and planners were forming industrial associations (*proizvodstvennye ob'edineniia*) and research and production associations (*nauchno-proizvodstvennye ob'edineniia*) to replace head administrations (*glavki*) of ministries and departments managing industrial subbranches. But, as usual, reform launched in the early 1970s was not completed by the end of the 1980s. There were 600 associations in 1970, accounting for 6.7 percent of total industrial output; in 1987, 4,300 associations accounted for half of manufacturing output. In 1988, after asserting that the old All-Union production associations "had not proven their worth," the chairman of the USSR Council of Ministers, Nikolai

I. Ryzhkov, stressed replacing "the still-existing head administrations" (*Pravda*, June 30, 1988) with research and production associations and new state production associations. He indicated interesting shifts in responsibilities between All-Union, republic, and local-level industries. All basic branches of the Soviet Union's industry—excluding the light and food industries—henceforth were to be under the All-Union ministries (including branches previously in union-republic ministries, that is, under the dual control of the center and a republic, such as the Coal Industry, Ferrous and Nonferrous Metallurgy, and Geology). Under republic and local agencies was left "everything having to do with the agrarian sector, light industry, food industry, trade, the service sphere, public health, and education" (cf. Gorbachev's closing remarks at the CPSU Central Committee Plenum, *Pravda,* April 27, 1989).

Concentration of state enterprises, transformation and expansion of associations, and continuing central control of the main manufacturing establishments is to be completed by further regrouping industry into *functional* complexes and instituting changes in the "territorial system of management" (existing territorial-production-complexes—that is, groups of industries within a geographical area, mainly Siberia, northern Russia, and in a few other regions). Since the late 1980s official statistics group heavy industry into the following functional complexes: fuel and power, metallurgy, machine building, chemicals, and lumber and construction materials. All of this reorganization does not seem to reduce the number of managers but only to reshuffle them. According to a State Statistical Committee Report (*Izvestia,* March 7, 1989), between 1985 and 1988 employees in the apparatus of ministries, departments, and other administrative agencies decreased by 23 percent, from 2.3 million to 1.8; but managerial personnel in the enterprises and organizations increased by 4.8 percent, from 12.5 to 13.1 million.

The drive toward concentration of the bulk of the large state enterprises, toward associations and complexes, has been guided by the center's wish to fit the main producing units into a system that would allow the "simplest" and "best" control of the country's basic activities. Conversely, the state enterprises have tried under all these changes to avoid exacting plans, accumulate reserves to offset uncertainties, and carry out only priority injunctions while evading other obligations. Eventually, both the center and the state enterprises have learned through experience that there were, unaccountably, many strategies and that an extensive form of the game—showing the complete move, information set, and payoff structure—could not be specified. Encasing the state enterprises in a hierarchical system with multiple objectives centrally defined—concerning volume, type, assortment, and the quality of goods, as well as financial indicators—led to *negotiation* between manipulators of the system and the enterprises, negotiation whose scope has shifted as manipulators have tried to change, at least in part, from plan indicators and assignments to economic levers.

Options and Hierarchical Dependence

During discussion on the draft of the Law on the State Enterprise Tat'iana Zaslavskaia and economist V. Efimov recalled in a cogent article in *Sovetskaia Rossia* (March 24, 1987) that what was wrong with the "old economic mechanism" was perpetuation of such "negative phenomena" as shortages of production, slow scientific and technical progress, low output, low quality, excessive inventories, large amounts of unfinished construction, and low labor productivity. They attributed these phenomena to three factors of the old system: *plan indices and assignments* for enterprises, backed by central allocation of resources; *formal economic accountability* relying on cost-based price formation and a uniform wage rate and salary system; and *multilevel management* with complex management procedures limiting the scope of independent decisions by the enterprises. To what extent have these factors been changed and their negative results been circumvented? Zaslavskaia and Efimov were not hopeful about favorable changes during discussion on the draft of the law, and their apprehensions have been substantiated.

Creators of the 1987 law undoubtedly set out to change the three factors, but what resulted after a variety of compromises was, in many respects, an ineffective hybrid. Consider the question of indices and assignments. The law stressed that "the enterprise works out and confirms its own plan" in accord with control figures (state plan), state orders, long-term normatives and ceilings, and consumers' orders. Control figures were not supposed to serve either as mandatory targets nor as criteria of performance. But as Leonid I. Abalkin pointed out in an interview in *Izvestia* (March 1, 1988), traditional volume indicators continued to appear in the control figures and thus continued to orient the ministries toward fulfillment of physical targets. Further, ministries continued to bear responsibility for goods included in product lists. This role pushed them to increase state orders and set arbitrary quotas for enterprises. State orders, which by law were declared obligatory for the state enterprises, were supposed to concern only top-priority products; in practice, they were extended to all types of output and involved virtually the entire production of certain enterprises. In short, their use became a way of resuscitating the old system of central administrative planning. The same law gave the state enterprises the right to draw up their own plans, and the managers of enterprises, in accord with their labor collectives, tended to set targets below those of control figures. By understating their plans, managers created room for maneuver, accumulated inventories to offset unstable supplies and irregular deliveries, and shunned production of what they considered insufficiently profitable goods. This practice allowed them not only to avoid fines imposed for failure to deliver required outputs—fines that might outweigh the addition to profits—but to meet the plan 100 percent and get bonuses for achievement.

The new system has not curbed the widespread shortage of goods, undue accumulation of inventories, and low productivity. The contradictory mechanism put in place by the Law on the State Enterprise, of ministries pushing for quantity outputs and enterprise managers planning below potential, left the way open for negotiation between the higher-level agency and dependents, not only on range and volume of goods but also on prices. Well-known pro-Gorbachev personalities like Tat'iana Zaslavskaia, Leonid Abalkin, and S. A. Sitarian indicated that the situation could be remedied by limiting or, better, by *discarding the system of state orders*, which introduced priorities in supplies, handicapped the drive toward wholesale trade, and circumscribed the independence of the enterprises. Not long ago Gorbachev, quoting Vasilii S. Nemchinov, expressed hope that replacement of the old system of assignments with state orders would avoid negative phenomena. But Nemchinov had suggested that the state orders be given on the basis of competition among enterprises. And how can one have competition among state firms that operate under the same titulary agency and, as is often the case, when the large firm accounts for all of outputs?

The adoption on June 4, 1990, of the "Law on Enterprises in the USSR" expanded significantly the rights of organization and operation of all types of enterprises—individual, family, cooperative, partnerships, and joint stock companies. But it did not affect the hierarchical system of organization, nor the *modus operandi* of the state-owned enterprises. Furthermore, the nature and scope of norms (of centrally established financial indicators or regulators) concerning all enterprises' profits (income), on which is predicated the issue of full economic accountability of any enterprise, is still not fully settled. According to the Law on the State Enterprise, a state enterprise can, with authorization of its higher agency, choose either one of two models of accountability: one based on profit, the other on gross revenue. In the first, the state enterprise settles its accounts with the budget, the higher-level agency, and its bank, out of profits. The remaining *residual profit* can be allocated by the enterprise, according to norms, to funds for production and incentives. The wage fund (or pay fund) is determined separately, according to a wage-based norm related to output. Together the residual profit and wage fund form the so-called economic accountability income of the state enterprise. In the second model, after subtraction of material outputs from receipts, settlements are made with the budget, the higher-level agency, and the bank. What remains is the enterprise's economic accountability income. The *wage fund is a residual* of this income after the enterprise has provided for development and other funds according to the norms. Income of personnel is thus dependent on financial results of the firm.

Most state enterprises have adopted the first model; the largest and most profitable state enterprises have adopted the second, which Gorbachev proclaimed to be the more progressive. The indicated use of norms in either model fuels controversy. In devising norms, the planners have to account for real constraints, ceilings on capital investments and construction, and decisions on basic proportions governing the distribution of financial resources. The norms, supposed to be uniform for all state enterprises and to increase progressively each year over the five-year plan, have had to be individualized (adjusted) for each state enterprise and since 1987 have changed haphazardly from year to year. Setting a fixed norm as a tax for everyone—notwithstanding enormous technical differences between the state enterprises—might have favored certain state enterprises and overburdened others. Adjustment might seem appropriate but turn out to be arbitrary, subject to arduous negotiation between higher-level agencies and dependent state enterprises. In either case the new "primarily economic methods of guiding the enterprises" have not yielded satisfactory results.

One must not forget that there might be no relation between profits and investments. The state firms earning little or no profit can receive government-subsidized investments or investment credits. No matter how excellent profitability might be, no state enterprise can exceed a certain rate of growth by relying on its resources (including credits to be repaid from its development funds). According to the 1987 law on state enterprises, "profit is the generalized index of the enterprise's economic activity." But managers of state firms are not profit maximizers because such profits are taxed away. Moreover, managers know that profits are a limited and often uncertain measure of success. Prices are fixed by negotiation with titulary agencies. Still, state enterprises might have to produce loss-making products. Further, if profits at the disposal of a state enterprise are insufficient for its needs, difficulties can be bridged by adjustment of norms, subsidies, or credits.

Up to the end of the 1980s the share of the state budget in the profits of state enterprises has declined, while that of enterprises has increased. As seen from table 9-2, the share of the state budget in total profits has declined from 62 percent in 1970 to 55 percent in 1987. The share was scheduled to fall to 49 percent in 1989, a fact that, according to then-minister of finance, Boris I. Gostev, compounded state difficulties in a period of budget deficits. In his report to the Supreme Soviet Gostev observed with regret that old times were gone, and now "there can be no return to the methods by which enterprises monies were arbitrarily taken away" (*Izvestia,* October 28, 1988). As of the end of the 1980s, the two budgetary sources from profits were the tax on profits ("deductions from profits") and charges for the use of assets, each accounting for a quarter of the total. On the side of the enterprise's use of profits, besides funds for economic stimulation (bonuses), funds were to be allocated for production, "social development" (construction and maintenance), and repairs. In projects submitted to the Supreme Soviet, deductions from profits would change, and old categories (including charges on assets established with fanfare

TABLE 9-2. The Uses of Profits, Selected Years, in
Percentages

	1970	1980	1985	1987
Payments into the budget	62	60	58	55
Charge on fixed assets and				
working capital	17	24	26	25
Fixed payments (rentals)	5	1	5	—
Payments from residual profits	35	33	20	2
Deductions from profits	4	1	6	27
Left at the disposal of enterprises	38	40	42	45
For capital investments	14	4	5	1
For economic stimulation	14	17	15	21
For increasing working capital				
and financing plan losses	4	3	2	2
For other purposes	6	16	20	21

Source: Goskomstat SSSR, *Promyshlenost' SSSR (Soviet Industry)* (Moscow:
Finansy i statistika, 1988), 35.

by the reforms of 1965) would be replaced by a two-part levy; a flat tax of 35
percent of profit would be earmarked for the state budget, and a second part,
"not to exceed" 25 percent of the total, would be for republic budgets. The share
of the enterprises would thus fall to 40 percent.

The last factor, which, according to Zaslavskaia and Efimov, was responsible for many of the past negative phenomena—namely, multilevel management and managerial procedures limiting independence of enterprises—
continued to yield ambiguous results after adoption of the 1987 law on the
state enterprises. Restructuring was supposed to involve an ever broader use
of economic contracts between enterprises and associations. But as Alexei
Melentiev, editor of *Kommunist*, pointed out in *Economic Strategy of the
CPSU*, a study published in 1988 by the Soviet Academy of Sciences, such
contracts are not *direct* arrangements. They are entered into in conformity
with duties and rights created by economic planning. Contracting parties are
identified during the drawing up of plans by enterprises (preliminary planning
contracts). Contracts are signed and fulfilled within arrangements established
in the state plan. Supply and pricing are determined by higher-level agencies.
In a valuable 1987 study, *The Soviet Economic System: A Legal Analysis*,
Olimpiad S. Ioffe and Peter B. Maggs make a telling distinction between
execution and performance of contracts in market-directed economies and the
Soviet economy. In the former case, while contracts are regulated by legal
provisions, they result from economic inducements. In the Soviet case economic inducements are not sufficient; legal provisions are accompanied by

administrative coercion, which plays the critical role. The complex of these measures, called "economic discipline," involves three elements: *planning* discipline, *contractual* discipline, and *financial* discipline. Planning discipline concerns compliance with constraints established by the state plan and fulfillment of obligations toward the titulary agency specified by the plan drawn by the state enterprise. Contractual discipline refers to execution of contracts, that is, to nonperformance or improper performance, and to obligations of contractors toward their appropriate state agency. Financial discipline refers both to audits to ascertain state assets, as well as inspections and sanctions concerning conformity with norms, allocation of profits (income), and obligations toward the state budget and banks. In all cases, duties are imposed on signatories of contracts not in mutual relations but in relation to different supervisory agencies.

Ever broader use of economic levers stressed by the policy of restructuring and replacement of commands and assignments with norms, ceilings (on resources), and state orders has not eliminated one of the most frustrating features of the old system—namely, squabbling among agencies, ministries, and dependents concerning the volume, structure, and quality of output. It has only changed the *scope* of bargaining toward questions involving norms, prices, credits, and other financial issues. Paradoxically, while higher concentration of production was supposed to both simplify and strengthen top management—ministries and ministerial agencies—it may have strengthened managers of large establishments and associations in negotiation with higher-level agencies.

The Second Economy

The so-called second economy is comprised of legal, semi-legal, and illegal private sectors. Besides the expanding sphere of individual, family, and cooperative enterprises, of partnerships and possibly of joint-stock companies, the legal private sector includes personal subsidiary farms and joint enterprises with foreign participation. Legal foundations of individual and cooperative enterprises have been established by the Law on Individual Enterprise (of November, 1986), the Law on Cooperatives (of March, 1988), and the Decree on Leasing (April, 1988). Further legal dispositions on the formation, registration, and operation of all types of enterprises have been added by the Law on the Enterprises of the USSR of June 4, 1990.

According to the November 1986 law, individual and family enterprises were supposed to be formed by citizens "who have free time from their basic work"—housewives, disabled persons, pensioners, and students. These enterprises were supposed to engage in handicrafts and small-scale manufacturing production (clothing, footwear, furniture, and pottery) as well as in a variety of services concerning construction, households, and repair work.

According to the 1988 Law on Cooperatives, such enterprises, formed by three or more private entrepreneurs chartered to enter business or "spun off" by managers of state-owned enterprises—who convert some of these enterprises, departments, or sections—could be of two kinds: producer cooperatives, manufacturing and selling a product or technical service, and consumer services cooperatives such as restaurants, repair shops, and retail stores. Both individual and cooperative enterprises were forbidden to engage in certain activities also prohibited in market-directed economies (activities competing with state monopolies, notably, manufacturing and marketing of alcohol, narcotics, as well as the organization of lotteries and gambling). Other prohibitions reflected views of leaders of the Soviet system about activities they considered "ideologically, socially and morally dangerous," including the organization of schools, the publishing of books, communication equipment, and the buying and selling of precious metals and stones. A peculiarly ill-defined area was the latitude granted private professional services with regard to medical assistance, the work of engineers, agronomists, and designers. Activities prohibited for cooperatives could be exercised, however, if carried out on the basis of linkage with a state enterprise. While the law of June 4, 1990, expanded the rights of the private firms in regard to size and output diversification, it did not cancel the basic dispositions of the preceding laws of 1986 and 1988.

Already in 1989, in a speech delivered before the Supreme Soviet in the name of the Soviet government, Leonid Abalkin stated that the development of private firms expressed the government's wish to go beyond the "general statification of the economy," which had served as the "foundation of the administrative-command system," that the government intended to create "equal conditions of competing existence" among state, local (communal), cooperative, and individual management, and that the government's encouragement of these changes was "not a maneuver," "not a subterfuge," but an important element in renewal of the economic system (*Ekonomicheskiaia gazeta*, October, 1989). In the government's view, "cooperatives make the first serious step toward the formation of the socialist market of which we talk so much and accomplish little." Abalkin's assertion of neither maneuver nor subterfuge bolstered the confidence of private entrepreneurs and checked the bureaucrats' propensity to set roadblocks to formation of private firms. Not all private entrepreneurs who recall or have been told about disbanding industrial cooperatives in the 1950s may feel confident, however, that the government's view about private enterprise has fully changed. The Central Union of Consumer Societies (*Tsentrosoiuz*) has continued to exist but under state control, and new consumer cooperatives can now be constituted but not without difficulties, under either the executive committees of the local Soviets or the old system of *Tsentrosoiuz*.

While enterprises of the second economy are supposed to operate on equal footing with those of the first, the situation is, of course, far from equal. Enterprises of the second economy face numerous hurdles. They must operate under discretionary supervision of the hierarchy of Soviets who can withhold authorization, impose licensing charges, provide or deny raw and other materials, tools, and property, and vary their tax bill. Moreover, as a contributor to a 1989 study, *Cooperatives of the New Type* (*Kooperativy novogo tipa*, edited by A. G. Pevzner) puts it, Communist bureaucrats tend to "look down on cooperatives like the feudal lords looked down on trade, as being below their dignity."

Private ownership of buildings and expensive tools is permitted but rare. The practice of individual or cooperative enterprises is to lease fixed assets. Creation of a lease obligation is crucial to a cooperative. Since adoption of the Decree on Leasing, land and natural resources, as well as any property of state, agricultural cooperatives, or other social enterprises and organizations, are leasable. A state enterprise can now lease all or part of its structural units or working capital, as well as other material or financial resources. Properties of offices and departments, districts, and social organizations are defined as leasable. At the beginning of the 1988 leasing policy, the idea was to place in the hands of private entrepreneurs the small, "sick," unprofitable enterprises, particularly those engaged in production of consumer goods and services. Since 1989 the concept has been enlarged to encompass unprofitable and profitable enterprises, for, as P. Bunich, a deputy of the Supreme Soviet, put it, leasing should take "a mass character" because it is "the most powerful means for increasing efficiency" (*Ekonomicheskaia gazeta*, May, 1989).

Unfortunately, the system is not as attractive as some Soviet leaders assume. Leases are still not true-term obligations; the lessee operates at the day-to-day pleasure of the lessor, while maximum duration of leases and the scope of rules in republics is left in the dark. There are no effective mechanisms for updating and modernizing leased enterprises, and lessees have little incentive to reinvest to fuel the growth of the enterprise, even though buildings or additions made by the lessee legally remain his or her property. Private enterprises face crucial difficulties in regard to raw materials, equipment, and parts, given shortages besetting the economy. Only cooperatives associated in one form or another with a state enterprise have fewer problems in this regard, though they might have to pay many times over the mandated price at which state-owned enterprises obtain supplies. Either the individual or cooperative enterprises have to get materials in ways that are not exactly legal. Acquisition of surplus and unused assets and nonquota waste products from state-owned enterprises raises difficulties. Finally, cooperatives cannot legally obtain imported goods of a high technological level. Individual or cooperative enterprises are not really outside planning. When making plans, they must take account of the state's long-term norms concerning levels of prices of production, rates of interest, rates of taxation, and other indicators. While they are independent—unless directly tied to a state-owned enterprise—and while they plan their production and financing, they function in a planned economy that affects them through innumerable channels.

Credits to finance growth in fixed assets, working capital, and inventories are hard to come by, due to state priorities that take precedence. Equity investment is not available except as accumulation of associates of the cooperative. The effectiveness and ability of the banking system to cope with these problems is uncertain. Cooperative banks are as yet few, and annual interest rates are of course far higher than those of state banks. Cooperatives pay all kinds of taxes and/or proxy taxes; they pay a virtual tax in the form of a markup on state materials and a graduated value-added tax that in some cases borders on confiscatory levels, and members pay a tax on earnings. Value-added tax rates and the tax rates on income can and do force cooperatives to lower output.

The principal customer of most privately owned firms is the state-owned wholesale distribution system. For these sales, prices are not higher than those charged by state-owned enterprises. The price structure is different for consumer goods and services in restaurants, photo labs, repair shops, and other such establishments, given the high price of inputs. These prices, as well as the appearance of all kinds of speculators, increase public hostility toward the private firms, whose owners are often branded as "thieves, profiteers and speculators." In this atmosphere of hostility and fear, racketeers feel free to prey on private business, knowing that often the police will look the other way.

Notwithstanding all these handicaps, the number of individual and cooperative enterprises has been rapidly increasing, if at rates lower than expected when laws were adopted. As of early 1989, the number of people engaged in individual enterprises was 750,000. Personnel of cooperatives amounted to close to three million, of which one million also held other jobs. It is interesting to consider these figures in relation to what Nikolai Shmelev called a pressing problem, how to release and absorb "existing but hidden surplus manpower," which, according to some estimates, is as high as a quarter of the work force, not to speak of pensioners, unemployed housewives, and students, all of whom were supposed to engage in individual and cooperative enterprises (*Novyi mir*, 1988). The growth of cooperatives in output of goods and services is projected to increase from less than 2 percent in 1989 to as much as 25 percent by the end of the century.

Whatever the possible growth of private business, it already affects state-owned enterprises, and this effect is bound to grow. Big industrial cooperatives spun off by state-owned industries—which might employ as many as two thousand workers—set telling examples in regard to productivity, salary scales, incentives, and worker morale. While in many state-owned enterprises wages have degenerated into a sort of socialist rent, cooperatives set new standards. Further, private business might help state enterprises fulfill obligations concerning production of consumer goods and, when needed, provide them on short order with technical and engineering design, nonstandard equipment and instruments, and reconditioning and improvement of existing equipment. However, symbiotic existence between a cooperative and a state-owned enterprise might also have negative results for both establishments. The state-owned enterprises could use affiliated cooperatives as channels to and from black markets. In turn, affiliated cooperatives might fall under arbitrary control of patron enterprises and lose independence and economic purpose.

Prospective Reform

Economic debates and systemic reforms (those that took place as well as those that were aborted) in Eastern European countries from the 1950s to 1980s have exercised an important and often ignored influence on planning in the Soviet Union. In two remarkable articles in *Acta Oeconomica* in 1982 and 1984, the Hungarian economist Laszlo Szamuely classified the reforms debated in Hungary and Eastern Europe, excluding Yugoslavia, into two groups or "waves." The first wave took place in the late 1950s and early 1960s. First attempts at desocialization of land and decollectivization in Hungary were crushed by Soviet military intervention. The object of the economic debates and reforms of the late 1950s—notably, in Poland and Hungary—was not to change socialist economy, but to improve planning. While during the debates some economists questioned the centralist administrative system of mandatory instructions from the center to enterprises, there was a consensus "against any attempt whatsoever of giving up the advantages given by the possibility of central planning"—to use a conclusion reached at the time by the Polish economist Wlodzimierz Brus (*Zycie gospodarcze,* 1957). Reformers concerned themselves with the "rational" organization of *channels of management* from the top to the bottom of the economy and *linkages* between physical and value terms of plans and between instructions and indicators of performance and incentives. In regard to management rationalization and coordination, reforms led to vast amalgamations of state enterprises and liquidation of private, small-scale enterprises to reduce the tasks of central control. In regard to plan formulation and implementation, debate and reform focused on determining rational prices and issues related to the reduction of instructions, allocation of investment, integration of physical and value balances, and democratization of the entire system by creation of workers' councils (representing personnel and controlling executives). In the early 1960s the hopes and illusions attached to mathematical methods to achieve better planning and better system coordination attained their highest level. The economic literature gave increased prominence to mathematical modeling and cybernetics studies searching to devise optimal plans and efficient, automated servomechanisms.

However, as results with respect to efficiency, growth, technological change, and standard of living continued to be disappointing all over Eastern Europe, a second wave of debate and reform attempts developed in Czechoslovakia and Hungary. This time attention shifted from improvement of the mechanism toward a new economic management system. In the search for and definition of new management, Czechoslovak and Hungarian economists made valuable analyses and evaluations of the old system and interesting suggestions. The Czechoslovak attempt at reform was cut short by the intervention of Soviet troops. Hungarian reforms, fashioned cautiously and modestly by policymakers and economists, took hold.

Hungary's reforms changed management of the economy from *directive* planning to an *indirect* regulatory economic management system, that is, to a system without central prescription regarding volume and output. The center in this system was to decide on division of income into consumption and investment, allocation of investment, and direction of the economy. In Marxian parlance, the center would decide "expanded reproduction" (growth) and relegate to enterprises the task of "simple reproduction" (maintenance of outputs at the same level). Without changing the system and without contemplating an increase in private initiative, the center would control financial regulations concerning taxation, prices, wages, credits, and foreign exchange through norms. Prices were liberalized, trade was encouraged between enterprises in materials and products, and obstacles to cooperatives were removed. But reform did not dismantle the hierarchical relations between the center, manipulator of economic levers, and enterprises and did not bring about self-regulatory market relations except in a marginal way. The old single channel of dependence of state-owned enterprises was replaced by dependence on several control agencies. The new system reflected a new illusion, that everything will work if, instead of prescription, the center would, as Laszlo Antal put it, "feed the still rather detailed and uncertainly formulated (although less rigid) expectations into the enterprise price and profit conditions, the subsidy and credit terms, wage regulations, assuming that these goals can be achieved more efficiently if, instead of prescribing them, they are made into the interest of the enterprise" (*Acta Oeconomica*, 1982). Under changes brought by the late 1960s reforms, Hungarian enterprises started to calculate prices, credits, interest rates, and exchange rates but within a manipulatory system of dependence between state administrators and managers. Instead of a market-regulated economy, Hungary produced a peculiar coordinating mechanism with, as Tamas Bauer once remarked, "mutual courtesy and permanent bargaining over rules and exceptions." The highly monopolized nature of the domestic market and state protection of producers and administrators, the protectionist seclusion of the market, increased wastefulness, and inefficiency and squandering of resources pushed the country further toward stagnation, technological retardation, alienation, and erosion of work morale.

The various East European debates and waves of reform had a profound but *delayed* effect on the Soviet system. Essentially, the first wave hit the USSR in the mid-1960s. The so-called Kosygin reform focused on improving central planning via the administrative rationalization of prices and use of sales instead of gross outputs and profit and profitability as indices for evaluating enterprises. But all this had to coexist with "the obligatory condition" of fulfillment by enterprises of "planned contractual deliveries in *physical* form with respect to quantity, quality and assortment," as the well-known Soviet economist, Evsey G. Liberman, put it in *Economic Methods and the Effectiveness of Production* (1971). Ultimately, the middle to late 1960s Soviet reforms, referred to as the "New System of Planning and Economic Incentives," brought a massive administrative price overhaul, emphasized "substantiation" of draft plans and increased responsibility of suppliers for products, restructured budgetary profit deductions (with charges of enterprises for use of state assets), and proposed better accounting at all levels. As in Eastern Europe, the period was marked by great illusions about mathematical modeling and cybernetics for straightening both management and planning. "Planometrics," or, as someone facetiously put it, "computopia," was at hand. Many Soviet economists, partisans of an "optimally functioning system" and "optimal planning," associated with the Scientific Council for Optimal Planning and Management and the Central Mathematical Institute (both part of the Academy of Sciences), contributed studies and essays now forgotten. The results were disappointing, and, eventually, "cardinal" principles of the reform were circumvented.

The second wave of reforms in Eastern Europe in the middle to late 1960s, entirely spent there by the beginning of the 1980s, hit the USSR in the mid-1980s, and many of its tenets were incorporated in Gorbachev's perestroika. As previously noted, Gorbachev also proclaimed the end of the system of detailed central injunctions on inputs, outputs, and performance of enterprises. He emphasized central decisions on "enlarged reproduction"— volume and allocation of investable resources—while leaving "simple reproduction" to the republic and local enterprises. He decided to replace injunctions with norms in regard to profits, prices, and credits and affirmed that the "autonomy" of the state-owned enterprises was necessary but only within the same old hierarchical setup. He aimed at increasing "democratization" by placing the authority of the manager on the somewhat shaky basis of the authority of each state-owned enterprise's Workers' Council. He encouraged private business as a market adjunct to the central system. To gauge the prospects of the perestroika, it is obviously important to understand why the second wave of reform yielded only disappointing results in the country where it was first applied, namely, Hungary. Put differently, Hungary's experiences will likely shed light in regard to both the limits and results of such reform and, thus, on prospective changes in the USSR.

Many factors explain the ups and downs of the Hungarian economy at this or that moment, from the timing, extent, and consequences of its indebtedness in the 1970s to the errors and miscalculations of its leadership. But one has to look to deeper causes to understand how that economy was run to a halt. The objectives of reform of the late 1960s were never reached. As Marton Tardos pointed out in a perceptive study published in *Acta Oeconomica* (1982), adjustments and readjustments of regulatory instruments (norms) failed to allow development of the enterprise autonomy; democratization via Workers' Councils asserting authority in regard to the enterprise's executives failed to materialize; expansion of commercial channels did not supersede material allocations through compulsory channels; prices failed to reflect supply and demand; and a closer connection between production and foreign trade failed. From the early 1980s it became evident—at least to a number of economists—that the hybrid system of central decision plus "uniform," indirect (often ad hoc) regulations could not regulate markets. Hungarian economists such as Marton Tardos and Tamas Bauer stressed the need to liberate enterprises from tutelage; break up large enterprises and eliminate monopoly positions; develop free trade among all enterprises, including state-owned ones; let supply and demand determine prices; eliminate subsidies and budget levies; separate central banking from commercial banking; enlarge the second economy; expand contracts with foreign markets, and divest the center from "ownership attributes" in one manner or another (creating holding companies), even if privatization did not seem expedient (or politically or socially acceptable).

The third wave of reforms foreshadows many directions in which the USSR will have to move if it is to yield more acceptable economic results. The main problems still concern the scope of central authority with respect to planning basic proportions of the economy, the sectoral interrelations and the allocation of investments, and the maintenance of the authority of tutelary organs over the state-owned firms. They concern the role of the budget and banks in regard to investment and money and the income level among profit-making and loss-making state enterprises. They posit the need to overhaul the tax system, discard the absurd bifurcation of money, liberate commercial banking from the state bank's tutelage, and build an interbank monetary market. They demand dismantling the central supply system and liberalizing prices. They require a vast expansion of access to foreign markets of all Soviet firms and expanded influence of the foreign markets on domestic production. Whatever the personal fortunes of Gorbachev, perestroika is necessarily a way station on the road to further structural economic transformation.

Concluding Comments

United States industry is still viewed as the preferred model, even though many American manufacturing branches face a strong and at times severe challenge in international markets. A comparison of industrial bases of the United States and the USSR shows interesting similarities as well as deep and perhaps unbridgeable differences. According to *A Comparison of the U.S. and Soviet Industrial Bases*, released in May, 1989, by the U.S. Directorate of Intelligence, the Soviet industrial labor force is twice as large as that of the United States. During the period 1971–86 the Soviet industrial labor force increased by 6.6 million, that is, by one-fifth. The United States relies on labor-saving technologies, while the USSR's industrial enterprises employ low-skilled manual workers. In terms of output per worker, the Soviets reach about half of the U.S. level. The stock of productive capital is huge in both countries, but the USSR has obsolete, backward plants and equipment. Soviet industry remains behind the United States in manufacturing technologies and lags in the use of computers and microelectronics. The Soviet leaders' hope of completely retooling the economy on the basis of domestic production and of massive imports of machinery and machine tools is not attainable. Several years of Gorbachev's program have yielded little progress. Efforts to raise the technology and quality of Soviet industrial products have not been successful. Even if the rapid retirement rates of equipment envisaged by Soviet leaders are carried out, the country will have aged equipment. Although the Soviet Union holds the lead in output of many industrial commodities, its goods are below standards prevailing in Western markets—a fact that has prevented Soviet goods from gaining appreciable share in these markets. While manufacturing products make up more than three-fourths of U.S. exports, only about a third of the USSR's sales abroad are manufactured goods.

Restructuring and retooling Soviet industry, while reshaping the economic framework—changing the scope and power of central authority, curtailing central agencies, combining state ownership with a vast range of private activities, injecting market relations, and enlarging the second economy—require prolonged efforts. Unifying conditions in the first and second economies in regard to access to inputs and production and breaking monopolies of state-owned firms in the prevailing condition of general shortages and suppressed inflation might require more time, adroitness, and maneuvering than the present leadership can muster.

CHAPTER 10

Agroindustry

Farming Organization and the Food Problem

Soviet leaders have assumed for a long time that they could radically alter the geophysical and socioeconomic characteristics of the countryside. They would dominate nature, scientifically harness the country's notoriously poor soil, unreliable rainfall, and unpredictable, short growing season. They would eradicate the peasantry "as a class," smooth out the differences between town and country, and integrate the farms into vast expanses of mechanized state holdings operating as grain and meat factories in the fields. In terms of power, the Soviet regime was established in the name of the urban industrial proletariat. While Soviet policymakers asserted that the peasants were the workers' "allies," they never ceased to look upon these allies as treacherous and undependable. Marxian theoreticians have looked down on the peasantry, deemed by them a backward and anachronistic leftover of social change—an individualistic, greedy, grubby, religious product of what Marx had called the "idiocy of rural life."

The Bolsheviks first allowed the "forms of land-use to be totally free" ("Law on Land," October 26, 1917), then tried to take back this freedom (Decree of the All-Russian Central Executive Committee, "On the Socialization of Land," February 19, 1918). Under so-called War Communism (1918–21), they confiscated whatever the peasants eked out of their land. When the "leap into communism" led to generalized famine, the New Economic Policy (1921–28) ended the outright confiscation of harvests and replaced it with the famous tax in kind (*prodnalog*). Agricultural output took off and the peasantry prospered, but, by the end of the 1920s, Stalin returned to the idea of regimenting not only the countryside but the cities as well. As the compendium, *Agriculture of the USSR* (1988), indicates, the collectivization of the peasantry increased from 3.9 percent in 1929 to 96.9 percent in 1940. The far-off isolated remnants of individual peasantry disappeared from Soviet statistics by 1970.

Because industrialization and urbanization demanded an increasing amount of agricultural produce for the expanding towns, and because adequate increments in agricultural output could not be secured either from state-

189

owned farms or through sufficient investments, the agricultural setup had to be adjusted to allow the largest possible increase in the *marketed* share of agricultural produce, notably, of grains, even if output remained stationary or was decreasing. This paradoxical result was secured by putting agriculture into a different mold from that suggested by the basic communist blueprints. Private property was liquidated, but on its ruins were established not highly mechanized state farms, but *group*-owned collective farms, compelled to distribute their output to members only after deliveries to the state were met. From the early 1930s on, however, a small portion of the state land had to be allocated for the personal use of collective and state farmers. Thus, three sectors developed in the agrarian economy of the USSR: the sector of collective farms (*kolkhozy*), or cooperative sector; the sector of state farms (*sovkhozy*); and the sector of private plots, subsequently called "personal subsidiary farms" (*lichnoe podsobnoe khoziastvo*).

Soviet constitutions defined the cooperative ownership as a *variety* of socialist ownership. Traditionally, the collective farm cooperative ownership was described as superior to private ownership but inferior to state ownership, since, allegedly, the latter belonged to the whole people, while the collective farm ownership was vested in the juridical entity composed only of collective farmers. Eventually, the collective farms were supposed to grow into fully state-owned agricultural exploitations, while the private plots were supposed to lose all economic significance. Over time, many collective farms were consolidated, and some of them were indeed transformed into state farms. But the private plots, far from losing their importance, continued to play a decisive role in agricultural output and trade.

The process of amalgamating smaller collective farms and absorbing some of them into the state-farms sector started in the early 1940s. The 235,000 collective farms of 1940 were consolidated into less than one-fifth as many by 1960, just 44,000. The process continued unabated until the mid-1980s when the total number of collective farms fell to 26,200. Since then their total number has fluctuated within narrow margins. Concomitantly, the number of state farms grew from 4,200 in 1940 to 7,400 in 1960 and then to more than three times that number by the middle and late 1980s. Between 1970 and 1987 alone, the total farm land in the hands of the collective farms shrunk by 35.3 million acres (from 204.5 million to 169.2 million hectares), while state-farm land expanded by 57.0 million acres (from 307.5 million to 364.5 million hectares). From 1940 to the 1980s the number of collective farmers engaged in collective farm work fell from 29 million to 12.4 million and that of workers and employees on the state farms rose from 1.8 million to 12.6 million (see table 10-1).

Under Soviet law the collective farms do not own land: they have the right, however, to possess, use, and dispose of their property, which is com-

TABLE 10-1. Collective and State Farms, Selected Years, 1940, 1960–87

	1940	1960	1970	1980	1987
Collective farms[a] (thousands)	235.5	44.0	33.0	25.9	26.6
State farms (thousands)	4.2	7.4	15.0	21.1	23.3
Interbranch agricultural enterprises (thousands)	—	3.1	4.6	9.6	7.2
Collective farmers[b] (millions)	29.0	22.3	17.0	13.5	12.4
Employment in state farms (millions)	1.8	6.8	10.0	12.0	12.6
Employment in interfarm associations (millions)	—	—	0.0	0.5	0.4
Additional employment from other enterprises (millions)	0.1	0.5	0.6	1.3	1.4
Total employed in all the branches of agriculture (millions)	30.9	29.6	27.6	27.3	26.8

Source: Narodnoe khoziaistvo SSSR, for 1985, 179; and 1987, 251, 259.
[a] Excluding collective farm fisheries.
[b] Employed in collective work.

prised of enterprises, buildings, installations, livestock, and equipment. (The right to own equipment was granted to them in 1958.) This property can be used subject to legal dispositions and not to free decisions. The collective farm *household*—there were some 12.6 million households in the 1980s in the collective farms—is entitled to a personal plot of land and owns a dwelling house, farm buildings, livestock, and equipment for working the personal plot. At least one member of the household must contribute labor to the collective. The basic task of the collective farm is to produce and market agricultural produce. But the collectives are also encouraged to combine resources with other state and collective farms, or with other cooperative organizations, to form production associations. They are also invited to contract with various organizations in order to form units for the production of manufactured goods on the collective farm. Further, the collective farm can enter into various forms of work contracts—collective, family, individual, and other forms—whenever its needs so require.

According to regulations, the highest authority of the collective is the general assembly of its members. With the increase in the size of the collectives, however, the general assembly has been replaced by an assembly of elected delegates. The latter, in principle, elect the chairman and executive board of the collective; in practice, the state administration "recommends" the chairmen, dismisses or transfers them, and places whom it wishes in key administrative posts. Like the state enterprise, the collective farm drafts and confirms its own five-year and yearly plans. The key elements of such plans are the state orders embodying contracted deliveries of produce to the state at state procurement prices. Once these deliveries are fulfilled, the collective farm is free to fix its own prices for products sold through the collective farm markets, consumer cooperatives, or other organizations. The 1988 Model Charter specifies, just as for the state enterprise, the ways in which the collective farm can distribute its income. The charter defines as gross product the total yearly product at its sales price. Net product is derived after subtracting the cost of material inputs, current repairs, and depreciation allowances. Net income is then obtained after further deductions of labor payments, social security, and insurance. From the net income are paid out taxes and other contributions to the state, the remainder being allocated according to centrally defined norms to various funds of the farm, such as growth of assets, incentives, and reserves.

The state farm, the agricultural homologue of the industrial enterprise, has a status similar to that of the manufacturing enterprise. It is managed by a director appointed by the republican agricultural ministry. The director carries the full responsibility for performance and hires personnel except for a deputy and other main agricultural specialists, who are appointed by higher authorities but upon the director's recommendation. As in industrial enterprises, the director discharges tasks with the help of appropriate functional and operational departments. State farms engaged in the same type of production can be grouped into trusts acting under the authority of a ministerial administration. Each state farm is divided into a number of basic production units, such as tractor brigades and livestock brigades, as its particular specialty requires. The units in this sector correspond to the shops into which the industrial firm is organized. The leaders of the basic unit are assisted by mechanics and various other skilled workers, as well as by unskilled laborers, a number of whom are only seasonally employed. In accordance with state and regional planning directives and on the basis of its contracts with procurement, trade, and marketing organizations, the state farm establishes its preliminary targets for sales, costs, profits, and capital construction. The higher administrative organs modify and adjust only the indices concerning sales, wage fund, and profits for the farms on so-called full business accounting and set limits in the budget for financing working capital and capital construction. As in the case of the industrial enterprise, the state farm operates on the basis of full cost (including fixed costs), pays capital charges, and is authorized to retain various shares in profits for the material incentive funds, the sociocultural fund, insurance, and farm expansion. On the basis of these decisions, state farms draw up their own output financial plans, which need no further approval by higher authorities.

The three agricultural sectors are very unequal in size. According to the official statistical data released in 1988, the collective farms controlled less than 23 percent of the land used in agriculture and about 31 percent of total farmland. In contrast, state farms and other state agricultural producing enterprises controlled 76 percent of the total agricultural land and over 68 percent of the farmland. As for the personal auxiliary farms—of the collective farmers and workers and employees of the state farms, as well as those granted to urban dwellers—their claim amounted to less than 1 percent of the total land used in agriculture and less than 1.5 percent of farmland. For livestock, the situation was significantly different; the collective and state farms each accounted for about 40 percent of the head of cattle, the private sector for about 20 percent. State farms continue to exceed collective farms in the size and quality of their lands, the concentration of technology, levels of qualified personnel, and degree of specialization. State farms vary significantly between areas; grain-growing farms are found mostly in the Black-Earth and virgin lands, namely, in the steppe zones of the south and southeast, as well as in Siberia and Kazakhstan, which produce most of the marketable grain. The great cotton-raising farms are in Central Asia. Sheep breeding is concentrated in vast farms in the dry steppelands. Other state farms that engage in pedigree livestock and poultry and in variety crops are scattered in various parts of the country.

As Brezhnev's agricultural secretary, Gorbachev was one of the principal architects of the so-called Food Program for the 1980s, adopted in May 1982 by the Central Committee of the CPSU (*Pravda*, May 24, May 28, 1982). The program affirmed that "the food problem is, both economically and politically, the central problem of the current decade" and set as objectives an "accelerated, steady increase in grain production," the meeting of the country's growing requirements of high-quality food and feed grain, increases in yields "everywhere," increases in meat, vegetables, fruits, and processed foods, and expansion of the trade in foodstuffs. To carry out the program, policymakers decided to effect a changeover in the planning and management of the agro-industrial complex as a single whole at all levels and to proceed with a vast increase and reallocation of capital investments.

To what extent was the indicated changeover implemented? In which ways did the subsequent policy, perestroika, reassess the goals and the results of the 1982 policy? Have the old pressure methods of procurement of agricultural produce been abandoned? Which basic directions emerged in regard to the restructuring of the organization of agriculture on the threshold of the 1990s?

The Soviet definition of the agro-industrial complex (as determined by a decree of the Central Committee of the CPSU of November 14, 1985) comprises a material production sphere, including agriculture and forestry, state procurement, food- and fiber-processing industries, trade and public catering, repair of agricultural machinery, construction, and nonmaterial services—supporting branches, including supply, transportation, scientific services, training, and managerial personnel. As of 1987, the material sphere employed 39 million people, the nonmaterial sphere, 3.2 million. This enormous complex accounted, then, for not less than one-third of the country's gross value of output, one-third of its work force, and one-third of its fixed assets. The organization of an agro-industrial complex might have been seen as very useful from the standpoints of planning and production organization. From the standpoint of planning, it might indeed be helpful to ascertain the basic demand and supply interdependencies as well as the effect of certain investment allocations. One can view the agro-industrial complex as depending on the industrial complex (that is, the rest of all industry) largely for investment needs (notably, tractors and other kinds of agricultural machinery and machinery for food and fiber processing, as well as for chemicals, oil, and medicinal preparations for livestock). On the other hand, the agroindustry's output is directed essentially toward consumption needs. From a planning standpoint it might be useful to ascertain what increases in the gross material output of the industrial complex (brought about by increases in investment) would increase the deliveries of the agro-industrial complex to consumer demand by, say, an x amount. This and other divisions of the economy's matrix can, of course, disclose many other important structural interdependencies.

The organization of the agroindustrial complex at all levels was motivated, however, by objectives other than the ascertaining of such interdependencies. The main objectives were the application by the farms of a more uniform pattern of norms (concerning the allocation of income), reorganization of the financial conditions and supervision of all financial activities of all types of farms and other rural enterprises, coordination of the ministries in charge with the supply of agricultural machinery and equipment, and, last but not least, the desire to stimulate production and marketing of agricultural products. A resolution of the Central Committee of the CPSU of November 23, 1985, created a Union-republic USSR State Agro-industrial Committee (*Gosagroprom*), subsequently condemned as inefficient and scheduled to be replaced by yet another centrally organized superagency, namely, a State Commission for Agricultural Purchase and Food. In the meantime, the November 23 resolution, complemented by a supporting resolution of March 29, 1988, shifted the responsibility for agricultural output onto the Union-republic ministries and their republic, territory, province, and district agro-industrial committees, while, as usual, retaining at the center the task of "planning for the agro-industrial complex as a whole."

In trying to carry out the objectives of the Food Program, Gorbachev first concentrated the ministerial setup and then shifted a share of investments away from the farms toward expansion of various industries in charge of the supply of capital goods and other resources to the agro-industrial complex, and toward sorely needed repairs and improvements in the complex's infrastructure. To visualize what all these measures implied, it might be interesting to note that the supply of producer goods to the complex involved no less than five ministries (Tractors and Farm Machinery, Animal Husbandry and Feed Production Machinery, Machinery for Light and Food Industries, Mineral Fertilizer Production, and Microbiological Industry). These ministries were supposed to coordinate their own activities in the Gosagroprom with those of other ministries (Grain Products, Land Reclamation and Water Resources, and Fish Industry) and with other committees or chairmen of committees (for Planning, Forestry Science and Technology, Material-Technical Supply, Gosbank, Central Statistical Administration, and many more, not least the Ministry of Finance). All these administrative changes, however, did not increase either output or the supply to the consumer. To increase output and, above all, state purchases, the Central Committee of the CPSU authorized markups of 50 percent above the established procurement prices for produce sold to the state through 1990 over the average levels of deliveries reached in previous years (*Pravda,* March 29, 1986). But as these prices were not always competitive with the market prices, deliveries to the state did not increase. The state continued to heavily subsidize staples (milk, meat, and bread), keeping their prices low in relation to those of other products planned that were deliberately high. This measure continued to increase the unsatisfied demand for "cheap" goods and, thus, further frustrate the consumer.

By March 15, 1989, Gorbachev had to concede (in his Report to the Plenary Session of the CPSU Central Committee) the complete failure of the Food Program, which, as noted, had been described in 1982 as "the central problem of the current decade." In the report Gorbachev stated, "the reality is this: we do not produce enough agricultural output. The state is forced to make large purchases abroad of grains, meat, fruit, vegetables, sugar, vegetable oil, and other products. We continue to trail behind developed countries—large and small—in labor productivity, in crop yields from fields, in livestock productivity and in the variety and quality of foodstuffs. The gap is not getting smaller, it is growing . . . . Up to now, we have been unable to resolve the food question in a fundamental way" (*Pravda,* March 16, 1989). The Food Program had posited the need for an accelerated, steady increase in grain production and projected a level of grain production of 238–43 million tons during the Eleventh Five-Year Plan (1981–85) and of 250–55 million tons during the Twelfth Five-Year Plan (1986–90). Grain output had been on average on the order of 205 million tons between 1976 and 1980. In the following five years, instead of increasing, grain output fluctuated below the 200 million tons mark. It reached 211 million tons in 1987 and fell again to 198 million tons in 1988. (Incidentally, this drop did not deter Gorbachev from asserting [*Pravda,* March 24, 1988] that the grain harvest must increase in the Thirteenth quinquennium to "260 to 280 million tons," which only shows how "realistic" such plans actually are.) Concomitantly, the potato crop was the smallest in over a third of a century, and the production of vegetables and fruits remained stationary. Except for hogs, stocks of cattle, sheep, and goats continued to slide until they were down to their 1983 levels. All indicators concerning labor productivity and the fields' fertility were decreasing in most regions. In addition, as Gorbachev observed in his March 15, 1989, report, "mismanagement carried off up to 20 percent of everything produced in the countryside—and for some products the figure is as high as 30 to 40 percent." To cope with this catastrophic situation Gorbachev had to formulate a broader and more complex approach to agriculture, in general, and the food problem, in particular.

Keys to the Food Problem

Gorbachev's strategy in regard to the food problem has grown in a number of directions since he became the party secretary in charge of agriculture. For the 1990s this strategy concerns a complex set of issues, from the interaction of the forms of ownership in this sector to the restructuring of the collective and state farms, labor organization and rewards, relations of the farms with the state planning and management hierarchy, and the scope of investment allocations to agricultural production and to the countryside in general.

Since the end of the 1980s Gorbachev has had to reject both theoretical and practical implications of the traditional Soviet division of the forms of ownership into "higher" and "lower." In practice, the division has meant a privileged status for state ownership (the highest form) and an underprivileged status for the peasant auxiliary economy (the lowest form). Gorbachev has started to assert "the equality of different forms of socialist ownership of the means of production and methods of economic management based on them" (*Pravda,* March 15, 1989). He has urged that the meaning of perestroika in the countryside "should consist in offering peasants broad opportunities for showing independence, enterprise and initiative"—an offer that goes against deeply ingrained antipeasant Soviet policies and bureaucratic habits. Though Gorbachev has not accepted the idea of land denationalization, he has suggested the need for changes in the ways the state exercises "the rights of the socialist owner." The basic thrust of his approach has been to encourage the development of a diversified network of inter- and intrafarm connections, erasing in time the dogmatic barriers between collective, state, and peasant farms. Interfarm organizations should mingle the different kind of farms into various forms of organizations, including agricultural combines, agricultural-manufacturing, agricultural-construction, and other agricultural-nonagricultural enterprises and workshops. He has also insisted on the need for "a new approach to family and individual peasant enterprise."

Inter- and intrafarm organization and management are also to be reshaped by a broad application of leasing, imaginatively combined, on the one hand, with various forms of cooperativization and, on the other, with the use of contracts with labor collectives. In a speech to the Fourth All-Union Congress of Collective Farmers (*Pravda*, March 24, 1988), Gorbachev illustrated with a few telling examples his vision of a restructured agriculture in which cooperatives and contractual arrangements would play an expanded role. For the purpose he quoted the case of a large state farm (of the Novosibirsk province) that created no less than thirty-three primary cooperatives for carrying out various production and service tasks. Each cooperative had three to five people engaged according to need in growing grain, feed production, and raising fur-bearing animals. The system freed a large number of workers who were transferred to other activities. In other cases, top priority was given to cooperatives encompassing the entire cycle, namely, production, processing, sale of products, technological service, and research. Referring to yet another case (in Chita province), he pointed to the association of a number of collective farms and a state farm with various kinds of industrial enterprises, a consumers' cooperative, and the Agro-industrial Bank and run by a council headed by a manager and operating through some three hundred primary labor collectives functioning on contractual arrangements and economic accountability principles. In another case he drew attention to the potential formation at a province level (in Tula) of a cooperative association grouping branch cooperative unions for the production, processing, and sale of various agricultural produce, and for the provision of housing and road services. Block by block, Gorbachev thus constructed at the farmers' congress his own grand design for transforming the organizational system in the countryside. In this grand conception, leasing, cooperativization, and contracting are ultimately to yield a "restructured agro-industrial complex conceived of as a single, multilevel cooperative, beginning with the family small-group, team, brigade, rental-contract and contract collective and running through the collective and state farms, as cooperatives of primary-level cooperatives, through the district association, agricultural firm or agricultural combine, and culminating in the province agro-industrial association."

Contracting with teams and work collectives in respect to crops or livestock has important implications for the reorganization of rural labor and for methods of remuneration. As Karl-Eugen Wädekin has recalled in an admirable study on Soviet agriculture (in a volume on *The Soviet Economy on the Brink of Reform*, edited in 1988 by Peter Wiles), the underlying objectives and principles of the formation and utilization of the so-called contract brigades and normless links, resurrected since the early 1980s, are the same as those that already prevailed under Stalin. It has always been the intent of Soviet policy to measure performance of a collective in terms of final product. While this measure is difficult to achieve in large-scale agriculture, it is possible up to a point at least to relate effort and final results for small groups and remunerate them accordingly. Stalin intended to make smaller collectives within the farm and relate performance and remuneration. For a number of reasons—particularly, the low level of rewards—such a connection proved ineffective. Eventually, after a number of wage reforms were carried out, the system was resurrected. Such an arrangement makes sense, according to Wädekin, if the contracts are negotiated and concluded on equal teams, the teams have a choice of inputs, they enjoy genuine autonomy in regard to decisions concerning work scheduling, and each group is kept sufficiently small for mutual social control. One can hardly assume that all these conditions could be met in most situations in Soviet agriculture. One can point out, moreover, that in agriculture, intrinsic as well as extrinsic factors play equally unpredictably for small groups' performances just as for the larger system. Be that as it may, according to official Soviet statistics, close to 500,000 contract brigades and independent teams, including contracts with family and individual workers, were in operation in the collective and state farms in the late 1980s and comprised some eleven million workers.

In theory, the reform's goal in regard to the relation of the collective and state farms with the central planning and management organs is the same as the one embodied in the Law on the State Enterprise concerning manufacturing establishments. The objective is to free the collective and state farms from mandatory task assignments from above and to let these farms achieve autonomy and economic accountability based on cost recovery and self-financing. The autonomy of the workers' teams requires the autonomy of the entire farm, and vice versa, otherwise the latter would only redistribute tasks assigned to it by its own supervisory agency. But abandoning the old and tried pressure methods of procurement is not as easy as it might seem. While Gorbachev himself had recognized that the new system of state orders (compulsory for those to whom they are addressed) was in fact resurrecting directive commands—or, as Gorbachev put it, "a hidden form of directive planning" (*Pravda,* July 30, 1988)—he could not redress the situation. Subsequently, he asserted that the system of state orders had to continue for a transitional period, a period "objectively" conditioned by such intractable factors as the bad state of the economy, its finances and monetary circulation, and, last but not least, the difficulties of formulating a satisfactory price reform (*Pravda,* March 16, 1989).

At the beginning of the implementation of the Food Program, it seemed that coordination and retooling in the industries supplying agriculture with machinery, equipment, and other products, and a shift in the state investments from agricultural production to the industries processing agricultural produce and to rural infrastructure, would rapidly increase agricultural output. In time, it became evident that the agro-industrial complex needed large investments for a vast number of purposes. Funds were needed not only to modernize the obsolete and decaying equipment of the processing industries and to stave off the terrible drains represented by losses during harvests, transportation, storage, and processing of output but also to mechanize certain agricultural branches—for example, vegetable, sugar beet, cotton, and flax growing, as well as livestock sections with up to 80 percent manual labor. They were needed, furthermore, for reorganizing the entire socioeconomic rural life, which was increasingly alienating the old as well as the younger populations of the countryside. Such reorganization required not only new funds for improving the social security and pension allowances of collective farmers but also huge outlays for providing modern utilities, schools, hospitals, and other services to long neglected, vast areas of the country. Clearly, such state investments are not available, and Gorbachev had to place his hope on the future development of better municipal managerial efforts and a larger scope of rural cooperatives' entrepreneurship.

All the indicated keys for the food problem appear thus in some respects inadequate and, in others, problematic and beyond available means. The official recognition of equality among collective, state, and personal auxiliary farms is probably welcomed in the villages but is as yet of limited import. The means at the disposal of these different categories of farms are vastly different. Much would have to be done in favor of the personal auxiliary farms in order to significantly increase their potential. Certain measures, like the leasing of livestock, for instance, could turn out to be either inapplicable or ineffective. The brilliant dissident writer Vladimir Bukovsky remarked derisively in an interview published in 1988 (in *Can the Soviet System Survive Reform?* edited by G. R. Urban), "What fascinates me is the reformers' almost cynical determination to stick to the framework and language of Marxism . . . . The *muzhik* is being encouraged to rent cattle. *Rent* cattle! The peasant family is given the option of renting a cow. Why this particular reform? Because renting a cow is not ownership; the peasant can exercise some of the ownership functions of having a cow—he can milk her and sell her product, but cannot own her." In fairness, it should be added that the new Law on Ownership allows the lessee to acquire leased property—including Bukovsky's cow, though this may not be the case in all circumstances. In any case, private acquisition of land is still not encouraged.

The development of a vast, all-embracing movement of cooperativization of the farms—the crucial concept of Gorbachev in regard to agroindustrial restructuring—is far from acquiring the dimensions envisaged by the architects of perestroika. Not only is rural entrepreneurship far from ready for the great onrush, but, moreover, deep resistance among rural party bureaucrats and the farms' specialists and scientists, who would lose their jobs, hampers any grand transformations. Mikhail Gorbachev condescendingly admonished the bureaucrats to "restructure their psychology" and not to forget that the time when the district party committee issued orders on what to plant, what to cultivate, and when reaping should begin "has gone, never to return." And he told the specialists that they better "overcome their arrogance, and some of them their laziness" and understand that there is no reason "to be ashamed of real labor for the glory of the fatherland" (*Pravda*, May 15, 1988). All this is well and good, but it does not either generate entrepreneurship or overcome resistance. In fact, as a chairman of a remote provincial agro-industrial association (of the Slavgorod district in the Altai territory), G. A. Bekker, told Gorbachev a few months later, everybody knows that the system of state orders, confirmed by the USSR Council of Ministers, means that "the state order is transmitted to the territory, and the territory transmits it to the agro-industrial committees, firms, and associations, and all that's left for the farms is to 'stand at attention' and carry out the directives from above" (*Pravda*, January 15, 1989). So much for the principle of autonomy of farms and the brigades at their order. While the architects of perestroika have been able to draw imaginative projects, they have not been as successful either in finding the means for carrying them out or in bridging the gaps between projects and realities on the ground, gaps that have affected the Food Program from its inception.

Personal Subsidiary Farms

To understand the present limitations and the future prospects of the "personal subsidiary farms" (PSFs), one must evoke briefly the official attempts made during the period preceding the adoption of the Food Program, from the early 1960s to the late 1970s, to modernize the countryside and to stem an "uncontrolled emigration" from the villages. In a well-documented 1987 study on the "Persistence of the Peasant in Soviet Society," Theodore H. Friedgut of the Center for Soviet and East European Research of the Hebrew University of Jerusalem recalls how timetables were set at the end of the 1950s for the transfer over a period of twenty years of the population of some 585,000 Soviet villages, officially proclaimed nonviable ("futureless"), to some 120,000 central villages of allegedly high development potential. As the years went by, the results of the program became increasingly devastating. Emigration from the rural areas swelled rather than receded, the capital assets of nonviable settlements were wasted, labor productivity declined, and the food crisis deepened. As part of the rural upheaval, numerous PSFs were abandoned and thousands of areas of small fields reverted to brush and swamps. By the beginning of the 1980s the party and government reversed themselves, abandoned the resettlement program, and instructed the authorities to place the PSFs legitimately within the framework of collective and state farms, to provide credit, fodder, and fertilizer on reasonable terms for them, to increase the sale of young livestock for personal use, and to facilitate their marketing of food through state channels. Yet, in 1989, in his reports on agriculture (particularly, in *Pravda,* March 16 and 24, 1989) Gorbachev noted that the rural situation continued to be hopeless and that "in many regions people were simply abandoning land and leaving the villages." He then added that abandoned farms abounded in the Russian Non–Black-Earth Zone, Belorussia, and the Baltic states, that the official policy of distortions had led many peasants to curtail their private farming and that even on collective and state farms "a third of the families keep no livestock, and more than half keep no cows and raise no pigs."

According to data released in 1988 by the State Statistical Office, in *The Agricultural Economy of the USSR,* the number of family users of personal plots was on the order of 45 million: 12.4 million families of collective farmers; 12.6 million families of workers and employees of state farms; and some 20 million families of workers and employees and retirees from other rural and urban enterprises and organizations. All told, these families worked less than 1 percent of the total agricultural land in use (that is, only some 8.7 million hectares), comprising, respectively, about 1.5 percent of the country's farmland (plowland, orchards, vineyards, meadows, and pastures) and about 2.7 percent of the country's sown areas. On their sown areas, the farmer families allotted close to 70 percent to potatoes, an area equivalent to as much as 46 percent of the total potato areas of the country.

To understand and properly evaluate the contribution of these minifarms—each of from one-fifth to one-third of a hectare—one must distinguish between de jure and de facto economic relations. The holders of PSF in the collective and state farms can lease pastureland from the large farms and can also obtain from them grain, fodder, and young livestock under various conditions. The personal minifarms are correctly described as auxiliary farms; some 80 percent of the families running them depend for work as well as for the wherewithal for cultivation on the collective and state farms. The PSF are called personal, not private, farms. A kind of division of labor occurs between them and the socialized sectors; the large farms are in some respects capital-intensive, the minifarms are labor intensive. The PSF provide industry and consumers with important quantities of crucial products—meat, milk, eggs, and wool—while, at the same time, they allow some peasant families to acquire the extra margin of food needed for subsistence and permit some other families additions to their income. Given the ability to lease or contract for pastureland use and fodder, as of 1988 the PSF raised some 19 percent of the country's horned cattle, 13 percent of its cows, 14 percent of its pigs, and 33 percent of its sheep and goats.

Over the years, the relative contributions of collective farms and the PSF to the total outputs of meat, milk, eggs, and wool have tended to decline, while that of the aggrandized state farms increased. Yet, as of 1987, the PSF alone contributed between 26 to 27 percent of each of the indicated outputs for the USSR as a whole. Important differences exist among regions in this respect, however, due to natural conditions and various approaches developed by local authorities. Notwithstanding these impressive results, without a vast change-over from leasing to broad privitization, the PSF are condemned to remain an appendage of socialized farms—too small, too backward, and too poor to have access to other technology than that of the sickle, pick, and shovel.

"Merchants" vs. "Cavalrymen"

A long, complex, wide-ranging, and at times acrimonious debate has been waged in the Soviet Union about the so-called peasant question, the party's agrarian policy, and the rationale of the transitions from War Communism to the NEP and then to Stalin's system. The launching of perestroika has added fuel to the polemics, along with a set of new questions, such as, What exactly are we reconstructing? How is perestroika related to Bolshevik theory and tradition? To what extent does perestroika represent a continuation of pre-Stalin policies—particularly, in regard to the peasant question and the role of markets?

The question "What exactly are we reconstructing?" was raised (in *Oktiabr*, June, 1989) by G. Vodolazov of the Academy of Sciences, in a philosophical-sociological commentary entitled "Lenin and Stalin" on Vasilii Grossman's novella, *Everything Flows* (*Vsio techiot*). The problem explored by Grossman in this extraordinary book, published twenty-five years after his death, raises an issue now dominant in the intellectual and political life of the USSR—namely, as Vodolazov puts it, "Don't all the terrible deformations which have so severely crippled post-October generations have their origin in that original 'plan' [created by Marx, Engels, and Lenin]?"

The debaters of this and all the previously mentioned issues cluster conveniently around the answers they give to *one* fundamental issue, namely, are markets compatible or incompatible with Marxism-Leninism? Those who stress the idea of incompatibility affirm that Lenin was certainly not a defender of market ideals and that the differences between him and Stalin were only marginal. Those who assert the concept of compatibility affirm not only that Lenin was the first to stress the connection between markets and Marxist-Leninist principles but that in the country's disastrous economic conditions only the establishment of broad market relations can provide a way out of chaos.

Even the partisans of the first school might be for or against Marxism and Lenin's interpretation of it. Vasilii Seliunin, for instance, a partisan of the school unsympathetic to Leninism, contends that "when it comes to socialist revolution the elimination of market-based production [*tovarnoe pro-izvodstvo*] is not just a deviation from the goal but the goal itself" (*Novyi mir,* May, 1988). According to Seliunin, the harsh measures taken under War Communism against the peasantry were not due to famine and economic devastation but had a theoretical basis, specifically, Lenin's fear that, unless market-based production is destroyed and the peasant is forced to surrender his or her surplus to the "workers' state on loan to help the hungry worker" rather than to "speculate," the revolution would perish. Only the miserable results of War Communism forced Lenin to frame the New Economic Policy and end the grain requisitions and replace them with a fixed tax in kind on peasants' output. Subsequently, the platform of the "leftist" adversaries of the NEP, who believed that "the socialist system has no place for market-based private production and who wanted to finance industrial growth by taxing the peasantry directly or indirectly," was taken over by Stalin and implemented by him. Now, affirms Seliunin, in order to succeed, perestroika must break completely with Stalin's conception. Moreover, it should be done in a single sweep; the architects of the new policy should remember that "an abyss must be crossed in a single leap—you can't make it in two." A similar opinion concerning Leninism and markets is advanced by someone apparently more favorable to Marxist principles, namely, L. Popkova, who thinks that "social-ism is incompatible with a market in terms of essence, in terms of founders' intentions, and in terms . . . of those who applied its tenets in real life and those who continue to apply them" (*Novyi mir,* May, 1987).

Opposition to this line of argument comes from partisans of perestroika who wish to assert not only the compatibility of markets (or commodity-money relations) with socialism but also the existence of continuity between Lenin's agrarian policy during the NEP and Gorbachev's policies. Such ideas have been advanced, with interesting variations, by Nikolai Shmelev (in *Novyi mir,* June, 1987), the Social Sciences Section of the presidium of the USSR Academy of Sciences (*Pravda,* July 14, 1989), and, of course, by Gorbachev himself, in particular, in his report on agrarian policy (*Pravda,* March 16, 1989).

Shmelev affirms that, initially, Lenin assumed that capitalism had al-ready created all that was necessary for socialism and that the Bolsheviks had only to suffuse all this with a new socialist content. As the disastrous eco-nomic results of the approach became evident, Lenin formulated the NEP. At the center of his plan of transition to *normal conditions* were commodity-money connections—to start with, in agriculture, preferential usage of eco-nomic levers, full cost accounting in all activities, and the development of cooperative property in all the economy's sectors. After Stalin's destruction of the NEP and his brutal application of War Communism's methods to the economy as a whole, it has again become imperative, just as in 1921, to apply

NEP policies; the market must be invigorated, the economy must be revitalized, and, first of all, a quick turn must be taken "for healthy, normal commodity-money relations in the agrarian sector."

The social scientists of the Academy of Sciences also stress the need to return "to Lenin's concept of socialism (the NEP period)." But, interestingly, the scientists add that liberating the society requires more than just cleansing it of Stalin's "vulgarizations." What is needed is a reexamination of property forms, methods of management, mix of social protection and efficiency, and timing of the expansion of market relations. According to these scientists, the creation of "socialism's new face" demands a restructuring and decentralization of the ownership forms leading to a multistructured society with state, cooperative, private, and mixed forms of property. It further requires a new balance between "the content of the issues taken on by the center" and the activities of the state-owned enterprises. Moreover, it poses the need for a judicious mix between social guarantees in regard to unemployment and the search for economic efficiency. Finally, it welcomes market expansion in many directions, but only after the questions of shortages and inflation dangers have been solved and "the art of the markets' systematic regulation" has been acquired.

Mikhail Gorbachev also affirms the necessity of mastering the use of the levers of commodity-money relations. The latter expression, both a restrictive and equivocal substitute for the term *markets*, still implies, as it did under the centralist system, that commodity production could arise only at the junction of two different forms of ownership, state and collective farms, and at the junction of state production and private consumption. In the official Soviet textbooks on economics, interstate enterprises' transactions are still alleged to involve only products, rather than commodities in the full sense of the term. Be that as it may, in the language of Soviet polemics, Gorbachev is counted among the so-called merchants, that is, the partisans of a mercantile approach to the stimulation and coordination of economic activities, as opposed to the so-called cavalrymen's approach, based on administrative-command methods and the belief that head-on attacks can solve any and all issues. In his report on the CPSU agrarian policy (*Pravda,* March 16, 1989) Gorbachev placed the peasant question at the center of the party's policy "both from the standpoint of revolutionary theory and from the standpoint of the tasks of building a new society." He then went on to say that the changeover to the NEP had been dictated by the need to preserve the worker-peasant alliance and save the "gains" of the revolution. After Stalin's methods of extraordinary coercion had done "enormous damage to agriculture," it became necessary to return to the methods of the NEP.

There is, indeed, similarity between certain measures envisaged by perestroika and those proposed by Lenin—namely, diversity in managing the land, use of norms for taxing peasants' incomes, free trade for peasants' surpluses, and wide scope for the development of cooperatives. Gorbachev wished thus to convey the impression not only that Soviet history had already furnished a viable alternative to Stalin's system of brutal coercion, but also that perestroika was simply reinstating that alternative after a distressing and unfortunate hiatus. One might point out, however, that there is a serious drawback to this kind of interpretation; Gorbachev hesitates to break up the main "achievements" of Stalin's coercions—that is, the full nationalization of the land and collectivization of the peasants. He is ready to transform Stalin's legacy, via the leasing of land and the transformation of state and collective farms into a vast network of cooperatives with subordinated cooperatives, but he still hesitates to reconsider the question of land ownership and reverse Stalin's collectivization policies. (These issues will be examined in more detail in part 4.)

Leasing can do many things in respect to family teams and even individual contractors. But, as before, leasing leaves the peasant utterly dependent on the transformed collective-state network, not having the ability to acquire his or her own land, deprived of the capacity to give free rein to initiative, and lacking the right to acquire modern technology and develop his or her primitive, auxiliary mini-exploitation into a *complete farm* in the Western sense of the term.

Traditionally, the partisans of administrative commands, the cavalrymen, were worried that the market could somehow hurt the state. They were particularly concerned with what would happen to the state procurement of agricultural produce. The merchants never worried about commodity-money or market relations. But they still continue to hold onto the collectivization system and hesitate to depend only on spontaneous ways of acquiring farm products. Perhaps the real fight between cavalrymen and merchants, which concluded with the apparent victory of the latter, still continues to linger indecisively in the consciousnesses of Soviet party and government leaders.

Concluding Comments

What happens in regard to agricultural restructuring and output growth will decisively determine the extent of the revitalization of the Soviet economy as a whole. As previously noted, at the end of the 1980s agroindustry produced about one-third of the country's gross product, commanded one-third of the country's productive assets, and employed about one-third of its labor force. Farm output alone claimed about 20 percent of annual investment and 20 percent of employment (not including the part-time labor of housewives, retirees, and students working on personal subsidiary farms), as compared to 5 percent each in the United States. Given the already indicated drawbacks, to which one has to add also unfavorable soil and climatic conditions, Soviet farms used one-third more land than in the United States, but the value of output per hectare was only about half that in the United States. The agricultural productivity of labor continues to range between 10 and 25 percent of that in the United States. Yet, increasing output per unit of inputs is imperative for increasing food supplies, reducing the high resource cost per unit of farm productions, and decreasing the heavy Soviet dependence on imports of agricultural products, particularly, grain.

Soviet policymakers are fully aware of the enormous difficulties that confront the farms and the agro-industrial complex as a whole. Gorbachev himself has stressed in his report on agrarian policy (*Pravda*, March 16, 1989) and his speech at the Fourth All-Union Congress of Collective Farms (*Pravda*, March 24, 1989) the numerous problems that hamper the Food Program, including the deficient performance of the sectors supplying agroindustry, along with the complex questions of incentives, infrastructure, quality of housing, and numerous other factors that handicap production and Soviet rural life in general. Notwithstanding the awareness of Soviet policymakers, however, the prospects for rapid, radical changes remain dim. Investments are bound to fall short of the sector's immense needs. The inefficiency of the entire system prevents timely delivery of equipment, fertilizers, and other inputs. Finally, self-financing and collective contracting cannot function effectively for years to come while prices fail to reflect supply and demand conditions.

CHAPTER 11

Supply and Trade

Industrial Purchasing

In a market- or plan-directed economy, every industrial activity requires materials, supplies, and equipment to work with, but, between the two, the processes of obtaining these supplies are vastly different. The changeover from the system that prevails in the USSR of allocation of these so-called producer goods to a system of competitive purchasing dominant in market-directed economies demands more than a Supreme Soviet decree enjoining such a transformation. The vast and complex networks of warehouses and distribution centers of this system of allocation could certainly be "ordered" to engage in wholesale trading. But to carry out such operations effectively—that is, via purchases from competitive suppliers at competitive prices—would require that the state-owned producing enterprises be entirely free from tutelary controls and obligations concerning their outputs, a measure that, as noted, is not on the policymakers' reconstruction agenda.

In market-directed economies, purchases of the needed industrial inputs must, as a rule, be made at the lowest cost consistent with quality and service requirements in order to guarantee the firm suitable profits and an advantageous selling position. In competitive markets, supplies can be obtained from various sources, and sound purchasing consists in selecting the quality and quantity needed at the lowest available price, at the proper moment, and from the best source. Yet, as Stuart F. Heinritz points out in his standard work, *Purchasing, Principles and Applications,* this rule is not fixed. In certain cases it might be economical to buy more expensive materials or equipment if the additional cost is offset by manufacturing economies. In other cases it might be more appropriate to incur some additional manufacturing costs in order to take advantage of cheaper materials that are adequate for the purpose. In other cases still it might be more profitable to abandon certain manufacturing operations when the parts produced can be bought from outside at lower costs. Purchasing requires flexibility and continuous attention to both production needs and wholesale market opportunities. Purchasing can affect end products' cost in many ways and not only through direct expenditure on materials. Delays due to lack of materials on hand, or to lack of uniformity and the dimensions and workability of the built inventories, can add to the hidden costs of production and can also result in excessive waste and rejections. In sum, purchasing must be adjusted to keep supplies attuned to current demand, while at the same time it is coordinated with production activities to achieve the goal of profitable operation of the firm.

In principle, in Soviet planning the basic goal is to achieve a *perfect fit* between scheduled production and deliveries of industrial supplies and scheduled demands for these goals. In practice, the attempts of matching supply and demand in the absence of markets is both elusive and cumbersome. Organizationally, the Soviet supply of producer goods combines the principles of branch organization of industry and territorial organization of the channeling of supplies in an unwieldy fashion. This combination has been the result of an awkward overlapping of various economic reforms preceding perestroika. The prevailing system is comprised of four structures: two principal systems, plus two specialized ones concerning, respectively, oil and oil products (*Goskomnefteprodukt SSSR*) and agricultural technical supplies (*Goskomsel'khoztechnika SSSR*). The main distribution channels of producer goods are the centralized interbranch system and the departmental system.

The *centralized interbranch network* of supply and distribution, organized under the USSR Council of Ministers, is headed by the USSR State Committee for material-technical supply (Gossnab SSSR). The task of Gossnab is to plan, together with Gosplan, the supply needs of the national economy and the distribution of supplies among its branches, republics, and territories. Under Gossnab SSSR function the All-Union Main Administrations for Supply, the All-Union Main Administrations for Equipment and Construction, territorial administrations for supply, and the Gossnab of the republics (excluding the Russian republic, the RSFSR) (see fig. 11-1). Each of the main administrations of the first group organizes the supply and distribution of one (or a group) of the basic intermediate products, for example, coal, metals, chemicals, lumber, cement, and machinery. Each of the main administrations of the second group is in charge of completing and equipping great construction projects or the reconstruction of enterprises for various branches of manufacturing, such as machinery, metals, foodstuffs, and building materials. The territorial administrations under Gossnab SSSR (for the RSFSR regions) and under the republics' Gossnabs (for the regions of the Ukraine and Kazakhstan) control the regional distributions, utilization of supplies by enterprises and associations, and distribution points (supply centers and storage).

The second main system of supply and distribution, the *departmental system*, functions under the All-Union and republic ministries and departments. It duplicates only in some respects the centralized interbranch network; its main focus is on the supply and distribution needs of transport and

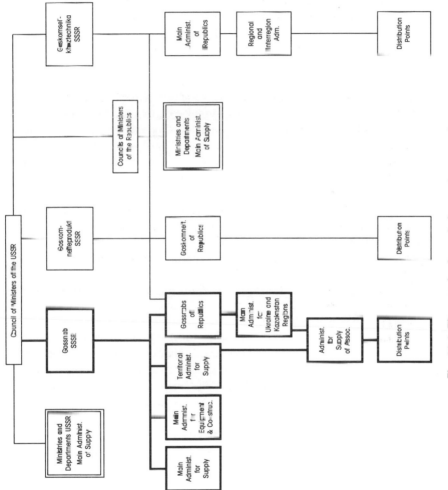

Fig. 11-1. The supply channels for producer goods

communications and of the nonmaterial sphere (housing, hospitals, and schools), as well as of the needs of industries of republic and regional importance. The departmental system involves a very large number of organizations and employees and clears the bulk of the supplies and distribution of producer goods. As of 1987, the crucial centralized interbranch network under Gossnab SSSR, the pivot of interindustry transactions, controlled only 15 percent of all supply-distribution organizations, 23 percent of their total personnel, and 42 percent of the circulation of producer goods.

The planning of the production and supply of industrial goods and the matching of suppliers and users are both astounding and disconcerting in their complexities. The plan of industrial supplies included in the national plan of economic and social development is comprised of three types of balances: *material balances, distribution balances,* and *interrepublic and interregional balances.* The schemata for matching suppliers and users must pay as close attention as possible to the timing of deliveries to insure keeping the scheduled paces of development throughout the economy.

As indicated in chapter 3, the leaders of perestroika have decided to move away as much as possible from direct assignments of inputs and injunctions on outputs. But they have not created free wholesale markets for producer goods. The distribution systems, ministries, departments, producers, and users sign contracts of purchase and delivery, but the movement of goods is not mapped out by the contracts. This movement is still determined by a complex set of still indispensable physical balances, even though the latter are officially supposed to play only a subsidiary role.

As pointed out in a Soviet book, *Planning the Economic and Social Development of the USSR,* edited by A. G. Zav'ialkov in 1987, the material balances (of production and use) have continued to be constructed for two vast categories of products: the balances of raw materials, fuels, and intermediate products—in Marxian terms, the balances of the "objects of work"—and the balances of machinery and equipment, the so-called balances of the means of work. To these two groups of balances must necessarily be tied all the other balances of distribution that need to be interconnected among themselves in a variety of ways.

The distribution balances fall into five groups. The first group, involving the balances of the key products necessary to national production, in 1987 covered some three hundred products. These balances were approved by the USSR Council of Ministers. The second group comprised balances for some fifteen hundred products. These balances were under only Gosplan's supervision. The third group was constructed on the basis of Gossnab's classification and concerned an additional thirteen thousand products—twenty-five hundred directly under Gossnab's control, the rest under the territorial administrations of supply. The fourth group included the distribution plans of the ministries and departments and entailed the construction of some forty thousand separate balances. Finally, the plans for interrepublic and interregional supplies involved a further vast number of balances and distribution schemata.

The architects of Soviet reconstruction programs have often stated their will to put an end to this system of planning and distribution of producer goods and to change over to a system of wholesale trade and freely negotiated contracts among producers and users. As an article entitled "Allocate? No. Sell" put it, "the USSR is the only country where central material and supply agencies directly manage the sale of producer goods and are given administrative and allocative functions" (*Izvestia,* January 3, 1989). Yet, while Soviet leaders and the Soviet press repeat incessantly that trade in producer goods must play "a decisive role" in the formation of the socialist market, progress in this direction is extremely slow. As of the end of the 1980s, the changeover to wholesale trade was supposed to combat two evil tendencies of the producers, namely, to accumulate inventories far in excess of input needs and to plan outputs below the Control Figures, that is, below their real production potential. Specially devised experiments for the account of the Ministry of Machinery, Road Construction, and Municipalities have been carried out with the aim of rectifying these situations. But the experiments have failed; the state enterprises' inventories continued to increase rather than diminish, and their managers continued to plan below the production potential. The trouble with such "experiments" is that they are tried within the broadly unchanged framework of central allocations. And every manager knows full well that, within that system, if one turns down unneeded resources, one does not get the same amount the next time around. While the central authorities are prone to command one day, "Make your own deals: Look for Partners," they are also prone the next day to announce that the state orders for output have priority, that materials needed to fill these orders will be allocated centrally, and that only *what is left over* is available for sale. Ultimately, the contracts between producers and users of producer goods continue to be based entirely on the Control Figures.

Changeover from the central system of allocation, and of matching producers and users, to a system of industrial purchasing even remotely similar to the one prevailing in market-directed economies is stymied by innumerable difficulties, among which the continuation of the system of state orders represents only one element. A purchaser of goods in a real market of producer goods—as in any other kind of market—must know and weigh the terms on which alternatives are offered by various suppliers. He or she must know and evaluate brand names, qualities, price-quantity relations, and the extent to which necessary credits can be secured and at what rates. The sellers of manufacturing products must, for their part, estimate the various levels of demand for their range of different products of different qualities and quantities. In the Soviet situation this type of data cannot be furnished either by the ponderous Gossnab or the entire cumbersome system of material-technical supply or the banks.

The raison d'être of Gosplan, Gossnab, and Gosbank has been to try to control the vast concentration of enterprises and match the producers with specially designated users of their products. In most cases, the suppliers are monopolistic producers created by the policy of centralized controls of vast industrial concentrations. The power of the producer to dictate price and terms, including what is to be delivered, when, and in what state of workability, cannot be challenged in the prevailing Soviet conditions. The changeover to wholesale trade cannot be achieved without industrial deconcentration, the surge of competitive suppliers, and the wide opening of the economy to world market influences. The changeover to wholesale trade in producer goods is in fact hampered not only by the sheer weight of this extensive system of planning-balancing supply and of demand-matching of producers and users, but also by the fear of both policymakers and the bureaucracies of these networks of *losing control* over the movement of material resources and bringing about a total economic collapse. As pointed out, the leaders of perestroika have started to restrict the scope of central planning and have often stressed the need to develop wholesale trade in capital goods. But, as in the case of agriculture, where they proved to be afraid of giving up the procurement of agricultural produce at administered prices, so in respect to producer goods, they seem to be afraid of relying on the spontaneity and unpredictability of the market. Moreover, the central bureaucracies are not the only ones afraid of the plunge. The managers of state enterprises, though endowed with only limited decision-making powers, also cling to the game they know: excessive inventories, low output plans, and bonuses for overfulfilling the targets. Even perestroika, with its still modest transformations, cannot easily shake their inertia. As S. A. Sitarian, vice chairman of the Commission on Improving the Economic Mechanism, put it in an interview in *Pravda* (January 5, 1989), "we are still encountering not just an economic but what I would call a psychological unreadiness on the part of many economic executives, engineering and technical personnel and even economists at various enterprises for working under the new arrangements." In other words, the changeover to wholesale trade requires much bolder steps forward than those needed by the adjustments to the arrangements introduced since the mid-1980s.

Marketing and Retail Sales

In developed, market-directed economies the role of marketing is now viewed in ways much different than in the early 1900s. At the turn of the century, industrial firms were production-oriented. They believed that a good product, defined in terms of its physical quality, would sell itself. Because goods were in short supply, the problem of finding potential customers was not very significant. Here is how the late chairman of the board of Pillsbury Company described the general attitude of his company in its early years: "We are professional flour millers. Blessed with a supply of the finest North American wheat, plenty of water power, and excellent milling machinery, we produce flour of the highest quality. Our basic function is to mill high-quality flour, and of course (and almost incidentally) we must have salesmen to sell it, just as we keep accountants to keep itn books" (*Journal of Marketing*, January 1960). This production-oriented philosophy dominated business for decades. As mass production capabilities expanded and supply increased, the problem of distribution became important. Emphasis was put on finding the best methods of getting the products from where they were produced to where they were consumed. Eventually, the emphasis shifted again toward increasing sales volume, so that the continuously expanding manufacturing capacity could be used efficiently and costs could be kept down. Long before the twentieth century has drawn to a close, the emphasis in marketing has shifted again from sales volume per se to the best ways to satisfy consumer needs and achieve long-term satisfaction of both consumers and society.

The production-oriented philosophy, which had receded in the West before World War I, continues to reign supreme in the state-owned enterprises, albeit in a simplified version. The emphasis there is not on production of the highest quality but rather on the production quantity needed to fulfill plan targets. In an economy in which shortages prevail for almost everything, problems such as distributing products more efficiently, increasing sales volume so as to use efficiently the manufacturing capacities available, and satisfying the consumer are as yet not seriously taken into account in the state sector. In the national economic plan, a great number of projections based on highly elaborated calculations are dutifully established for "the branch of trade and public dining." These projections concern the volume of trade through the retail outlets of the state and through those of the cooperatives (of *Tsentrosoiuz* also belonging to the state) for the USSR and the republics. They also involve calculations of the balances of production and distribution of food and nonfood products for the country as a whole, as well as the plans for capital construction projected for the entire branch. Forecasts are connected with the basic data regarding the scheduled outputs of manufacturing and agroindustry, the targets of the Food Program, development of transportation, estimates of the growth and structure of incomes and outlays of the population, budget receipts (particularly, the turnover tax) and expenditures (particularly, subsidies), and correlated activities of the State Bank.

The planning of the structure of trade is based on the analysis of past trends, estimates of inventories and scheduled imports, and projections of the patterns of demand. Various methods are used for these forecasts, including an array of norms for the "rational utilization" of food and nonfood products, estimates of the shifts in income and outlays of various categories of the population, and projected output targets. Extremely detailed calculations are made in both physical and value terms of the balances and supply and distribution by groups and subgroups of commodities and specific commodities, for example, for food (meat and meat products, milk and milk products, eggs, sugar, vegetable oil, potatoes, vegetables, fruits, bread and cereals, and alcoholic and nonalcoholic beverages), nonfood (fabrics, clothing, knitwear, hosiery, footwear, soap, and tobacco), and a special subgroup of goods for so-called cultural and household services (watches, electronic products, printed materials, cars and other motor vehicles, furniture, rugs, glassware and ceramics, and lumber and other building materials). Further calculations are made on the specific forecasted purchases from the retail trade network (stores, stands, and pharmacies), public catering enterprises (canteens, restaurants, snack bars, and teahouses), custom tailor shops (for all types of work including repair and remodeling), and warehouses (for producer goods). Estimates are also made of the nonplanned goods entering into retail purchases via the collective farm markets, and detailed projections are also constructed for the various types of outputs forthcoming from personal subsidiary farms.

Special plans are also drawn up for the eventual expansion of the state-run retail network, supported by calculations concerning output expansions, changes in the size of the population, and ad hoc norms for establishing the number of outlets, sales floor surface, and personnel needed for manning such facilities in the towns or in rural areas. In practice, however, the actual expansion of the state retail network has been slow, irregular, notoriously inadequate, and primitive. According to the statistical yearbook for 1987, retail outlets per 10,000 inhabitants increased from 21 in 1940 to 28 in 1970 and then fell back to 26 in 1987 (roughly one-fifth of the number of outlets available in the United States). There were some 727,000 retail trade enterprises comprised of 559,000 stores (half of them in towns) and 168,000 stands (two-thirds of them in towns). The number of stores in towns increased by 21 percent in relation to 1970, in the rural areas by only 4 percent. The number of stands decreased in towns and stayed about the same in the countryside. Out of the 559,000 stores, some 60 percent belonged to Tsentrosoiuz, but these stores were quite small—they cleared only one-quarter of total retail trade, while the balance of 40 percent of stores belonging to the state system cleared two-thirds of retail trade. Between 1970 and 1987 the store floor space increased by some 75 percent, and the average floor space per store rose from sixty-three square meters to ninety-three square meters, still a very small surface for a store (roughly ten-by-nine meters). The total personnel employed in retail trade increased also by 33 percent, from 3.7 million to 5 million, and the average per store rose from 5.5 persons to 7 persons in 1987. In addition to these networks, there were some 6,087 collective farm markets (of which less than one percent were covered)—20 percent less than in 1970—clearing some 5 percent of total retail trade and 9 percent of the trade in foodstuffs only.

According to a study by A. Shokhin, A. Guzanova, and L. Liberman (published in *Literaturnaia gazeta*, September 14, 1988), there are considerable differences in the use of sales channels depending on where one lives and what his or her per capita income is. The authors point out first that there are significant price and quality differences between the same types of goods purchased in various distribution channels. At the time a kilogram of meat sold for two rubles in the state stores, but for two, three, or four times more for meat of a lower quality in cooperative trade ([Tsentrosoiuz] and the collective farm markets). Residents of Moscow, Leningrad, and adjoining oblasts shop mostly in the state stores. In the oblast centers less than half of purchases can be made in state stores; the rest has to be made in other markets. The greatest access to the state stores is for people living in large cities. In addition, managers and other members of the hierarchy have access to special stores with lower prices and a wider assortment. The lower the income, the more the consumer must resort to smaller, poorly provided, and more expensive shops of the cooperatives and to expensive collective markets.

The system of public catering is the most neglected branch of the system of distribution and is in dire need of better sanitation, amelioration, and expansion. As of 1987 the Soviet Union had some 345,000 public dining establishments of which two-thirds were restaurants (some 60 percent of them in cities), the rest factory canteens and snack bars. Again about one-quarter of all public catering was carried out through Tsentrosoiuz. In terms of personnel, public dining employed 2.7 million persons in 1987, as against 1.9 million in 1970, with the average per unit decreasing from 8.3 persons to 7.9 persons. As Gorbachev himself put it in a report to the CPSU plenum on July 29, 1988 (*Pravda*, July 30), "While accomplishing the task of increasing the amounts of consumer goods and paid services, we should also deal in a serious way with the improvement of the entire system of distribution above all of trade and public catering . . . . Many shortcomings in this sphere are linked to a lag in material facilities, and in many cases to the neglect of these facilities."

Most planning of services is carried out in relation to the plans of various complexes, for example, construction, communications, health, physical culture, and social insurance. As already pointed out, private housing is "the most acute problem of the USSR." According to official data, the floor area of private housing built in each five-year plan period from the Eighth Five-Year Plan onward (1966–70) oscillated around 520–550 million square meters.

The share of private housing built by the population in the towns decreased constantly from some 153 million square meters in the Eighth Five-Year Plan to 120 million in the Ninth, 91 million in the Tenth, 80 million in the Eleventh, and 37 million during the first years (1986 and 1987) of the Twelfth Five-Year Plan. In regard to medical facilities, one must note not only the extraordinary inadequacies of hospital buildings and other health care facilities but also the pervasive "deficits" concerning equipment, instruments, medicines, and shortages of specialized personnel. The Soviet pharmacy system is equally handicapped by the absence of adequate buildings, chronic deficit of medicines, and short supply of specialized labor. Soviet leaders are well aware of the appalling situation in retail trade as a whole, the cramped facilities, sudden "vanishing" of the most elementary products from retail trade (such as salt, sugar, flour, and soap), the long consolidated lists of "deficit medicines" established by each pharmacy, the poor quality of service, and the widespread phenomenon of long waiting lines. As Gorbachev affirmed in the July, 1988, report quoted above, "The Central Committee and the government are now receiving requests that various premises be made available for use in expanding the sphere of trade and of consumer services . . . . In general, comrades, we must more resolutely get rid of various kinds of offices, reduce their number, and turn their premises over to trade and consumer-service enterprises and medical institutions." But such exhortations are rarely followed by action.

Finally, it is interesting to note that the large differences between the republics over budgetary outlays per capita (refer back to table 6-2) are also present in regard to the system of trade, public catering, and medical services. According to the data furnished by the 1987 statistical yearbook, the Soviet republics could be grouped as follows on the basis of their per capita yearly retail trade levels. The highest level, namely above 2000 rubles, was registered in two republics, Estonia and Lithuania. Next in the retail trade per capita scale, with levels between 1500 and 1900 rubles, came four republics, Latvia, Moldavia, Belorussia, and Georgia. The per capita retail trade turnovers of Russia and the Ukraine were close to the average of 1480–1490 rubles. Below the average came in decreasing order the other seven republics, namely the Tadzhik, Armenian, Turkmen, Kazakh, Kirkhiz, Uzbek, and Azerbaijan republics. Such data are the best proxies available for absent per capita income levels.

The Shadow Economy

As pointed out previously (particularly, in chap. 2), a vast amount of buying and selling is carried out under multiple semi-legal and illegal forms in what the Soviets call shadow markets. How are these markets related to Soviet planning priorities and Soviet economic regulations? Which licit and illicit transactions harbor these markets? Why keep such markets expanding, particularly in the conditions of perestroika?

As O. V. Osipenko and Iu. G. Kozlov remind us in *Ekonomika i organizatsia promyshlennogo proizvodstva* (EKO—1989), the Soviet economy lives not according to laws but according to a substatutory complex of normative acts—statutes, directives, orders, and letters of instructions—that need not be based on a specific law. Hundreds of frequently contradictory directives and orders, which suggest impracticability of their implementation, open a variety of loopholes and allow all kinds of subterfuges, including cheating, fraud, and misappropriation of state resources at all levels of the administration. The increased alienation of the population manifests itself by widespread indifference toward public property. Uncertainties generated by breakdowns in many institutional rules and organizational forms in a period of reconstruction and reshufflings of personnel facilitate the development of various illicit channels of distribution outside the officially established framework. Increasingly, the shadow economy becomes a part of the daily processes of acquiring needed goods and services.

Illicit methods of acquiring goods can involve special administrative allocations and closed distributions with special rules and at favorable prices. M. Berger remarked that a true "wave of regulated distribution of goods is washing over us with increasing force" (*Izvestia,* March 29, 1989). Berger referred to distributions with coupon invitations bearing the stamps of given institutions—coupons more valuable than bank notes—entitling the bearer to obtain scarce goods diverted for the use of personnel (and their friends) of large enterprises and influential organizations (such as trade union committees). Networks of distribution with their own rules thus emerge along the established trade channels. Given arbitrary discrepancies between domestic and foreign market prices, all kinds of illicit deals are carried out by firms and cooperatives. Instead of engaging in the production for consumers specified in their charter, some cooperatives turn to middleman activities, including not entirely legitimate export-import operations. G. Yastrebtsov tells (in *Pravda,* April 20, 1989) of a company, Technika, which, instead of conforming to its charter, purchased scarce goods on the domestic market and exported them in order to import electronic equipment that it sold at a good price to . . . the Ministry of Justice. These export-import operations were licitly carried out through the agencies of the Ministry of Foreign Relations.

Since the center's priorities deviate substantially from the population's wants, and since the main flows of the economy do not move in accordance with changing needs, people are increasingly skeptical about the possibility of acquiring goods they need in official trade channels and at official prices. A. D. Smirnov indeed remarked that "the ruble is more like a lottery ticket than a bank note: if you are lucky you can buy something" (*Pravda*, October 21, 1989). This lottery extracts a heavy price under the forms of "low efficiency, mismanagement, lines and waiting lists, corruption, speculation, and the growth of public apathy." The discrepancy between state priorities and public wants engenders curious paradoxes in regard to money holding; the producer does not want rubles, and the consumer cannot spend them as he or she wishes. Working within a system of rationed inputs and controlled sales, rubles mean relatively little for the enterprises. What matters more for them are the reserves of raw materials and equipment that they accumulate, part of which they can use as a hedge against plan pressures, and part they can swap with other enterprises for other materials they might need. Barter in illicitly accumulated inventories plays a big role in the shadow auxiliaries of planning.

Rubles accumulate in the hands of the consumer for a variety of reasons beside the mismatching of the basic planned flows of production and income. Widespread bribe taking, traffic of influence, report padding, setting unwarranted pay and bonus levels, as well as all kinds of absurd prohibitions and regulations, push people and deals into the shadow. According to Osipenko and Kozlov (in the EKO article quoted above), "the bribe occupies the central place in the code of unwritten behavior norms for agents in the shadow economy." Consider the role of bribing in the undemocratic mechanism of selecting and promoting certain officials. The mechanism, which allows placing even unreliable people—including ex-convicts—in "income yielding places," functions according to the principles of dedication to superiors, ethnicity, nepotism, and a well-publicized bribing scale. Bribes are also needed from the lowest to the highest echelon of the ladder for the delivery of any good and any service—"from the meat cutter at the market, the waiter in the restaurant, the store clerk to urban trade director, . . . the members of the collegium of the respective ministry and oblast party committee secretaries."

A host of incongruous or outright farcical provisions push into the shadow activities that in fact need no regulation at all. Osipenko and Kozlov recall that until September, 1987, when the limits on keeping livestock on personal plots were lifted, a farm worker with five cows could legitimately draw income from the sale of milk of only three of his cows. The use of equipment with more than seven horsepower was also considered illegal. Self-employed persons continue to hide in the shadow because of the absurdities of taxation, the dogmas concerning the stability of prices and the rates charged for services, and the callousness, sluggishness, and sloppiness of state enterprises in providing certain goods and services (for example, construction materials and all kinds of repair work). Construction and housing repair stand out among services in which the shadow market is very active. According to T. I. Koriagina (in *Trud*, August 12, 1988, and in EKO, 1989) the population pays billions of rubles to the private providers (*chastniki*) of house repair services, who work quickly, better, and, when needed, at prices far higher than those listed in the state sector. Only 20 to 25 percent of orders for parts and spare parts are satisfied by auto-repair enterprises, and only 50 to 60 percent for automotive services—without regard to speed and quality, which again opens a wide field to the chastniki. Considerable sums go for other types of repairs for household appliances, television sets, and radios. Important amounts of money are also spent for shadow services in rentals of housing, tailoring, weddings and funerals, transport, and medical services (for private practitioners and more attentive care from doctors, dentists, and nurses). New kinds of illegal earnings are gained from the underground manufacture and sale of scarce means of production and a growing traffic in narcotics.

It is interesting to recall here the special role that branches of the defense industry play in regard to the provision of goods of mass consumption. The defense industry has a quasi-monopoly in the production of so-called technically complex goods. According to I. S. Belousov, chairman of the State Military-Industrial Commission, enterprises in the defense-industrial complex (VPK) supply 100 percent of the All-Union output of television sets and household sewing machines, more than 97 percent of refrigerators and tape recorders, over half of the motorcycles, and about 70 percent of the vacuum cleaners and washing machines (*Pravda,* August 28, 1989). In addition, the defense establishment is scheduled to engage in the production of a whole range of equipment for the agro-industrial complex, the light industry, trade and public catering, up-to-date medical machines, and work for an integrated information network for the country as a whole. But the defense establishment will not relinquish its converted facilities to civilian ministries. It will expand current outputs and engage in new lines of production—just as it did in previous conversion processes, in 1945–47 and 1961—and keep the plants in the VPK. While defense industries are scheduled to increase the provision of technically complex goods for civilian use during the Thirteenth Five-Year Plan (1991–95), nobody thinks that this will end the scarcity of a wide range of goods or that it will affect the expansion of shadow markets in a lesser measure than in the past.

Soviet planners assert that at the end of the 1980s, the unsatisfied consumer demand for goods and services exceeded seventy billion rubles. The population's monetary incomes were continuing to rise far faster than the growth rates of output, and the inflationary pressures were mounting. According to Nikolai Shmelev (*Izvestia,* October 30, 1989), at the time there were 500 to 550 billion rubles of "free money" in the country, part of which had been amassed by the enterprises and part by the public. Of these, 300–350 billion were cumulated deposits by the consumers for major long-term purchases, such as a house or car. The rest, so-called hot money, was ready to be spent, but no goods were available. As the ruble continued to depreciate, people started to buy in panic whatever they could get their hands on, including two to three television sets, appliances, and other durables, thus further increasing both scarcities and the scope of shadow markets. All kinds of suggestions were made for absorbing the hot money and coping with the scarcity of goods—including rationing, selling land for housing in the cities, issuing bonds, and differentiating interest rates on deposits—but to no avail.

Faced with shortages that incessantly engulf even elementary staples, the country's leaders have continued to focus on all kinds of equally ineffective administrative measures without knowing how to encourage the expansion of regulated markets. Gorbachev expressed this bureaucratic quandary very well in his speech to the party's Central Committee plenum in July, 1988 (*Pravda*, July 30, 1988): "When information is received that salt, sugar, flour, and many other goods that are not in short supply are continuously vanishing from the trade network in various places, one automatically gets the idea that someone has a stake in maintaining a shortage, or at least is totally devoid of any sense of responsibility to people." And Gorbachev concluded, "All these questions must be placed under the control of Party and Soviet agencies, under the control of working people."

Linkages to Suppliers and Customers

In the discussion on marketing, we recalled that, as the American industrial firms grew and expanded their production facilities, they shifted from a production-oriented to a distribution-oriented philosophy. Analyzing the historical process of development of the American firm, Alfred Chandler focused inter alia in his *Essays toward a Historical Theory of Big Business* on the interrelation between the changing functions of the manufacturing enterprises and the expansion of their decisions in regard to both supply and distribution. Chandler suggested the following sequence in the historical development of American enterprises and their functions: first came the single-product, single-function firm; next, the single-product, multifunction enterprise; finally, the multiproduct, multifunction industrial concern. The oldest type of enterprise fulfilled one specific function; the mercantile house bought and sold goods, the shipping company dealt with shipping, and the mining company was involved only in mining. Between the Civil War and the turn of the century, larger and larger firms, while still operating within the confines of one industry, started to produce one major line of products as well as a few by-products both at the center and at different locations. Many of these companies, whose output expanded rapidly thanks to mechanization, sought to achieve economies of scale not only in production but also in the acquisition of inputs and the distribution of their products.

The development of backward linkages (toward input sources) and forward linkages (toward storing, wholesaling, and retailing) took place in both older and newer industries. In the older industries dependent on agriculture, these types of linkages developed for the processors of goods like meat, beer, bananas, and tobacco, which required quick transportation or storage for high-volume distribution. In the newer metals and machinery industries, revolutionized by high-volume output techniques, the development of their own sales organizations was motivated particularly by the need to provide initial demonstrations of models, consumer credit, and repair and service. These firms provided examples for other manufacturers, who continued to rely on existing wholesale networks, but many factory owners hesitated to follow them. A number of factors, including the great merger movement at the turn of the twentieth century, led to the emergence of vast multiproduct, multifunction firms through combination, consolidation, and integration. As high-volume producers, the newly consolidated enterprises also found that they could not rely on the fragmented distribution facilities of independent wholesalers. Therefore, they also set up their own wholesale and retail outlets, as well as their own purchasing organization handling their input needs. In a few broad strokes, Chandler's brilliant analysis thus tied the expansion of manufacturing and its diversification and integration to the growth of the distribution system and its transformation and adjustment to consumer demand in order to forge the mass American market.

In light of Chandler's analysis, one can better grasp both the damaging impacts of Soviet organizational concepts concerning manufacturing and distribution and the difficulty of overcoming them. As noted earlier, Soviet planners aimed constantly at completely severing manufacturing from both supply and distribution. The latter were placed in the hands of Gossnab and the other distinct administrations of supply, while retail trade was channeled through the state and cooperative (Tsentrosoiuz) networks. The system has prevented the integration of certain input-output operations as well as the carrying out of efficient choices among competitive suppliers of different (or similar) types of goods at different prices. On the other hand, the system has precluded mutually interacting effects between the expansion of manufacturing along various production lines and growth, firm by firm, of appropriate wholesale and retail channels. The state-owned firms have not felt the need to focus their attention on such problems as presentation and adjustment of models to consumers' needs, systematic supply of spare parts and accessories, and guaranteed repairs—facts that, incidentally, opened the door to shadow markets.

The transformation of Gossnab and related supply and distribution systems into a free wholesale network accordingly raises enormous difficulties. The party's decisions first assumed that, by 1989, 30 percent of the trade in capital equipment will be carried out through wholesale trade, while 70 percent will still be distributed in the usual administrative fashion. By 1990 wholesale trade was to account for 60 percent and by 1992 for 80–90 percent. Actually, wholesale trade reached only 3–5 percent by the end of the 1980s. More importantly, one must ask what the Soviet bureaucracy means by wholesale trade. In his book *Inside Perestroika* (1989), the leading economist Abel Aganbegyan notes that some Soviet people "believe that wholesale trade is simply a version of the old administrative system." To which Aganbegyan retorts that "trade is the free, multifarious commercial intercourse of equal partners" that takes place either through direct contacts between producer and consumer enterprises or through an intermediary, such as some wholesale trading office.

Aganbegyan's definitions are certainly the right ones. The question, however, is how exactly the state-run manufacturing establishments are to connect their production programs with the appropriate wholesale-retail extensions. In order to be efficient, the process cannot be carried out as a mechanical soldering of two ill-assorted parts. The process supposes an organic, reciprocally influencing development in which mutual adjustments must be made and in which time and trial and error play important parts. The planned figures on the transformation of the old supply-distribution administrative system into a new free wholesale network are totally unrealistic and reveal a complete misunderstanding of the complex linkages involved. One of the main prerequisites for the emergence of effective, adjustable wholesale networks responsive to both producer and consumer needs is the liberation of state producers from any tutelary controls. Only such freed enterprises could reshape from the vestiges of the old administrative system their own appropriate wholesale-retail extensions oriented toward the consumer and attentive to his or her needs.

Concluding Comments

A previous discussion (in chap. 2) sketched the main constraints under which the Soviet household operates and the hurdles this household faces when it sets out to get the goods and services it needs. Two valuable studies, one directed by Gertrude E. Schroeder and the other by Igor Birman, which completes Schroeder's in various respects, provide a quantitative foundation for evaluating Soviet personal consumption in comparison with that in the United States. The Schroeder study, which was prepared for the Joint Economic Committee of the U.S. Congress and entitled *Consumption in the USSR: An International Comparison,* was released in 1981. It built the indicated foundation using a mass of complex computations of carefully selected data. Goods and services that provide a comparison of consumption were

TABLE 11-1. Soviet per Capita Consumption as Percentage of American Consumption

Commodity Groups	Schroeder Study			Birman Corrections		
	Rubles	Dollars	Geometric Mean	Rubles	Dollars	Geometric Mean
Food	50	57	54	42	46	44
Soft goods	32	48	39	29	43	36
Durables	10	18	13	9	16	12
Household services	14	22	18	12	19	15
Education	63	93	77	79	116	94
Medicine	17	65	33	29	91	51
Total	28	43	33	21	38	28

Source: Igor Birman, *Personal Consumption in the USSR and USA* (New York: St. Martin's Press, 1989), 157.

Note: Figures have been rounded.

divided into groups: for goods (food, durables, and all other so-called soft goods) and for services (household and communal services). Each of these groups were divided into subgroups, and sample goods (services) were selected for each subgroup. Then, ruble-dollar price ratios were calculated for each sample good. Finally, for each group a price parity (exchange rate) was computed, allowing consumption comparison for each group (namely, how many rubles must be spent in the USSR to buy the quantity of goods that can be purchased for one dollar in the United States). The Birman critique (*Personal Consumption in the USSR and the USA*, published in 1989) evaluated and adjusted *some* of the price ratios and price parities used in the Schroeder study in order to determine the volume and structure of Soviet consumption.

It is interesting to recall in this connection that the 22d Congress of the CPSU had promised some twenty years earlier that by 1980 the Soviet Union would provide the highest standard of living (consumption) compared with any capitalist country. The Schroeder study pointed out that, in fact, by 1980 Soviet per capita consumption reached about a third of that in the United States (less than 30 percent according to Birman) and that the Soviet pattern of consumption conformed in many respects to that of a less developed country. The study added that "little progress toward a modern pattern" had been made there in recent decades. As can be seen from table 11-1, as a rule, education and food have tended to account for the highest consumption shares, durables and household services for the lowest.

The situation in regard to personal consumption has not improved since then, nor has its pattern changed in any way. In many respects consumption conditions have deteriorated since the late 1970s and early 1980s. To a great extent, the perception of this continued deterioration deepened the alienation of the Soviet population and ushered in waves of proposals for reform and restructuring. As the Organizational Committee of the All-Union Scientific-Practical Conference put it in its new proposals for Radical Economic Reform, "the situation of the consumer market has deteriorated noticeably, the population's mistrust of the state has grown, and outbreaks of speculative demand have become more frequent" (*Ekonomicheskaia gazeta,* October, 1989). But the committee estimated that a balanced consumer market could be achieved only after a series of reforms involving almost each and every part of the entire economy, a balance allegedly reachable by the beginning of the second half of the 1990s.

CHAPTER 12

Foreign Trade

Access to Markets

In market-directed economies, foreign trade is shaped by the perceptions and decisions of importers and exporters regarding the opportunities for gains from international trade, the governments' commercial policies concerning restrictions and regulations on the flow of trade, and the prevailing conditions in foreign exchange markets and the balance of payments. Opportunities for trade are evaluated on the basis of the prices of commodities. Differences in relative commodity prices across nations reflect the comparative advantage of engaging in trade, advantage due to differences in the productivity of labor (according to David Ricardo) or to differences in resource endowments and/or technology reinforced by differences in tastes (according to Gottfried Haberler). Commercial policies cover a vast gamut of measures involving tariffs, quotas, voluntary export restraints, and technical-administrative and other regulations. Tariffs, the most important trade restrictions, are often applied to exports by the less developed countries in order to raise their prices and, by the advanced industrial countries, to imports in order to protect some labor-intensive industries under various pretexts. The foreign exchange markets are the places where, say, dollars are bought and sold for other currencies. The exchange rate is the domestic price of foreign currency for which dollars are exchanged. The equilibrium rate is determined at the intersection of the nation's aggregate demand and supply curves for the given foreign currency. The balance of payments, the (yearly) accounts of exports, imports, and capital transfers, can adjust automatically through price, income, and monetary adjustments, or through direct controls and policies affecting production, employment, and national income. Foreign trade flows and the actual movement of capital, labor, and technology across frontiers are a substitute for one another, though they affect the nations involved differently. Foreign investments involve either financial assets (stocks and bonds) or real investments in capital goods, factories, inventories, and land. For many decades now, direct investments have been the main channel of private capital flows.

The underlying theories and practical approaches dominant in market-directed economies in regard to international trade, commercial policies, exchange rates, balance of payments adjustments, and flows of productive resources across frontiers were rejected in toto by Soviet policymakers, planners, and theoreticians from the inception of the Soviet system. For Marxists, by definition, market prices reflect in a distorted fashion the intrinsic, hidden values. In international trade, given the differences in facilities of production between trading countries, the more developed country receives commodities containing more labor content (hence, more value) than the less developed country. Restating Ricardo's theory of comparative advantage, Marx noted that "an advanced country is enabled to sell its goods above their value even when it sells them cheaper than the competing countries," while a less developed country "may offer more materialized labor in goods than it receives, and yet it may receive in turn commodities cheaper than it may produce them" (*Capital*, vol. 3). The theory of an implicitly unequal exchange, distrust of the commercial policies of advanced industrial countries, suspicions concerning flexible exchange rates and foreign automatic or specific adjustments of the balance of payments, and, finally, peculiar ideas about the movement of capital across frontiers, coalesced into a nightmarish conception of the "exploitation" of underdeveloped nations.

On the basis of this conception, the Soviet Union made foreign trade a state monopoly and erected a foreign trade organization meant to ward off capitalist economic penetration, provide maximum protection to domestic capital formation, and turn all foreign trade transactions into subservient instruments of the overall economic plan. This organization and its underlying principles were not affected by any major economic restructuring until 1986. None of the planning and management reforms undertaken in the Soviet Union included foreign trade in their purview. To understand to what extent the measures taken from 1986 onward affected the old system and to what extent they left some of its parts standing, even though they had been built on admittedly obsolete concepts, let us consider its main historical characteristics.

In the traditional system of Soviet foreign trade, the objectives of the overall economic plan were commanding the dynamics of imports, which, in turn, were conditioning the dynamics of exports. The government took upon itself the tasks of determining the overall volume, structure, and direction of the country's trade. Tariffs were reduced to a secondary role. The Ministry of Foreign Trade, the head of the foreign trade system, was empowered to plan all the relevant elements of foreign transactions as a function of the domestic output plan and various policy considerations and commitments. It prepared and participated in the negotiation of foreign trade agreements and controlled and directed state-chartered foreign trade corporations authorized to enter the field of foreign trade.

The planning department of the ministry prepared the draft plan of trade in close contact with the State Planning Commission, which transmitted it to the state-chartered corporations. Constructed within the directives of Gosplan, the draft took into consideration the basic proportions planned for the economy as a whole, existing commercial commitments, and the foreign exchange available. It specified the volume, prices, transport cost, structure, and direction of foreign trade. The importing and exporting corporations drafted, in turn, their specific plans on the basis of the physical balances (output and its allocations in physical terms) submitted to them by the producing organizations and their selling and purchasing departments. The corporations of foreign trade suggested, fitted in, or completed modifications of the basic blueprint, which they presented to the planning department of the ministry. The coordinated, yearly, or long-term (five years) plan could then be established by the ministry and submitted for final approval to the Council of Ministers. The foreign exchange and finance department of this ministry, which kept in close contact with the State Bank, concerned itself with balance of payments problems. The administrative-economic department prepared the budget of the ministry and planned and surveyed the expenditure of foreign trade organs. The contract department studied market trends abroad, prepared the projects for interstate negotiations, and drafted instructions for the foreign trade organizations carrying out contracts after their signature. The accounting and auditing department checked and controlled financial accounts of the ministry and its organs.

The ministry conducted its domestic activities through foreign trade commissioners and monopolistic corporations. The latter were defined as "governmental agencies operating under special status," that is, state-owned organizations placed on a self-accounting basis. Each was established as an independent legal entity, organized under a charter specifying its endowment by the state for the pursuit of its assigned business. In carrying out the tasks assigned by the plan and transacting purchases and sales at the prices established by the government, each organization was expected to produce planned or above-plan profits in agreement with scheduled costs and planned profit margins. The state did not guarantee their obligations, since they were established as independent legal entities. The relation with the production enterprises was that of customer and supplier, regulated by special contracts. Once the overall economic plan was approved, these contracts were concluded within the framework of the plan by the corporations and the selling or purchasing organizations of the economic ministries or the trusts and associations, specifying prices and terms of delivery.

A chamber of commerce, not directly included in the system of the Ministry of Foreign Trade, assisted foreign customers in all matters connected with trade, sent delegations abroad, arranged participation in foreign trade fairs, and obtained patents for its citizens. To it were also attached arbitration commissions. The Ministry of Foreign Trade carried on its operations abroad through trade delegations (in Russian, called *torgovye predstavitel'stva*—in short, *torgpredstva*). The torgpredstva were treated as state delegations and enjoyed full diplomatic immunity in socialist countries, since foreign trade was considered by these countries to be a state function. The torgpredstva controlled the commercial activity carried on abroad by their national foreign trade corporations and insured that it conformed to national laws of the foreign trade monopoly, granted the documents needed for the agreed commercial operations, and also studied the general business trends in each country with respect to trade possibilities. In some countries, including the United States, where the torgpredstva were not accepted as state delegations, the Soviet Union and its various satellites maintained commercial agencies directly subordinated to their respective ministries of foreign trade.

The creation of the "socialist camp," that is, the existence of a group of Soviet-type economies, led to the appearance of a *special foreign trade market* distinct from the rest of the world market—namely, the inter-planned-economies market. Stalin proudly (and erroneously) asserted that this was "a second world market" destined, in time, to reach and surpass in importance the first (intercapitalist) world market. In order to coordinate its activities at the level of trade and, eventually, at the level of output, the participating countries formed (in January, 1949) a Council of Mutual Economic Assistance (CMEA) in which the Soviet Union was to play the dominant role. The interstate commercial treaties concluded between these socialist countries were based on agreements of "friendship and mutual aid" and had both a political and commercial aim. The stated political aim was to help the signatory countries to "construct communist societies," while the commercial aim was to provide a well-defined framework for commercial agreements. The commercial treaties included provisions for most-favored-nation treatment with respect to physical and juridical persons of a signatory power, export and import operations, transport of freight or passengers, and customs duties. They contained further provisions concerning arbitrage competence, exchange of specialists, organization of trade fairs, and other points of secondary importance.

Let us now follow a whole foreign trade operation as it was carried out in practice, first with the socialist countries, then with the other countries of the world. On the basis of the plan, contracts were concluded between exporting corporations and the appropriate domestic organizations selling commodities earmarked for export. The prices paid by the exporting corporations were the factory price f.o.b., not including the turnover tax. For certain scarce commodities, a special purchase authorization was also needed. Payment to the producer was done via the so-called acceptance form—that is, acceptance by the purchasing exporting corporation of documents indicating that the goods have been sent to it by the producer. The commodity was forwarded by the exporting agency to the foreign importing agency via appropriate channels. The settlement was made through the system of "incasso with direct payment." The export organization was paid by its central bank from the account of the buyer upon receipt of the export documents. The bank then sent the documents to the central bank of the importing country, which, in turn, credited the account of the exporter and then presented the documents for collection of payments to the importing organization. In case of refusal of the buyer to accept the goods, the banks notified one another and adjusted their accounts accordingly.

With the capitalist countries, trade agreements were concluded in the same way, but the values involved were expressed in the currency of the partner country or in dollars. Again, these were bilateral agreements, with accounts carried in clearing, just as in the case of trade with the socialist countries. The balance of such accounts could be covered either by gold or foreign exchange or by the shipment of additional commodities, as was also done among socialist partners. In countries with which no clearing accounts were established, payments were made through foreign accounts kept by the central banks with various foreign banks. Whatever the case, the trade settlements with nonsocialist countries were done via the usual letter of credit (and not through the incasso form). The exporter received payment from a specially agreed bank at the presentation, under specified conditions, of export documents. Up to June, 1957, the clearing ruble played only the role of a bookkeeping unit of account. After June, 1957, the State Bank of the Soviet Union started to act as a clearinghouse for intersocialist multilateral compensations. Given that the bulk of trade continued to flow on the basis of bilateral agreements and through bilateral channels, the amount multilaterally compensable remained rather small for a long time. The amount was built up by purchases above the minimums provided for by the bilateral agreements, purchases of various consumers' goods, and various obligations arising from services. Various elements—the necessity of insuring planned supplies and, hence, the preference for bilateral arrangements, the scarcity of exportable goods over and above plan, and the impossibility of using accumulated, convertible clearing rubles for doing business with another CMEA country— kept multilateral compensations within narrow margins. No foreign currency, be it of a socialist or nonsocialist country, circulated within these countries, and taking the domestic currency abroad was strictly prohibited. It was officially stated that the rate of exchange of these domestic currencies was established in "a planned fashion." Actually, the rate was fixed at an arbitrary level, since neither changes in the domestic wholesale and retail prices nor changes in the world prices of the goods exported or imported by these countries affected the planned rate of exchange.

Since domestic prices were looked upon as an element that could be extensively manipulated in order to meet various planned objectives, prices reflected only in part the underlying endowment of factors. Since various rates of exchange were established at arbitrary levels, the planner of foreign trade was handicapped when trying to ascertain the efficiency of the foreign trade system as a whole, though he or she might have been able to relate in a crude manner the profitability of one transaction to that of another. Each socialist country used a different method in this field, though all these methods were qualified as extremely deficient by their users.

While over the years there has been much talk about a large division of labor among CMEA countries, various factors either prevented it or rendered it marginal and arbitrary. The intersocialist division of labor progressed little, first of all because each of these countries attempted to build the same structure of production as that of the Soviet Union. Each conceived its industrialization as a process in which the producer goods industries must develop at a faster rate than the consumer goods industries, regardless of the impact this policy might have on the standard of living. Each country held dogmatically to the Marxian schema of enlarged reproduction, positing that certain branches must develop faster than others, whatever the underlying endowments of factors might be. Eventually, it was perceived that each country need not develop *all* the branches of heavy industry and that cooperation was achievable without changing in any way the basic tenets of enlarged reproduction within each economy. This division of labor was not arrived at, however, on the basis of direct contacts between the exporting and importing concerns of the countries involved. Rather it was achieved on the basis of attempts of centralized coordinations of the production plans and administrative decisions passed on down to the producing enterprises. This kind of coordination did not function well. A variety of factors played against it. A major obstacle was the impossibility of establishing some meaningful relation between the distorted interior prices and the accounting prices of the goods to be traded. Another handicap was the inbuilt tendency of each plant, industry, sector, region, or country in the area to forego trade and insure its supplies by accumulating stocks or producing spare parts or any other goods needed for the fulfillment of the domestic output plan. (Self-sufficiency becomes a virtue within a planning system whose basic emphasis is the fulfillment of given physical output targets.) Finally, the Soviet Union itself was reluctant to agree to any scheme that would have implied a weakening of its central position in CMEA, a reduction of its control over its own output plan, or a sharing with other socialist countries of its own investable resources.

As the policies of economic restructuring started to unfold, the traditional concepts of foreign trade as an instrument for balancing plan requirements and a shield of national independence, as well as the ideas on CMEA's role as a second world market, came under increasing official scrutiny. Yet no serious in-depth public discussions were devoted to the examination and re-buttal of the old theoretical tenets that had guided Soviet foreign trade policies for decades. The traditional policies and their rationales were dispatched to oblivion via a series of decrees. The debates on past methods were perfunc-tory, with mention here and there of their "incorrectness" and their damaging impact. The second world market itself was soon and just as unceremoniously demoted to the unsavory role of "the garbage can" of the socialist countries, in need of a complete overhaul of trading policies and structure on a new, hard-currency basis.

The official theoretical downgrading of past policies and practices took place at a roundtable on "What is Slowing Us Down?—Foreign Economic Ties, Reality and Prospects" (*Izvestia*, October 10, 1987). A number of econ-omists of the USSR Academy of Sciences' Institute of Economies of the World Socialist System—Vladimir Shastitko, Viacheslav Dashichev, and Val-eri Karavaiev—forcefully rejected the old Soviet theories on foreign trade and summarily condemned CMEA for its inability to foster a meaningful division of labor. In the words of Shastitko, "the incorrect ideas that prevailed for many years concerning the place of foreign trade in the national economy" stemmed from the perception of foreign ties "only as a means of eliminating the imbalances that were constantly arising in the economy." Dashichev pro-claimed that "to restrict one's participation in the international division of labor is to doom oneself to economic and technical backwardness," and he added for good measure that CMEA's integration efforts, which occurred "at the upper level—at the level at which all the plans have been coordinated—and from which administrative decisions have been sent down to the enter-prises," were inefficient and damaging in regard to a real division of labor, which can be properly achieved "primarily through direct ties among the enterprises." By that time, a series of decrees changing the organization of Soviet foreign trade had already been adopted by the USSR Council of Minis-ters, and CMEA had been warned by Nikolai I. Ryzhkov, the chairman of the USSR Council of Ministers, that it had to be fundamentally restructured and had to take steps "toward a collective monetary unit convertible into western currencies"—in short, that it had to cease its existence as a sui generis market functioning only on the basis of rigid, bilateral barter exchanges.

Expansion of Options

While maintaining the principle of the monopoly of foreign trade—that is, that foreign economic activities are part of the overall national economic plan—the Gorbachev leadership has proceeded from 1986 on to the dis-mantlement, restructuring, and redefinition of components of the centralized system of foreign trade management.

On August 19, 1986, the Central Committee of the CPSU adopted two joint decrees that profoundly changed the system that had prevailed for over half a century in the administration of Soviet foreign economic relations. The direction and coordination of foreign economic activities, scheduled to become broader and more complex than ever before, was placed henceforth in the hands of a newly formed State Foreign Economic Commission (SFEC) attached to the USSR Council of Ministers. The commission was empowered to direct the work of the Ministry of Foreign Trade, the State Committee for Foreign Economic Relations (which had been managing and implementing economic and technical cooperation with the CMEA countries), Intourist, the Foreign Trade Bank, the State Custom Administration, all ministries and departments that will be active in foreign trade, and the delegations to intergovernmental commissions. SFEC was also granted the right to examine the drafts of current and long-term plans and exercise oversight over all their connections to foreign economic operations. Further, the monopoly rights of foreign trade organizations were curtailed and dispersed. A number of ministries, departments, enterprises, and associations received the authorization to engage directly in import-export operations starting January 1, 1987. Financial measures were adopted, giving enterprises and associations direct involvement in foreign currency transactions. The formation of joint ventures with nonsocialist firms was authorized. On January 13, 1987, legislation was enacted to elaborate the framework of such joint enterprises and to spell out the procedures governing their operation. A further reform introduced on January 15, 1988, merged the USSR Ministry of Foreign Trade and the USSR State Committee for Foreign Economic Relations into a new All-Union Ministry for Foreign Economic Relations (MFER) under the SFEC. The MFER was charged with drafting the foreign trade plan, taking into account the draft plans of all the entities authorized to engage in foreign trade—namely, ministries, departments, specialized foreign trade organizations, and certain enterprises and associations.

The shakeup has left the majority of the old-type specialized foreign trade organizations under the MFER and has placed the others within the systems of various ministries and departments. Despite the fact that each of these organizations is a juridical person and therefore has an independent balance sheet, each is placed under a higher authority empowered to keep track of its activity, reorganize it, merge it, divide it, or liquidate it. In addition, those placed within the system of a ministry or a department in order to keep their activity closer to production must function also under the close supervision of the MFER; this second linkage is supposed to preserve the integrity of the controls over foreign trade. A further complicating element of the organizational structure of foreign trade is a December, 1986, decision authorizing the formation of economically accountable foreign trade firms (FTF) within both types of specialized foreign trade organizations and within a production association, enterprise, or autonomous organization. While within its specific sphere of activity the FTF can function in ways similar to a foreign trade organization, it cannot act in its own name, since it is not a juridical person and therefore does not have a separate balance sheet. Finally, in accord with the 1987 Law on the State Enterprise, which asserted that foreign economic activity was an integral part of an enterprise's work, the USSR Council of Ministers granted, as of January 1, 1989, the right to engage in import-export operations if their products or services are competitive on foreign markets to *all* enterprises, associations, production cooperatives, and other organizations (including the agricultural cooperatives). Moreover, the Council of Ministers allowed the formation on a voluntary basis of various types of foreign trade organizations, including interbranch associations, consortiums, joint-stock companies, trading and other associations with the participation of banks and supply and marketing organizations. The SFEC acquired the right to suspend the import-export operations of enterprises, associations, production cooperatives, and other organizations only upon a representation by the MFER in cases of "unscrupulous competition" or of activities "damaging to state interests."

The broad openings of these innumerable channels toward the world markets, in principle still coordinated centrally so as to preserve the state's monopoly of foreign trade while creating new trade opportunities, also generated confusion and new difficulties. This monopoly continues to be accompanied by the old monopoly of foreign exchange—that is, the enterprises are still not the genuine masters of the foreign currency that they earn. As B. Flodorov pointed out the system of so-called foreign currency funds is maintained, whereby, instead of the actual foreign currency, the exporters receive rubles and a right to a part of the foreign currency they have earned (*Izvestia*, December 23, 1988). In practice, the enterprises are thus compelled to sell part of their revenues to the state at the official exchange rate. The enterprises have still not been given the right to take the foreign currency remaining at their disposal and deposit it in foreign currency accounts at interest rates comparable to those of Western banks. As far as the foreign currency markets are concerned, provision was made, as previously noted, for the free exchange of foreign exchange fund entitlements and the sale and purchase of these entitlements for Soviet rubles at negotiated prices at foreign currency auctions organized by the USSR Bank for Foreign Economic Relations.

The indicated restructuring of the managerial system and procedures in foreign trade had seriously affected inter-CMEA business deals, their structure, prices, and the currency used to carry them out. From 1987 on, discussions on these issues in CMEA had become increasingly contentious among the financial and commercial representatives of the countries involved (the USSR and its former satellites—East Germany, Czechoslovakia, Hungary,

Poland, Rumania, Bulgaria—plus Cuba, Mongolia, and Vietnam). Various proposals were put forward in this council by the Soviet Union in order to improve its own terms of trade, including a "new configuration of specialization and structure of the national economies." As for prices and the currency to be used, the Soviet Union had suggested already at the forty-third meeting of CMEA in 1986, that the participating countries should plan for an eventual changeover from "mutual convertibility of national currencies, to the creation of a collective monetary unit that will be convertible into freely convertible currencies" (*Pravda,* October 14, 1986). However, East European policymakers and planners were reluctant to further skew their economies to fit the actual or supposed needs of the USSR. They had long since lost the illusion that the import possibilities of the USSR were limitless, or that the import obligations contracted in CMEA on the basis of agreements predicated on poorly collated plans were stable and reliable. They were in favor of a kind of tacit agreement that would allow them to shift, year after year, as much of their exports as possible toward other markets. But the Soviet representatives had set their minds on thoroughly changing the relations that had prevailed in CMEA, shifting the terms of trade in favor of their country, reshuffling CMEA's structure of trade, and aligning its prices on the world market. As one after another of the East European countries were breaking their former Communist bonds, the Soviet premier Nikolai I. Ryzhkov proposed on December 13, 1989, that CMEA should be restructured, that its accounting system should be based on hard currency, and that trading should start to be carried out at world market prices from 1991 on. Thus, as CMEA was disintegrating, the USSR put each of its former allies on notice that it did not intend any more to receive in exchange for its oil exports, priced at world market levels, shoddy East European manufactured goods priced higher than they could fetch anywhere else. Such a move, at a moment of vast political upheavals, economic instability, and deep uncertainty about the future, was bound to accentuate the fears of further deep dislocations of the former satellites' heavy industries.

Paradoxically, while the former allies of the Soviet Union experience enormous pressures to shake off Soviet domination and change the rationale, direction, and structure of their political systems, some of their provisional governments continued to cling to the USSR and each other as economic partners for the immediate future. Indeed, none of these countries could contemplate serenely the rapid closing down of obsolete factories and increased unemployment, and none—excluding, of course, vanishing East Germany—could complacently face the attendant social dislocations as the Soviet Union was shifting its exports toward the world market. Expanding Soviet ties to markets other than those of the moribund CMEA gave a push toward a fall in the prices of certain inter–East European traded goods and toward the production and sale of better products on these markets. But this latter change involves a process of adjustments in which other factors will necessarily come into play, downgrading the orientation toward the inter–East European markets and decreasing their attraction. In the meantime, the shift to world market prices further deepens the postsocialist woes of the East European economies.

Joint Ventures

The architects of perestroika clearly intend not only to multiply direct contacts between Soviet and foreign companies on the world markets, but also to encourage foreign investments in the Soviet Union itself and establish a broad base for the formation of joint foreign-Soviet enterprises on the territory of the USSR. In regard to foreign investments, they can point to important historical precedents during the NEP period (1921–28)—namely, the formation with foreign and Soviet capital of so called mixed companies and the granting to foreign capital of concessions contracts (that is, leasing to foreign enterprises of Soviet forests, mines, and oil fields). These policies led to the formation of some 160 mixed companies and about 130 concessions. In 1930 Stalin ordered the dissolution of the mixed companies and sharply curtailed the operation of concessions. By 1936 there were about ten concession contracts still in force. The last concession, Japanese fisheries in the Sea of Okhotsk, was ended in 1944.

The Soviet Union again engaged in the formation of mixed companies, but this time in conquered Eastern Europe after World War II. Most of these companies were established on the basis of reparations and former German assets that came under the control of the USSR in the former enemy countries of Hungary and Rumania. There were six joint companies in Hungary and fifteen in Rumania, besides numerous other Soviet-controlled undertakings in these countries and in East Germany (then the Soviet Occupation Zone), whose entire economy was managed by the Soviet occupation administration. At the time the Soviet Union also established some other joint partnerships, notably, with the Bulgarian and Yugoslav governments. The entire system started to unravel from 1949 on. First, Yugoslavia broke its agreements with the USSR and dissolved the joint companies with Soviet participation. East Germany was proclaimed an independent state (the *Deutsche Demokratische Republik*—DDR) in October, 1949. Finally, the Soviet-Hungarian and Soviet-Rumania mixed companies were dissolved between 1954 and 1956. Not until 1971 did CMEA countries envisage again the formation of intersocialist companies with Soviet participation. But no such companies were established on the territory of the USSR. The Soviet Union secured, however, various investments from the East European countries in its own oil explorations and installations and the building of the necessary transport facilities (such as the Friendship Pipeline) for delivering oil to "friendly" countries.

The decisive move to lay the foundation for the formation and functioning of joint enterprises on Soviet territory was the adoption on January 13, 1987, of a decree of the USSR Council of Ministers on the creation of "Joint Enterprises, International Associations, and Organizations with the Participation of Soviet and Foreign Organizations, Firms, and Agencies of Administration." Two subsequent amendments (of September 17, 1987, and December 2, 1988) enlarged the original dispositions, simplified registration procedures, clarified tax provisions, and provided for important changes with respect to the ratio of foreign ownership, the nationality of the chairman and the director, and the employment and dismissal of staff. The Soviet decrees specify that joint enterprises established on a contractual basis between one or several Soviet enterprises (or associations) and firms of capitalist or developing nations can function on Soviet territory with the authorization of the Soviet Council of Ministers. No restrictions will be placed on the Western partner's ownership percentage. In his valuable legal treatise, *Joint Ventures in the Soviet Union* (1989), Kaj Hober points out that the Western companies' contributions will most likely consist of technology and know-how in various forms, while the Soviet contribution will consist mostly of rights to use buildings, real property, water, and natural resources as well as labor.

The highest body within a joint venture is the board of directors; according to Soviet decrees, the chairman of the board *or* the director of the company can be foreign citizens. The joint companies are empowered to conduct export and import operations independently and function, in practice, outside the planning framework, since they are not allotted any plan tasks and their market is not guaranteed. Yet they do depend, of course, in various degrees on planning decisions concerning materials, fuel, power, and other products. The monetary assets of joint ventures can be held in rubles or foreign accounts with Soviet state banks. Interest on foreign currency accounts will depend on world market rates and in ruble accounts on Gosbank rates. Joint enterprises pay a 30 percent tax on the portion of profit left after deductions for reserves and other funds. They are exempt from taxes during the first two years of their activities. Profits and other amounts due foreign specialists must be obtained from the sale of products on the foreign market.

The Soviet partner can offer to the manager of the joint enterprises extensive experience in dealing with Soviet bureaucracy. The Western partner can offer extensive experience in dealings with foreign customers, competitors, and government officials. On the negative side, it is difficult to unify management and avoid conflicts of interests. The Soviets' aim, of course, is to make the joint companies primarily exporting entities. Western partners might wish to focus rather on the Soviet market, promote the importance of import substitution, and avoid competition with their own products in other markets. These differing motives have already caused many negotiations to falter. Yet in time both the Soviet Union and Western entrepreneurs might find it in their interest to expand the scope, diversity, and number of joint enterprises in the USSR. The Soviet Union is deeply interested in acquiring not only hard currency but also Western technology, Western management expertise, and Western techniques—which can certainly be better acquired and assimilated in day-to-day practice than in seminar lectures at some American university. Western partners might hope not only to get a foothold in the Soviet market but also to have access to a highly skilled stratum of technicians and lower production costs.

Between 1987 and 1989 some seven hundred joint ventures were formed in the USSR. While there were some sizable creations, the majority of the companies were small or, at best, middle sized. They now function in such fields as computers, control systems for plants, machine tools, grain-processing machinery, and shipbuilding, and, eventually, they could include business jets production, as well as lumber, wood products, and various consumer goods. Among the most important joint Soviet-American deals was the signing at the end of the 1980s of an agreement between the Soviet government and a high tech concern, the Phoenix Group International, Inc., of Irvine, California, to set up a computer factory at Pensa (southwest of Moscow). The factory, with 50–50 Soviet-American ownership, American management, and Soviet technicians, will assemble millions of IBM-compatible personal computers to be placed in schools, factories, and offices throughout the Soviet Union over the first half of the 1990s. It is also interesting to note that the Kansallis Bank of Finland and four Western European and three Soviet banks have formed the International Moscow Bank to assist Western companies in the Soviet Union. But the main lever for the development of such companies will become, in time, the expanding Soviet-German cooperation scaled after the liquidation of the former Soviet satellite, East Germany, and its absorption by West Germany.

Prospects

The new policies on foreign trade—broader access to foreign markets opened to all Soviet enterprises and access to joint partnerships on Soviet territory opened to Western investors—will exercise in time an important impact on the Soviet economy and the centralized combination of plan and market mechanisms. As of now what comes into focus in the Soviet Union are tensions between tendencies toward liberalization and the strictures of domestic planning and the difficulties that such a situation engenders for Western companies. As Kaj Hober points out in his treatise on joint ventures, the earlier centralized system was in some respects comfortable for Western companies. For them it was easy to keep in touch with a small number of representatives of the Ministry of Foreign Trade and the foreign trade organizations. In the process of decentralization, some of the latter entities have disappeared or have been placed under a ministry, and the old contacts are no longer maintainable. New channels have been opened, and new contacts will have to be established. It is difficult to know exactly who the new decision makers really are. Much of the foreign trade expertise had accumulated in the old organizations, and many of the experts have now been dispersed (one does not know exactly where). Inexperience and uncertainty with respect to responsibilities and functions created by the reorganization will cause all kind of delays. In certain cases, one can see conflicts of interest among the thousands of entities that have been granted foreign trade rights. Clearly, competition for transactions with foreign companies already exists among all these Soviet organizations. In the past, Western companies complained that they could not reach the end users of imported goods in the Soviet Union; now, opportunities have been created for breaking into the Soviet market, but firms may be confused about where exactly to begin. Patience and endurance will still be needed when negotiating trade transactions or joint ventures.

For the Soviet Union itself a massive reorientation of trade away from the old CMEA arrangements will be neither simple nor easy to carry out. The orientation of Soviet trade toward CMEA's markets has been irrepressible for a number of decades. From the 1950s to the end of the 1980s, between 50 to 60 percent of its exports went to CMEA's members, and 50 to 60 percent of its imports came from them. Trade with the less-developed countries, on the one hand, and with industrial countries, on the other, have by and large failed to develop vigorously from the 1970s on. Trade in both directions with industrial countries has been fluctuating between 15 to 20 percent, except at the time of higher oil prices, when these shares almost doubled (see table 12-1). Many of the factors that have shaped this pattern of trade will still be present even if the Soviet Union succeeds in changing a number of the parameters that have hemmed in its trade with the industrial countries. For the past decades, the Soviet Union has exported mainly oil and gas, diamonds, and other materials to the West and has imported mainly chemicals, heavy machinery, and vehicles.

A vast number of Western restrictions and controls in regard to both imports from and exports to the Soviet Union and the socialist countries have been in place since the late 1940s and early 1950s. The United States was the first to set in place lists of restrictions on so-called strategic exports, soon followed by similar controls established by the other NATO members and monitored by a famous Coordinating Committee (COCOM) on Multilateral Exports Controls. Though the levels and stringency of these controls have

TABLE 12-1. USSR's Foreign Trade by Groups of Countries, in Percentages

	1950	1960	1970	1980	1987
Exports					
Socialist countries	83.6	75.7	65.4	54.2	64.9
of which CMEA	55.7	56.0	54.3	49.0	59.7
Industrial countries	14.6	18.2	18.7	32.0	20.8
Developing countries	1.8	6.1	15.9	13.8	14.3
Imports					
Socialist countries	78.0	70.7	65.1	53.2	69.4
of which CMEA	59.5	50.1	57.0	48.2	64.0
Industrial countries	15.6	19.8	24.1	35.4	22.8
Developing countries	6.4	9.5	10.8	11.4	7.8

Source: Narodnoe khoziaistvo SSSR v 1987, 614.

declined since the 1950s, they have continued to limit in a variety of ways Soviet access to world markets. The upheavals in Eastern Europe, the changes in the Soviet Union itself under perestroika, and the Soviet-German rapprochement of July, 1990, are, however, likely to bring about significant modifications in the nature and extent of Western trade restrictions. Calling for "a common European economic space," already in December, 1989, the Soviet Union signed its first commercial agreement with the twelve-nation European Economic Community (EEC). Under the agreement the European community will phase out quotas on Soviet manufactured products in three stages up to 1995 and then reevaluate the remaining quotas. The agreement provided for cooperation in various areas, including food processing, tourism, banking, insurance, oil and gas, and nuclear energy. The basis of a much broader cooperation has been laid, since then, between Germany and the USSR. This understanding will likely bypass all the restrictions remaining on the COCOM lists. The Russians now seem inclined to be very flexible in regard to possible agreements with the West on trade and military matters and are also ready to join such respectable and moderating international institutions as the General Agreement on Tariffs and Trade (GATT), the International Monetary Fund (IMF), and the World Bank.

Concluding Comments

A debate has been raging in the Soviet Union concerning the advisability and timing of ruble convertibility. Those opposed to the free exchange of the ruble fear inflationary consequences of the currency's depreciation, massive unemployment, speculation, the importation of business cycle disturbances, and other calamities. Those who view convertibility as necessary but who are in favor of cautious moves in this direction assert that prudence might be beneficial, at least in some respects. Thus, they point out that even a modest first step, namely, the reduction in the exchange value of the ruble for Soviet citizens travelling abroad—a measure taken in October, 1989—has already had a salutary impact on Soviet exchange rates for virtually all export transactions. Eventually, they add, after internal price reforms, a single exchange rate will likely come into force, offering the enterprises consistent, market-based incentives for earning hard currency. They stress that the main obstacle to immediate convertibility is the pent-up demand for hard currency; convertibility would lead to a massive flight of capital, in effect, to a vote of no confidence in the restructuring policy.

Those who reject the go-slow theory and the idea that convertiblility should cap the restructuring reforms argue—as does, for instance, A. D. Smirnov in an interview in *Pravda* (October 21, 1989)—that it is not enough to reorganize the bureaucratic machine, abolish some ministries, and streamline some administrations. What needs to be eliminated once and for all is the central apportioning of assignments in physical units, and what must be guaranteed is the free movement of resources. Convertibility is necessary for that. The hundreds of billions of rubles "not backed up by goods," now in the hands of enterprises and consumers, will not make the monopolistic producers reduce costs, increase productivity, and work more conscientiously. The only way to end low efficiency, mismanagement, waiting lines, corruption, speculation, and apathy is to make the ruble worth earning and saving. Paradoxically, Western advisers of the supply-side economics persuasion tell the Russians that the only thing that can make the ruble have a realistic value is to tie it to a fixed quantity of gold, that is, link it to the country's gold reserves. The advisers have found Russian listeners, but such a move is clearly not politically acceptable. Be that as it may, finally, the Russian leadership has firmly understood what some East European economists such as the Hungarian Tibor Liska told it long ago (in *Kozgazdasagi Szemle* in 1963)—that even a socialist economy "has to be developed as guided by the world market and not in seclusion behind national frontiers, or else it would unavoidably fall behind in modernization, in technological progress, in the level of social productivity. World market orientation has to determine the internal financial, market orientation and other value mechanisms, including the need for a convertible currency."

Part 4
"Workable" Alternatives?

Part 4 focuses on the rationale and consequences of Soviet attempts to suppress the market or reduce market mechanisms to subsidiary roles, while relying instead on the direct allocation of material resources for production and distribution with or without administratively determined prices.

The opening chapter of part 4 presents first the basic schemata of the workings of a socialist economy, as conceived by Marx and Engels. While Marx contended that he had no intention to prepare "recipes for the cooking pots of the future," he and especially Engels defined very clearly some recipes and these particular cooking pots. It was Engels who spelled out in his "mature" theoretical work, *Anti-Dühring* (1878), the essential features of the society that allegedly would emerge from the evolution and demise of capitalism. According to Engels, as soon as "the proletariat takes possession of the means of production in the name of society" market anarchy would be replaced by a "plan conforming conscious organization of society." Value, prices, and money would tend to vanish as soon as market spontaneity was replaced by physical planning "without the intervention of much vaunted 'values.'" Marx's conception certainly coincided with that of Engels. Indeed, in his famous *Critique of the Gotha Program* (1875), he indicated that, within "a co-operative society based on common ownership of the means of production," producers would not exchange their products; values (and prices) would not exist. The individual producer would simply give to the society his or her "individual quantum of labor" and would receive back from it, after certain deductions, exactly what had been given to it. Similarly, in the exchange of commodities, a given amount of labor would be exchanged for "equal amounts of labor in other forms." (Within such a framework, a term such as *market socialism* is an oxymoron.)

During the period of War Communism, the Bolshevik government extended state ownership and the direct authority and scope of its administration to the maximum, proclaimed a general obligation of work for all, and put into place a system of forced allocation of labor, centralized management of production, grain monopoly, and a distribution of goods through rationing and allocation in kind without trade. Starvation and the utter collapse of these economic arrangements forced a retreat from the goal of the "naturalization of economic

241

life" and the banishing of commodity and money relations. A new economic policy (NEP) and the resort to a whole set of changes in respect to taxes (in agriculture), local markets, money and prices, and the principles of management of the state property eventually revived the economy. By the end of 1928 the NEP was discarded as Stalin, in agreement with a large segment of the Bolshevik leadership, strengthened and expanded the application of the key principles of economic organization embodied in the Marxian schema and the economy of War Communism. Part 1 has already described the following features: full integration under the party's command of the state administration and the economy, the expansion of socialization to all sectors, the establishment of overall planning in physical terms using commands in regard to production and distribution, and the rigorous enforcement of policymakers' priorities over the wishes of the consumer, with the help of arbitrarily manipulated prices and limited and distorted market transactions reduced to subsidiary supports of the plan. After detailing various comparisons with War Communism, chapter 13 examines the main proposals made both by Soviet economists and foreign theoreticians for improving economic calculations in the system, by mimicking market supply and demand, better coordinating the plan's overlapping and poorly integrated supporting balances, and refining the scope of controls in the interactions between planners and managers of the enterprises. An examination of the causes and consequences of the utter failure of the Marx-Engels schema of economic organization, even after "improvements," as critically assessed by post-Stalin writers, concludes this chapter.

Chapter 14, the final chapter of part 4, presents the sequence of steps necessary for dismantling the Marx-Engels system in order to render possible the development of effective market relations and economic calculations. To start with, measures on the side of production organization are examined—notably, those related to the necessary dismantling of administratively created monopolies, the liberation of enterprises, the breakup of the walls between supply, production, and distribution, and the expansion of real competition and market relations in all directions. In regard to financial spheres, the chapter looks at the liquidation of barriers between transactions among enterprises, the population, and in foreign trade, and to the roles of banks, the stock market, and the budget in these processes. Then, the measures are contrasted with the dilemmas faced by the architects of restructuring as they try to rely, cautiously and marginally only, on market relations. Both during War Communism and Stalin's centrally administered model, as well as under NEP and the new reconstruction policies, the fundamental flaw of socialism remains that of the incapacity of this system to carry out effective *economic calculations*—be it with the help of "artificial markets," "artificial competition," a reduced scope of central allocation of capital and labor, clever price manipulations, or intermittent attention to the ever-changing relations between supply and demand over time and space.

CHAPTER 13

Suppression of the Free Market

Conceptual Frameworks

To a large extent the structural patterns of organization of the Soviet economy have been shaped by Marx and Engel's conception of socialism. While the founders of so-called scientific socialism did not systematically set out blueprints of a socialist future, they did indicate their views about the *principles of organization* of a socialist society. Their ideas about the socialization of the means of production and its impact on the centralized allocation of machinery and equipment, their theories on planning and on the harmonization of all economic activities, on incentives and productivity, as well as their concepts about the elimination of the market and the economic significance of prices and wages, income accounting, and distribution, have affected the ways of thinking of the Communist leaders and continue to influence their decisions about possible modifications of this system.

These ideas, extensively expounded by Engels in a series of theoretical articles published in a socialist journal in 1877 (and reprinted the next year in a book entitled *Anti-Dühring*), had first been formulated by Marx in a number of sources, particularly, in his well-known *Critique of the Gotha Program* (1875). Essentially, Engels asserted that the enormous expansive force of modern industry comes into continuous conflict with patterns of consumption and sales and with the absorptive capacity of the market. These collisions bring about overproduction and crises and compel the state—"the official representative of the capitalist society"—to become a "national capitalist," assuming the direction of production and converting great establishments for production and distribution into state property. This, however, is only a preliminary step to the complete takeover of all production forces "open and directly" by society itself. When this socialized appropriation occurs, the artificial restrictions on the expansion of production are eliminated and waste and devastation of productive forces and products are ended. With socialization, production of commodities—that is, production for the market—"is done away with," "anarchy in production is replaced by plan-conforming conscious organization," the productive forces "dovetail harmoniously into each other on the basis of one single vast plan," and industry is distributed "over the whole country in the way best adapted to its development." In such an economy accounting is done on the basis of the labor content of each product "without assigning value to products," that is, without prices in the conventional sense of the term.

In the *Critique of the Gotha Program*, Marx had indeed specified that in the "cooperative society based on the common ownership of the means of production," which will emerge from the capitalist society, the "producers do not exchange their products." The labor employed on their products does not appear anymore as the value of these products. In the new conditions, the producer (the worker) simply receives for a given "quantum of labor" (after certain social deductions) the same amount of labor in the form of products. The disappearance of value and money is stressed forcefully also in Marx's *Foundations [Grundrisse] of the Critique of Political Economy* (1857–58) where he states: "There can be nothing more erroneous and absurd than to postulate the control by united individuals of total production on the basis of exchange value, of money."

The ideas of organizing socialist society on the pattern of the German *Kriegswirtschaft* (the German war economy of World War I)—as a vast industrial enterprise run in a planned fashion without prices and money—were adopted by the leaders of German socialism and then taken over and adapted in various ways by Russian socialists of all tendencies. Their eventual implementation was feverishly debated during the short, intense, fast-moving period immediately *preceding* and immediately *following* the Bolshevik revolution—from the February revolution and the so-called accession to power of Russian capitalism, through a transitory period of state capitalism and workers' control following the October revolution, up to the disintegration of these controls, by the time of the Treaty of Brest-Litovsk and the first decrees of nationalizations of whole industries. During the period preceding October, the Mensheviks and Bolsheviks clashed over the functioning of the short-lived Russian capitalism. The former stressed what the French usually define as "*étatisme*" and "*dirigisme*" (jointly)—or, in free translation, "statism" and "fiscal and monetary steering." The Bolsheviks advocated "worker's control over the capitalists"—a position that they were preparing to carry over into the next period, that is, after their own seizure of political power. The economic proposals of the Mensheviks in May 1917 emphasized the powers of the state and its economic controlling and regulatory functions. They proposed the formation of state trading monopolies (for grain, meat, salt, and leather), state regulation of certain trusts (coal, oil, metal, sugar, and paper), state participation in the distribution of materials and finished products, price controls, and state surveillance over credit institutions. The Bolsheviks supported these proposals but with the special proviso that "the workers must request the immediate realization of real controls, first of all *by the workers themselves*"; this, according to the Bolsheviks, was the way to avoid "imminent economic catastrophe."

As Richard Lorenz points out in *The Beginnings of the Russian Industrial Policy* (1965), the Bolsheviks based their policy on the idea of the realization of state capitalism *with and through the system of Soviets*—as a central prerequisite for any other reforms. In other words, Lenin, and the Bolshevik leaders who supported him, at the time conceived as both possible and necessary the coexistence of capitalism in the economic sphere—under workers' control—and of socialist (that is, Bolshevik) power in the political sphere. The rationale of this coexistence is to be found in Lenin's thesis that, though it is easier to seize power in a less developed than in a more developed country, it is more difficult to bring about the crystallization of socialist economic relations there. To Lenin, the speed of revolutionary takeover was inversely proportional to the "ripeness of capitalist relationships," and what was decisive was *not* the immediate expropriation of the expropriators—to use Marx's well-known formula—but the establishment of an all-embracing workers' control over the capitalists in order to keep the economic machine in operation. In Lenin's writings of the time (for example, *State and Revolution*), the entire economy must become a "*single factory* and *a single* office" under the control of the "armed workers." He conceived workers' control as a means of coercing the capitalists to cooperate with Soviet power. The workers would hire the technicians, bookkeepers, and managers, and later, as the operations of economic control become increasingly simple, and, "as anyone who can read and write and who knows the first rules of arithmetic" becomes able to perform them, a new system would eventually emerge. The functions of bookkeeping and management would be performed by each in turn, would become a habit, and would finally "die out as the special function of a special stratum of the population."

Lenin's policy in the winter of 1917–18 thus aimed to reorganize the economy with the *help of the capitalists*. But not all the Bolsheviks agreed with this policy. For some, the question of the socialization of industry was already on the agenda; for others, workers' control was a necessary step in that eventual direction. The conflict between the partisans of outright state socialism and those of state capitalism did not last long in practice. The capitalist entrepreneurs did not feel at the time that they could work efficiently under workers' control; on the other hand, the Bolsheviks in the factories were drawn more and more toward the formation and coordination of a system of economic Soviets—similar to the system of political Soviets—rather than toward the utilization of the old managerial machine. Finally, on December 2, 1917, the Bolsheviks formed the Supreme Economic Council (VSNKh) under the Council of People's Commissars with the precise task of organizing the economy as a whole and of coordinating inter alia every form of workers' control at all levels. Yet the chaotic situation in industry continued, with some factories confiscated, others closed down or abandoned by their owners, and others engaged in trading with the peasants instead of with other factories. By the beginning of 1918 the illusion of an economy based on private property under workers' control was fast disappearing. What was taking its place was a war economy crudely patterned on the German war economy. By May–June, 1918, acute shortages of commodities and widespread famine, along with various war imperatives, pushed the Soviet government toward the full implementation of what became known as War Communism—a complex of measures concerning the nationalization of even small-scale industries, outright requisition of peasants' so-called grain surplus, state-organized distribution of products instead of trade, and the abolition of money within the state sector, along with vast currency emissions to cover the state's own purchases on the legally nonexistent free market. Thus, the collapse of state capitalism, the civil war, and the Communist war economy tended to bring about a deep correspondence between the earlier theoretical assumptions about the characteristics of the socialist society and the actual everyday Bolshevik policies and practical arrangements in the period from 1918 to the beginning of 1921.

Patterns of Organization

The decree of December, 1917, that established the VSNKh empowered it to "work out the general norms and plan regulation of the economic life of the country." Eventually, the country's production, transportation, and distribution were organized under the presidium of the VSNKh and under various commissions and departments along branches of activity. Except for small undertakings, enterprises lost all autonomy. In principle, branches and enterprises were financed by state budget allotments, and, in turn, they were supposed to hand over to the state any and all monetary receipts. However, as economic relations became increasingly "naturalized"—that is, as centralized allocations and corresponding requisitions of materials and products became the rule—the financial dispositions lost all significance. On November 2, 1918, a Committee for Utilization—prefiguring the Material-Technical Supply System—was given the task of assessing, on the one hand, the expected supply of certain resources (for example, grain, oil, and gas) and, on the other hand, their expected allocation. These first balanced estimates were submitted to and approved by the VSNKh. An ever-increasing number of products became subject to central control, with the respective allocations determined either on the basis of norms or of rations. By the end of 1919 forty-four categories of products—ranging from salt and sugar to felt boots and woolen cloth—were centrally allocated. By 1920 the central balances involved fifty-five product categories with three hundred fifty articles. The simple statistical accounting procedure of balancing supply and distribution eventually became the heart and soul of Soviet planning. A crucial theoretical and practical step in regard to the possible coordination of these product-specific, independent balances was made in 1924–25 when the Central Statistical Office published the *Balance of the National Economy of the USSR for 1923–24,* the pioneering input-output work prefiguring the American input-output theory and analysis of Wassily Leontief.

The suppression of free markets—that is, the naturalization of the economy—had its main roots in the decision of the Bolshevik government in May 9, 1918, to requisition the so-called surpluses of grain "hidden" by the peasants—surpluses over and above the compulsory deliveries of grain paid at meaningless, officially fixed prices. The peasantry tried to resist these arbitrary confiscations in whatever ways they could. Proclaiming a "food dictatorship," the Commissariat for Food then launched a brutal campaign in the countryside aimed at making the peasants "disgorge" their allegedly hidden resources. (In many ways this campaign prefigured Stalin's brutal attack on the villages a decade later.) By November 21, 1918, a government decree simply did away with the system of compulsory deliveries at fixed prices. As the official decree put it, "In order to replace the machinery of private trade and to supply the population in a planned manner through Soviet and cooperative units of distribution, the Commissariat for Food must collect every necessary product for personal consumption and for households." Commenting on this decree, Laszlo Szamuely rightly noted (in a 1974 study on the *First Model of the Socialist Economic Systems*) that with this the government took a crucial step; thereby, trade was in fact officially "liquidated and all free market transactions prohibited." With the "moneyless" system of interfirm allocations and product exchange, the official cessation of market relations between the towns and the countryside, the introduction of ration books and payment of the workers in kind, and the obligation for every citizen with some state or cooperative shop to obtain his or her ration, market relations became illegal. Yet illegal exchanges continued even in the interstices of the state complex. The state itself continued to issue depreciating currency to cover its expenses in illegal markets, though it assumed that in due time it will "put an end to the expiring monetary circulation." As Nikolai Bukharin and Eugenii Preobrazhensky put it in *The ABC of Communism* (written in 1919 but published in 1922), in time, "even in private trade among the peasants, money will pass into the background" as corn will be exchanged only for such products in kind as clothing, utensils, and furniture. "The increasing depreciation of currency" was, according to the Bolsheviks, "essentially an expression of the annulment of monetary values."

War Communism ended in disaster. As Lenin put it in October 17, 1921, in his report, "The New Economic Policy and the Tasks of the Political Education Departments" (*Collected Works,* vol. 33), up to the spring of that year the Bolsheviks had assumed "uncalculatingly" that "there would be a direct transition from the old Russian economy to state production and distribution on

Communist lines." This, however, added Lenin, was a mistake. The error consisted of having tried to bypass "a prolonged, complex transition through socialist accounting and control," a prolonged phase of state capitalism. Having suffered a severe economic defeat, the only solution left was "a strategical retreat." It is important to note that Lenin did not reject the socialist schemata embodied in War Communism; he merely asserted that its fiasco was due to an unwitting impatience to use the so-called direct Communist approach for "developing the productive forces which the program of the party regarded as vital and urgent." Alas, this impatience actually "hindered the growth of productive forces and proved to be the main cause of the profound economic and political crisis that we experienced in the spring of 1921."

The question of what strategy would be able to produce the development of large-scale industry, "which the program of the party regarded as vital and urgent," was arduously debated in the 1920s. It divided the Communist leadership, and then the entire party, into sharply varying factions and ultimately shaped for decades to come both Soviet economic policy and the organization of the Soviet economy. (I have examined these debates in detail in *Soviet Strategy for Economic Growth* [1964].) The Soviet goal of modern economic development—namely, creating a powerful military-industrial complex, increasing overall productive capacity, changing the technology, raising productivity, and sharply increasing total and per capita income—was connected also with a number of ideological approaches to the questions of ownership forms and the uses of trade and market mechanisms.

The drive for the expansion of productive capacity was linked to various theses concerning, notably, the liquidation of "precapitalist and capitalist forms of production," particularly in agriculture, the nature of the terms of trade between the towns and the countryside, and the possibility of achieving and of maintaining "socialism in one country." Briefly, the party's left-wingers, led by Leon Trotsky, affirmed the need to establish the "dictatorship of industry" as the unique lever of vast internal socioeconomic changes and as a means of consolidating the "dictatorship of the proletariat," increasing the importance of workers in the total labor force, and changing the relationship between state-owned industry and privately owned agriculture. The right-wingers, led by Nikolai Bukharin, emphasized instead the needs to strengthen "the workers' and peasants' alliance" as a means of consolidating the Soviet regimes and expanding agricultural production as the best support for a systematically growing industry. The left-wingers claimed that the capitalist danger was ever present, that time was of the essence, and that socialism could not triumph in the USSR if the revolution did not spread further in industrialized Europe. The right-wingers dismissed these contentions and asserted that full socialism could be constructed in isolation in the USSR even at a "turtle's pace." Those who, like Stalin, fluctuated between the two tendencies, but who had complete faith in the political might gathered by the party machine in the USSR, embarrassed themselves little with theories about the pace of world revolution. They focused instead on what could be done at home to further strengthen and consolidate the party's hold over all aspects of the country's activity and transform the USSR into a world power.

Stalin took over from the left the ideas of the dictatorship of industry and the necessity for agriculture to pay "tribute" for the purpose. He took from the right the idea that full socialism could indeed be constructed in the USSR, but he added that this could be done only at an accelerated rate of economic development. The 15th Party Conference—already controlled by Stalin—affirmed at the end of October, 1926, that "all the efforts of the party and of the state" would be directed toward the aim of catching up with and surpassing the level of the most advanced industrial countries" within "a minimal historical period." In the drive to catch up, Stalin resorted to War Communism's methods. He pushed the expansion of socialization in all directions, the virtual elimination of all private production and trade, the massive diversion of investable resources to heavy industry at the expense of agriculture and the consumer, and the achievement of the fastest rate of growth possible in industrial capacity and output.

Just as War Communism's leaders had looked upon the peasantry as both the enemy of the system and the source of funds for industry, so Stalin looked upon the private peasant as the biggest and most troublesome challenge to his great industrialization drive. In a speech on "Grain Procurement and the Prospects for the Development of Agriculture" (*Collected Works*, vol. 11) delivered in January, 1928, Stalin announced his decision to proceed at breakneck speed toward the collectivization of agriculture. Alleging that the Soviet Union could not rest "upon two heterogeneous foundations. upon united socialized industry and upon individual small-peasant economy based on private ownership of the means of production," Stalin argued that the moment had come "to pass from the socialization of industry to the socialization of agriculture." Collectivization was the means not only of liquidating private property but also of removing the danger that the peasant would not deliver his grain in the amounts and at the ridiculous prices fixed by the state. In July, 1928, in a speech cynically entitled "On the Bond between Workers and Peasants" (*Collected Works*, vol. 11), Stalin affirmed that the peasant must not only pay the usual direct and indirect taxes and "overpay relatively high prices for manufactured goods," but also must accept being "underpaid for agricultural produce." This, added Stalin, was "an additional tax levied on the peasantry for the sake of promoting industry . . . . It is something in the nature of a 'tribute,' of a supertax which we are compelled to levy for the time being in order to preserve and accelerate our present rate of industrial development."

In 1921 Lenin had asserted that, for "restoring large-scale industry," the

Bolsheviks were forced "to borrow from the peasants a certain quantity of foodstuffs and raw materials by requisitioning" (Lenin, *Collected Works*, vol. 33). The new and much more heavy borrowing of Stalin's regime could not be carried out by direct requisitioning; it required the concomitant uprooting, killing, or deporting of tens of millions of so-called Kulaks (rich peasants), who left the countryside in a disastrous state for decades. By January 26, 1934, in his report to the 17th Party Congress (*Collected Works*, vol. 13), Stalin was hypocritically advising his henchmen, busy with the brutal mopping up of the last vestiges of private property in the countryside, not to be "dizzy with success . . . now that the country has been transferred on to the lines of industrialization and collectivization," since many difficulties still lie ahead.

Some nine months after the launching of the First Five-Year Plan, Stalin, praising his successes, closely tied his policies with those of War Communism. In a "Year of Great Change" (*Collected Works*, vol. 12), he noted, "We may therefore say that our Party succeeded in making good use of our retreat during the first stage of the New Economic Policy, in order, in the subsequent stage, to organize the change and to launch a successful offensive against the capitalist elements." And Stalin then recalled that Lenin had stated in 1921 (in Lenin, *Collected Works*, vol. 27), "We are now retreating, going back as it were; but we are doing this in order, by retreating first, afterwards to take a run and make a more powerful leap forward. It was on this condition alone that we retreated in pursing our New Economic Policy." Stalin then went on to say that the five-year plan was accelerating the production of the means of production, was placing the country on an "iron-and-steel basis," and was finally transforming the country from an agrarian to an advanced industrial one.

While nationalization was engulfing agriculture and all-round planning was taking its grip on the whole economy, the offensive against market relations took a somewhat different course than during War Communism. According to Stalin, the NEP had two orientations in regard to private trade; on the one hand, unlike War Communism, it aimed at "ensuring *a certain freedom* for private trade"; on the other hand, it took measures "directed *against complete freedom* for private trade," aimed at ensuring the role of the state as "regulator of the market" ("The Right Deviation in the CPSU," April, 1929, *Collected Works*, vol. 12). According to Stalin, since the beginning of 1929, the market as such had not been suppressed, but it had become "a special type of trade," namely, a trade without private capitalists and speculators, a trade involving primarily state industry with the collective and state farms—in short, a trade at centrally administered prices between centrally manipulated traders. But trade involves commodities and money relations. In Stalin's conception, commodities would continue to exist but *only* in the relations between the state sector and the collective farms, not within the state sector itself. Within the latter, products would be transferred on the basis of bookkeeping accounts, allegedly without involving money. The goal of a completely moneyless economy, as Engels had suggested and War Communism had tried to achieve, had to be shifted to some point into the future.

When Lenin had been forced by "objective conditions" to abandon War Communism and to accept the idea of trade, he stated: "Communism and trade? It sounds strange. The two seem to be unconnected, incongruous, poles apart." Yet, he added, trade is "not more removed from Communism" than "the small peasant is" ("The Importance of Gold," November, 1921, *Collected Works,* vol. 33). Stalin justified the continuation of trade under socialism essentially with the same kind of reasoning. As he put it in 1952 in his *Economic Problems of Socialism in the USSR,* the collective farmers simply do not want to alienate their goods other than as commodities; and, because of this, "commodity production and trade are as much a necessity with us today as they were thirty years ago, when Lenin spoke of the necessity of developing trade to the utmost." Stalin remained faithful to the Marxian tenet that the free market must be suppressed; indeed, he noted in the same work, "of course, when instead of the two basic sectors, the state and the collective farm sector, there will be only one all-embracing production sector, with the right to dispose of all consumer goods produced in the country, commodity circulation, with its 'money economy' will disappear as being an unnecessary element in the national economy."

In short, after the collapse of War Communism and the shifting into the future of the idea of a completely naturalized, moneyless economy, Stalin's system, constructed after the retreat of the NEP, exhibited a *dichotomous* character. On the one hand, it relied on what its leaders believed to be moneyless transactions among the state enterprises; and, on the other hand, it accommodated itself with commodity relations and with "cash" transactions in regulated markets with the peasant economy and with households. As far as the state sector was concerned, this system was fully consistent, in the minds of its creators, with both the Marx-Engels conceptual framework and with War Communism. As such, it functioned virtually unchanged until the mid-1980s.

Commands and Soviet "Economic Accounting"

As the investment requirements of industrialization grew continuously from the launching of the First Five-Year Plan, the policy-making center had to focus its attention not only on the expansion of the means of production and the physical targets of the economic plan, but also on the levels of capital accumulation and the practices of cost accounting. As Stalin indicated in an important speech delivered on June 23, 1931, at a conference of Soviet business executives ("New Conditions—New Tasks in Economic Construction," *Collected Works,* vol. 13), the country faced the need not only to recondition and restructure old factories, but also to create entirely new, technically well-equipped industries. In the recent past, he noted, "we got the millions of rubles we needed" from the light industry, agriculture, and budget savings. Now, he continued, we need to concentrate on economic accounting. Costs had to be brought down, wages had to be largely differentiated by skills and productivity, and business organizations, "which have long ceased to keep proper accounts, to calculate, to draw up sound balance-sheets," had to change their ways. It was necessary "to introduce and reinforce business accounting, to increase accumulation in industry."

Could meaningful business accounting be practiced within an economy devoid of free markets—that is, meaningful prices—for the means of production? Could the obligatory fulfillment of physical, quantitative plan targets set for the production enterprises be made consistent with accurate monetary accounts? Could the economy function, on the one hand, as a strict command economy and, on the other, as a coordinated entity based on real economic accounting (*khozraschet*)? Soviet policymakers and planners tried both to perfect the specificity and coherence of the often overlapping and contradictory physical plan instructions *and* to render khozraschet congruous and operational on the basis of arbitrarily manipulated prices. The objective proved unattainable on both counts. Recall the oscillations in regard to the channels of chains from the center to the production units; the emphasis was first on the principle of branch organization, then regional organizations, then back to the branch but, within them, with various regional reinforcements. Recall too the efforts deployed in order to make the central instructions fewer, consistent, and capable of motivating the enterprises' managers in the ways desired by the center. In regard to plan consistency, enormous efforts were made in the search for optimality. Extensive research was carried out in appropriate institutions applying cybernetic concepts, linear programming, system engineering, and operations research methods. Most of these academic exercises, predicated as they were on unreliable data and often approximate methods of calculation, had little impact either on the center or the enterprises. As Michael Ellman noted in his 1971 study, *Soviet Planning Today,* "as a practical activity optimal planning is concerned with obtaining bad answers to questions to which worse answers are obtained by other methods." But the planning bureaucrats were sticking anyway to the old and tried "worse" answers obtained by the traditional methods. In any case, as Ellman added, "it would be a mistake to suppose that the compilation of optional plans is an alternative to the expansion of *khozraschet.*"

Enormous efforts were also invested in respect to economic accounting. Much was done in order to develop ways of eliciting more truthful information from the managers of the enterprises on their real output capacities, actual output mixes, and real costs. As George N. Halm recalls in a cogent article,

"Allocation and Motivation in the Socialist Economy" (1968), which focused on the Liberman plan and the Kosygin reform of the 1960s, uncertainties and risks in terms of interrupted production processes and pressures of meeting targets induced managers to shy away from innovations, to understate production capacities, to overstate their needs for materials, fuel, and equipment, and to handle khozraschet as a kind of obligatory method of misinformation. In a much heralded paper, Liberman proposed in the early 1960s the introduction of an incentive system based on profits and on greater freedom of maneuver for the enterprises' managers. This changeover to the broader use of economic levers was to rely on profits—on a "profitability rate" expressing profits as a percentage related to the value of productive assets and a long-term "profitability norm" established centrally for every branch of production. Since all this depended on arbitrarily set prices, they could hardly straighten out khozraschet. Profit rates, in Liberman and Kosygin's sense, were meaningless when figured out on the bases of wrong cost prices and capital values. Further, the attempt to achieve consistency among the operations of a non-market interindustry state sector, through a plan based on physical targets but supported with credits as needed, appeared doubtful even to Stalin when he was stressing the need of khozraschet. Indeed, as he put it in his 1931 speech to Soviet business executives: "It is a fact that in a number of enterprises and business organizations such concepts as 'regime economy,' 'cutting down unproductive expenditure,' 'rationalization of production' have long gone out of fashion. Evidently they assume that the State Bank 'will advance the necessary funds anyway.'" Nothing, alas, has really changed in this regard since then.

As early as the turn of the twentieth century, some Western economists seriously questioned Marx and Engel's conception of a socialist economy, which could allocate its resources efficiently simply on the basis of the "quantities of labor required for each product" and "without assigning any value to products." In 1902 in the "Problems of Value in a Socialist Society" (reprinted in Friedrich A. Hayek's 1938 collection *Collectivist Economic Planning*), a Dutch economist, N. G. Pierson, and the Italian Enrico Barone in 1908 (in "The Minister of Production of a Socialist State," included in the same collection) showed that the rationale that led to rational allocation in a perfectly competitive capitalist economy would apply equally to a socialist one. Barone demonstrated how the indicated minister would have to calculate the equivalents that satisfy the "equations expressing the physical necessities of production," reintroduce, no matter under what name, "all the categories of the old regime . . . prices, salaries, interest, rent, profits, savings, etc.," and then also observe the conditions that characterize free competition, namely, "minimum cost of production and the equalization of price to cost of production," if he wanted to achieve efficient allocation in the socialist state.

The discussion took a more dramatic turn in 1920 when Ludwig von

Mises (in "Economic Calculation in the Socialist Commonwealth," also included in the Hayek volume) asserted flatly that "where there is no market, there is no price mechanism; without a pricing mechanism, there is no economic calculation." Von Mises stressed the idea that, even if the prices of finished goods were determined by the market, they could not be properly related to costs in a system where, by definition, the market for producer goods was eliminated. Von Mises emphasized subsequently in various studies that he did not question the ability of a socialist society to order the production "of cannons or clothes, dwelling houses or churches, luxuries or subsistence," but rather its ability to ascertain how its productive resources could be used more effectively to produce these goods. If Barone had essentially attempted to refute the "fantastic doctrine" that optimally efficient production in a collectivist state could be ordered differently than a free-market production, von Mises challenged the very existence of objective standards of rational orientation under socialism. Before going further, it is worth noting that Barone had been absolutely right that any attempt at economic calculation in a socialist society posited the need to use "the categories of the old regime . . . prices, salaries, interest, rent, profits, savings, etc." The Soviet Union reintroduced all the old categories—allegedly, with new social connotations but, in the absence of markets for producer goods, the absence of competition, and the arbitrary manipulations of the prices and wages, they did not yield proper results.

Two basic answers were formulated in response to von Mises's challenge. The first one, associated with the name of H. D. Dickson but common also to a number of German economists, asserted that socialism was *not* incompatible with markets for producer goods, which simply eliminated the very issue to which an answer was supposed to be given. The second answer, associated with Oskar Lange (in an essay, *On the Economic Theory of Socialism,* 1936), provided for a special procedure for ascertaining the proper relative prices of producer goods. Lange suggested that the socialist Central Planning Administration (CPA) could find these prices by assuming the functions of a competitive market. The CPA could start from a set of prices picked at random and adjust them periodically by successive approximations so as to strike a balance between supply and demand. Each manager would be instructed to regard the accounting prices as being independent of his own output or expansion decisions. This so-called competitive, *market-socialist* solution was criticized by Hayek in two important articles ("On the Economic Theory of Socialism" [1936] and "The Competitive Solution" [1940]) in which he argued that the amount of information needed by the CPA would be overwhelming and, secondly, and more importantly, that market prices result from complex interactions among individuals with dissimilar types of interests and knowledge and not from parametric data available to passive pricetakers.

This Western academic debate found interesting and important rejoinders from East European economists, who witnessed both the inner workings and the limitations of the CPAs in their own countries. The Czech economist, Karel Kouba, for instance, drew attention (in "Plan and Market in the Socialist Economy" [1967]) to the diverging interests and motivations of the planning organs and the managers of the enterprises. Planners' data collection and processing, he noted, are not purely technical matters. These data, furnished by the enterprises' managers, involve the latter's material interests concerning earnings, prices, and "social funds," and the credibility of such data is highly questionable. Conversely, the data adjusted and supplied as commands by the planners are also distorted in order to convey a variety of instructions and are not accepted passively by the managers. Hungarian economist Marton Tardos dismissed Lange's solution (in "The Conditions of Developing a Regulated Market" [1986]) as a "ramification of hypotheses alien to reality." According to Tardos, Lange's model, "built upon total centralization of price fixing, and upon centrally set rules of behavior, harmonizes well with the [Walrasian] general equilibrium model," but, in reality, in a capitalist economy a center is not needed, while in a command socialist economy could function only a center "with special knowledge and decision abilities" (decisions that far exceed price fixing). And Tardos concluded that this model was "called without justification, the market model of socialism." Another Hungarian economist, Janos Karnai, also asserted (in "The Hungarian Reform Process" [1986]) that Lange had made his conjectures in "the sterile world of Walrasian pure theory." He then drew attention especially to Lange's "erroneous assumptions" concerning the behavior of both planners and enterprises' managers. Lange's planners, affirmed Kornai, "are reincarnations of Plato's philosophers, embodiment of unity, usefulness and wisdom. They are satisfied with doing nothing else but strictly enforcing the 'Rule', adjusting prices to excess demand. Such an unworldly bureaucracy never existed in the past and will never exist in the future." Then, like Kouba, Kornai stressed that organizations, and leaders who identify themselves with organizations, "have deeply ingrained drives" concerning the survival, growth, expansion, power, and prestige of their organizations. Society "is not a parlor game where the inventor of the game can arbitrarily invent the rules." In short, no fully convincing argument, either theoretical or practical, has been adduced against von Mises's clear and lapidary formula.

On Stalin's "Economics" Heritage

Soviet analyses and evaluations of the connections between Stalinism and Leninism and their relations to both Marx and Russia's traditions, history, and revolutionary movements, as well as to Stalin's theories of economics and to his practical way of running his administrative-centralist state, are vast and far reaching. Given the great impact of some of these discussions and the probing questions they raise, however, a brief summary of some salient points on the roots of these policies, the principles of these economics, and the functioning of the centralist system seem in order.

G. Vodolazov remarked (in *Octiabr,* June, 1989) in the analysis of Vasilii Grossman's novella, *Everything Flows,* that the roots of both Stalinism and Leninism go back to the violent ideas of the "barracks communism" (*kazarmennyi kommunism*) of Sergei Nechaev and Peter Tkachev and not to the beliefs in reason, truth, and human decency of Nikolai Chernishevski, as is usually and erroneously asserted. The authoritarianism and voluntarism typical of both War Communism and Stalin's system involved, according to Vodolazov, in the former case "the naïveté of the revolutionary masses" but embodied in the latter case the bureaucracy's own interests—a bureaucracy that perceived in them "ideal tools" of government. Grossman himself actually traced even farther the roots of Leninism-Stalinism, namely, to the "traditional national, millennial unfreedoms" in which Russia has been plunged since the beginnings of its history—a contention sharply criticized by an increasing crop of vocal nationalist writers.

But could something else other than barracks communism be built on a noncommodity-nonmarket foundation? asks the philosopher Alexander Tsipko (in *Nauka i zhizn,* nos. 11, 12, 1988, and no. 1, 1989). Could sound guarantees of individual freedom and democracy actually exist "when all members of society work for the proletarian state and have no independent sources of existence?" Does not the very idea of a revolutionary vanguard lead necessarily "to new forms of social inequality?" As Tsipko rightly points out, Stalin's concepts did not differ *in essence* from those of the "mortal enemy" of the Bolsheviks, the German socialist theoretician Karl Kautsky, nor from the views of Leon Trotsky, who also had faith "in the possibility of a noncommodity, nonmarket economy." And Tsipko asks bitterly whether there was a real, imperative need for the massive crimes committed in the campaign of "expropriation of the kulaks," or, for that matter, the policy of industrialization itself, a policy based not on "calculations of any sort" but only on arguments "strictly normative in nature," none of which, he claims, were based on facts.

In a critical examination of Stalin's economics, Tina Dzokaeva recalls that, when Stalin assumed the role of "supreme judge" in this and other disciplines, socialism was glorified as a "conflict-free economic system" in which all the principles that activate any other economic system were said to have little or no play (*Pravda,* May 6, 1988). The Soviet system was supposed to function according to the "specific laws of socialism, headed by the law of conformity to the plan," which explained and justified everything. It was on these and other similar simplistic contentions—about "the absence of wage labor," "the work force automatically ceasing to be a commodity," "the directly social nature of labor under socialism"—that were constructed dozens of economics textbooks, including the latest, which came out in the 1980s. And another economist, Boris Bolotin, remarks (in an article included in *The Stalin Phenomenon*, a pamphlet published in Moscow in 1988) that Stalin's fixation with "production relations" (the relations of the workers to the socialized enterprises as both owners and producers) and his peculiar conception of commodities and money (which continued to exist allegedly only because of the persistence of collective farms) "shaped economic thinking not only among a considerable number of our managers but also among our scholars." Ownership relations within the countryside determined, in short, the existence or nonexistence of the theoretical blueprint drawn by Marx and Engels, and the peasants themselves were accordingly treated as a terrible hindrance—to be disposed of, as Tsipko had noted, like the infidels in other kinds of societies. Of course, many of these criticisms of Stalin's economics had been put forward long before, in extensive and remarkable analyses in Eastern Europe—notably, in Poland in the 1950s and in Czechoslovakia and Hungary in the 1960s where each and every aspect of the implications of Stalinism have been perceptively dissected. Yet what is crucial to note is that these ideas are finally getting such great exposure in the USSR itself.

One of the most probing analyses of Stalin's centralist system is perhaps to be found in an early 1960s novel by Alexander Bek, *New Appointments*, which Gavriil Popov examines insightfully in "From an Economist's Point of View" (*Nauka i zhizn*, reprinted in *The Stalin Phenomenon*). What does such a system involve? As Bek reconstructs it around the fictitious character Onisimov, "chairman of the State Committee for Metallurgy and Fuel," and as Popov cogently points out, it involves first of all absolute subordination to the top (Stalin and, eventually, his successors) and rigorous and utter execution of all the directives handed down. To carry out the tasks, the chairman relies on the absolute subordination of his staff. He issues detailed instructions and concrete assignments for the staff, design offices, and scientists and controls everybody continuously and relentlessly. All along the pyramid the favorite slogan is "no arguing"—what matters is the execution. Harsh words, reprimands, and swinging blows are employed, but each one thinks that's how it should be, it is the rule, the usual order of things. The system needs workers who have stamped out all individual traits except those that are necessary to insure that the system works. The defects of the system are overloading of the top, the isolation of its members from real life, and the incapacity of those trained at any given echelon to take up higher responsibility when needed; each cog fits perfectly at a given spot and nowhere else in a machine that does not work. The enforced blending of diligence with personal loyalty at each step of the ladder is reinforced by a "subsystem of fear"—of dismissal and even physical liquidation. The entire system is no good for other decisions than totally centralized ones; it proves more and more rigid, unbending, and incapable of dealing on a day-to-day basis with what matters most in an economic system, *choice among alternatives*.

Concluding Comments

At the turn of the last century, Eduard Bernstein, the German social democrat who became the bête noire of many other socialists and of the Communists, cogently dismissed Marx and Engel's conception of a harmoniously directed society on the basis of a "plan-conforming conscious organization" rendered possible by the socialization of the means of production. In the lyrical terminology of Engels (in *Anti-Dühring*), through socialization "the whole sphere of the conditions of life" now comes under "the dominion and control of man, who for the first time becomes the real, conscious lord of nature, because he has now become master of his own social organization." In *Prerequisites of Socialism and the Tasks of the Social-Democracy,* Bernstein prosaically pointed out that, if one wished to expropriate all undertakings in Germany "say of twenty persons and upwards, be it for state management altogether or for partly managing and partly leasing them," he would set for himself a gigantic task. "What abundance of judgment, practical knowledge, talent for administration, must a government or a national assembly have at its disposal to be even equal to the supreme management or managing control of such a gigantic enterprise."

As we said, the Bolsheviks were not deterred by the needs of abundant judgment, practical knowledge, and talent for administration. Before the revolution and during War Communism, Lenin assumed (in *The State and Revolution*) that "after the overthrow of the capitalists and the bureaucrats, it is quite possible to proceed immediately, overnight, to replace them in the control of production"; that all citizens would become "employees and workers of a single countrywide 'syndicate'"; and that all that was required was that "they should work equally, do their proper share of work, and get equal pay." The German social democrat Karl Kautsky—dubbed by Lenin as a renegade and a traitor—answered (in *The Labor Revolution* [1921]): "No, a social apparatus of production which is of so simple a nature that anybody can organize and direct it, and in which the manager has nothing to do except to supervise work and pay everybody an equal wage—that is a prison, not a factory. Even the simplest factory places greater demands upon its managers, to say nothing of the collective social work." And Kautsky added for good measure that such "crude economic ideas" reveal "a fabulous ignorance" of the immense difficulties involved in such schemes. Indeed, War Communism led to ruin and utter disaster.

Stalin, who absolutely dominated the party, state, and economy, assumed that he alone could perfectly well determine the appropriate patterns of organization of the economy, set the pace of its growth, trace the path of its development, and lay down the line to be followed by the population and the country as a whole. As he put it in a "reply to discussion" on his report to the 16th Party Congress (July, 1930, *Collected Works*, vol. 13), "There is of course no need to dwell on the correctness of the propositions expounded in the report. There is no such need because, in view of its evident correctness, the Party line stands in no need of further defence at this Congress." Deriding this fatal conceit, Friedrich Hayek reminds us (in *The Fatal Conceit: The Errors of Socialism*, Collected Works, vol. 1) not only that "there is not and never could be a single directing mind at work," but also that any attempt at control beyond the immediate direct purview of any central authority required enormously complex, evolving, and interacting information. Order and control could be achieved only if each of the participants—controllers as well as local managers—"who could gauge visible and potential resources were also currently informed of the constantly changing relative importance of such resources, and could then communicate full and accurate details about this to some central planning authority," which, in turn, would be able to tell them what to do in light of other information reaching the planners from other sources, and so on, again back to the planners.

Alexander Tsipko pointed out another type of conceit also involved in Stalinism, the conviction that pure socialism and progress toward a "non-contradictory state" were at hand. According to Tsipko, the Russians succumbed to the temptation of believing that they could create "something that no one else ever had." History, says Tsipko, had set a trap for them: "People sincerely believed that we were a special people and a special country created to work wonders, 'to make reality the fable.' And Stalin made masterful use of this conceit of people who had worked the wonder of revolution." We turn now to the immense difficulties involved in the dismantling of such a system, even when its disastrous results are apparent to almost everyone.

CHAPTER 14

Rehabilitation of the Market

Issues In the Reversion to Markets

For a long time the economic transformations made by the Communist regimes—the creation of powerful centralist governments, socialization of the means of production, exclusive state ownership in manufacturing, banking, transportation, and trade, and replacement of the market with commands and central allocations—were proclaimed to be *irreversible*, the unalterable, final outcomes of historical processes started under capitalism. Actually, all kinds of alterations had to be practiced from time to time in these allegedly unalterable and irreversible outcomes. Indeed, many modifications were made in the institutional fabric of the Soviet Union, and then of the East European countries, long before the complete collapse of the latter's Communist regimes.

To establish standards against which one could better ascertain the specific changes envisaged or practiced under the policy of perestroika and, in order to sketch the further indispensable measures of restructuring, the following discussion will first present step-by-step the measures taken to change a primarily market-directed economy into a centrally administered one. It will then present in reverse order the measures needed to dismantle such a system. At the 102d meeting of the American Economic Association in December, 1989, one of the panels focused on the supposed absence of a specific literature indicating how a centrally planned economy could be transformed into a market-directed one. Actually, it seems that any elementary economics textbook contains useful indications in this respect.

Let us then recall briefly first the sequence of the main measures implemented by the Communists and the criteria used in the elimination of market relations. While some of these measures have been taken concomitantly in a number of sectors, for the purpose of clarity, it is helpful to follow them *sector by sector*. Consider the process of nationalization—more accurately, the statification (from the French "étatisation") of manufacturing undertaken in the USSR, first haphazardly during War Communism and then again in a systematic fashion during the NEP period. Nationalization and reorganization involved, to start with, the large-scale industries of producer and consumer goods and were extended subsequently to small-scale industries, cooperatives, and artisanal workshops. Nationalization without compensation encompassed all assets—buildings and auxiliary installations, machinery and equipment, stocks of raw materials, patents and trademarks, and checks and deposits. The term *large-scale* was applied on the basis of various criteria such as number of workers and employees, output capacity, and share in total output in a given area. In regard to small-scale enterprises, various distinctions were considered appropriate at different points in time concerning, notably, the capacity and equipment of workshops, number of hands employed, type of work (repair or services), and old or new lines of production. The reorganization of manufacturing, as described before, proceeded on the basis of the principle of the submission of the enterprise's operation to a higher authority within a branch (or territorial setup).

According to official Soviet data (*Narodnoe khoziastvo*, 1956), by the end of the NEP in 1928, the state industry owned 69.4 percent of total industrial establishments, the cooperatives 13 percent, and the "capitalist and small production" 17.6 percent. By the end of the Second Five-Year Plan, the shares had shifted to 90.3 percent, 9.5 percent, and 0.2 percent. In regard to agriculture, domestic and foreign trade, and various other sectors, the pace of nationalization varied significantly. In Tsarist Russia the peasantry owned roughly two-thirds of the land, the landowners a little over one-third. By the end of the NEP, less than 2 percent of peasant households were collectivized; by 1937, this figure stood at 93 percent. The total agricultural land was absorbed either into the state farms or into collective farms. As far as private retail trade was concerned, it accounted for over three-quarters of the total in the early 1920s; by 1935 this type of trade had ceased to exist, and only the private trade of collective peasants in the collective farm markets remained legal. In regard to foreign trade, the Bolsheviks established the state monopoly of imports, exports, and foreign exchange from the moment of their accession to power, and the system remained virtually unaltered until 1986. Concomitant with these transformations, the Communists extended the nationalization in transportation and communications, much of which was already state owned, as well as into the nonproductive sphere in education, health care, and related services.

In order to cement the central role of the Soviet government in the economy, the state undertook radical restructuring of the financial sector. It nationalized the banks and consolidated them into a monobank of issue and economic control over the entire economy. Secondly, it changed the role of the state budget and the structure of government receipts and expenditures, increased the shares extracted from certain industries and then redirected them toward other industries. It then separated the monetary circulation into three distinct and differently controlled compartments (interindustry flows, cash flows to households, and foreign trade). Finally, it established, mainly from

1925 on, a consolidated centralized economic planning system—concerning first the nationalized industries and then, from 1929 on, the economy as a whole (on the basis of physical instructions on inputs and outputs supported by state credits and centrally administered prices and wages). As time went on, pressing needs of coping either with deep and disastrous economic break-downs or with a markedly faltering economic performance brought about major reversals of policy and structural reorganizations (as in 1921 and 1928) and all kinds of reforms concerning the scope of centralized commands, autonomy of the enterprise, types of incentives, and structure of prices. In essence, however, the centrally administered system did not change.

Which specific measures would be necessary to *convert* such an economy to a market-directed one? Put differently, which steps would have to be taken in order to dismantle the inner frame of the centralized system of the Soviet type and establish in its place a debureaucratized economy functioning on the basis of free markets? For the purposes of simplicity, it is useful to consider the fundamental issues involved under the following headings: ownership rights, business organization and motivation, labor and industrial relations, and functions of the government and ways of discharging them. Which basic steps would have to be taken within *each* of these domains? In mapping out this broad design, the main issues involved and their interconnections can be cataloged, thus, helping to dispel the illusion that this or that single step taken or scheduled to be taken by the architects of perestroika would by itself effectively achieve the transition from the centrally administered system to a free market-directed one.

Let us focus first on ownership rights. The institution of private property is the foundation of market-directed economies. As Richard Posner stresses in *Economic Analysis of Law* (1973), an efficient system of property rights is one that creates incentives for the efficient use of resources. The criteria within a legal framework for such efficient use are universality, exclusivity, and trans-ferability. The first principle implies that *all resources* should be ownable by an individual or group of individuals, except resources so plentiful that everybody can consume as much of them as they wish without reducing the consumption of anyone else. The second principle posits the right of the owner to exclude anyone (except, in certain cases, the government) from using the given resource. The third principle implies the absence of prohibition on the transfer of that resource through voluntary exchange. In the Soviet case, the creation of incentives for the efficient use of resources posits the need to dismantle nationalizations, beginning with the involuntary collective farms, which mortgage most of the land, and the granting of individual and group property rights in all spheres of economic activity from production to trade.

Consider next business organization and motivation. A free market economy is predicated on *free enterprise*—freely constituted individual proprietorship, joint partnerships, cooperative ownership, joint-stock companies, and holding companies—engaging for profit in domestic activities or foreign trade. In the Soviet case, a move toward free market economics posits the need to dismantle the bureaucratic organizational setup in manufacturing, for instance, by ministries, departments, branches, administrations, and other forms of tutelage and compulsory production associations. It posits the freeing of all enterprises to serve the consumer—not production targets set by central planners. Concomitant processes would have to dismantle the state supply and distribution systems and the free reorientation of various of its components toward cooperation with restructured, decentralized industrial establishments. To insure an orderly debureaucratization, stop the tragedy of neglect, misuse, destruction, and pilfering of state property, and promote judicious choices in the patterns of *privatization*, detailed, conscientious analyses and recommendations of the specific forms and expected results of denationalizations, the criteria used, and the firms selected would have to be prepared by some ad hoc State Property Agency. With the help of qualified experts, the agency would have to determine, notably, the criteria for pricing state assets, the incentives used to encourage the purchase of these assets, and the intended use of the proceeds. Complex issues are also bound to arise in the transition to private ownership concerning credit conditions for acquiring denationalized properties and the necessary initial working capital, for which a number of modalities would have to be devised.

Consider next the problems involving labor and labor relations. The necessary guarantee to enterprises of the freedoms of hiring and firing and of bankruptcy, the systematic expansion of the purchases of inputs and sale of outputs in free markets, the cessation of the channeling of profits (by the state budget and state banks) from the profit-making to the losing enterprises, and the end of state subsidies (particularly, for staples) involve deep changes in the status and condition of labor. These changes posit, on the one hand, the need for guaranteed freedom of labor movement (nonexistent today) and the right of free trade union organization and, on the other hand, the provisions of unemployment compensation along with the creation of various forms of labor retraining.

The restructuring of government activities, and the redefinition of the nature and scope of its actions in regard to the banks and other financial institutions, the producing and trading enterprises, and households, involves vast processes of change in the Soviet case. (These processes might be further complicated, as they could also concern the independence of certain republics of the former union.) The changes require first of all that the central government organs relinquish the conception that they are the *owners,* in the name of the workers or the people, of the enterprises and banks and that they are charged with their day-to-day administration. The Central Planning Administration would have to be dissolved or possibly integrated into the Central Statistical Office. The fiscal system would have to be overhauled with emphases shifting to direct taxation, uniformization of the taxes on profits, and permission of private savings and investments. In regard to the monetary system, its three distinct circuits would have to be unified, the monetary overhang sharply reduced, and the currency's convertibility guaranteed. This change would require a controlled reduction of the monetary overhang, perhaps along with exchange of new money against old money at some arbitarily determined rate. Banking would have to be privatized, and markets would have to be created for capital and securities. The government would also have to dismantle its price administration and rapidly reduce the domains of centralized or (administratively) decentralized but controlled pricing. While largely opening the ways of access for foreign capital into the domestic markets, the government would also have to seek admission to such organizations as the IMF, the World Bank, and GATT.

Even if the Soviet Union were to lose some of its republics, the problems of finding the proper paths toward free market–determined patterns of work and organization would be the same for itself as well as for the newly independent republics. The example of the East European countries clearly shows that these paths are neither self-evident to everybody nor as easily implementable, at the same pace, in each of the countries breaking away from a Soviet-type organization. Restriction of the scope of centralized capital construction, reduction of the domain of centralized pricing, expansion of commercial banking, and revamping of the system of taxation are certainly significant steps away from the traditional Soviet system. Devolutions of certain economic powers to the republics, regions, and local authorities, however, do not by themselves transform the USSR from a centrally planned economy into a market-determined one.

Dynamics of NEP and Perestroika

Mikhail Gorbachev has often referred to Lenin's NEP as a kind of blueprint of perestroika. This identification with NEP is valid to the extent that it implies a commitment to the idea of freedom of operation within well-defined limits of certain *regulated* markets at the borders of state administered complexes. The identification is not valid as far as the rationale and dynamics of the two policies are concerned.

As noted, the calamitous results of War Communism forced Lenin to formulate the New Economic Policy, stop the confiscation of peasants' grain, and replace it with a fixed tax in kind. But, notwithstanding the contentions of certain contemporary partisans of perestroika, in Lenin's conception, the change did not imply his abandoning of War Communism's ideas and commitments. As already indicated, for him War Communism was a mistake *but* only in the sense that the leaders of the revolution had underestimated the strengths of the "capitalist fortress." Their error had been "in assuming that we could proceed straight to socialism without a preliminary period in which the old economy would be adapted to a socialist economy." This adaptation of the old economy was to consist, in Lenin's views, in a sui generis form of state capitalism, that is, of capitalist relations stimulated within well-defined and controlled limits by the Communist government. These so-called capitalist relations were to consist of substitution of the tax in kind for the requisitions in the countryside, freedom of trade in the surplus of grain left over after the tax, development of small commercial enterprises, and the leasing of state enterprises, "thereby giving capitalism freedom to develop." As Lenin put it (in "The Importance of Gold Now and After the Complete Victory of Socialism," November 5, 1921, *Collected Works,* vol. 33) "we have been adopting . . . a reformist method: not to break up the old social system—trade, petty production, petty proprietorship, capitalism—but to revive trade, petty proprietorship, capitalism, while cautiously and gradually getting the upper hand over them, or making it possible to subject them to state regulation only to the extent that they revive." The idea of a *temporary retreat* and marginal restorations of what Lenin calls state capitalism—namely, of small-scale domestic production and trade and the leasing mainly of some state mineral resources to foreign capital—to be chocked off at the appropriate time is clearly apparent from even a cursory examination of the scope and dynamics of these forms of ownership and activity during the NEP.

According to a Soviet study by Iu. Poliakov, V. Dimitrenko, and N. Shcherban (*The New Economic Policy* [1982]), at the beginning of the NEP, a time of restructuring and concentration of the nationalized large-scale industries under state head-administrations (the *glavki* under the Supreme Council of the National Economy—VSNKh), the state could effectively man and directly control only about one-third of the nationalized industries. It offered to lease the other two-thirds to either cooperatives or private entrepreneurs but did not often find takers. These two-thirds comprised industries abandoned by their former owners and their top personnel that the state could not reactivate. As far as the census industry is concerned—that is, industries excluding small-scale establishments—the share of the state rose continuously, and that of the private sector conversely decreased as the NEP unfolded. The state share, which amounted in 1920 to 88 percent of these industries, rose in 1924–25 to 89.4 percent and in 1926–27 to 91.8 percent, the private sector decreased sharply, while the cooperative share rose also during some of the indicated years, namely, from 3.7 to 6.3 percent and then hovered around 6 percent in 1926–27. The same dynamics are apparent in retail trade. In 1922–23 three-quarters of the total retail trade was carried out by private traders ("nepmen"). The percentage fell in 1924 to 53 percent, in 1925 to 43, in 1926 to 41, in 1927 to 35, in 1928 to 24, and in 1930 to less than 6 percent. In agriculture, collectivization started only after 1929. Already during the NEP, however, the state managed to extract tribute from the peasants under the form of unfavorable terms of trade between state manufactured goods and the peasants' produce. This practice led to a major crisis in 1923—the first so-called scissor crisis—the first major discrepancy between the rising manufacturing prices and falling agricultural prices. The crisis was overcome by temporary price changes. A similar crisis in 1928 precipitated the collectivization drive.

The continuous preparation during the NEP of the establishment of a fully centralized planning system is clearly indicated by a number of well-known facts. After partial plans, like the famous Lenin plan for the electrification of Russia (GOELRO), important theoretical and practical steps were taken toward overall economic coordination. Among the preparatory technical steps, one can count the *Balance of the National Economy of the USSR for 1923–24* (which Stalin later dismissed as "a game with figures") and the *Control Figures for 1925–26* (in which Trotsky thought he heard "the music of the future"). The directives for the First Five-Year Plan were established at the 15th Party Congress in 1927, and the plan was launched in 1928 (after numerous corrective stepping ups of the growth rates of the scheduled industrial production and gross social product) for the period 1928–29 to 1932–33. The plan was proclaimed fulfilled in four years, in 1932. Throughout the NEP the state marginalized the private sector's sphere of operation by using both administrative constraints and economic levers (such as price and credit manipulations), never losing sight of the ultimate objective of submitting the entire economy sooner rather than later to its full control. If one considers the rationale of the NEP, as formulated by Lenin in 1921, and takes into account the final goals this policy aimed at, one cannot but judge it an overall success. Soviet industry reached its prewar output level in 1926 and the small crafts and small-scale industry did so in 1927. By 1928 the sown areas in agriculture rose to around 95 percent of the sown areas of 1913 (in the post–World War II territory); a less favorable situation was registered in regard to livestock, but there too obvious improvements had taken place. All in all, using 1913 as a base, according to official data (*Statistical Yearbook for 1956*), in 1928 the number of workers employed in the national economy attained the level of 95 percent; basic assets in the economy rose to 136 percent; gross industrial output stood at 132 percent; and the national income reached 119 percent.

Consider now the rationale, dynamics, and preliminary results of perestroika through the 1980s. This policy of restructuring was also a reaction to a continuous decline and a disastrous economic situation. Nevertheless, its objectives and dynamics unfolded under conditions significantly different from those of the NEP. By 1985 the manifest popular revulsion against the inflexible and inefficient system of administrative commands, growing lack of confidence in the party and in its patently incapable leading gerontocracy, and the pent-up pressures for change in political, economic, social, and ethnic relations became increasingly difficult to contain. Not long after his accession to power, in a celebrated speech published in *Pravda* (August 1, 1986), Gorbachev stressed that the scale of transformation he was envisaging was "not smaller than that of the NEP." Indeed, he said that he equated perestroika with "a *revolution* in the entire system of societal relations, in the psychology and understanding of the present period, and above all, in the tasks engendered by rapid scientific and technological progress." As a prerequisite to this reconstruction, he posited the need to reduce the role of the Communist party's bureaucracy in the economy and society. Against this background, he defined the main axes of his policy as consisting of the acceleration and intensification of production and the transformation of management structures. As noted in preceding chapters, Gorbachev subsumed under acceleration the ending of stagnation and inertia, the retooling of industry and the raising of the rate of economic growth, reaching a new, quality growth, and the "solving of the food problem." He subsumed under managerial transformation the curtailment of the party's role, new patterns of ministerial centralization, reductions in the scope of central planning, and expansion of enterprises' autonomy and their self-financing. In regard to agriculture, he directed his efforts mainly toward popularizing the idea of leasing of land and various state premises.

In fact, throughout the 1980s, perestroika did not revolutionize the scope of *ownership rights*, the established *patterns of business organization and motivation,* the traditional *labor and industrial relations*, nor the key economic *functions of government* in any significant way. Progress toward even centrally regulated markets was consequently limited mostly to a slow and as yet marginal development of cooperatives. This less-than-revolutionary beginning does not mean that many of these issues will not be raised in explosive ways throughout the early 1990s and beyond. The question of private ownership remains especially explosive, particularly in agriculture—where, incidentally, the NEP confronted with hostility an unruly peasantry still master of its land, while Gorbachev confronts with anxiety an indifferent, alienated, collectivized countryside, debt-ridden and inefficient, whose organizational structure he is reluctant to change.

Development under perestroika of private, individual, and cooperative production and small-scale trade has been far less impetuous through the 1980s than through the first years of the NEP. Without broad changes in access to state premises, assets, raw materials, and credits, the prospects for development of legalized private business are slim. On the other hand, with regard to the organization and functioning of state enterprises, without sharp, effective reductions to the scale of centralized capital construction—still the heart and soul of the state plan—without the abandonment of the scope of central tutelage and centralized price fixing, without real expansion of the role of all enterprises in regard to their own investments and expansion, economic accountability and self-financing will remain as they have always been, imperfect and unreliable. In fact, the architects of perestroika have not yet given up the idea of supertutelage and superconcentration of the state enterprises. What Gorbachev thought in this respect, at least in the 1980s, he stated clearly in 1987 in his "Report to the Plenum of the Central Committee of the CPSU" (*Pravda*, June 26, 1987). He indicated then that what was really needed was the administrative *concentration* "of the 37,000 enterprises included in the plan, into a few thousand major branches, interbranch associations capable of carrying out the entire research-investment-production-marketing-servicing." A certain progress was registered during these years in labor and industrial relations. The scope of enterprise management was increased in regard to hiring and firing of labor and in respect to the realignment of wages with productivity. All this was tempered, as noted earlier, by the rights extended to workers' collectives concerning the election and control of managerial personnel, rights hampering the effectiveness and the initiative of the plant's hierarchy. Finally, in respect to the functions of government, the fiscal system was not overhauled in the 1980s, the process of transferring resources from the profit-making to the losing enterprises was not stopped, subsidies were not discontinued, expenditures were not brought into balance with receipts, and the budget deficits continued to grow. However, promises are on record concerning consistent reductions in spending on defense and administration in the 1990s, along with other restructuring measures involving the tax system, the credit system, state purchase prices of agricultural output, and the elimination of "subjectivism on the part of ministries, departments and Union republics in determining the size of the enterprises' payments into the budget"—as the chairman of the Council of Ministers, Nikolai I. Ryzhkov, wrote in his "Report to the Second Congress of the USSR's People's Deputies" on the Thirteenth Five-Year Plan for 1990–95 (*Pravda*, December 14, 1989).

Barring deep sociopolitical changes, the prospects for a clear-cut departure from the conception of a centrally planned and managed commanding heights, combined with decentralized administrative responsibilities and expanding but controlled markets are not encouraging. This prognosis is evident if one takes Ryzhkov's report to the letter. According to it, "starting in 1993 the market is to receive increasingly tangible development." What kind of market, and what kind of development? Ryzhkov spoke of two kinds of measures in this connection. In the first place, he spoke of "a major structural maneuver," thanks to which more investments will be directed toward the production of consumer goods in order to reduce the ruble overhang and normalize both the consumer market and monetary circulation. This normalization is to be achieved by establishing early in the plan the state orders for consumer goods (in terms of value and volume) "that will ensure a balance between planned trade turnover and commodity resources," with lists "in physical units for the most important products." In the second place, state orders will be reduced to 90 percent of the output of fuels, chemicals, and building materials, with ceilings on the distribution of resources only for the outputs produced as part of these state orders: "all the rest will be bought and sold through free trade." Clearly the conception about what free markets mean was less developed in the late 1980s under perestroika than it was in the early 1920s under the NEP. At the time of the drafting of the Thirteenth Five-Year Plan, at the end of the 1980s, the attention of the country's leadership was still fixed on the size and impact of state orders in regard to both consumer and producer goods production, rather than on the necessity to rapidly free the state enterprises and expand market relations. Thus, while the NEP succeeded in meeting its targets, the architects of perestroika ended its first phase with poor results regarding its goals for the pace of retooling, growth rates of output, food problems, disciplining of the work force, and subduing ethnic centrifugal forces.

Mikhail Gorbachev repeated often during the 1980s that the policy of restructuring was neither "a cosmetic repair of the existing economic mechanism" nor "a retreat from socialism." He and the other architects of perestroika also wished to convey the impression that they believed that, mutatis mutandis, the Soviet economic crisis was akin to the one the United States experienced during the Great Depression. And, just as the United States had surmounted its crisis in the 1930s, the Soviet Union would do so in the 1990s *without changing the very essence of its system*. Put differently, perestroika would be a kind of Soviet New Deal, and Mikhail S. Gorbachev a Soviet version of Franklin D. Roosevelt. These analogies, suggested notably by Gorbachev's minister of foreign affairs, Eduard A. Shevarnadze in an address to the American Foreign Policy Institute of New York (*New York Times*, October 4, 1989), should, however, not be taken to the letter. The Great Depression was a sharp yet transitory downward deviation from the trend, in terms of output and employment, while the Soviet Union is experiencing a chronic economic retardation of unprecedented depth, marked by, among other things, a long-term decline in growth rates and the structural development of all its economic sectors. Roosevelt's problem was to put the economy back on track; Gorbachev's is to find out not only what track to bring the economy back to, but also how and at what speed the rest of society can be put in the same tracks as well.

Impacts of Glasnost

Glasnost—openness for public opinion in public affairs—is viewed by Gorbachev as part and parcel of the process of restructuring, an indispensable instrument for identifying the causes of the calamitous situation of the country, combating and surmounting stagnation, inertia, and alienation, and democratizing the polity, society, and the economy. As he put it (in a report to the plenary of the Central Committee of the CPSU, January 27–28, 1987), "We need democracy like air . . . . We need now more light, so that the Party and the people can know everything, so that no dark nooks are left to become overgrown with mold again." Glasnost has allowed the publication of long-suppressed critical data on a variety of aspects of life in the Soviet Union. It has helped to demythologize a number of Soviet tenets about the dictatorship of the proletariat, the system's founding fathers, Soviet planning, and socialist humanism and equity. It has also brought into the limelight deep divisions about the paths now open to the Soviet Union as a whole, to Russia proper, and to other of its republics and numerous ethnic groups.

The demythologizing of the dictatorship of the proletariat and the party's role as the unique "teacher, guide, and leader" of the working class has been officially sanctioned, as already noted, by the party's platform of February, 1990, endorsing the abolition of the party's constitutional monopoly on political power. In *The State and Revolution,* Lenin contended that this dictatorship was the *state* of the "proletariat organized as a ruling class," a class taught, guided, and led by the Marxist-educated vanguard. In his speech on the platform (February 5, 1990), Gorbachev asserted (without referring to 1968's leader of Czechoslovakia, Alexander Dubček) that, henceforth, the Soviet ideal was "a humane, democratic socialism," an ideal that required the abandonment of "the ideological dogmatism that had become ingrained during the past decades," a change in "the party's relations with state and economic bodies," and the eventual creation of "a law-based state and a self-governing society." The demythologizing of the founding fathers—namely, of Lenin himself, Trotsky, Bukharin, Stalin, and Lenin's entire central committee— has been carried out not so much by the party's leadership, as by an ever-growing number of books and publications (some of which have already been discussed)—an atonement exercise whose novelty has still not worn off.

The demythologizing of Soviet planning has been carried out on various levels, including, notably, reevaluations of the actual rates of growth, actual consequences of the strategy of development (which "extremely deformed the structure of social production" [as Soviet premier Nikolai I. Ryzhkov observed in *Pravda,* December 14, 1989]), the actual state of the collectivized and victimized peasants, and the wide differences between the salaries, pensions, and perks of the nomenklatura. Conflicts of interests that were supposed to have disappeared come to the surface of Soviet society, and alienation, which allegedly could not exist when the means of production were nationalized, is now officially recognized as widespread and intractable.

As Leon Aron pointed out (in *Commentary,* November, 1989), glasnost has also destroyed the myth of "social protection," a myth according to which the Soviet system protected its citizens from the ills of capitalism, such as neglect of children, hunger, poverty, disease, unemployment, crime, prostitution, drugs, and hopelessness. Data on schooling facilities and health care conditions, for instance, are particularly revealing of the true situation. Soviet children attend schools, of which half have no heat, running water, or sewage systems; children as young as ten work twelve-hour days harvesting potatoes; and thousands of children are crippled in labor accidents. About one-third of Soviet hospitals have no running water and indoor toilets; the lack of medicines is widespread, and, as already indicated, the army has a monopoly in the production and delivery of medical instruments and equipment, still in very short supply. Finally, official data, now collected and released by the historian V. Zemkov (in an interview in *Argumenty i fakty,* November 11–17, 1989), add some statistical dimensions to an appalling creation of the centralized planning system, the concentration camps, whose immense tragedy and frightening domain have been so magnificently identified and analyzed by Alexander Solzhenitsyn in the *Gulag Archipelago.* According to official data, as of March 1, 1940, the gulag comprised 53 camps, 425 corrective labor colonies, and 50 colonies for juveniles. The yearly arrivals of prisoners (*zeks,* in Gulag terminology) in the camps rose between 1934 and 1941 from 510,000 to 1.5 million and then fell between 1942 and 1947 (the last year for which we have the data) from 1.4 million in 1942 to 808,000 in 1947. A report by the Soviet State Security Committee (*Komitet Gosudarstvennoi Bezopasnosti*—KGB) released by Tass News Agency on February 13, 1990, indicates that three-quarters of a million people were shot to death as enemies of the people from 1930 to 1953. This figure does not include the millions who died on the way to and in the labor camps and prisons or in the famines during the collectivization drive in the 1930s. The official Tass release also specified that 3,778,234 people were sentenced for "counterrevolutionary activity" from 1930 to 1953, the year Stalin died.

Glasnost has taken the lid off pent-up pressures involving ugly and unfathomable interethnic conflicts and has also brought into the limelight again a host of familiar problems with widespread and intricate roots in Russian and Soviet history. Among the issues again in debate are the nature and role of the Russian state, the "messianic" role of Russia (Christian or proletarian Russia), Western versus Slavic values, and, last but not least, the nagging question of who must bear the responsibility for the Communist revolution and of its disastrous aftermath, the Russians themselves or the minorities, above all, the Jews. Stalin, who fancied himself to be an expert on the nationalities question, asserted (in "The National Question and Leninism," *Collected Works,* vol. 11) that "the new Soviet nations which developed and took shape on the basis of the old, bourgeois nations, after the overthrow of capitalism . . . differ radically from the corresponding old, bourgeois nations of the old Russia" in "structure, spiritual complexion and in social and political interests and aspirations." These old articles of faith of the Soviet catechism have long since lost any plausibility. The open, widespread revolt of various Soviet republics began at the end of the 1980s, and the increasingly bloody conflicts among neighboring ethnic groups, have sealed the fate of the old Soviet nationalities policy.

What is interesting to note is that the tearing apart of the Soviet Union—that is, of the former, immense Russian empire—has brought to the fore violent nationalistic, chauvinistic, and in some respects mystical religious Russian movements long disenchanted with what crude modernization, brutal industrialization, and barbarian collectivization has done to the spiritual fabric and the "soul" of old Russia. This disenchantment has found perhaps its first and most telling expression in Vasilii Rasputin's novel *Farewell to Materaia* (published for the first time in 1976 in *Nash sovremennik*). In the novel, Rasputin, a leader of the so-called new peasant-nationalist Russian literature, likens Russia's agony to that of a Siberian village located on a tiny island in the middle of the Angara River, waiting to be submerged by the waters of a new power station and dam constructed upstream across the great river. The Russians, like the old people of *Materaia* (a word close to the Russian *mater* [mother]), do not understand what befell them and feel forgotten and abandoned.

Paradoxically, in 1990 Rasputin has been coopted in Gorbachev's first Presidential Council—in principle, the highest policy-making entity in the land. How far *Materaia* is from the pompous Stalinist literature of the 1930s that glorified the beginnings of the onslaught of Soviet industrialization! In two brilliant analyses of *Materalu* and of other works of nationalistic writers—who, according to Solzhenitsyn, now represent the authentic Russian culture and national renewal—Mikhail Agurski pointed out in the early 1980s that this new Russian literature is imbued with unbound hatred for everything "cosmopolitan," the "Westernist" intelligentsia, industrial-urban society, and the Soviet system as a whole, which destroyed "the bases of Russian life" in order to create a monster, a world superpower. Just as in the rest of Soviet society, various nationalist currents are engaged in their own radical reexaminations of the civil war, collectivization, political terror, the history of the two world wars, and Stalin's personality and reign.

In the conditions of glasnost many nationalists claim openly that Jewish participation in the revolution and in the social and political life of postrevolutionary Russia has been extremely harmful. They perceive the Jewish element as a bearer of cosmopolitanism incompatible with Russian civilization—just as Stalin and his acolytes had asserted when it seemed expedient—and claim that Stalin himself was manipulated by Jews such as his henchman Lazar Kaganovich. The strident conflict around the "responsibility of the Jews" reached a new peak at the end of the 1980s, notably, after the publication of Grossman's novella *Everything Flows*. Written between 1955 and 1963 (one year before the death of its author) and published only in June, 1989, in *Octiabr,* Grossman's book asserts that the "Freedom-less" Soviet state is in essence none other than "the Russian state system, born in Asia but arraying itself in Western clothing." It is in fact a *suprahistorical* phenomenon, "a system in which the law is a weapon of tyranny only, and in which tyranny is the law"; it is this system that found a perfect embodiment in both Lenin's intolerance and fanaticism and Stalin's brutal methods. Grossman's thesis— which might have reminded some people of the famous 1840 verse of Mikhail Lermontov, "Farewell, unwashed Russia, land of slaves, land of masters"— has become the target of many Russian nationalists, who, while detesting the centralist-administrative Stalinist system, nourish a deep affection for a vast, centralist, multinational, powerful state, similar in many respects to the one that preceded the revolution.

Grossman's thesis (and Grossman himself as a Jew) have been violently attacked by Igor Shafarevich, the well-known mathematician and dissident, whose book, *Russophobia,* published in 1989 in *Nash sovremennik* (the official organ of the Writers' Union of the Russian Republic), has become the catechism of the nationalists. In his old writings and his newest, Shafarevich asserts that the "russophobes" look down upon the Russians as "a people of slaves," claim that Russia has "no other choice" than a Western-type democracy or an authoritarian state, and contest that Russia could not only save itself but also show others the way out of the modern impasse. According to Shafarevich, Grossman's and other Russian Jews' hatred of Russia is due to their sense of belonging to another nation, the Jewish nation. Their past responsibility for the revolution and Stalin's system weighs heavy on them. To fight the Westernist threat they embody, Russia must return to a broad-based, strong, multinational state with small-scale industry and small, community-run agriculture.

It is interesting to recall that in one of his earlier essays ("Separation or Reconciliation—the Nationalities Question in the USSR," published in 1974 in a book edited by Solzhenitsyn, *From Under the Rubble*), Shafarevich affirmed that "a common history has welded the nations of our land together," that the internationalists have instigated the creation of small states and hostile cultures, and that Russia and its peoples, who have suffered under Communism, have the "historic mission" of showing the world "the way out of the labyrinth in which mankind is now lost." Among the answers to Shafarevich, it might be appropriate to recall here the remarks (in *Moskovskie novosti,* October 8, 1989) of the famous Soviet songwriter, Bulat Okudzhava. Behind the patriotic posturing of the nationalists, notes Okudzhava, one discerns the simple thought that "it is not the many centuries of serfdom . . . not a lack of legal and democratic habits, not all this aggravated by the pressures of the seventy years" (of the Bolshevik regime) that are to blame but, rather, that the Jews are the ones who brought Russia to the brink of catastrophe. And Okudzhava adds derisively that there is no need to engage in fruitless searches; all that is needed is to "set out to suppress that enemy [the Jews] with banners bearing the cross of St. Andrew" [the naval ensign of imperial Russia]—listening to the familiar songs of the rabid Black Hundreds and of Goebbelses. What is interesting to note here is that this renewed chauvinism and antisemitism coalesces with the apprehensions of a part of the Communist apparatus and perhaps also part of the military opposed to the policy of restructuring and glasnost. This shared sentiment might explain at least up to a point why the Gorbachev regime has not launched a vigorous campaign against the antisemites, even though its reluctance is not well received outside the USSR.

From another point of view, the well-known dissident writer Vladimir Bukowsky asserts ("In Russia, Is It 1905 Again?" *Wall Street Journal,* November 27, 1989) that, to "the leadership, glasnost and *perestroika* signal a change of policy," but to the people "they are a chance to change the system." And, Bukowsky concludes, "a crack in the prison wall is always perceived by a prisoner as an opportunity to escape, not as an improvement in the ventilation." As the saying goes, *si non e vero, e ben trovato.*

"No" to Convergence

Given the changes introduced by the architects of reconstruction, particularly in regard to the position of the Communist party, and given the scheduled changes in the economy, can one speak of a tendency toward the convergence of Soviet socialism with Western capitalism? In order to properly reply, one has to define as clearly as possible the terms involved, namely *convergence, socialism,* and *capitalism.* Indeed, few terms have been so used and abused that, without preliminary definitions, one cannot know exactly in which specific frame of reference their interrelations are supposed to be examined.

The term *convergence* is applied in biology, or in paleontology, to an important and interesting evolutionary phenomenon. It concerns the evolution of unrelated animals that evolve astounding similarities in a limited number of parts as they adapt to similar conditions of life. Natural scientists caution, however, that one can be led astray if one focuses only on a small number of convergent features while ignoring the absence of alteration in many other complex and largely independent parts. To cite an example once given by the naturalist Stephen Jay Gould, an ichthyosaurus, for instance, is still a reptile, not a fish, despite its convergent dorsal and caudal fins. Similar kinds of comparisons can certainly be made also in the social sciences, provided one does not forget there too the caveat indicated by the natural scientists.

In the Marxian frame of reference, socialism means the abolition of the private property of the means of production and the transfer of the latter to society. The socialist community cannot but exercise a unitary control over the means of production, no matter which ways this unitary control is exercised. Recall, as Engels put it in *Anti-Dühring,* that, "as soon as society has taken possession of the means of production and applies them to direct social production," it will "quite easily decide everything," taking into account, on the one hand, the means of production at its disposal and, on the other, "the amount of labor inherent in any product" as revealed by experience. As Iu. V. Shishkov reminds us (in "Perestroika and the Phantom of Convergence," in *Rabochii klass i sovremennyi mir,* 1989), "all our friends, and all our ennemis throughout the entire world have for many decades considered the USSR a socialist country." Throughout Soviet history this association was due precisely to the transfer to the state of the bulk of the means of production "and to their unitary control by the Soviet State." Conversely, capitalism implies the private ownership of the means of production and the absence of centralized unitary control over their use. This specific difference has made the Soviet system distinct from any other, be it a so-called socialist country led by a socialist political party, Marxist or non-Marxist, or a capitalist country (no matter how many companies might have been nationalized within it and no matter how much dirigisme might have prevailed).

Numerous Western writers representing many disciplines have propounded convergence theories. It is sufficient to limit the present discussion to economic theories, wherein the main forces that are alleged to make for convergence are the complex and widely ramified impact of the technical-scientific-managerial-revolution in large-scale production and large-scale organization. Separately, or in conjunction with these main forces, other factors are also alleged to make for convergence in the "mature" industrial states: notably, tendencies of systems' adaptability; the influences of experience and of each system upon the other; and a "changeover from ideology to rationality" in tune with the technico-scientific changes themselves. These tendencies are alleged to have effected a number of systemic changes, particularly, the significance and role of large-scale industry in the economy; the importance and functions of the state; the nature and inner workings of the abstract institutions that carry out society's goals—property rights, markets, and the degree of centralization and decentralization in production decisions and prices; the ways in which the production process is run, coordinated, and expanded; and the nature, uses, and scope of information and the manner it affects the system in its entirety. Among the most representative modern contributors to the economic theories of convergence—theories with roots both in early socialist concepts and in the capitalist paradigms of the historicists and institutionalist schools—have been W. W. Rostow, John Kenneth Galbraith, and Jan Tinbergen.

In *The Stages of Economic Growth: A Non-Communist Manifesto* (1960), Rostow has asserted that *all societies* lie "in their economic dimensions" within one of a specific number of stages or steps on a ladder of economic growth and development. Starting with traditional society, the first step involves, in Rostow's conception, preconditions for takeoff, then the takeoff, the drive to maturity, and the stage of high mass-consumption. Beyond that, "it is impossible to predict," although one can foresee some of the issues. The indicated stages have nothing to do with the question of public or private ownership. They are defined only in terms of real per capita income growth and of patterns of income distribution between consumption, savings, and investment, as well as in terms of leading sectoral complexes of production. Allegedly, all countries move normally along the indicated sequence. Communism is a kind of harsh "last resort," a *possible* form of organization, capable of launching and sustaining the growth process. Put otherwise, "it is a kind of disease which can befall a transitional society if it fails . . . to get on with the job of modernization." Then, as income per capita reaches a certain level, the communist society, like the capitalist societies before it, enters into the phase of high mass-consumption. Provided the consumers' income elasticity of demand is not frustrated by public policy, the communist society will also eventually develop the typical "sectoral complexes" of this stage, namely, the "automobile sectoral complex" and the related industries and services associated with it.

According to John Kenneth Galbraith (*The New Industrial State* [1967]), the economic nucleus of the mature industrial state—be it capitalist or socialist—is formed by the complex of large corporations, which Galbraith specifically designates as the industrial system, or the modern economy. This complex is in fact the locus of key decisions for the economy in its entirety and the society at large. The "brain" of the corporation is not, as is usually assumed, its management, but the specialized knowledge, talent, and experience of the firm's technicians—engineers, product planners, market researchers, and sales executives—which management mobilizes through continuously constituted and reconstituted committees. This so-called technostructure is the society's guiding intelligence. To implement its decisions, the technostructure binds the consumer to its needs, brings under its control the supply of capital and labor, unions, and universities, and extends its influence deep into the state. It is to its planning—that is, to its control of demand, supply, and capital—that the state's own policies and instruments, from taxing to spending, civil or military, are closely attuned. At the borders of the industrial system and its large-scale processes is the world of small firms. It is within this world only, and up to a point in some of its interactions with the industrial system, that market relations and "consumer sovereignty" function. Galbraith asserts that, for effective performance, the corporation *must* defend

278 Restructuring the Soviet Economy

its own decisions—that is, its power and autonomy for implementing decisions against the challenge of any authority (public or private, or both, as the case may be) in either a capitalist *or* a socialist economy. In the Soviet Union, there are two major sources of interference with this autonomy: the state central planning apparatus and the Communist party. However, even in the Soviet system, the managers emphasize the need for autonomy, and the result is an uneasy compromise between the manager and the party, so that, ultimately, "the resolution of the problem of authority in the industrial enterprise is not unlike that in the West—although no one can be precisely sure."

In a number of writings in the 1950s and 1960s, Jan Tinbergen stressed the existence of convergence in regard to both property rights and decision-making authority. Starting from the "most striking difference" between East and West, namely, the respective sizes of the public sector, Tinbergen pointed to the expansion of this sector in the West via what he calls "stepwise nationalization" and to the continuous limitations of various attributes of property rights. He then noted that ownership can be visualized as a "bunch of decision rights each of them showing a range of alternatives." These rights have been progressively narrowed, as capitalism has evolved, via public legislation. Converging tendencies might manifest themselves by different approaches to the question of the scope of public ownership under socialism as well as by the shifting of decision powers from the state to state-owned production units. In Tinbergen's vision, the imperatives of technological development, experience, and adaptability inexorably push the capitalist and socialist systems toward a similar mix of goals, controlling devices, processes, and information use. The "West" moves from the traditional factor optimization and management to the complex organization and coordination of "hundreds of thousands of simultaneous actions" for entire industries, sectors, and, finally, for the economy as a whole. The "East" moves through growth and experience from the narrow military concepts of a sui generis war economy and from extreme scarcity to different patterns of organization and accelerated growth. In the natural search for optimality it revises its commitments to total nationalization of the means of production, comprehensive planning, tight centralization, and direct instrumentalities. Thus, West and East converge toward an optimum that can be rationally determined and sought after.

Soviet and other pro-Soviet writers have systematically rejected the convergence theories of Rostow, Galbraith, and Tinbergen (as well as the theses of other Western economists) as involving wrong historicist-deterministic sequences, an abstraction called the industrial state independent of the underlying predominant forms of ownership, and the existence of a single optimum for differently structured societies. As a French Stalinist philosopher, Merleau Ponty, proclaimed sententiously in the early post–World War II years, "Marxism is not a philosophy of history, it *is* the philosophy of history and to reject it is to reject historical reason." Any attempt to formulate a different stage theory is thus dismissed a priori. As for the absence of emphasis of the convergence theorists on differences in the forms of ownership, a collective of Soviet economic writers observed (in the *Socialist Economic System* [1984]) that such theories ignore the changes in production relations that are brought about by fundamental changes in ownership forms and that they erroneously look upon the latter only in a "formalistic-juridical way." In short, what the Soviet writers have consistently affirmed—and, I believe, rightly so—is that the convergence theorists can focus on a certain number of convergent features while overlooking the absence of alteration in other, more important divergent characteristics, for example, the still-predominant state ownership of the means of production in the USSR, the importance for the economy as a whole of central capital constructions and the resources devoted to them, and the marginal character of tolerated and highly controlled markets.

Now, on these issues, the architects of perestroika seem to subscribe to certain Marxist-"revisionist" theories, such as those propounded by Wlodzimierz Brus, formerly of the University of Warsaw. In *The Market in a Socialist Economy* (1972), Brus suggested that one must distinguish between production relations and the mechanisms that activate the operations of the economy based on them. Following Stalin's definition, which Brus accepted at the time, production relations depend on the forms of ownership of the means of production, the status that this ownership confers on various social groups, and the principles that this ownership implies in income distribution. In the case of a society based on the public ownership of the means of production, the existence of a planning-cum-management center is a sine qua non element for formulating the chief economic decisions and coordinating such an economy. This does not mean, however, that the forms of organization of social production and the mechanism that they condition cannot differ within and between such societies. Brus then specifies that such differences could concern the degrees of administrative centralization and decentralization, the forms of management, and the leverage allowed to workers' councils, the system of incentives, industrial policies, labor policies, and the extent of use of market mechanisms.

I believe that the *directions* of the changes mapped out by the central Soviet government correspond in many respects to the basic lines identified by Brus. They still concern only the mechanisms of activating the economy and managing and controlling it, but *not* rather than the public ownership foundations on which so-called production relations are predicated—namely, the status of the state enterprises, the primary role of the state in the economy's planning-managing organisms, the absence of a decisive role for private capitalists and entrepreneurs, and the limited importance and functions of private profits, interest, and rent. However, immense pressures have been building in the Soviet society against this orientation. While the center tries to cling to the ineffective remnants of centralized planning, leaders such as Boris Yeltsin and economists such as Stanislav Shatalin advocate a lightning passage to massive privatization and to "full market relations." This "counterplan," to be carried out in five hundred days flat, is unfortunately not realistic. Decades, not five hundred days, may be needed to convert state property into private property, to control the money supply, to unravel the maze of overlapping networks created under the administrative system. It was once assumed that only two five-year plans would be necessary for creating a socialist world of plenty. Now, for new dreamers, only Five Hundred Days would be needed to bring about capitalist prosperity and abundance. There seems to be something strangely fascinating in Soviet policy-making about the figure 5.

Concluding Comments

In his celebrated book, *Socialism: An Economic and Sociological Analysis*, first published in 1922 and reissued and expanded since then in many editions and in many countries, Ludwig von Mises stated that the socialization of the means of production precluded rational economic calculation and, thus, that socialism was not a *workable* system. "Everything brought forward in favor of Socialism cannot make Socialism workable." Neither artificial markets nor artificial competition can provide ways out of the problem of rational allocation of resources. Guidance of the economy by the market implies the organization of production and the distribution of the product according to individual wishes as influenced by the supply and demand conditions in the factors and goods markets—markets reflecting in their prices the ceaseless search for profit. Neither Lange, Liberman, Kosygin, nor Gorbachev and the perestroika economists can perform the task of consistent price determinations across factors and goods and solve the problem of rational resource allocation and adequate labor or management incentives. Decentralization—but with limits on the concentration of centrally determined capital construction involving the bulk of economic resources, centrally normed profits and wages, and centrally determined prices—cannot yield efficient answers to the problem of economic calculation and cannot put an end to the misallocation and wastage of resources.

For years, the Communist leaders of the East European satellites of the USSR have imagined that they could solve key issues by reducing the scope and detail of central plan instructions, introducing leasing, authorizing more or less limited markets at the borders of the state's commanding heights while holding in their grips large-scale industry, banking, transportation, and trade. Their experience has shown over and over again that they could not devise better workable alternatives to the obviously inefficient and impractical fully centralized system. Their experience has also shown that state ownership of the key means of production—the crux of the Marxian theory and of the Bolshevik revolution—created insurmountable obstacles to the channeling of investable resources toward the firms that produced the best returns (because they responded to consumer demands) rather than to the loss-making enterprises that were built according to planners' preferences. The calamitous economic legacies left by the former Soviet satellite regimes and the turning of these countries toward the establishment of market-directed economies— that is, toward economics in which the market and its function in regard to price formation are not divorced from private property and the freedom of its owners to dispose of it as they see fit—certainly contain lessons that the main leaders of Soviet perestroika still overlook. In the very difficult economic situation in which the Soviet Union finds itself as it attempts to restructure the polity, society, and the economy, the question of whether the Western powers decide or not to help with freer trade, credits, and subsidized grain imports is certainly of capital importance. This aid cannot attenuate for long, however, nor alone can it solve the deep, basic *systemic* crisis of a disintegrating economy and agonizing society in which the property of the bulk of the means of production still remains in the shaky hands of an enfeebled state.

References and Bibliography

Russian sources are given in Russian whenever a translated text was not available to me. Translations of various Soviet articles are usually published in *Current Digest of the Soviet Press* (CDSP) and *Problems of Economics* (PE).

Chapter 1

Party, State, and the Economy

Hahn, W. Jeffrey. *Soviet Grassroots, Citizen Participation in Local Soviet Government*. Princeton, N.J.: Princeton University Press, 1988.

Hill, Ronald J. *The Soviet Union, Politics, Economics and Society from Lenin to Gorbachev*. Boulder, Col.: Lynne Rienner Publishers, 1985.

Hough, Jerry F., and Fainsod, Merle. *How the Soviet Union Is Governed*. Cambridge, Mass.: Harvard University Press, 1974.

Kerblay, Basile, and Lavigne, Marie. *Les soviétiques des années 80*. Paris: Armand Colin, 1985.

Lavigne, Pierre, and Lavigne, Marie. *Regards sur la Constitution soviétique de 1977*. Paris: Economica, Collection Politique Comparée, 1979.

"O proekte platformy TsK KPSS k XXVIII s'ezdu partii" (On the Draft Platform of the CC of the CPSU for the 28th Party Congress—[with discussion]). *Pravda*. February 6, 7, 8, 9, 1990.

"Proekt odobrennyi fevral'skim 1990 Plenumom TsK KPSS k gumannomu, demokraticheskomu sotsializmu (Platforma TsK KPSS k XXVIII s'ezdu partii)" (Draft, approved by the February 1990 Plenum of the CC of the CPSU on Humane, Democratic Socialism [Platform of the CC of the CPSU for the 28th Party Congress]). *Izvestia*, February 13, 1990.

Trotsky, Leon. *The New Course*. New York: New International Publishing Co., 1943; Shachtman, Max. *The Struggle for the New Course*. New York: New International Publishing Co., 1943.

Extent and Consequences of "Socialization"

Aganbegyan, Abel. *The Economic Challenge of Perestroika*. Bloomington: Indiana University Press, 1988.

Gorbachev, Mikhail S. *Reorganization and the Party's Personnel Policy*. Report and Concluding Speech at Plenary CPSU Central Committee, January 27–28, 1987. Moscow: Novosti, 1987.

————. *Restructuring—A Vital Concern of the People*. Speech at the 18th Congress of the Trade Unions of the USSR, February 25, 1987. Moscow: Novosti, 1987.

Kapustin, E. I., et al., eds. *Ekonomicheskii stroi sotsializma* (The Socialist Economic System), vol. 1. Moscow: Ekonomika, 1984.

Marx, Karl, and Engels, Friedrich. "Manifesto of the Communist Party." In *The Marx-Engels Reader*, ed. Robert C. Tucker. 2d ed. New York: Norton, 1978.

Sik, Ota. "Enterprise Interests without Erroneous Ideological Prejudices." In *Organizational Alternatives in Soviet-type Economies*. Ed. Nicolas Spulber. Cambridge: Cambridge University Press, 1979.

Organization and Steering Methods

Aganbegyan, Abel. *The Economic Challenge of Perestroika*. Bloomington: Indiana University Press, 1988.

Becker, Abraham S. *Soviet Central Decision making and Economic Growth: A Summing Up*. Santa Monica: Rand Corporation, 1986 (R–3349-AF).

Bukharin, Nikolai. *Ekonomika perekhodnogo perioda* (Economics of the Transition Period). Moscow: Gosizdat, 1920.

Bukharin, Nikolai, and Preobrazensky, Eugenii. *The ABC of Communism* [1919]. Ann Arbor: University of Michigan Press, 1966.

Gorbachev, Mikhail S. "O zadachakh partii po korennoi perestroike upravleniia ekonomikoi" (On the Tasks of the Party on the Radical Reconstruction of the Economy). Report to the Plenum of the CC of the CPSU, June 25, 1987. *Pravda* (June 26, 1987).

Ignatovskii, P. A. *Ekonomicheskaia zhizn' sotsialisticheskogo obshchestva* (The Economic Life of Socialist Society). Moscow: Ekonomika, 1983.

Kapustin, E. I., et al., eds. *Ekonomicheskii stroi sotsializma* (The Socialist Economic System), vol. 1. Moscow: Ekonomika, 1984.

Kolesov, N. D., Gorlanov, G. V., and Poliakov, R. I., eds. *Edinyi narodnokhoziaistvennyi kompleks i sovershenstvovanie razvitogo sotsialisticheskogo obshchestva* (The Single National Economic Complex and the Perfection of the Developed Socialist Society). Leningrad: Leningrad University, 1984.

Moiseev, A.V., and Petrosian, K. Ts. *Khoziaistvennyi mekhanizm: 100 voprosov i otvetov* (The Economic Mechanism: 100 Questions and Answers). Moscow: Politlit., 1981.

Peschon, John, ed. *Disciplines and Techniques of Systems Control*. New York: Blaisdell Publishing, 1965.

Popov, Gavriil. *Management of the Socialist Production*. Moscow: Progress Publishers, 1986.

Singh, Madan G. *Dynamical Hierarchical Control*. Amsterdam, North-Holland, 1977.

"Laws," Policies, and Priorities

Bukharin, Nikolai, and Preobrazhensky, Eugenii. *The ABC of Communism* [1919]. Ann Arbor: University of Michigan Press, 1966.

Marx, Karl. *Capital, A Critical Analysis of Capitalist Production* [1887]. 3 vols. Moscow: Foreign Publishing House, 1954–62.

Spulber, Nicolas. *Organizational Alternatives in Soviet-type Economies.* Cambridge: Cambridge University Press, 1979.

Stalin, J. V. *Economic Problems of Socialism in the USSR.* New York: International Publishers, 1952.

Concluding Comments

Spulber, Nicolas. *Organizational Alternatives in Soviet type Economies.* Cambridge: Cambridge University Press, 1979.

Chapter 2

Commodity Space

Kapustin, E. I., et al., eds. *Ekonomicheskii stroi sotsializma* (The Socialist Economic System), vol. 1. Moscow: Ekonomika, 1984.

Lapidus, Iosif A., and Ostrovityanov, K. *An Outline of Political Economy; Political Economy and Soviet Economics.* Trans. from Russian. New York: International Publishers, 1929.

Smirnov, A. D., Golosov, V. V., Maximova, V. F., eds. *The Teaching of Political Economy, A Critique of Non-Marxian Theory.* Trans. from Russian by H. Campbell Creighton. Moscow: Progress Publishers, 1984.

Constraints on Producers

Asselin, Jean-Charles. *Planning and Profits in Socialist Economies.* Trans. from French by Jill Rubery and John Andrew Wilson. London: Routledge and Kegan Paul, 1984.

Chandler, Alfred. *Essays toward a Historical Theory of Big Business.* Ed. Thomas K. McCraw. Boston: Harvard Business School Press, 1988.

Mixon, Wilson J., and Uri, Noel D. *Managerial Economics.* New York: Macmillan, 1985.

Palda, Kristian S. *Pricing Decisions and Marketing Policy.* Englewood Cliffs, N.J.: Prentice-Hall, 1971.

Scherer, Frederic M. *Industrial Market Structure and Economic Performance.* Boston: Houghton Mifflin, 2d ed., 1980.

Williamson, Oliver E. *The Economics of Discretionary Behavior: Managerial Objectives in a Theory of the Firm.* Englewood Cliffs, N.J.: Prentice-Hall, 1964.

———. "The Modern Corporation: Origins, Evolution, Attributes," *Journal of Economic Literature* 19 (December, 1981): 1537–68.

"Zakon SSSR, O predpriiatrakh v SSSR" (USSR Law on Enterprises in the USSR), *Ekonomika i zhizn,* no. 25 (June, 1990): 19–21.

Constraints on Households

"Comprehensive Program for the Development of Consumer Goods Production and the Service Sphere in 1986–2000," *Pravda* (October 9, 1985). Trans. in *CDSP* 37, nos. 41–43.

Fedorenko, N. P., and Rimashevskaya, N. M. "The Analysis of Consumption and Demand in the USSR." In *Essays in the Theory and Measurement of Consumer Behavior in Honor of Sir Richard Stone*. Ed. Angus Deaton. Cambridge: Cambridge University Press, 1981.

Kerblay, Basile, and Lavigne, Marie. *Les soviétiques des années 80*. Paris: Armand Colin, 1985.

Meney, Patrick. *La kleptocratie: La delinquence en URSS*. Paris: La Table Ronde, 1982.

Ruvinskaia, L. M. *Modelirovanie dinamiki potrebitel'skikh komplekxov* (Modeling the Dynamics of Consumer Complexes). Novosibirsk: Nauka, 1981.

Schroeder, Gertrude E., and Edwards, Emogene. *Consumption in the USSR: An International Comparison*. A study prepared for the Joint Economic Committee, 97th Congress of the United States, 1st sess. Washington, D.C.: GPO, 1981.

Tobin, James. *Essays in Economics*. Vol. 2, *Consumption and Econometrics*. Cambridge, Mass.: MIT Press, 1987.

Wellisz, Stanislaw, and Findlay, Ronald. "Central Planning and the 'Second Economy' in Soviet-Type Systems," *The Economic Journal* 96 (September, 1986): 646–58.

The Role of Prices

Cherkovets, V. N., ed. *Formy i metody sotsialisticheskogo khoziaistvovaniia* (Forms and Methods of Socialist Management). Moscow: Ekonomika, 1987.

Chubakov, G. N. *Uchet obshchestvennogo truda i tsena pri sotsializme* (Calculation of Social Labor and Price under Socialism). Moscow: Ekonomika, 1981.

Ezhov, A. N. *Ekonomicheskii mekhanizm planovogo upravleniia tsenami pri sotsializme* (Economic Mechanism of Planned Price Management under Socialism). Moscow: Vyshaia shkola, 1981.

Komin, A. N. *Ekonomicheskaia reforma i optovye tseny v promyshlenosti* (The Economic Reform and the Wholesale Prices in Industry). Moscow: Finansy, 1968.

Kovalevskii, G. T. *Zakonomernosti obrazovania stoimosti pri sotsializme* (Law-governed Formation of Value under Socialism). Minsk: Nauka i Tekhnika, 1982.

Kushnirsky, Fyodor I. "Methodological Aspects in Building Soviet Price Indices," *Soviet Studies* 37, no. 4 (October, 1985): 505–19.

Medvedev, V. A., et al., eds. *Politicheskaia ekonomiia* (Political Economy). Moscow: Politlit., 1989, pt. 3.

Nemechinov, Vasilii S. *"Sotsialisticheskoe khoziaistvovanie i planirovanie proizvodstva"* (Socialist Management and Planning of Production), *Kommunist*, no. 5 (March, 1964): 74–87.

Organizatsionnyi komitet radikal'naia ekonomicheskaia reforma (Organizational Committee of Radical Economic Reform). "Vsesoiuznaia nauchno-prakticheskaia konferentsiia po problemam radikal'noi ekonomicheskoi reformy" (All-Union

Scientific-Practical Conference on Problems of Radical Economic Reform), *Ekonomicheskaia gazeta*, no. 43 (October, 1989).

Petrakov, Nikolai. "Planovaia tsena v sisteme upravleniia narodnym khoziaistvom" (The Plan Price in the System of Management of the National Economy), *Voprosy ekonomiki*, no. 1 (1987): 44–55.

Sedyshev, Iu. A. *Stoimostnye formy v planovom upravlenii* (Value Forms in Planned Management). Moscow: Nauka, 1983.

Valtukh, K. K. *Marx's Theory of Commodity and Surplus Value, Formalized Exposition*. Moscow: Progress Publishers, 1987.

Concluding Comments

Posner, Richard. "An Economic Theory of the Criminal Law," *Columbia Law Review* 85 (October, 1985): 1193–1231.

Chapter 3

Planning Strategy

Frolov, Konstantin. *We Count on Machine Building*. Moscow: Novosti, 1986.

Konnik, I. I. *Denezhnoe obrashchenie v protsesse rasshirennogo sotsialisticheskogo vosproizvodstva* (The Circulation of Money in the Process of Expanded Socialist Reproduction). Moscow: Finansy i statistika, 1982.

Lenin, V. I. *Razvitie kapitalizma v Rosii* [1899] (The Development of Capitalism in Russia). Moscow: Foreign Language Publishing House, 1956.

Medvedev, V. A., et al. *Politicheskaia ekonomiia* (Political Economy). Moscow: Politlit., 1989, pt. 3.

Robinson, Joan. *An Essay on Marxian Economics*. London: Macmillan, 1942.

Spulber, Nicolas. *Soviet Strategy for Economic Growth*. Bloomington: Indiana University Press, 1964.

Zalkind, A. I., et al. *Narodno-khoziaistvennye proportsii—dinamika, metodologiia, planirovanniia* (National Economic Proportions—Dynamics, Methodology, Planning). Moscow: Ekonomika, 1984.

Proportions and Balances

Berri, L. Ya., ed. *Planning a Socialist Economy*. Moscow: Progress Publishers, 1977.

Kornai, Janos. *Mathematical Planning of Structural Decisions*. Amsterdam: North-Holland, 1967.

Nemchinov, V. S. "The Use of Statistical and Mathematical Methods in Soviet Planning." In *Structural Interdependence and Economic Development*. Proceedings of an International Conference on Input-Output Techniques. Ed. Tibor Barna with William I. Abraham and Zoltán Kenessey. New York: St. Martin's Press, 1963.

Spulber, Nicolas, ed. *Foundations of Soviet Strategy for Economic Growth*. Bloomington: Indiana University Press, 1964.

Treml, Vladimir G., ed. *Studies in Soviet Input-Output Analysis*. New York: Praeger, 1977.

United Nations, Department of Economics and Social Affairs. *Basic Principles of the System of Balances of the National Economy: Studies in Methods*, ser. F, no. 17. New York: United Nations, 1971.

Controls and Optimization

Cave, Martin, McAuley, Alastair, and Thornton, Judith. *New Trends in Soviet Economics*. Armonk, N.Y.: M. E. Sharpe, 1982.

Cherkovets, V. N., ed. *Formy i metody sotsialisticheskogo khoziaistvovaniia* (Forms and Methods of Socialist Management). Moscow: Ekonomika, 1987.

Conyngham, William J. *The Modernization of Soviet Industrial Management*. Cambridge: Cambridge University Press, 1982.

Ellman, Michael. *Planning Problems in the USSR, The Contribution of Mathematical Economics to their Solution, 1960–1971*. Cambridge: Cambridge University Press, 1973.

————. *Soviet Planning Today, Proposals for an Optimally Functioning Economic System*. Cambridge: Cambridge University Press, 1971.

Fedorenko, N. P., Leibkind, Iu. R., and Maiminas, E. Z., eds. *Problemy metodologii kompleksnogo sotsialno-ekonomicheskogo planirovaniia* (Methodological Problems of Complex Social-Economic Planning). Moscow: Nauka, 1983.

Kantorovich, Leonid V. *Essays in Optimal Planning*. White Plains, N.Y.: International Arts and Sciences Press (IASP), 1975.

Kantorovich, Leonid V., Albegov, M., and Bezrukhov, V. "Shire ispol'zovat' optimizatsionnye metody v narodnom khoziaistve" (Use on a Wider-Scale Optimization Methods in the National Economy), *Kommunist*, no. 9 (1986): 44–54.

Kapustin, E. I., et al., eds. *Ekonomicheskii stroi sotsializma* (The Socialist Economic System). vol. 1. Moscow: Ekonomika, 1984.

Kushnirsky, Fyodor I. *Soviet Economic Planning*. Boulder, Colo.: Westview Press, 1982.

Schroeder, Gertrude. "The Soviet Economy on a Treadmill of Reforms." In *Soviet Economy in a Time of Change*. A compendium of papers submitted to the Joint Economic Committee, Congress of the United States, 96th Congress, 1st sess. vol. 1. Washington, D.C.: GPO, October, 1979.

Seliunin, Vasilii. "Istoki" (Sources), *Novyi Mir*, no. 5 (May, 1988): 162–89.

Sutela, Pekka. *Socialism, Planning and Optimality, A Study in Soviet Economic Thought*. Helsinki: Finnish Society of Science and Letters, 1984.

Overhauling the Directive Center

Abalkin, Leonid I. "Novaia kontseptsiia tsentralizma" (New Conception of Centralism), *Ekonomicheskaia gazeta*, no. 50 (December, 1987): 2.

Iun', O. "Razvivaia planovyi mekhanizm khoziaistrovaniia" (Developing the Planning Mechanism of Management), *Kommunist*, no. 13 (1985): 41–51.

"Korenaia perestroika upravleniia ekonomikoi" (Radical Restructuring of the Management of the Economy) [Round Table Discussion in Gosplan], *Planovoe khoziaistvo*, no. 9 (September, 1987): 16–31.

Kushnirsky, Fyodor I. *Soviet Economic Planning*. Boulder, Colo.: Westview Press, 1982.

Litvin, Valentin. "On *Perestroika*: Reforming Economic Management," *Problems of Communism* (July–August, 1987): 87–98.

"Novoe kachestvo tsentralizovannogo planirovaniia" (The New Quality of Central Planning), *Ekonomicheskie nauki*, no. 10 (1987): 69–77.

Ryzkhov, Nikolai I. *Guidelines for the Economic and Social Development of the USSR for 1986–1990 and for the Period Ending in 2000*. A report to the 27th Congress of the CPSU. Moscow: Novosti, 1986.

Concluding Comments

Voznesensky, Andrei. "Prophecies of a Greedy Observer" (on Chekhov), *The New York Times Book Review* (November, 27, 1987): 3, 35.

Chapter 4

Planning Capital Formation

Abalkin, Leonid I. *Kursom uskoreniia* (The Course toward Acceleration). Moscow: Politlit., 1986.

Berri, L. Ya., ed. *Planning a Socialist Economy*. Moscow: Progress Publishers, 1977.

Gorbachev, Mikhail S., "The Five-Year Plan: 1986–1990; The Economic and Social Development of the USSR and the Tasks of the Party Organizations in Carrying it Out." Speech delivered in Moscow, June 16, 1986. In Mikhail S. Gorbachev, *Mandate for Peace*. Toronto: Paper Jacks, 1987.

———. "Korennoi vopros ekonomicheskoi politike partii" (Fundamental Issue of the Party's Economic Policy), *Kommunist*, no. 9 (June 11, 1985): 13–33.

Ryzhkov, Nikolai I. "Efficiency, Consolidation and Reform are the Paths to a Healthy Economy" (Report [on the Aims of the Thirteenth Five-Year Plan, 1991–1995]), *Pravda* (December 14, 1989). Trans. in *CDSP* 41, no. 51 (January 17, 1990).

———. *Guidelines for the Economic and Social Development of the USSR for 1986–1990 and for the Period Ending in 2000*. A report to the 27th Congress of the CPSU. Moscow: Novosti, 1986.

Sarkisyants, G. S., ed. *Soviet Economy, Results and Prospects*. Moscow: Progress Publishers, 1977.

Capital Budgeting

Koval', N. S., and Miroshnichenko, B. P. *Planirovanie narodnogo khoziaistva SSSR* (Planning the National Economy of the USSR). Moscow: Vyshaia shkola, 1968.

Lebedinskii, N. P., ed. *Metodicheskie ukazaniia k sostavleniu gosudarstvennogo plana razvitiia Narodnogo khoziaistva SSSR* (Guidelines on Methods for the Compilation of the State Plan for Development of the USSR National Economy). Moscow: Ekonomika, 1969.

Mixon, Wilson, Jr., and Uri, Noll D. *Managerial Economics*. New York: Macmillan, 1985.

Planirovanie razmeshcheniia proizvoditel'nykh sil SSSR—Osushchestvlenie politiki KPSS na etapakh sotsialisticheskogo stroitel'stva (Planning the Distribution of the Production Forces of the USSR—Carrying out the Policy of the CPSU on the Stages of Socialist Construction). Moscow: Ekonomika, 1986.

"Acceleration" vs. Bottlenecks

Berry, M. J., and Cooper, Julian. "Machine Tools." In *The Technological Level of Soviet Industry*. Ed. Ronald Amann, Julian Cooper, and R. W. Davies. New Haven, Conn.: Yale University Press, 1977.

Cohn, Stanley H. "Soviet Intensive Economic Development Strategy in Perspective." In *Gorbachev's Economic Plans*. Study Papers Submitted to the Joint Economic Committee, Congress of the United States, 100th Congress, 1st sess. vol. 1. Washington, D.C.: GPO, 1987.

Frolov, Koustantin. *We Count on Machine Building*. Moscow: Novosti, 1986.

Goskomstat. SSSR (State Statistical Office, USSR) *Material'no-technicheskoe obespechenie narodnogo khoziaistva SSSR* (Material-Technical Supply of the National Economy of the USSR). Moscow: Finansy i statistika, 1988.

Gregory, Paul R. "Industrial Modernization." In *Gorbachev's Economic Plans*.

Miller, R. F. "Organizing for the Scientific and Technical Revolution." In *Political and Administrative Aspects of the Scientific and Technical Revolution in the USSR*, T. H. Rigby and R. F. Miller. Canberra, School of Social Science, Australian National University, Department of Political Science, Occasional Paper no. 11, 1976.

Norms and Achievements

Kapustin, E. I., et al., eds. *Ekonomicheski stroi sotsializma* (The Socialist Economic System). vols. 2 and 3. Moscow: Ekonomika, 1984.

Malygin, A. A. *Planirovanie vosproizvodstva osnovykh fondov* (Planning the Growth of Basic Assets). Moscow: Ekonomika, 1985.

Mazurin, L. I. *Sovershenstrovanie proektno-smetnogo dela* (Improvement of Project Estimates). Moscow: Finansy, 1980.

Sorokin, G. "Tempy rosta sovetskoi ekonomiki" (Growth Rates of the Soviet Economy)," *Voprosy ekonomiki*, no. 2 (1986): 11–21.

Concluding Comments

Keller, Bill. "Inertia and Apathy Collide with Change in Stalin's 'Iron City,'" *The New York Times*, August 16, 1988.

Perevedentsev, Viktor. "Where Does the Road Lead?" *Sovetskaia Kultura* (October 11, 1988). Trans. as "Was the BAM a Wise Investment?" *CDSP* 40, no. 46 (December 14, 1988).

Pryde, Philip R. "The 'Decade of the Environment' in the USSR," *Science* 220 (April 15, 1983): 274–79.

Chapter 5

Balances of Manpower

Feshbach, Murray. "Manpower Management in the USSR." In *Soviet Resource Management and the Environment*. Ed. W. A. Douglas Jackson. Columbus, Ohio: American Association for the Advancement of Slavic Studies, 1978.

Koval', N. S., and Miroshnichenko, B. P. *Planirovanie vosproizvodstva osnovykh fondov* (Planning the Growth of Basic Assets). Moscow: Ekonomika, 1985.

Lebedinskii, N. P., ed. *Metodicheskie ukazaniia k sostavleniu gosudarstvennogo plana razvitiia Narodnogo khoziaistva SSSR* (Guidelines on Methods for the Compilation of the State Plan for Development of the USSR National Economy). Moscow: Ekonomika, 1969.

Spulber, Nicolas, and Horowitz, Ira. *Quantitative Economic Policy and Planning, Theory and Models of Economic Control*. New York: Norton, 1976.

United Nations, Department of Economics and Social Affairs. *Basic Principles of the System of Balances of the National Economy: Studies in Methods*, ser. F, no. 17. New York: United Nations, 1971.

Zagorodnevoi, A. M., ed. *Osnovy planirovaniia ekonomicheskogo i sotsial'nogo razvitiia SSSR* (Bases of the Economic and Social Planning of the Development of the USSR). Moscow: Izd. Mosk. Universiteta, 1983.

Labor Market and Wages

Arnot, Bob. *Controlling Soviet Labour, Experimental Change from Brezhnev to Gorbachev*. Armonk, N.Y.: M. E. Sharpe, 1988.

Godman, Ann, and Schleifer, Geoffrey. "The Soviet Labor Market in the 1980s." In *Soviet Economy in the 1980s: Problems and Prospects*. Selected papers submitted to the Joint Committee, Congress of the United States, 97th Congress, 2d sess., Washington, D.C.: GPO, 1982, pt. 2.

Gorbachev, Mikhail S. *Reorganization and the Party's Personnel Policy, Report and Concluding Speech*. Plenary CPSU Central Committee, January 27–28, 1987. Moscow: Novosti, 1987.

———. *Restructuring—A Vital Concern of the People*. Speech at the 18th Congress of the Trade Unions of the USSR, February 25, 1987. Moscow: Novosti, 1987.

Kahan, Arcadius, and Ruble, Blair A. *Industrial Labor in the USSR*. New York: Pergamon Press, 1979.

Kunelskii, L. E. *Zarabotnaia plata i stimulirovanie truda* (Wages and Work Incentives). Moscow: Ekonomika, 1981.

McAuley, Alastair. *Women Work and Wages in the Soviet Union*. London: Allen and Unwin, 1981.

Trenènkov, E. M. *Organizatsiia oplaty truda rabochikh i sluzhashchikh* (Organization of Labor Payment of Workers and Employees). Moscow: Profizdat, 1986.

Salaries of Employees, Professionals, and Executives

Carrère d'Encausse, Hélène. *Confiscated Power, How Soviet Russia Really Works*. New York: Harper and Row, 1980.

Chapman, Janet G. "Recent Trends in the Soviet Industrial Wage Structure." In *Indus-*

trial Labor in the USSR. Ed. by Arcadius Kahan and Blair A. Ruble. New York: Pergamon Press, 1979.

Lane, David. *Soviet Economy and Society*. London: Blackwell, 1985.

Nove, Alec. *Marxism and "Really Existing Socialism."* London: Harvard Academic Publishers, 1986.

Scherbakov, V. I. "Kardinal'naia perestroika oplaty truda" (Fundamental Restructuring of Wages), *Ekonomika i organizatsiia promyshlennogo proizvodstva*, no. 1 (1987): 37–52.

Voslensky, Michael. *La Nomenklatura, Les privilegies en URSS*. Paris: Pierre Belfond, 1980.

Yanowitch, Murray. *Social and Economic Inequality in the Soviet Union*. White Plains, N.Y.: M. E. Sharpe, 1977.

Zaslavskaia, Tat'iana. "Chelovecheskii faktor razvitiia ekonomiki i sotsial'naia spravedlivost'" (Social Justice and the Human Factor in Economic Development), *Kommunist*, no. 13 (1986).

Inequality and Economic Welfare

Chapman, Janet G. "Are Earnings More Equal under Socialism: The Soviet Case with Some United States Comparisons." Paper delivered at the Charles Haywood Murphy Symposium, Tulane, 1978. In *Income Inequality*. Ed. John R. Moroney. Lexington, Mass.: Lexington Books, Heath and Co., 1978.

Gladky, Ivan. *Social Programmes Benefit from Economic Restructuring*. Moscow: Novosti, 1986.

Kasimovskii, E. "Sotsial'naia spravedlivost' i sovershenstvovanie raspredelitel'nykh otnoshenii v SSSR" (Social Justice and the Improvement of Distribution Relations in the USSR), *Ekonomicheskie nauki*, no. 12 (1986): 3–13.

Khabibi, R. I. *Mekhanizma raspredeleniia obshestvennykh fondov potrebleniia* (The Mechanism of Distribution of the Social Consumption Funds). Moscow: Ekonomika, 1986.

Lane, David. *The End of Social Inequality? Class, Status, and Power under State Socialism*. London: Allen and Unwin, 1982.

McAuley, Alstair. *Economic Welfare in the Soviet Union, Poverty, Living Standards, and Inequality*. Madison: University of Wisconsin Press/Allen and Unwin, 1979.

Osipov, G. V., ed. *Industry and Labour in the USSR*. London: Tavistock Publications, 1966.

Pavlova, N., and Rimashevskaia, N. "Sistema pensionnogo obespecheniia" (The System of Pension Security), *Voprosy ekonomiki*, no. 10 (1987): 21–31.

Smirnov, A. D., Golosov, V. V., Maximova, V. F. *The Teaching of Political Economy, A Critique of Non-Marxian Theories*. Moscow: Progress Publishers, 1984.

Zakharov, Mikhail, and Tsivilyov, Robert. *Social Security in the USSR*. Moscow: Progress Publishers, 1978.

Concluding Comments

Gregory, Paul R., and Collier, Irvin L., Jr. "Unemployment in the Soviet Union: Evidence from the Soviet Interview Project," *The American Economic Review* 78, no. 14 (September, 1988): 613–32.

Kostiakov, Vladimir G. "Polnaia zaniatost'. Kak my ee ponimaem?" (Full Employment: How Do We Understand It?), *Kommunist*, no. 14 (1987): 16–25.

Kostin, L. "Perestroika sistemy oplaty truda" (Restructuring the System of Labor Payment), *Voprosy ekonomiki*, no. 11 (1987): 41–51.

Lane, David. *Labour and Employment in the USSR*. Brighton, U.K.: Wheatsheaf Books, Harvester Press, 1986.

Osipenko, O. "Netrudovye dokhody i formy ikh proiavleniia" (Unearned Incomes and Forms of Their Manifestation), *Ekonomicheskie nauki*, no. 11 (1986): 63–70.

"Resolution: On Ensuring Effective Employment," *Pravda* (January 19, 1988). Trans. in *CDSP* 40, no. 4 (February 24, 1988): 1–4.

Chapter 6

Nature and Scope of the State Budget

Allakhverdyan, D. A., ed. *Soviet Financial System*. Moscow: Progress Publishers, 1966.

Babashkin, L. E. *Pokazatel' effektivnosti v usloviakh perspektivnogo finansovogo planirovaniia* (Indices of Effectiveness in Conditions of Perspective Financial Planning). Moscow: Finansy i statistika, 1982.

Bazarova, G. V., ed. *Rol' finansov v sotsialno-ekonomicheskom razvitii strany* (The Role of Finances in the Country's Social-Economic Development). Moscow: Finansy i statistika, 1986.

Gallik, Daniel, Jesina, Cestmir, and Rapawy, Stephen. *The Soviet Financial System: Structure, Operation, and Statistics*. Washington, D.C.: U.S. Bureau of the Census, Internal Population Statistics Reports, ser. P, 90, no. 3, 1968.

Newcity, Michael A. *Taxation in the Soviet Union*. New York: Praeger, 1986.

Senchagov, V. K., ed. *Finansovye resursy narodnogo khoziaistva* (Financial Resources of the National Economy). Moscow: Finansy i statistika, 1982.

Principles and Structure of Soviet Taxation

Dyrdov, S. N., and Avdoshina, E. A. *Spravochnik po nalogam s naseleniia* (Manual on Taxes on the Population). Moscow: Finansy i statistika, 1984.

Gallik, Daniel, Jesina, Cestmir, and Rapawy, Stephen. *The Soviet Financial System: Structure, Operation, and Statistics*. Washington, D.C.: U.S. Bureau of the Census, Internal Population Statistics Reports, ser. P, 90, no. 3, 1968.

Holzman, Franklyn D. *Soviet Taxation: The Fiscal and Monetary Problems of a Planned Economy*. Cambridge, Mass.: Harvard University Press, 1955.

Orlov, V. E. "O sovershenstvovanii praktiki planirovaniia i postupleniia platezhei v biudzhet" (On Improving Planning Practice and Budgetary Receipts), *Finansy SSSR* (January, 1987): 13–19.

Newcity, Michael A. *Taxation in the Soviet Union*. New York: Praeger, 1986.

Sorokin, V. A. *Platezhi predpriiatii v biudzhet* (Budgetary Payments of the Enterprise). Moscow: Finansy i statistika, 1983.

Structure of Outlays and the Budget Deficit

Birman, Igor. *Secret Incomes of the Soviet State Budget*. The Hague: Nihoff, 1981.
Gostev, V. I. "Gosudarstvennyi biudzhet SSSR na 1989 god i zadachi po ego isp-olneniiu" (USSR State Budget for 1989, and the Tasks for its Execution), *Finansy SSSR* (January, 1989): 3–17.
Hutchings, Raymond. *The Soviet Budget*. Albany: State University of New York Press, 1983.

The State Budget in Historical Perspective

Bahri, Donna. *Outside Moscow; Power Politics and Budgetary Policy in the Soviet Republics*. New York: Columbia University Press, 1987.
Birman, Igor. *Secret Incomes of the Soviet State Budget*. The Hague: Nihoff, 1981.
Hutchings, Raymond. *The Soviet Budget*. Albany: State University of New York Press, 1983, (Appendix).
Ministry of Finance of the USSR. *Gosudarstvennyi biudzhet SSSR*, 1971–75, 1976–80, 1981–85 (USSR State Budget, 1971–75, 1976–80, 1981–85). Moscow: Finansy i statistika, 1976, 1982, 1987.
Panskov, V. G. "O formirovanii biudzhetov na normativnoi osnove" (On the Formation of Budgets on a Normative Basis), *Finansy SSSR* (April, 1988): 29–35.

Concluding Comments

Abalkin, Leonid I. "Restructuring of the Economic Mechanism." In *The Economic Strategy of the CPSU*. Moscow: USSR Academy of Sciences, Institute of Economics, "Social Sciences Today," Editorial Board, 1988.
Shmelev, Nikolai. "Novye trevogi" (New Anxieties), *Novyi mir*, no. 4 (1988): 160–75.

Chapter 7

The Rules of the Game

Cherkhovets, V. N. *Formy i metody sotsialisticheskogo khoziaistvovaniia* (Forms and Methods of Socialist Management). Moscow: Ekonomika, 1987.
Gerashchenko, V. S., ed. *Denezhnoe obrashchenie i kredit SSSR* (Monetary Circulation and Credit in the USSR). Moscow: Finansy, 1976.
Kapustin, E. I., et al., eds. *Ekonomicheskii stroi sotsializma* (The Socialist Economic System), vol. 3. Moscow: Ekonomika, 1984.
Konnik, I. I. *Denezhnoe obrashchenie v protsesse rashirennogo sotsialisticheskogo vosproizvodstva* (Monetary Circulation in the Process of Expanded Socialist Reproduction). Moscow: Finansy i statistika, 1982.
Lavigne, Marie. "The Creation of Money by the State Bank of the USSR." In *Soviet Industrialization and Soviet Maturity*, ed. Keith Smith. London: Routledge and Kegan Paul, 1986.

Oblat, G. "Exchange Rate Policy in the Reform Package," *Acta Oeconomica* 39, nos. 1–2 (1988): 81–93.
Portes, Richard. "Central Planning and Monetarism: Fellow Travellers." In *Working Papers Series No. 782*. New York: National Bureau of Economic Research, 1981.

Money Bifurcation and Circular Flows

Estigneeva, L., and Perlamutrov, V. "Finansovo-kreditnye otnosheniia v usloviakh intensifikatsii" (Financial Credit Relations in the Conditions of Intensification), *Voprosy ekonomiki,* no. 12 (1985): 36–46.
Gerashchenko, V. S., ed. *Denezhnoe obrashchenie i kredit SSSR* (Monetary Circulation and Credit in the USSR). Moscow: Finansy, 1976.
Mamonova, I. D. *Rol' kredita v stimulirovanii ekonomii material' nykh resursov* (The Role of Credit in the Stimulation of Economies in Material Resources). Moscow: Finansy i statistika, 1984.
Sverdlik, Sh. B. "Predpriiatie i bank" (The Enterprise and the Bank), *Ekonomika i organizatsiia promyshlennogo proizvodstva*, no. 7 (1986): 100–116.

From Monobank to Complex Banking

Alkhimov, V. S., ed. *Gosbank SSSR i ego rol' v razvitii ekonomiki strany 1921–1981* (The USSR State Bank and its Role in the Country's Economic Development, 1921–81). Moscow: Finansy i statistika, 1981.
Barkovskii, N. D., et al. *XXVII s'ezd KPSS i razvitie denezhno-kreditnoi sistemy SSSR* (The 27th Congress of the CPSU and the Development of the Monetary-Credit System of the USSR). Moscow: Finansy i statistika, 1987.
Bokros, L. "The Conditions of the Development of Businesslike Behavior in a Two-Tier Banking System," *Acta Oeconomica* 38, nos. 1–2 (1987): 49–60.
Bunich, P. G. "Novyi khoziaistvennyi mekhanizm i kreditnaia reforma" (The New Economic Mechanism and the Credit Reform), *Ekonomika i organizatsiia promyshlennogo proizvodstva*, no. 3 (1988): 3–18.
Garemovskii, N. V. "Bankovskaia sistema na novom etape razvitiia" (The Banking System in the New Stage of Development), *Deng'i i kredit*, no. 1 (January, 1988): 3–14.
Gerashchenko, V. S., and Shabanova, N. N. "Komercheskii kredit: za i protiv" (Commercial Credit: For and Against), *Deng'i i kredit*, no. 11 (November, 1988): 26–35.
Kogan, M. L. "Gosudarstvennyi bank SSSR kak glavnyi bank strany" (The State Bank as the State's Central Bank), *Deng'i i kredit*, no. 11 (November, 1988): 14–25.
Tardos, Marton. "Can Hungary's Monetary Policy Succeed?" *Acta Oeconomica* 39, nos. 1–2 (1988): 61–79.
Zakharov, V. S. "Kredit i samofinansirovanie" (Credit and self-financing), *Ekonomika i organizatsiia promyshlennogo proizvodstva*, no. 3 (1988): 18–28.

The Unplanned Financial Disequilibria

Bazarova, G. V. *Rol' finansov v sotsialno-ekonomicheskom razvitii strany* (The Role of Finances in the Country's Social-Economic Development). Moscow: Finansy i statistika, 1986.

Belkin, V. D., and Ivanter, V. V. *Planovaia sbalansirovannost': ustanovlenie, poder-zhanie, effektivnost'* (Planned Balance: Establishment, Maintenance, Effectiveness). Moscow: Ekonomika, 1983.

Bleaney, Michael. *Do Socialist Economies Work? The Soviet and East European Experience*. London: Basil Blackwell, 1988.

Bogomolov, O. "Passion over Prices: How Much Money Costs," *Literaturnaia gazeta* (September 16, 1987). Trans. in *CDSP* 39, no. 43 (November 25, 1987).

Margolin, N. S. "Voprosy sovremennogo sostoianiia denezhnogo obrashcheniia" (Problems of the Contemporary State of Monetary Circulation), *Deng'i i kredit*, no. 12 (December, 1988): 9–14.

Senchagov, V. N. *Finansovye resursy narodnogo khoziaistva* (Financial Resources of the National Economy). Moscow: Finansy i statistika, 1982.

Concluding Comments

Feldstein, Martin. "Why Perestroika Isn't Happening," *The Wall Street Journal* (April 21, 1989).

Hanson, Philip. "Inflation versus Reform," *Report on the USSR* [Radio Liberty] 1, no. 16 (April, 1989): 13–18.

Chapter 8

Soviet Accounts of Income and Product

Sidorov, M. N., and Fedotov, A. A. *Natsional'nyi dokhod, Faktory rosta, structura, metody prognozirovaniia* (National Income, Growth Factors, Structure, Forecasting Methods). Moscow: Ekonomika, 1984.

United Nations. *Comparisons of the System of National Accounts and the System of Balances of the National Economy*. New York: United Nations, Department of International Economics and Social Affairs, Studies in Methods, ser. F, no. 20, pt. 2, 1981.

Western Alternative Measures

Bergson, Abram. *Soviet National Income and Product in 1937*. New York: Columbia University Press, 1953.

Central Intelligence Agency (CIA). *The Soviet Economy in 1988: Gorbachev Changes Course*. Washington, D.C.: CIA, April 14, 1988.

———. *Soviet Gross National Product, 1960–80*. Washington, D.C.: CIA, March, 1983.

United Nations. *Comparisons of the System of National Accounts and the System of Balances of the National Economy.* New York: United Nations, Department of International Economics and Social Affairs, Studies in Methods, ser. F, no. 20, pt. 2, 1981.

From Slowdown to "Acceleration"?

Abalkin, Leonid I. "Socialism has no Ready-made Pattern," *Pravda* (June 30, 1988). Speech of the Director of the USSR Academy of Sciences' Institute of Economics. Trans. in *CDSP* 40, no. 27 (1988): 7–8.
Aganbegyan, Abel. "Acceleration: A Turning Point." In *The USSR: Acceleration of Socio-Economic Development.* Moscow: USSR Academy of Sciences, Institute of Economics, Soviet Economic Science Series No. 3, "Social Sciences Today," Editorial Board, 1987.
————. *The Economic Challenge of Perestroika.* Bloomington: Indiana University Press, 1988.
Kirichenko, V. N., ed. *Uskorenie sotsialno-ekonomicheskogo razvitiia i perspektivnoe planirovanie* (Acceleration of the Social-Economic Development and Perspective Planning). Moscow: Ekonomika, 1987.
Kulikov, V. "Accelerated Socio-Economic Growth as a Basis for Social Progress." In *The USSR: Acceleration of Socio-Economic Development.* Moscow: USSR Academy of Sciences, Institute of Economics, Soviet Economic Science Series No. 3, "Social Sciences Today," Editorial Board, 1987.
Sorokin, G. "Tempy rosta sovetskoi ekonomiki" (Growth Rates of the Soviet Economy), *Voprosy ekonomiki*, no. 2 (1986): 11–21.
"The Soviet Growth Slowdown. Three Views" (of Stanislaw Gomulka, Padma Desai, and Vladimir Kontorovich), *The American Economic Review*, (May, 1986): 170–185. Papers and Proceedings of the Ninety-Eighth Annual Meeting, New York (December 1985).

Consumption and Its Relation to Income

Aganbegyan, Abel. "Debate: Uphill or Downhill," *Pravda* (February 6, 1989). Trans. in *CDSP* 40, no. 6 (March, 1989): 1–4.
Central Intelligence Agency. *Revisiting Soviet Economic Performance Under Glasnost: Implications for CIA Estimates.* Washington, D.C.: CIA, September, 1988.
Kapustin, E. I., et al., eds. *Ekonomicheskii stroi sotsializma*, vol. 1. Moscow: Ekonomika, 1984.
Ofer, Gur, Vinokur, Aaron, and Bar-chaim Yechiel. *Family Budget Survey of Soviet Emigrants in the Soviet Union.* Santa Monica, Cal.: Rand Corporation, Paper Seires (P–6015), July, 1979.
Seliunin, Vasilii. "Glubokaia reforma ili revansh biurokratii?" (Great Reform, or Revenge of the Bureaucracy?), *Znamia* (July, 1988): 155–67.

Concluding Comments

Bornstein, Morris. *The Soviet National Income Accounts for 1955*. Ann Arbor: Center for Russian Studies, University of Michigan, 1962.

Ofer, Gur. "Soviet Economic Growth: 1928–1985," *Journal of Economic Literature* 25, no. 4 (December, 1987): 1767–1833.

Spulber, Nicolas. *Soviet Strategy for Economic Growth*. Bloomington: Indiana University Press, 1964.

Chapter 9

State Enterprises, Associations, and Complexes

Dellenbrant, Jan Ake. *The Soviet Regional Dilemma: Planning, People, and Natural Resources*. Armonk, N.Y.: M. E. Sharpe, 1986.

Freris, Andrew. *The Soviet Industrial Enterprise: Theory and Practice*. New York: St. Martin's Press, 1984.

Goskomstat. SSSR (State Statistical Office, USSR). *Promyshlennost' SSSR* (The Industry of the USSR). Moscow: Finansy i statistika, 1988.

Lavrikhov, Iu., Panfilov, M. P., Sidorov, N. Kh., and Andreev, U. N., eds. *Proizvodstvennye ob'edineniia organizatsiia, effektivnost', perspektivy razvitiia* (Production Associations: Organization, Effectiveness, Perspectives of Development). Moscow: Ekonomika, 1982.

Ryzkov, Nikola I. Report on "Restructuring the Management of the National Economy," *Pravda* (June 30, 1987). Trans. in *CDSP* 39, no. 27 (1987): 8–11, 24.

Options and Hierarchical Dependence

Abalkin, Leonid I. "Restructuring of the Economic Mechanism." In *The Economic Strategy of the CPSU*. Moscow: USSR Academy of Sciences, Institute of Economics, "Social Sciences Today," Editorial Board, 1988.

Aganbegyan, Abel. "Programma korennoi perestroiki" (The Program of Radical Restructuring), *Ekonomika i organizatsiia promyshlennogo proizvodstva*, no. 11 (1987): 3–19.

Ioffe, Olimpiad S., and Maggs, Peter B. *The Soviet Economic System: A Legal Analysis*. Boulder, Colo.: Westview Press, 1987.

"Law on the State Enterprise," *Pravda* (July 1, 1987). Trans. in *CDSP* 39, no. 30 (1987): 8–14; and *CDSP* 39, no. 31 (1987): 10–17, 28.

"Za novoe ekonomicheskoe myshlenie" (For New Economic Thinking [Roundtable of *Nova mysl* and *Kommunist*]), *Kommunist*, no. 15 (1988): 91–104.

The Second Economy

Belkindas, Misha. *Privatization of the Soviet Economy Under Gorbachev*. Berkeley, Calif.: Berkeley-Duke Occasional Papers on the Second Economy in the USSR, Paper no. 14, April, 1989 (mimeo).

Bunich, P. "Bez polumer!" (Without Half-measures!), *Ekonomicheskaia gazeta*, no. 20 (May, 1989).

Butler, W. E. *Soviet Law*. 2d ed. London: Butterworths Legal Publishers, 1988.

Center for Privatization et al. *Soviet Cooperatives: A Force for Major Economic Development*. U.S., issued by the Center for United Nations Industrial Development Organization. New York. September, 1989.

"Law on Individual Enterprise," *Pravda* (November 21, 1986). *CDSP* 38, no. 46 (December 17, 1986): 6–8.

"Resolution: Regulation of Certain Types of Activities of Cooperatives," *Izvestia* (December 31, 1988). Trans. in *CDSP* 41, no. 1 (1989).

Prospective Reform

Abalkin, Leonid I. *Novyi tip ekonomicheskogo myshleniia* (New Type of Economic Thinking). Moscow: Ekonomika, 1987.

Antal, Laszlo. "About the Property Incentive" (Interest in Property), *Acta Oeconomica* 34, nos. 3–4 (1985): 275–86.

———. "Thoughts on the Further Development of the Hungarian Mechanism," *Acta Oeconomica* 29, nos. 3–4 (1982): 199–224.

Bauer, Tamas. "Deceleration, Dependency and 'Departernalization': Some Considerations Concerning the Changes of the Soviet Union and Eastern Europe in the Coming Decades," *Acta Oeconomica* 39, nos. 1–2 (1988): 155–69.

Liberman, Evsey G. *Economic Methods and the Effectiveness of Production*. White Plains, N.Y.: International Arts and Sciences Press, 1971.

Marer, Paul "Market Mechanism Reforms in Hungary." In *Market Reforms in Socialist Societies*, ed. Peter Van Ness. Boulder, Colo.; Lynne Rienner Publishers, 1989.

Sarkozy, T. "Problems of Social Ownership and of the Proprietory Organization," *Acta Oeconomica* 29, nos. 3–4 (1982): 225–58.

Spulber, Nicolas. *Organizational Alternatives in Soviet-type Economies*. Cambridge: Cambridge University Press, 1979.

Szamuely, Laszlo. "The First Wave of the Mechanism Debate in Hungary (1954–1957)," *Acta Oeconomica* 29, nos. 1–2 (1982): 1–24.

———. "The Second Wave of the Economic Mechanism Debate and the 1968 Reform in Hungary," *Acta Oeconomica* 33, nos. 1–2 (1984): 44–67.

Tardos, Marton. "Can Hungary's Monetary Policy Succeed?" *Acta Oeconomica* 39, nos. 1–2 (1988): 61–79.

———. "Development Program for Economic Control and Organization in Hungary," *Acta Oeconomica* 28, nos. 3–4 (1982): 295–315.

Concluding Comments

Central Intelligence Agency. *A Comparison of the US and Soviet Industrial Bases*. Washington, D.C.: CIA, May, 1989.

Chapter 10

Farming Organization and the Food Problem

Butler, W. E. *Soviet Law.* 2d ed. London: Butterworths Legal Publishers, 1988.
Doolittle, Penelope, and Hughes, Margaret. "Gorbachev's Agricultural Policy: Building on the Brezhnev Food Program." In *Gorbachev's Economic Plans*, vol. 2. Study papers submitted to the Joint Economic Committee, Congress of the United States, 100th Congress, 1st sess. Washington, D.C.: GPO, 1987.
Goskomstat, SSSR (State Statistical Office, USSR), *Sel'skoe khoziaistvo SSSR* (Soviet Agriculture). Moscow: Finansy i statistika, 1988.
————. *Trud v SSSR* (Labor in the USSR). Moscow: Finansy i statistika, 1988.
Ioffe, Olimpiad S., and Maggs, Peter B. *The Soviet Economic System: A Legal Analysis.* Boulder, Colo.: Westview Press, 1987.
Kapustin, E. I., et al., eds. *Ekonomicheski stroi sotsializma*, vol. 2. Moscow: Ekonomika, 1984.
Litvin, Valentin. *The Soviet Agro-industrial Complex.* Boulder, Colo.: Westview Press, 1987.
"On the Further Improvement of the Mechanism of Economic Management in the Country's Agro-industrial Complex," *Pravda* (March 29, 1986). Trans. in *CDSP* 38, no. 14 (1986): 10–15.
Severin, Barbara. "Solving the Soviet Livestock Feed Dilemma: Key to Meeting Food Program Targets." In *Gorbachev's Economic Plans*, vol. 1. Study Papers Submitted to the Joint Economic Committee, Congress of the United States, 100th Congress, 1st sess. Washington, D.C.: GPO, 1987.
"The USSR Food Program for the Period up to 1990," *Pravda* (May 27, 1982). Trans. in *CDSP* 34, no. 21 (1982): 9–13, 23; and *CDSP* 34, no. 22 (1982): 7–11.

Keys to the Food Problem

Abalkin, Leonid I. "The Fate of the Reform: The Government's Tactics and Strategy" (interview with Abalkin), *Izvestia* (September 22, 1989). Trans. in *CDSP* 41, no. 39 (October 25, 1989): 12–14.
Brada, Joseph C., and Wädekin, Karl-Eugen. *Socialist Agriculture in Transition: Organizational Response to Failing Performance.* Boulder, Colo.: Westview Press, 1988.
Bukovsky, Vladimir. "The Quiet Exit of Soviet Communism." In *Can the Soviet System Survive Reform?* ed. G. R. Urban. London: Pinter Publishers, 1989.
Gorbachev, Mikhail S., "Develop Leasing, Restructure Economic Relations in the Countryside," *Pravda* (October 14, 1988). Trans. in *CDSP* 40, no. 41 (November 9, 1988): 1–6.
————. "On the CPSU's Agrarian Policy in Today's Conditions," *Pravda* (March 15, 1989). Trans. in *CDSP* 41, no. 11 (April 12, 1989): 3–6; and *CDSP* 41, no. 12 (April 12, 1989): 10–16.
————. "Put Cooperative's Potential in the Service of Restructuring," *Pravda* (March 24, 1988). Trans. in *CDSP* 40, no. 12 (April 20, 1988): 1–7.

————. Speech at CC meeting on the "Rental Contract," *Pravda* (May 14, 1988). Trans. in *CDSP* 40, no. 20 (June 15, 1988): 1–6.

Gustafson, Thane. *Reform in Soviet Politics: Lessons of Recent Policies on Land and Water.* Cambridge: Cambridge University Press, 1981.

Seliunin, Vasilii. "Istoki," (Sources) *Novyi Mir*, no. 5 (May, 1988): 162–89.

Shmelev, Nikolai. "Avansy i Dolgi" (Advances and Debts), *Novyi Mir* (June, 1987).

Tedstrom, John, and Hanson, Philip. "Supreme Soviet Issues Decree on Leasing," *Report on the USSR* [Radio Liberty] 1, no. 16 (April, 1989): 6–8.

Timmerman, Heinz. *Gorbatschow-ein Bukharinist? Zur Neubewertung der NEP-Periode in Moskau.* Köln: Bundesinstitut für Ostwissenschaftliche und Internationl Studien, 1988.

Urban, G. R., ed. *Can the Soviet System Survive Reform?* (Seven Colloquies about the State of Soviet Socialism). London: Pinter Publishers, 1989.

Wädekin, Karl-Eugen. "Soviet Agriculture." In *From Brezhnev to Gorbachev: Domestic Affairs and Soviet Foreign Policy*, ed. Hans-Joachim Veen. Hamburg: Berg, 1984.

Personal Subsidiary Farms

Friedgut, Theodore H. *The Persistence of the Peasant in Soviet Society.* Jerusalem: Hebrew University, The Marjorie Mayrock Center, Research Paper No. 64, May 1987.

Goskomstat, Sel'skoe khoziaistvo SSSR (Soviet Agriculture). Moscow: Finansy i statistika, 1988.

Kalinkin, A. F., ed. *Lichnoe podsobnoe khoziaistvo* (Personal Subsidiary Farms). Moscow: Kolos, 1981.

Nikiforov, L. V. *Sotsialno-ekonomicheskii potential sela* (Social-Economic Potential of the Village). Moscow: Nauka, 1986.

"O sobstvennost' v SSSR. Proekt zakon SSSR" (On Ownership in the USSR: Draft Law). *Sotsialisticheskaia industria* (November 18, 1989).

Shmelev, G. I. *Lichnoe podsobnoe khoziaistvo: Vozmozhnosti i perspektivy* (Personal Subsidiary Farms: Possibilities and Perspectives). Moscow: Politlit., 1983.

Wädekin, Karl-Eugen. *The Private Sector in Soviet Agriculture.* Ed. George Karcz. Berkeley: University of California Press, 1973.

————. "Soviet Agriculture: A Brighter Prospect?" In *The Soviet Economy on the Brink of Reform*, ed. Peter Wiles. Boston: Unwin Hyman, 1988.

"Merchants" vs. "Cavalrymen"

Gorbachev, Mikhail S. "On the CPSU Agrarian Policy in Today's Conditions," *Pravda* (March 15, 1989). Trans. in *CDSP* 41, no. 11 (April 12, 1989): 3–6; and *CDSP* 41, no. 12 (1989): 10–16.

Seliunin, Vasilii. "Istoki," (Sources), *Novyi Mir*, no. 5 (May, 1988).

Shmelev, Nikolai. "Avansy i Dolgi" (Advances and Debts), *Novyi Mir* (June, 1987).

"Toward a Contemporary Concept of Socialism," *Pravda* (July 14, and July 16, 1989). Trans. in *CDSP* 41, no. 31 (August 30, 1989): 4–8.

Concluding Comments

Central Intelligence Agency. *Modeling Soviet Agriculture: Isolating the Effects of Weather*. Washington, D.C.: CIA, August, 1988.

Severin, Barbara. "Solving the Soviet Livestock Feed Dilemma: Key to Meeting Food Program Targets." In *Gorbachev's Economic Plans*, vol. 1. Study papers submitted to the Joint Economic Committee, Congress of the United States, 100th Congress, 1st sess. Washington, D.C.: GPO, 1987.

Chapter 11

Industrial Purchasing

Aganbegyan, Abel. *The Economic Challenge of Perestroika*. Bloomington: Indiana University Press, 1988.

Borzova, K. A., *Osnovnye dogovornye formy material'no-technicheskogo snabzheniia promyshlennosti* (Basic Bargaining Forms of Industrial Material-Technical Supply). Minsk: Izd. BGU, 1983.

Geronimus, B. L., Shlefrin, V. I., and Shurenkov, I. V. *Optimizatsia planirovaniia material'no-technicheskogo snabzheniia Souiznoi Respubliki* (Optimization of the Planning of the Material-Technical Supply of the Union Republic). Minsk: Belarus, 1978.

Heinritz, Stuart F. *Purchasing: Principles and Applications*. 3d ed. Englewood Cliffs, N.J.: Prentice-Hall, 1959.

Lagutkin, V. M., and Iakobi, A. A., eds. *Organizatsiia i planirovanie material'no technicheskogo snabzhenie i sbyta v narodnom khoziaistve* (Organization and Planning of Material-Technical Supply and Sale in the National Economy). Moscow: Metallurgiia, 1977.

Mikaliunas, L. V., and Minkin, Z. S. *Material'no technicheskoe snabzhenie: novyi mekhanizm khozaistvennogo rascheta* (Material-Technical Supply: The New Mechanism of Economic Accounting). Moscow: Ekonomika, 1989.

Schroeder, Gertrude E. "Organizations and Hierarchies: The Perennial Search for Solutions." In *Reorganization and Reform in the Soviet Economy*, ed. Susan J. Linz and William Moskoff. Armonk, N.Y.: M. E. Sharpe, 1988.

Zakruzhnyi, A. A. *Organy snabzheniia i sbyta* (The Organs of Supply and Sale). Minsk: Vysheishaia shkola, 1983.

Zav'ialkov, A. G., ed. *Planirovanie ekonomicheskogo i sotsiialnogo razvitiia SSSR* (Planning the Economic and Social Development of the USSR). Moscow: Vyshaia shkola, 1987.

Marketing and Retail Sales

Bazarova, G. V., ed. *Rol' finansov v sotsialno-ekonomicheskom razvitii strany* (The Role of Finances in the Country's Social-Economic Development). Moscow: Finansy i statistika, 1986.

Belokh, N. V., and Rusakov, V. P. *Planovaia sbalansirovannost' sprosa i pre-*

dlozheniia potrebitel'skikh blag (Planning the Balancing of Supply and Demand for Consumer Goods). Moscow: Nauka, 1986.

Boone, Louis E., and Kurtz, David L. *Contemporary Marketing*. 3d ed. Hinsdale, Ill.: Dryden Press, 1980.

Denton, Elizabeth. "Soviet Consumer Policy: Trends and Prospects." In *Soviet Economy in a Time of Change*, vol. 1. A compendium of papers submitted to the Joint Economic Committee, Congress of the United States, 96th Congress, 1st sess. Washington, D.C.: GPO (October, 1979).

Kapustin, E. I., et al., eds. *Ekonomicheskii stroi sotsializma*, vol. 3 (The Socialist Economic System). Moscow: Ekonomika, 1984.

Lazer, William, and Culley, James D. *Marketing Management*. Boston: Houghton Mifflin, 1983.

Lebedinskii, N. P., ed. *Metodicheskie ukazaniia k sostavleniu gosudarstvennogo plana razvitiia Narodnogo khoziaistva SSSR* (Guidelines on Methods for the Compilation of the State Plan for Development of the USSR National Economy). Moscow: Ekonomika, 1969, pt. 5.

Levin, A. I., and Iarkin, A. P. *Ekonomika potrebleniia* (Economics of Consumption). Moscow: Nauka, 1984.

The Shadow Economy

Alexeev, Michael V., and Sayer, Ali. "The Second Economy Market for Foreign Made Goods in the USSR." In *Studies on the Soviet Second Economy*. Berkeley: Berkeley-Duke Occasional Paper on the Second Economy in the USSR, no. 11 (December, 1987).

Belousov, I. S. "Conversion: What it Means" (interview), *Pravda* (August 28, 1989). Trans. in *CDSP* 41, no. 35 (September 27, 1989): 1–5.

Grossman, Gregory. "A Tonsorial View of the Soviet Second Economy." In *The Soviet Economy on the Brink of Reform*, ed. Peter Wiles. Boston. Unwin Hyman, 1988.

Korotkov, P. "Trudnyi put' k rynku" (Difficult Road to the Market), *Ekonomicheskaia gazeta*, no. 42 (October, 1989): 1, 3.

Osipenko, O. V., and Kozlov, Iu. G. "Chto obrasyvaet ten'?" (What Casts a Shadow?), *Ekonomika i organizatsiia promyshlennogo proizvodstva*, no. 2 (1989): 47–59.

Linkages to Suppliers and Customers

Chandler, Alfred. *Essays Toward a Historical Theory of Big Business*. Ed. Thomas K. McCraw. Boston: Harvard Business School Press, 1988.

Shokin, A., Guzanova, A., and Liberman, L. "Tseny glazami naseleniia" (Prices Through the Eyes of the Population). *Literaturnaya gazeta* (September 14, 1988): 11.

Concluding Comments

Birman, Igor. *Personal Consumption in the USSR and USA*. New York: St. Martin's Press, 1989.

Moskvin, A. I. *Narodnoe potreblenie v usloviiakh razvitogo sotsializma* (National Consumption in the Conditions of Developed Socialism). Kiev: Naukova dumka, 1984.

Chapter 12

Access to Markets

Barkovskii, N. D., et al. *XXVII s'ezd, KPSS i razvitie denezhno-kreditnoi sistemy SSSR* (The 27th Congress of the CPSU and the Development of the Monetary-Credit System of the USSR). Moscow: Finansy i statistika, 1987.

Brabant, Jozef M. van. *Adjustment, Structural Change, and Economic Efficiency: Aspects of Monetary Cooperation in Eastern Europe.* Cambridge: Cambridge University Press, 1987.

Konstantinov, Iu. A. *Novyi valiutno-finansovyi mekhanizm i perestroika upravleniia vneshekonomicheskimi sviazami SSSR* (The New Financial-Foreign Currency Mechanism and the Restructuring of the USSR Foreign Economic Ties). Moscow: Finansy i statistika, 1987.

Sokoloff, Georges. *The Economy of Detente: The Soviet Union and the Western Capital.* Trans. from the French by Jean Kirby. New York: Berg, distributed by St. Martin's Press, 1987.

Spulber, Nicolas. *Socialist Management and Planning: Topics in Comparative Socialist Economics.* Bloomington: Indiana University Press, 1971.

————. "The Soviet-Bloc Foreign Trade System," *Law and Contemporary Problems* (Summer, 1959): 420–34.

Expansion of Options

Boguslavski, M. M., and Smirnov, P. S. *The Reorganization of Soviet Foreign Trade.* Ed. Serge L. Levitsky. Armonk, N.Y.: M. E. Sharpe, 1989.

Butler, W. E. *Soviet Law.* 2d ed. London: Butterworths Legal Publishers, 1988.

Cherepanov, A. "Izvestia Round Table: What is Slowing Us Down," *Izvestia* (October 10, 1987). Trans. in *CDSP* 39, no. 41 (November, 1987): 7–8.

Clement, Hermann. "Changes in the Soviet Foreign Trade System," *Soviet and Eastern European Foreign Trade* 24, no. 4 (Winter, 1988–89): 3–61.

"Decrees of the CPSU Central Committee and the USSR Council of Ministers of August 19, 1986," *Soviet and Eastern European Foreign Trade* 24, no. 4 (Winter, 1988–89): 62–75.

Marer, Paul. "The Economies and Trade of Eastern Europe." In *Central and Eastern Europe: The Opening of the Curtain?* Ed. William E. Griffith. Boulder, Colo.: Westview Press, 1989.

Schroeder, Gertrude E. "Gorbachev's Economic Reforms." In *Gorbachev's New Thinking: Prospects for Joint Ventures.* Ed. Ronald D. Leibovitz. Cambridge, Mass.: Ballinger, 1988.

Vasilev, G. I., and Galanov, S. S. "Kreditno-raschetnoe obsluzhivanie novykh form vneshekonomicheskikh sviaze" (Credit-Accounting Service of the New Forms of Foreign Economic Ties), *Den'gi i kredit*, no. 7 (July, 1987): 19–26.

Joint Ventures

Clement, Herman. "Changes in the Soviet Foreign Trade System," *Soviet and Eastern European Foreign Trade* 24, no. 4 (Winter, 1988–89), ch. 6 and app. 4, On Procedures Governing the Creation and Operation of Joint Enterprises.

Csaba, Laszlo. "Restructuring of the Soviet Foreign Trade Mechanism and Possibilities for Interfirm Cooperation in the CMEA," *Acta Oeconomica* 39, nos. 1–2 (1988): 137–54.

Hober, Kaj. *Joint Ventures in the Soviet Union*. Dobbs Ferry, N.Y.: Transnational Juris Publications, 1989.

Kroll, Heidi. "Breach of Contract on the Soviet Economy," *The Journal of Legal Studies* 41, 4 (January, 1987): 119–48.

Prospects

McIntyre, Joan F. "Soviet Efforts to Revamp the Foreign Trade Sector." In *Gorbachev's Economic Plans*, vol. 2. Study papers submitted to the Joint Economic Committee, Congress of the United States, 100th Congress, 1st sess. Washington, D.C.: GPO, 1987.

Lavigne, Marie. "Soviet Trade with LDC's." In *Gorbachev's Economic Plans*, vol. 2.

Concluding Comments

"Debate Rostrum: Should We Look for a 'Philosophic Stone' in the Economy?" (interview with Professor A. D. Smirnov, conducted by V. Poshataev, *Pravda* [October 21, 1989]). Trans. in *CDSP* 41, no. 41 (November 8, 1989).

Wolf, Thomas A. *Market-Oriented Reform of Foreign Trade in Planned Economies* (mimeo). For presentation at the International Economic Association in Moscow, March 28–30, 1989.

Chapter 13

Conceptual Frameworks

Engels, Friedrich. *Anti-Dühring, Herr Eugen Dühring's Revolution in Science* [1878]. Moscow: Foreign Language Publishing House, 1959.

Lenin, V. I. "The State and Revolution," *Collected Works*. Vol. 25: June–Sept. 1917. Moscow: Progress Publishers, 1964.

Lorenz, Richard. *Anfänge der bolschewistischen Industriepolitik* (Beginnings of the Bolshevik Industrial Policy). Köln: Wissenschaft u. Politik, 1965.

Marx, Karl. "Critique of the Gotha Programme" [1875]. In Karl Marx and Friedrich Engels, *Selected Works*. 3 vols. Moscow: Progress Publishers, 1970.

Nove, Alec. *Marxism and 'Really Existing Socialism.'* London: Harvard Academic Publishers, 1986.

Sutela, Pekka. *Socialism, Planning and Optimality: A Study in Soviet Economic Thought*. Helsinki: Finnish Society of Science and Letters, 1984.

Patterns of Organization

Bukharin, Nikolai, and Preobrazhensky, Eugenii. *The ABC of Communism* [1919]. Ann Arbor: University of Michigan Press, 1966.

Spulber, Nicolas. *Soviet Strategy for Economic Growth*. Bloomington: Indiana University Press, 1964.

Szamuely, Laszlo. *First Models of the Socialist Economic Systems: Principles and Theories*. Budapest: Akademiai Kiado, 1974.

Commands and Soviet "Economic Accounting"

Antal, Laszlo. "Thoughts on the Further Development of the Hungarian Mechanism," *Acta Oeconomica* 29, nos. 3–4 (1982): 199–224.

Asselain, Jean-Charles. *Planning and Profits in Socialist Economies*. Trans. Jill Rubery and John Andrew Wilson. London: Routledge & Kegan Paul, 1984.

Ellman, Michael. *Planning Problems in the USSR: The Contribution of Mathematical Economics to their Solution 1960–71*. Cambridge: Cambridge University Press, 1973.

Halm, George N. "Mises, Lange, Liberman: Allocation and Motivation in the Socialist Economy," *Weltwirtschaftlisches Archiv* 100, no. 1 (1968): 19–39.

Hayek, F. A., ed. *Collectivist Economic Planning*. London: Routledge and Sons, 1938.

Kornai, János. "The Hungarian Reform Process: Visions, Hopes, Reality," *Journal of Economic Literature* 24 (December, 1986): 1687–1737.

Kouba, Karel. "Plan and Market in the Socialist Economy" [1967]. In *Organizational Alternatives in Soviet-Type Economies*, ed. Nicolas Spulber. Cambridge: Cambridge University Press, 1979.

Lange, Oskar. "On the Economic Theory of Socialism." In *On the Economic Theory of Socialism*, ed. B. E. Lippincott. Minneapolis: University of Minnesota Press, 1938.

Mises, Ludwig von. *Socialism: An Economic and Sociological Analysis*. Trans. J. Kahane. Indianapolis: Liberty Classics, 1979.

Tardos, Marton. "The Conditions of Developing A Regulated Market," *Acta Oeconomica* 36, nos. 1–2 (1986): 67–89.

On Stalin's "Economics" Heritage

The Stalin Phenomenon. Moscow: Novosti, 1988.

Concluding Comments

Bernstein, Edward. *Die Voraussetzungen des Sozialismus und die Aufgaben der Sozialdemokratie* [1894]. Trans. E. C. Harvey, *Evolutionary Socialism: A Criticism and Affirmation*. New York: Huebsch, 1909.

Hayek, F. A. *The Fatal Conceit: The Errors of Socialism*, vol. 1. Ed. W. W. Bartley III. Chicago: University of Chicago Press, 1988.

Kautsky, Karl. *The Labor Revolution* (1921). Trans. H. J. Steuning. New York: Dial Press, 1925.

Chapter 14

Issues in the Reversion to Markets

Posner, Richard. "Economic Analysis of Law" [1973]. In *Economic Foundations of Property Law*. Ed. Bruce A. Ackerman. Boston: Little, Brown and Co., 1975.

Revel, Jean-François. "Is Communism Reversible?" *Commentary* 87 (January, 1987): 17–24.

Dynamics of NEP and Perestroika

Atlas, M. S., et al. *Leninskoe ychenie o NEPe i ego mezhdunarodnoe znachenie* (Lenin's Teaching About the NEP and its International Significance). Moscow: Ekonomika, 1973.

Kushnirsky, Fyodor I. "Soviet Economic Reform: An Analysis and a Model." In *Reorganization and Reform in the Soviet Economy*, ed. Susan J. Linz and W. Moskoff. Armonk, N.Y.: M. E. Sharpe, 1988.

Poliakov, Iu. A., Dimitrenko, V. P , and Shcherban, N. V. *Novaia ekonomicheskaia politika* (The New Economic Policy). Moscow: Politlit., 1982.

Szamuely, L. "The After-Life of NEP," *Acta Oeconomica* 39, nos. 3–4 (1988): 341 55.

Yakovlev, Alexander. "Our Doctrine Is Strong by Virtue of Its Truth," *Rude Pravo* (November 16, 1988). Address to Prague Party School. Trans. in *FBIS*-Sov-88-231 (December 1, 1988): 82–90.

Impacts of Glasnost

Agursky, Mikhail. *Contemporary Russian Nationalism: History Revised*. Jerusalem. The Hebrew University, The Soviet and East European Centre, Research Paper No. 45, January, 1982.

―――. *The New Russian Literature*. Jerusalem: The Hebrew University, The Soviet and East European Research Centre, Research Paper No. 40, July, 1980.

Aron, Leon. "What Glasnost Has Destroyed," *Commentary* 88, no. 5 (November, 1989): 30–34.

Bukovsky, Vladimir. "In Russia, Is It 1905 Again?" *The Wall Street Journal* (November 27, 1989).

Documents and Materials. Nineteenth All-Union Conference of the CPSU, June 28– July 1, 1988. *Report and Speeches by Mikhail Gorbachev*. Moscow: Novosti, 1988.

Grossman, Vasily. *Forever Flowing*. Trans. Thomas P. Whitney. London: Collins Harvill, 1986.

————. *Life and Fate*. Trans. Robert Chandler. London: Collins Harvill, 1985.

Solzhenitsyn, Aleksandr, et al. *From Under the Rubble*. Boston: Little, Brown and Co., 1974.

Tarasulo, Isaac J., ed. *Gorbachev and Glasnost: Viewpoints from the Soviet Press.* Wilmington, Del.: SR Books, 1989.

"No" to Convergence

Brus, Wlodzimierz. *The Market in a Socialist Economy.* London: Routledge & Kegan Paul, 1974.

Gordon, Scott. "The Close of the Galbraithian System," *Journal of Political Economy* 76, no. 4 (July–August, 1968): 635–44.

Hahn, Jeffrey W. "Is Developed Socialism a Soviet Version of Convergence?" In *Developed Socialism in the Soviet Bloc: Political Theory and Political Reality*, ed. J. Seroka and M. D. Simon. Boulder, Colo.: Westview Press, 1982.

Heertje, Arnold. *Economic and Technical Change*. London: Widenfeld and Nicolson, 1977.

Kapustin, L. E., et al. *Ekonomicheskii stroi sotsializma,* vol. 1. Moscow: Ekonomika, 1984.

Shishkov, Iu.V. "Perestroika i prizrak konvergentsii" (Perestroika and the Ghost of Convergence), *Rabochii Klass i sovremennyi mir*, no. 1 (1989): 31–45.

Spulber, Nicolas. "Socialism, Industrialization and 'Convergence.'" In *Jahrbüch der Wirtschaft Osteuropas* 2 (1971): 392–424.

Wiles, P. J. D. *Economic Institutions Compared*. Oxford: Basil Blackwell, 1977.

Concluding Comments

Mises, Ludwig von. *Socialism: An Economic and Sociological Analysis*. Trans. J. Kahane. Indianapolis: Liberty Classics, 1979.

Index